Lecture Notes of the Institute
for Computer Sciences, Social Informatics
and Telecommunications Engineering   653

Editorial Board Members

Ozgur Akan, *Middle East Technical University, Ankara, Türkiye*
Paolo Bellavista, *University of Bologna, Bologna, Italy*
Jiannong Cao, *Hong Kong Polytechnic University, Hong Kong, China*
Geoffrey Coulson, *Lancaster University, Lancaster, UK*
Falko Dressler, *University of Erlangen, Erlangen, Germany*
Domenico Ferrari, *Università Cattolica Piacenza, Piacenza, Italy*
Mario Gerla, *UCLA, Los Angeles, USA*
Hisashi Kobayashi, *Princeton University, Princeton, USA*
Sergio Palazzo, *University of Catania, Catania, Italy*
Sartaj Sahni, *University of Florida, Gainesville, USA*
Xuemin Shen, *University of Waterloo, Waterloo, Canada*
Mircea Stan, *University of Virginia, Charlottesville, USA*
Xiaohua Jia, *City University of Hong Kong, Kowloon, Hong Kong*
Albert Y. Zomaya, *University of Sydney, Sydney, Australia*

The LNICST series publishes ICST's conferences, symposia and workshops.
LNICST reports state-of-the-art results in areas related to the scope of the Institute. The type of material published includes

- Proceedings (published in time for the respective event)
- Other edited monographs (such as project reports or invited volumes)

LNICST topics span the following areas:

- General Computer Science
- E-Economy
- E-Medicine
- Knowledge Management
- Multimedia
- Operations, Management and Policy
- Social Informatics
- Systems

Tiémoman Koné · Abdoulaye Sere ·
Koffi Fernand Kouamé
Editors

Towards New e-Infrastructure and e-Services for Developing Countries

16th International Conference, AFRICOMM 2024
Abidjan, Côte d'Ivoire, November 27–29, 2024
Proceedings, Part II

Editors
Tiémoman Koné
Université Virtuelle de Côte d'Ivoire
Abidjan, Côte d'Ivoire

Abdoulaye Sere
Université Nazi Boni
Bobo-Dioulasso, Burkina Faso

Koffi Fernand Kouamé
Université Virtuelle de Côte d'Ivoire
Abidjan, Côte d'Ivoire

ISSN 1867-8211 ISSN 1867-822X (electronic)
Lecture Notes of the Institute for Computer Sciences, Social Informatics
and Telecommunications Engineering
ISBN 978-3-032-01909-7 ISBN 978-3-032-01910-3 (eBook)
https://doi.org/10.1007/978-3-032-01910-3

© ICST Institute for Computer Sciences, Social Informatics and Telecommunications Engineering 2025

This work is subject to copyright. All rights are solely and exclusively licensed by the Publisher, whether the whole or part of the material is concerned, specifically the rights of translation, reprinting, reuse of illustrations, recitation, broadcasting, reproduction on microfilms or in any other physical way, and transmission or information storage and retrieval, electronic adaptation, computer software, or by similar or dissimilar methodology now known or hereafter developed.
The use of general descriptive names, registered names, trademarks, service marks, etc. in this publication does not imply, even in the absence of a specific statement, that such names are exempt from the relevant protective laws and regulations and therefore free for general use.
The publisher, the authors and the editors are safe to assume that the advice and information in this book are believed to be true and accurate at the date of publication. Neither the publisher nor the authors or the editors give a warranty, expressed or implied, with respect to the material contained herein or for any errors or omissions that may have been made. The publisher remains neutral with regard to jurisdictional claims in published maps and institutional affiliations.

This Springer imprint is published by the registered company Springer Nature Switzerland AG
The registered company address is: Gewerbestrasse 11, 6330 Cham, Switzerland

If disposing of this product, please recycle the paper.

Preface

We are extremely pleased to present the proceedings of the 16th EAI International Conference (EAI AFRICOMM 2024) on Internet Infrastructure and Services in Africa, organized by the Université Virtuelle de Côte d'Ivoire (UVCI) in collaboration with the European Alliance for Innovation (EAI). This conference was held in Abidjan (Côte d'Ivoire) from 27th to 28th November 2024 and brought together technologists, researchers, and practitioners around the world with a shared purpose: to shape Africa's digital future and strengthen its position in the global digital ecosystem.

The EAI AFRICOMM 2024 conference theme reflected the critical intersection of Africa's digital transformation with socioeconomic development. The aim of AFRICOMM 2024 was not only to showcase innovation but also to discuss real-world solutions that will lead to meaningful impacts in the lives of millions of Africans.

It gave the opportunity to celebrate the strides that have been made across Africa to build a connected, sustainable, and inclusive digital infrastructure and also to share expertise on emerging topics such as 5G, AI-driven solutions, cybersecurity, and smart infrastructure. These discussions came at a pivotal time as we continued to address both technical and policy challenges to further connect Africa and enhance digital services for all. It is through collaboration that we can catalyze Africa's tech sector, address digital divides, and leverage new technologies to foster economic growth, innovation, and inclusivity.

For this edition, AFRICOMM received 130 paper submissions, of which 52 were accepted after rigorous double-blind peer review, with submissions each receiving three review on average. Out of these, 44 registered papers were presented. The submissions come from a diverse group of authors representing several countries, including Burkina Faso, Benin, Cameroon, Côte d'Ivoire, Democratic Republic of Congo, France, Senegal, South Africa, and USA, showcasing the conference's pan-African and international significance.

The technical program also featured two keynote speakers: Claude Lishou from Université Cheikh Anta Diop, Senegal and Abdoulaye Sere from Université Nazi Boni, Burkina Faso. The coordination was done by the Tiemoman Koné, the General Chair, and Fernand Kouamé, the Local Chair. It was also a great pleasure to work with such an excellent organizing committee team for their hard work in organizing and supporting the conference. In particular, the Technical Program Committee, led by our TPC Chairs, Abdoulaye Sere, Bi Tra Goore, completed the peer-review process of technical papers and made a high-quality technical program. We are also grateful to Conference Managers for her support and to all the authors who submitted their papers to the AFRICOMM 2024 conference.

We strongly believe that AFRICOMM 2024 provided a good forum for all researchers, developers, and practitioners to discuss all science and technology aspects that are relevant to Africa Internet Infrastructure and Services.

Tiémoman Koné
Abdoulaye Sere
Fernand Kouamé

Organization

Steering Committee

Roch H. Glitho — Concordia University, Canada

Organizing Committee

General Chair

Tiémoman Koné — Université Virtuelle de Côte d'Ivoire, Côte d'Ivoire

General Co-chairs

Doumbia Vafi — Ministère de l'Enseignement Supérieur et la Recherche Scientifique, Côte d'Ivoire

Kouadio Nanan Kouassi Gilles-Ghislain — Délégation Permanente de la Côte d'Ivoire auprès de l'UNESCO, France

TPC Chair and Co-chair

Abdoulaye Sere — Université Nazi Boni, Burkina Faso
Bi Tra Goore — Institut National Polytechnique Félix Houphouët-Boigny, Côte d'Ivoire

Sponsorship and Exhibit Chair

Anoh Nogbou Georges — Université Virtuelle de Côte d'Ivoire, Côte d'Ivoire

Local Chair

Kouamé Koffi Fernand — Université Virtuelle de Côte d'Ivoire, Côte d'Ivoire

Workshops Chair

Asseu Olivier Pascal Kouamé — Ecole Supérieure Africaine des TIC, Côte d'Ivoire

Publicity and Social Media Chairs

Saley Mahaman Bachir — Université Félix Houphouët-Boigny, Côte d'Ivoire
Valère-Carin Jofack Sokeng — Université Félix Houphouët-Boigny, Côte d'Ivoire

Publications Chair

Abdoulaye Sere — Université Nazi Boni, Burkina Faso

Panels Chair

Kimou Kouadio Prosper — Institut National Polytechnique Félix Houphouët-Boigny, Côte d'Ivoire

Technical Program Committee

Adepo Joël Christian	Université Virtuelle de Côte d'Ivoire, Côte d'Ivoire
Affian Kouadio	Université Félix Houphouët-Boigny, Côte d'Ivoire
Anoh Nogbou Georges	Université Virtuelle de Côte d'Ivoire, Côte d'Ivoire
Asseu Olivier Pascal Kouamé	Ecole Supérieure Africaine des Technologies de l'Information et de la Communication, Côte d'Ivoire
Atiampo Kodjo Armand	Université Virtuelle de Côte d'Ivoire, Côte d'Ivoire
Babri Michel	Institut National Polytechnique Félix Houphouët-Boigny, Côte d'Ivoire
Banah Florent Degni	Institut National Polytechnique Félix Houphouët-Boigny, Côte d'Ivoire
Bassolé Didier	Université Joseph Ki-Zerbo, Burkina Faso
Brou Konan Marcellin	Institut National Polytechnique Félix Houphouët-Boigny, Côte d'Ivoire
Emran Anas	Centre Régional Africain des Sciences et Technologies de l'Espace en Langue Française affilié à l'ONU, Morocco
Gbegbe Raymond	Institut National Polytechnique Félix Houphouët-Boigny, Côte d'Ivoire

Gooré Bi Tra	Institut National Polytechnique Félix Houphouët-Boigny, Côte d'Ivoire
Kimou Kouadio Prosper	Institut National Polytechnique Félix Houphouët-Boigny, Côte d'Ivoire
Kouakou Ives Arsène Koffi	Institut National Polytechnique Félix Houphouët-Boigny, Côte d'Ivoire
Kouamé Abel Assielou	Institut National Polytechnique Félix Houphouët-Boigny, Côte d'Ivoire
Kouamé Appoh	Institut National Polytechnique Félix Houphouët-Boigny, Côte d'Ivoire
Kouamé Euloge François	Université Virtuelle de Côte d'Ivoire, Côte d'Ivoire
N'guessan Béhou Gérard	Université Virtuelle de Côte d'Ivoire, Côte d'Ivoire
Ouédraogo Frédéric	Université Norbert Zongo, Burkina Faso
Sadouanouan Malo	Université Nazi Boni, Burkina Faso
Saley Mahaman Bachir	Université Félix Houphouët-Boigny, Côte d'Ivoire
Sere Abdoulaye	Université Nazi Boni, Burkina Faso
Somé Michel	Université Nazi Boni, Burkina Faso
Talla Tankam Narcisse	Université de Dschang, Cameroon
Tanon Lambert Kadjo	Institut National Polytechnique Félix Houphouët-Boigny, Côte d'Ivoire
Tégawende Bissyande	Université Joseph Ki-Zerbo, Burkina Faso
Tiguiane Yelemou	Université Nazi Boni, Burkina Faso
Traoré Issa	Centre National de Calcul de Côte d'Ivoire, Côte d'Ivoire
Traoré Yaya	Université Joseph Ki-Zerbo, Burkina Faso

Contents – Part II

Big Data Analytic, Blockchain/Workshop - Emerging Technologies/PHD

A New Approach to Matching Big Data Sources in a Semi-structured Data Warehouse Context 3
   Anassin Chiatsè Mireille Patricia, Tounwendyam Frédéric Ouédraogo, and Saha Kouassi Bernard

Web Scraping for Competitive Intelligence: State of the Art and Case Study ... 13
   Edouard Ngor Sarr, Oumar Diagne, Abel Diatta, and Lamine Faty

Financial Cost Sensitive Feature Selection Method Based on Association Rule Applied to Credit Scoring 34
   Ghislain Dorian Tchuente Mondjo and Kely Maxime Motue Djoko

Blockchain as an Alternative for Transparency and Optimal Handling of Microcredits in the Democratic Republic of Congo 58
   Jonathan Kabemba Ntumbwa, Robert Makila Beni, and Patrick Mukala

Improving Smart Contract Security Using Sequential Models 71
   Rosaire Senou and Jules Degila

The Limit of Direct Modulation in an FTTH/GPON Architecture 81
   Zacharia Damoue, Mamadou Alpha Barry, Abdourahmane Ndiaye, and Mamadou Moustapha Ndiaye

Artificial Intelligence (AI) and Machine Learning (ML) Applications

Impact of Climate in Modeling the Evolution of COVID-19 Cases in Côte d'Ivoire 95
   Donilèmin Jules Silue and Ismael Kone

Preventing Typosquatting with IDN Conversion: A Siamese Neural Network Approach 113
   Evrard Cabrel Nguemeyou Tchouangang, Idrissa Sarr, Alex Corenthin, and Bassirou Kassé

Enhancing LoRaWAN Network Performance with Reinforcement
Learning: Mitigating Collisions and Reducing Energy Consumption 128
   *Pape Abdoulaye Fam, Ibrahima Faye, Papa Silly Traore,
and Mamadou Lamine Ndiaye*

Detection and Treatment of Various Rice Diseases in Benin Using AI:
From Bibliometric Analysis to Survey 143
   Alfred Adinsi and Pélagie Houngue

An Edge-AI-Based Monitoring of Rift Valley Fever Vectors Using Deep
Learning 162
   *Aboubacry Hamat Ba, Dame Diongue, Maissa Mbaye,
Ousmane Dieng, Nicolas Djighnoum Diouf, Mariama Sene-Wade,
Ndeye Mery Dia Badiane, Mamadou Ciss, and Assane G. Fall*

Detection of Malicious Android Applications Based on Verification
of Indicators of Compromise and Machine Learning Techniques 182
   *Theodore Dama, Aminata Sabane, Abdoul Kader Kabore,
and Tegawendé F. Bissyande*

Two Phases Feature Selection Method for Classification Problems Based
on Association Rules 197
   Ghislain Dorian Tchuente Mondjo and Kely Maxime Motue Djoko

Stationary Wavelet Transform Based Watermarking for Telemedicine
Image Security 220
   Aminata Ngom, Samba Sidibé, Ndeye Fatou Ngom, and Oumar Niang

Exploring Human Personality Traits in Phishing Success: Contextual
Cybersecurity Study 240
   Robert Makila Beni, Landry Mbale, and Antoine Bagula

Optimizing Real-Time Video Analytics for Resource-Constrained
Environments 256
   Rodrique Kafando, Aminata Sabané, and Tégawendé F. Bissyandé

A New Convolutional Neural Network Approach for Image Classification:
The Case of Tomatoes 267
   Kopoin N. D. Charlemagne, Koffi Dagou, and Zouneme Boris

Text-to-OWL: Automated Ontology Construction for Tuberculosis
Treatment Recommendation Using Generative AI 281
   *Zonabo Ouédraogo, Lydie Simone Tapsoba, Aminata Sabane,
Rodrique Kafando, Abdoul Kader Kabore, and Tegawendé F. Bissyande*

Using a Bidirectional Decoder Model with Attention Mechanisms for Biomedical Named Entity Recognition 295
   Brou Konan Marcellin, Samassi Adama, Kouamé Appoh, and Touré Kidjégbo Augustin

Detection of COVID-19 Using Machine Learning Techniques 304
   Diako Doffou Jérome, Johnson Grâce Yénin Edwige, Sandjé Marcelin, and Patrice E. Mensah

Text Mining for Thematic Keyword Extraction: Enriching a French Lexicon on Food Security 319
   Rabiatou Zampaligre, Aminata Sabane, Rodrique Kafando, Abdoul Kader Kabore, and Tégawendé F. Bissyande

Improving Web User Tracking Systems Through Browser Fingerprinting 334
   Goya Alama Désiré Dao, Abdoul Kader Kabore, Aminata Sabane, Rodrique Kafando, and Tégawendé F. Bissyande

Monitoring the Compliance and Response to the COVID-19 Lockdown in South Africa, and Analysing the Impact Thereof 344
   Avuya Shibambu, Nelisiwe Dlamini, Sthembile Mthethwa, Nenekazi Mkuzangwe, Motlatsi Mantsi, and Thato Boateng

Regression Model-Based Energy Prediction Approach for IoT Oriented System 363
   Khanyisile Mkhonza, Sizakele Mathaba, and Adigun Mathew

Author Index 375

Contents – Part I

E-Government and E-Service

Virtual Reality in Education: Addressing School Inaccessibility in Burkina Faso During Crisis 3
   Moustapha Bikienga, Manegaouindé Roland Tougma, Karzoum Arsène Sankara, and Boureima Zerbo

A Structured Metamodel for Architecture Debt Management 15
   Flavien Hervé Somda and Désiré Guel

Emerging Network

Digital Technology and the Crop Calendar for Efficient Agriculture in West Africa 37
   Ida Sèmévo Tognisse, Jules Degila, Marius Sounouvou, Frejus Ariel Sodedji, Valere Salako, Symphorien Agbahoungba, Eric Agoyi, Maurice Ahouansou, and Achille Ephrem Assogbadjo

Twenty Years of Research on Information-Centric Networking: Which Conclusions for the Next Version of the Internet? 52
   Mohamed Bobo Diallo, Vazoumana Fofana, Abderrahmane Maaradji, Nada Sbihi, Fatimatou Coulibaly, Jean Cyrille Koffi Angaman, Issagha Bah, Déthié Dione, Joseph Ndong, and Tounwendyam Frédéric Ouédraogo

Spatial Mode Multiplexing Using Soliton Microcombs for Next-Generation Network 66
   Douatia Koné, Koffi A. Kamenan, Niangoran Médard Méné, and Aladji Kamagaté

Harnessing ISM for Customer Churn in Mobile Telecom. Networks 87
   Jean-Claude Mudilu Kafunda, Marivaux Nzaji Bampende, Ange Taboria Baelongandi, Nicodème Kabongo Lungenyi, and Kyandoghere Kyamakya

Legal and Ethical Considerations in IoT Forensic Investigations: A Study on Global Perspective 105
   Norman Nelufule, Daniel Shadung, Pertunia Senamela, and Unarine Manari

Contribution to the Strategic Alignment of Artificial Intelligence
to the Personalized e-Learning Business Process 118
   Kragbi Olivier Petey, Tiémoman Kone, and Behou Gerard N'guessan

5G-NR PUSCH Receiver Optimization in Context of Intra/Inter-cell
Interference 142
   *Désiré Guel, Flavien Herve Somda, P. Justin Kouraogo,
and Boureima Zerbo*

Real-Time Vital Sign Monitoring of Contagious Diseases in West Africa's
Healthcare System Using Grafana and IoT Devices 159
   *Thierry Kondengar, Mamadou Ba,
Metouole Mwinbe Yves Ghislain Somda, and Samuel Ouya*

A Comparative Study of Road Traffic Simulators 172
   Abdoul-Rachid Dabo, Emile Nana, and Ferdinand Tonguim Guinko

Towards an Architectural Approach of Insurance Fraud Detection System 191
   Rasidatou Nabi, Yaya Traoré, and Ibrahima Diop

LoRaWAN Infrastructure to Support Wildlife Conservation 199
   Adalberto João, Eusébio Chicapa, and Joaquim Macedo

Cybersecurity

Verifying the Integrity of Hardcopy Documents: Proposed Solution 217
   Sthembile Mthethwa and Cynthia Hombakazi Ngejane

Towards an Efficient Framework for Risk Assessment of Personal Data
Protection in Mobile IoT 232
   *Venceslas M. Olowo, Sèmèvo Arnaud R. M. Ahouandjinou,
Adoté François-Xavier Ametepe, and Probus M. A. F. Kiki*

Securing Individual's Identity Using ZKP: Proposed System Architecture 249
   *Sthembile Ntshangase, Kedimotse Baruni, Siphelele Myaka,
and Oyena Mahlasela*

Cyber Physical Systems Dependability Using CPS-IoT Traffic Surveillance 263
   Landry Mbale and Antoine Bagula

Multi-scale and Programmable Anomaly Detection System for SDN-IoT 278
   Adama Coly, Fatoumata Thiam, and Maïssa Mbaye

Leveraging Network Reconfiguration to Mitigate Stealthy FDI Attacks
in Smart Grid SCADA Systems by Exploiting Attacker Uncertainty 293
   Aurélie Kpoze, Jules Degila, and Arnaud Ahouandjinou

Bibliometric Analysis on Cybersecurity and e-government 315
   Jean-Baptiste Gandonou, Jules Degila, Thierry Wandji,
   Théophile Dagba, Ida Sèmévo Tognisse, and Anziz Adehan

Author Index 329

Big Data Analytic, Blockchain/Workshop - Emerging Technologies/PHD

A New Approach to Matching Big Data Sources in a Semi-structured Data Warehouse Context

Anassin Chiatsè Mireille Patricia[1](✉) , Tounwendyam Frédéric Ouédraogo[2] , and Saha Kouassi Bernard[3]

[1] Université Alassane Ouattara de Bouaké, Bouaké 01 01 BP V18, Côte d'Ivoire
anassin.patricia@uao.edu.ci
[2] Université Norbert Zongo, Koudougou, Burkina Faso
[3] Ecole Normale Supérieure d'Abidjan, Abidjan, Côte d'Ivoire

Abstract. In this paper, we propose a new data model capable of helping to solve the problem of data mining and data quality, particularly in Big Data. The latter is a real challenge due to the structural and semantic variations in optimal warehouse management since the development of modern digital processing techniques. Source certainty plays an important role in the semi-structured data warehouse. In addition, for correspondence, the ETL (Extraction, Transformation and Loading) process must be mastered to reduce heterogeneity. The question is how to deploy Ant Colony (ACO) and Gradient Boosting Machine (GBM) algorithms. Then combine these for semi-structured reference data. And finally, make them efficient for schema enhancement. Experiments show that the hybrid approach outperforms the individual algorithms in terms of precision (98.9%), recall (97.8%) and F1-measurement (97.2%). This method is therefore significantly efficient in terms of scheme flexibility, while minimizing storage and processing costs.

Keywords: Big Data · ETL · semi-structured data · data quality

1 Introduction

Traditional data warehouses were designed to manage structured data from relational databases [1]. However, with the growing diversity of sources, such as social networks, IoT sensors and real-time feeds, it has become necessary to develop an architecture capable of handling this type of format (JSON, XML or similar). This requires advanced integration techniques to ensure their consistency and usefulness [2–4].

One of the main challenges is schema matching. These can vary considerably in terms of structure and semantics, complicating the process of alignment, fusion and accuracy for subsequent analyses. So, in response to the need to offer greater flexibility to better meet user requirements, a first approach [5, 6] was to propose a rule-based language called IRAH ("Intensional Redefinition for Aggregation Hierarchies") aimed at transforming pairings between aggregation levels within hierarchies. This allows users to build their own navigation paths by reorganizing the instances available to them. The second approach [7] presents an active warehouse-based system in which the user must specify the analysis through an ECA (Event - Condition - Action) mechanism.

In fact, these analyses are carried out on the warehouse and improve pre-processing. For performance efficiency, the authors focus on results to induce changes in the operational domain. With regard to multidimensional personalization, the authors [8, 9] drew on techniques for filtering information according to user profile to refine queries by adding predicates.

These contributions [10–12] has provided the user with a focus on his center of interest, while taking into account visualization constraints. It's not just about weights, but rather orders (qualitative representation of preferences). And this makes the task easier for the stakeholder. What's more, these orders are not expressed in absolute terms, but in relation to the context. It is therefore imperative to develop a new, automated and efficient approach, given their flexibility and complexity.

This paper proposes a new approach to matching Big Data sources in a semi-structured data warehouse context. The method uses advanced machine learning techniques such as the combination of ant colony (ACO) and gradient boosting machine (GBM) algorithms to automatically identify and align patterns. This approach aims to significantly reduce the time and effort required to integrate warehouses, while improving the accuracy and consistency of integrated data. In addition, the article presents an empirical evaluation of the effectiveness of this method through real-life case studies, demonstrating its relevance and potential in the field of Big Data.

The article is organized as follows: Sect. 2 presents the state of the art; Sect. 3, entitled presentation of the approach, highlights the proposed model; Sect. 3.5 compares our approach with others. Section 4 concludes.

2 State of the Art

This section reviews the literature on semi-structured data warehousing and the ETL process. Among these problems, we are first interested in the optimization of schema correspondences. Secondly, we take into account the ETL process to model a reference semi-structured data warehouse based on Big Data.

2.1 Semi-structured Data Warehouse

The design and construction of semi-structured data warehouses has been the subject of several studies. The authors [13–15] propose a semi-automatic approach to building data marts from XML sources. This approach consists of identifying one or more facts from an attribute tree. This tree is used to link and reorganize facts and dimensions to validate source documents. They implement a prototype that takes an XML schema as input and produces a logical schema of the warehouse as output.

Pursuing this idea, the authors [16, 17] propose a data structure called XML-Star-Schema. This introduces the notion of referential integrity constraints. In addition, some authors [18] have proposed XCubes for transferring data cubes between different companies. Others [19] have developed an XML-OLAP platform for online analysis of XML documents, eliminating the need for join operations between hierarchical levels.

Although semi-structured warehouses are useful for data reconciliation, they remain insufficient for the problem of optimal data utilization. In the following sections, we present the problems of generating the ETL process and querying on a data grid.

2.2 ETL Process

Constraint-driven generation has previously been studied in the field of engineering [20]. The context of this work is the analysis of mutation in a program, where there are several "Mutants" (i.e. program instances created with small rectifications of the original system). The approach analyzes the constraints that the "mutants" impose on program execution and generates data to guarantee the modified programs.

This problem has also been revised for the ETL process. The authors analyze both constraints during program execution. In the event of failure, both scenarios are covered. However, these works test the correctness of program executions and not its quality criteria. In databases, [21] presents an instance-based approach for application programs.

Some authors rely on dedicated SQL-based white-box testing. Given a statement, this defines a schema and the tester's requirements imposed on the constraint servers. If they are satisfactory, instances are provided.

These contributions of [22] presents a generic approach whose graphical representation supports customization with tributary dependencies. [23] proposes a multi-objective test set creation. This allows modeling not only on execution coverage, but also on additional objectives such as memory consumption criteria.

However, the above works focus solely on relational systems to solve the constraints of the existing system. To compensate, some authors [24] propose an important factor: tagging. They define loads while testing ETL to evaluate flows and measure quality satisfaction. These approaches do not provide any automatable means for reference data loads.

[25] on the other hand present a tool called Big Data Generator Suite (BDGS) while preserving 5V characteristics. Furthermore, in [26], a parallel framework is implemented. It uses XML configuration files for large-scale description and distribution. In this way, features can be used to compare standard DBMSs and large platforms (e.g. MapReduce platforms).

Nevertheless, most business process modeling tools do not provide comprehensive support for simulating the execution and analysis of relevant quality objectives. We will focus on simulation approaches in the general area of data-centric development processes (DCP) and quality criteria for the design of semi-structured data warehouses.

However, existing approaches to integrating semi-structured data have several limitations. Firstly, classic pattern-matching algorithms often focus on one particular aspect, such as accuracy, to the detriment of other criteria such as cost or scalability. Secondly, existing models are often best suited to structured data, which makes them less effective for handling semi-structured or unstructured data from diverse sources such as XML, JSON or IoT streams. Finally, as data volumes increase in Big Data environments, they struggle to scale efficiently and maintain stable performance in the face of massive quantities.

To overcome all this, we propose a new approach that optimizes not only the scalability of ETL match quality, but also the costs and performance of the process through the hybrid algorithm.

3 Our Approach

A methodology is proposed for integrating data sources into a warehouse. It consists firstly in formalizing a schema using semi-structured documents to express an interesting level of analysis abstraction. Then, using the ETL process, we define a correspondence between the various instances. Finally, optimize the parameters by combining algorithms.

3.1 Reference Data Warehouse Model

This model makes it possible to store semi-structured documents at a relevant level of abstraction in a reference warehouse. A collection is built from a unified schema. These then correspond to an OLAP fact and must satisfy certain constraints, such as meeting a minimum information requirement for the fact to be observed to be consistent.

Figure 1 summarizes the various stages. Initially, the user declares his analysis objectives in multidimensional form. These are transformed into an attribute tree. A comparison is then made in the following two cases: (1) If the input document contains the minimum required information, it is accepted. An instance is created and validated according to the schema. (2) If the input document does not contain sufficient information for an OLAP fact, it is rejected. Finally, all this is saved in an .XSD file. The aim is to obtain a homogeneous set of data with strict constraints on content, as well as native storage at the lowest possible cost.

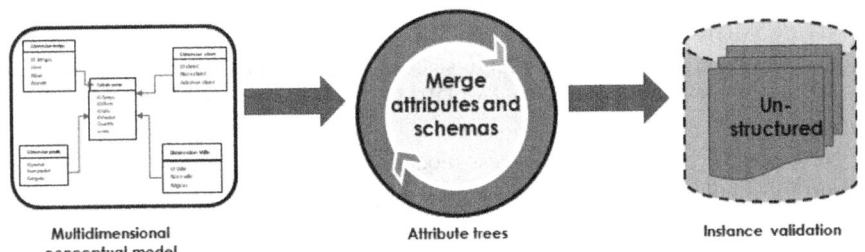

Fig. 1. Semi-structured data warehouse model.

3.2 ETL Approach

The implementation highlights the importance of each step in improving data quality and correspondence. Firstly, extraction, which involves the initial collection and preparation of data from a variety of heterogeneous sources. Each has its own format (semi-structured, unstructured, and structured).

The data is then transformed to become homogeneous and ready for analysis. Machine learning and automatic learning algorithms, such as boosting and ACO, are used. The ma Page normalizes, cleans and structures extracted data so that it is compatible with the data warehouse schema. In addition, the Passer: Indicates the processes or tools used according to the needs of the analysis. In addition, the path illustrates the flow before loading.

Finally, loading into a semi-structured warehouse, ready to be used for decision-making. The Fig. 2 describes all of the above.

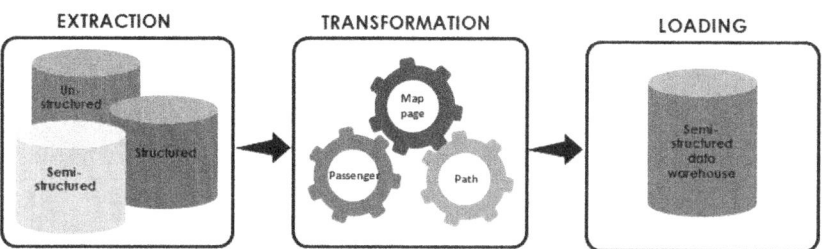

Fig. 2. ETL process for Big Data sources

3.3 Global Architecture

Figure 3 illustrates the integrated workflow from Big Data collection to advanced analysis. First, the data comes from diverse and heterogeneous sources, requiring careful extraction and preparation. Secondly, the UML model is used to conceptualize and structure the data prior to transformation. In addition, ETL is used for data integration and homogenization. In addition, the Semi-structured Data Warehouse is used to store and manage different formats efficiently. In addition, the Computing Grid ensures high processing capacity for voluminous data. Finally, OLAP analysis and Data Mining to analyze and uncover valuable insights.

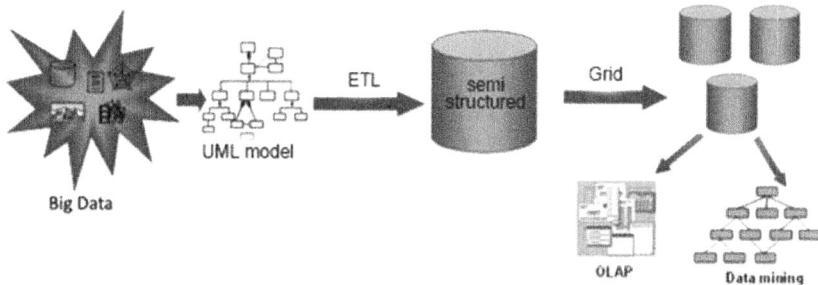

Fig. 3. Model architecture

3.4 Model Optimization

The objective is to maximize a function that evaluates the quality and cost of schema matching solutions. In other words, to find the best possible matches that offer high quality at optimal cost. Then to transform the aggregated costs and metrics into a unified measure of performance, facilitating comparison between different matching solutions. In addition, the cost function takes into account the costs associated with maintenance and processing, in order to assess the long-term viability of solutions. Finally, by aggregating data metrics, the function provides an overview of match quality for each attribute and source, enabling adjustments and improvements to be made.

So our optimization framework is as follows:

Maximize $\sum_{j} \sum_{i} \varphi(\pi_{ij}, \sigma_{ij})$.

Where
$$\begin{cases} \sigma_{ij}(\{d_{jk}\}) = \sum_{k=1}^{n_{ij}} \sigma_{ijk}/n_{ij} \\ \pi_{ij} = mc_i + mp_i \end{cases}$$

φ: quality/cost transformation function
π: cost function
σ: metrics aggregation function
d: data $i \in [1, |S|]; j \in [1, |A|]; k \in [1, |n|]$
n: number of data per attribute and per source
mc_i: maintenance costs
mp_i: Process cost.

The frame plays a central role in optimizing the algorithm proposed below (Table 1).

Table 1. Hybrid algorithm (ACO + GBM)

ALGORITHM 1: HYBRID ANT COLONY ALGORITHM	
1	Initialization of the parameters
2	**Repeat**
3	**For each** ant **in** the colony
4	Build an iterative solution based on GBM predictions and safeguard solution performance
5	Update phenomena to increase the attractiveness of the best local solution: local update
6	end
7	Calculate the Choquet's integral, identify the solution with the best performance and maintain this performance.
8	Update the phenomena rate for the components of the best solution: global update
9	**Until** a maximum number of iterations is reached
10	Identify the best solution across all iterations
12	**End**

This algorithm is described as follows:

First, step 0 represents the convergence thresholds or attractiveness factors used to guide the solution-finding process. Then step 1 constructs an iterative solution to the schema matching problem. This involves finding a path (a solution) that links the different components of the data schemas in an optimal way. Furthermore, quality could be measured by the accuracy of the schema matching, and cost by the time or resources required to find the solution. In addition, this local update allows subsequent ants to favor paths (solutions) that have been identified as good by previous ants. In addition, the Choquet integral is a measure used to evaluate the overall performance of solutions, taking into account the interactions between the various quality and cost criteria. Finally, step 2 identifies the best solution found over all iterations. This solution represents the best match of the semi-structured data schemas in terms of quality and cost.

3.5 Experimental Results

For constant data sizes equal to 2 GB, we list three sources: banking transactions (Kaggle), social networks (https://developer.twitter.com/) and Iot sensors (https://archive.ics.uci.edu/ml/index.php). We set the number of iterations to 100, assuming constant cost. We ran Pyton on a Core i7 computer with 16 GB Ram. We evaluate the performance of each algorithm according to the optimization framework.

For Ant Colony Algorithm. Performance metrics provide an assessment of match quality. The aggregated values and transformations show that the approach is moderately effective in optimizing match quality while minimizing costs in a semi-structured Big Data context (Table 2).

Table 2. Metric evaluation on ACO

Data set	Precision	Recall	F-measure	σ_{ij}	φ
1	0,85	0,80	0,82	0,83	0,13
2	0,75	0,70	0,72	0,73	0,10
3	0,90	0,88	0,89	0,89	0,13

For Gradient Boosting Machine Algorithm. The use of the boosting algorithm improves the performance metrics (Precision, Recall and F1-measure) for each data source, resulting in better matches. The values and transformations show that the boosting approach is moderately effective in optimizing match quality while minimizing costs in a semi-structured Big Data context (Table 3).

Table 3. Metric evaluation on GBM

Data set	Precision	Recall	F-measure	σ_{ij}	φ
1	0,90	0,88	0,89	0,89	0,13
2	0,85	0,80	0,83	0,83	0,12
3	0,95	0,93	0,94	0,94	0,13

For Hybrid Algorithm (Our Approach). The combination of the ACO and GBM algorithms delivers improved performance metrics (Accuracy, Recall and F1-measure) for each data source. The boosting algorithm (GBM) initially improves match predictions, while the ant colony-inspired algorithm (ACO) optimizes matches by refining solutions. Aggregate values and transformations show that this combined approach is highly effective in optimizing match quality while minimizing costs in a semi-structured Big Data context (Table 4).

Table 4. Metric evaluation on ACO + GBM

Data set	Precision	Recall	F-measure	σ_{ij}	φ
1	0,92	0,90	0,91	0,91	0,13
2	0,87	0,83	0,85	0,85	0,12
3	0,97	0,95	0,96	0,96	0,14

Figure 4 summarizes the various tables. It shows that our approach outperformed the others in almost every metric. This is the advantage of exploiting the strengths of each algorithm. The slight difference in the transformation function (0.13) does not significantly affect its overall performance.

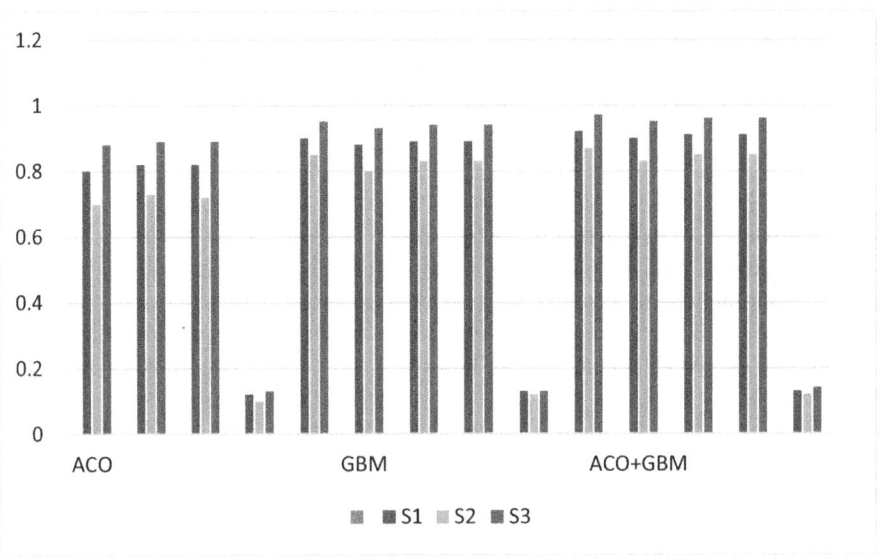

Fig. 4. Performance of different algorithms

4 Conclusion

In this paper, we have presented a new approach to Big Data source matching in a semi structured data warehouse context. By integrating optimization algorithms such as the Ant Colony Algorithm (ACO) and the Gradient Boosting Machine (GBM), our method aims to improve the quality of data matching while minimizing the associated costs. We have demonstrated that integrating these algorithms not only improves the precision and recall of data matches, but also reduces the aggregation function and maintains an acceptable error tolerance rate. This approach facilitates reliable analyses and sharp decisions for companies and organizations that have to deal with large quantities of data from different sources and formats. For future work, it would be interesting to explore other combinations of algorithms to evaluate the scalability and performance of our method in cloud environments.

References

1. Anassin, M.C., Aka, B., Brou, M.K.: Data extraction in the warehouse: a quality-based approach. Eur. J. Sci. Res. **150**(1), 14–20 (2018)
2. Azgomi, H., Sohrabi, M.K.: A game theory based framework for materialized view selection in data warehouses. Eng. Appl. Artif. Intell. **71**(125), 137 (2018). https://doi.org/10.1016/j.engappai.2018.02.018
3. Patricia, A.C.M., Bernard, S.K., Lagasane, K.: Correlations between big data and cloud in the transactions environment. Ingénierie des Systèmes d'Information **29**(3), 877–883 (2024). https://doi.org/10.18280/isi.290308
4. Daoud, M., Tamine, L., Chebaro, B.: Proposal of a session-based personalized IR system integrating a semantic user profile. Digit. Document **13**(1), 137–160 (2010). https://doi.org/10.3166/dn.13.1.137-160
5. Charalambidis, A., Troumpoukis, A., Konstantopoulos, S.: SemaGrow: optimizing federated SPARQL queries. In: Proceedings of the 11th International Conference on Semantic Systems - SEMANTICS '15, pp. 121–128 (2015). https://doi.org/10.1145/2814864.2814886
6. Nakucçi, E., Theodorou, V., Jovanovic, P., Abelló, A.: Bijoux: data generator for evaluating ETL process quality. In: Proceedings of the 17th International Workshop on Data Warehousing and OLAP - DOLAP '14, pp. 23–32 (2014). https://doi.org/10.1145/2666158.2666183
7. Weiping, Q., Dessloch, S.: Distributed snapshot maintenance in wide column NoSQL databases using partitioned incremental ETL pipelines. Inf. Syst. **1**, 11 (2017)
8. Wang, Y., Xia, Y., Fang, Q., Xu, X.: AQP++: a hybrid approximate query processing framework for generalized aggregation queries. J. Comput. Sci. **26**(419), 431 (2018). https://doi.org/10.1016/j.jocs.2017.05.001
9. Babu, S., Mohan, U.: An integrated approach to evaluating sustainability in supply chains using evolutionary game theory. Comput. Oper. Res. **89**(269), 283 (2018). https://doi.org/10.1016/j.cor.2017.01.008
10. Jaradat, A., Alhussian, H., Patel, A., Fati, S.M.: Multiple users replica selection in data grids for fair user satisfaction: a hybrid approach. Comput. Stand. Interfaces **71**, 103432 (2020). https://doi.org/10.1016/j.csi.2020.103432
11. Ningli, X., Qin, R., Song, S.: Point cloud registration for LiDAR and photogrammetric data: a critical synthesis and performance analysis on classic and deep learning algorithms. ISPRS Open J. Photogramm. Remote Sens. **8**, 100032 (2023)

12. Cheng, Y., et al.: Regional metal pollution risk assessment based on a big data framework: a case study of the eastern Tianshan mining area, China. Ecol. Indic. **145**, 109585 (2022)
13. Goldin, E., Feldman, D., Georgoulas, G., Castano, M., Nikolakopoulos, G.: Cloud Computing for Big Data Analytics in the Process Control Industry. European Unions Horizon Research and Innovation Programme under the Grant Agreement, 636834 (2020)
14. Jarosz, J.: Big data and cloud computing: roles and relationships, techniques and tools. J. Data Anal. **1**(1), 33–41 (2022)
15. Dorigo, M., Stützle, T.: Ant Colony Optimization. MIT Press, Cambridge (2004)
16. Singh, V., Chen, S.-S., Singhani, M., Nanavati, B., Kar, A.K., Gupta, A.: How are reinforcement learning and deep learning algorithms used for big data based decision making in financial industries–a review and research agenda. Int. J. Inf. Manag. Data Insights **2**, 100094 (2022)
17. Wu, B., Yang, L., Chen, Y.: An empirical study of purchase rate and dropout rate between mobile and PC customers. J. Syst. Manag. **29**, 924–933 (2020)
18. Agrawal, R., Srikant, R.: Fast algorithms for mining association rules in large databases. In: Proceedings of the 20th International Conference on Very Large Data Bases (VLDB'94), pp. 487–499 (1994)
19. Li, Z., et al.: DeepBSA: a deep-learning algorithm improves bulked segregant analysis for dissecting complex traits. Mol. Plant **15**, 1418–1427 (2022)
20. Friedman, J.H.: Greedy function approximation: a gradient boosting machine. Ann. Stat. **29**(5), 1189–1232 (2001)
21. Chen, F., Wang, H., Xie, Y., Qi, C.: An ACO-based online routing method for multiple order pickers with congestion consideration in warehouse. J. Intell. Manuf. **27**(2), 389–408 (2016). https://doi.org/10.1007/s10845-014-0871-1
22. Mavruk, T.: Analysis of herding behavior in individual investor portfolios using machine learning algorithms. Res. Int. Bus. Financ. **62**, 101740 (2022)
23. Zhanga, K., et al.: Modality analysis and algorithm design of stator short-circuit fault set for large compressed air energy storage generators. Energy Rep. **9**, 58–65 (2023)
24. Zhang, X., He, Y., Pan, L., Yao, Z.: Sales data analysis of cloud computing products based on big data. IFAC PapersOnLine **55–10**, 1404–1409 (2022)
25. Chouder, M.L., Rizzi, S., Chala, R.: Enabling Self-Service BI on Document Stores. DOLAP (2017)
26. Wua, B., Tiana, F., Zhanga, M., Zenga, H., Zenga, Y.: Cloud services with big data provide a solution for monitoring and tracking sustainable development goals. Geogr. Sustain. **1**, 25–32 (2020)

Web Scraping for Competitive Intelligence: State of the Art and Case Study

Edouard Ngor Sarr[✉], Oumar Diagne, Abel Diatta, and Lamine Faty

UFR SES, University Assane Seck de Ziguinchor (UASZ), Ziguinchor, Senegal
{edouard-ngor.sarr,abel.diatta,l.f}@univ-zig.sn,
o.diagne20160440@zig.univ.sn

Abstract. Data collection is a critical technique that involves extracting, organizing, and storing raw data from various sources, whether manual or automated. This article presents a state-of-the-art review along with a case study on the use of web scraping for competitive intelligence. In this study, we collected and merged data from different sources, performed cross-analyses, and visualized the results in informative dashboards to support decision-making. This information was then leveraged to formulate business recommendations aimed at enhancing the competitiveness of the companies studied. The study demonstrated that integrating web scraping into business strategies can improve market understanding and provide valuable insights to outcompete rivals. Additionally, we discuss the challenges associated with the use of web scraping for economic intelligence, while highlighting the potential contribution of artificial intelligence to enhance these systems.

Keywords: Web scraping · Data analysis · competitive intelligence · digital Marketing

1 Introduction

In a constantly changing world where the majority of Commercial activities are carried out online through web platforms (online stores/shops) more and more. The European Commission has launched a new initiative to the economical competitive intelligence has become very crucial for any company seeking to improve its competitiveness. Indeed, competitive analysis is defined when an organization X, which has similar activities to those of another organization Y, monitors the relevant activities of its competitors [1]. It is a powerful tool used by companies to analyze their environment [2]. The economical competitive intelligence is very essential for e-commerce businesses to remain competitive in a constantly changing market [3]. The success of such monitoring will necessarily depend on a good knowledge of its ecosystem and the implementation of data collection strategies in the websites of competitors.

This task, in the context of Web 2.0, has become very complex and time-consuming. Therefore, it's crucial to develop automated methods to optimize data acquisition [2].

Data acquisition involves collecting, organizing, and storing raw data with potential value from one or more sources. This information extraction process can be manual, automated, or semi-automatic and can include databases, digital files, or web pages. In this study, we focus on the automated acquisition of data from web pages: web scraping. Web scraping is a technique for retrieving data from web pages using a program or software. Thus, web scraping involves setting up computer programs to search, identify, and collect desired data from various web corpora and then presenting it in a more structured format for better decision-making. This technique has become widely used across various sectors, including healthcare, agriculture, e-commerce, communications, security, and even media. Various approaches, techniques, tools, and applications are also discussed in the literature [4].

In competitive intelligence, web scraping involves systematically and automatically [5] collecting relevant information about competitors' activities, products, services, strategies, and performance from their web platforms, especially their online stores. Scraping thus allows businesses to gain a competitive advantage by closely monitoring their rivals in the market [6]. In a nutshell, the objective of data scraping is to help industry actors to establish autonomous data acquisition systems to facilitate informed decision-making [7].

This article presents the state of the art and a case study on the use of web scraping for competitive intelligence in e-commerce in Senegal. The article is divided into four main sections. Section 2 addresses web scraping. Section 3 provides the state of the art of scraping in competitive intelligence. Section 4 is dedicated to our case study.

2 State of the Art

2.1 Approaches and Tools for Web Scraping

The literature presents five main approaches for web scraping, ranging from basic to sophisticated: regex-based web scraping, DOM-based web scraping, API-based web scraping, machine learning-based web scraping, and visual web scraping.

Regex-Based [8] Web Scraping: Firstly, this approach defines a set of specific search patterns in advance to guide the extraction process. A regular expression is a string of characters that describes a search pattern. Regular expressions are used to search and manipulate strings according to specific patterns. Patterns can be simple (a specific word or a special character) or complex (a string of characters, a date, or an email) [9]. Popular tools like ScrapeBox Email Scraper, Email Extractor, Sales Navigator, AeroLeads, or Prospect.io use this approach [10, 11].

DOM-Based Web Scraping: This approach leverages the hierarchical structure of web pages to extract the desired data [12]. The DOM (Document Object Model) is a hierarchical model that represents web documents as a tree of nodes, allowing developers to programmatically access and manipulate the content, structure, and style of web pages. The DOM provides a detailed representation of a page's structure, making it easier to navigate and manipulate its content [13]. JavaScript-based tools like JSDom [14] and its variants use this approach [15].

API-Based Web Scraping: This approach involves interacting directly with application programming interfaces (APIs) provided by websites to extract data in a structured manner and in compliance with data usage policies [16]. Platforms like Twitter, Facebook, or Reddit offer native APIs that allow access to user data legally and in a controlled manner without violating site terms of use [17].

Machine Learning-Based Web Scraping: This approach involves training algorithms to recognize and extract information from a page's DOM structure. It allows the creation of learning models for analyzing large amounts of data. These models [18], whether supervised, unsupervised, or reinforcement, enable intelligent and adaptive data collection, similar to search engine indexing robots [19].

Visual Web Scraping Based on Artificial Intelligence (AI): This approach uses computer vision and machine learning techniques to visually analyze web page content and extract relevant data [20]. Computer vision aims to automate the processing and analysis of digital images to extract meaningful information [21]. It includes tasks like object recognition, face detection, image segmentation, or 3D reconstruction. Tools like Diffbot [22] use AI algorithms to automatically recognize and extract data from complex web pages, including unstructured data like images or graphics [23] (Table 1).

Table 1. Advantages and Disadvantages of Different Web Scraping Methods

Web Scraping Methods	Web Scraping Methods	Web Scraping Methods
Regular Expression-Based Web Scraping	- Simple to implement	- Limited to text formats
DOM-Based Web Scraping	- Allows data extraction from HTML structure	- Requires knowledge of HTML/CSS
API-Based Web Scraping	- Provides structured and easy-to-use data	- Dependent on the existence of an API
Machine Learning-Based Web Scraping	- Ability to extract complex data	- Requires expertise in machine learning
AI-Based Visual Scraping	- Can extract data from visual content	- High technical complexity

Additionally, numerous libraries and frameworks are available in popular programming languages [24]. In JAVA, APIs like Jsoup, Selenium WebDriver, HTMLUnit, WebHarvest, Abot, HtmlCleaner, Jauntium, or WebCollector are used [25]. For Python, libraries such as Selenium, Requests-HTML, PyQuery, MechanicalSoup, Lxml, Requests, BeautifulSoup, or Scrapy are available [26]. JavaScript offers libraries like Cheerio, Puppeteer, Request-Promise, Axios, Node-crawler, AxiosScraper, or Simple HTML DOM Parser [27]. PHP also has tools like Goute, WebScraping.io, ScrapingBee, ScraperAPI, QueryPath, PHP Crawler, PHP Web Scraper, or PHP Web Scraper [28] (Table 2).

Table 2. Web scraping libraries and frameworks across different languages

Language	Library or Framework	Advantages	Disadvantages
Java	Jsoup	-Easy HTML parsing -Handles malformed HTML well	- Does not support complex JavaScript pages
	Selenium WebDriver	- Supports dynamic content - Works with multiple browsers	- Slower due to reliance on browsers
Python	BeautifulSoup	- Simple syntax - Ideal for small projects	- May be slow on large datasets
	Scrapy	- Fast and scalable - Excellent for large-scale scraping	- Slower learning curve
JavaScript	Puppeteer	- Ideal for dynamic content - Support for headless browsers	- Consumes a lot of resources
	Cheerio	- Lightweight - Syntax similar to jQuery	- Limited to static content
PHP	Goutte	- Easy to use - Lightweight for simple tasks	- Limited features for complex projects

The growing accessibility of web scraping tools for non-programmers is also worth mentioning, with user-friendly platforms [29] like import.io, Octoparse, Parsehub, ProWebScraper, Monzanda, or Web Content Extractor. These ready-to-use tools provide intuitive graphical interfaces and cloud or local scraping functionalities, allowing a broader audience to benefit from web scraping without advanced programming skills [30].

Several browsers offer extensions for web scraping. These extensions are lightweight applications that extend the capabilities of a web browser by adding specific features not integrated by default. These tools enable users to easily extract data from various web pages. They are particularly appreciated for their ability to convert extracted data into usable formats, such as forms or text files. Users can select elements to extract directly from their browser. For example, Chrome offers several practical extensions for web data collection, and similar extensions are available for other browsers like Mozilla Firefox and Microsoft Edge.

2.2 Forms of Competitive Intelligence

The literature distinguishes several forms of competitive intelligence based on objectives and targets. Competitive intelligence can be active or passive depending on the goal. It can also be direct or indirect depending on the target. We have:

- **Passive Competitive Intelligence**: This involves collecting information about competitors without a specific predefined objective. It involves observing and monitoring competitors' activities and performance without directly interacting with them [31].
- **Active Competitive Intelligence**: In contrast to passive intelligence, active competitive intelligence aims to obtain specific information to produce knowledge and guide concrete actions [32]. It involves direct interaction with competitors or their online resources.
- **Direct Competitive Intelligence**: This targets competitors offering similar products and services. The focus is on activities and performance of these competitors since they share the same target market [32].
- **Indirect Competitive Intelligence**: This focuses on competitors offering products or services that meet different customer needs, even if they are not direct competitors in the same market [33].
- **Mixed Competitive Intelligence**: This combines passive and active or direct and indirect approaches to gather comprehensive and in-depth information about competitors [34]. This allows businesses to obtain a more complete overview of the market and competitors.

Regardless of the form of intelligence used, web scraping is employed to collect data from various online sources while adhering to the specific objectives and targets of each approach.

3 Web Scraping for Competitive Intelligence

3.1 Challenges

In an environment where competition has become very fierce and where the landscape is characterized by the complexity and velocity of transactions through online stores, competitive intelligence has become indispensable and crucial for the continuity and survival of companies. Indeed, competitive intelligence encompasses a set of practices, methodologies, and tools aimed at systematically and proactively collecting, analyzing, and exploiting relevant data for the company [35]. It aims to anticipate changes in its environment, identify opportunities and threats, and make informed decisions. It is used by companies to analyze their environment and make decisions based on available data [2]. The data used in such intelligence often comes from competitors and requires a time-consuming and resource-intensive collection, especially if this data is in online stores. Hence the interest in using innovative data collection techniques such as web scraping. Web scraping in competitive intelligence plays a crucial role by allowing the search and extraction of data from competitors' sites, structuring it, and storing it in a usable format [36]. The stakes are multiple for companies, including:

- **Web scraping for good market trend monitoring:** Web scraping plays an essential role in collecting information on prices and events influencing these prices [37]. By analyzing historical product data and predicting future movements, companies can proactively adjust their strategies [38]. Through good intelligence, companies can offer discounts, increase production, or introduce new products, thus better meeting the needs and expectations of their customers [39].
- **Web scraping to improve competitive analysis:** By monitoring competitors' activities through web scraping, companies can gather valuable information about their strategies, performance, and innovations [40]. This data helps identify areas where competitors excel and those where they are vulnerable [41]. Consequently, organizations can adjust their own strategies to position themselves advantageously in the market, exploiting competitors' weaknesses and strengthening their own strengths [42]. In sum, web scraping helps the organization determine its strengths and weaknesses to minimize threats and maximize opportunities [43].
- **Web scraping to improve price analysis:** to monitor market supply and demand and assess cost flexibility. Through web scraping, companies can collect data on competitors' prices, as well as price variations based on demand and seasons [44]. This information helps adjust their own product prices competitively and strategically [45]. By understanding market price dynamics, companies can respond more effectively to supply and demand fluctuations, optimizing their positioning and profitability [46]. Also, respecting MAP (Minimum Advertised Price) is essential to ensure minimum pricing during product sales, ensuring fair competition and maintaining product value [47].
- **Web scraping to increase revenue:** To increase its revenue, organizations can implement the best frameworks based on available data. By analyzing this data, we can identify market opportunities, adjust our offerings, and optimize our processes to maximize sales and profitability [48].
- **Web scraping to retain customers:** Personalizing offers according to customer segments is crucial for creating lasting relationships [49]. By understanding the specific needs of each segment [50], we can offer products and services that precisely meet their expectations, thus strengthening customer satisfaction and fostering long-term loyalty [51]. For companies operating in the e-commerce sector, certain types of data are particularly sought after [52].

3.2 Difficulties

Optimal use of web scraping in competitive intelligence faces several challenges, including:

- **Diversity of data and sources (distribution of data across different sources):** This advanced approach involves using multiple servers or scraping instances to collect data on a large scale simultaneously [53]. This method accelerates the collection process and efficiently manages large volumes of data. Distributed scraping presents several difficulties, such as coordination and synchronization of tasks in parallel launches, error management, scalability of different sources, and data standardization and aggregation.

- **Bypassing anti-scraping measures and tools:** Companies often face limitations imposed by target websites, such as the use of CAPTCHAs [54] and anti-scraping tools. CAPTCHAs are designed to distinguish humans from bots. Integrating CAPTCHA resolution services increases the cost and complexity of data collection. Detection and rotation of proxies are crucial to avoid blocks, and resolution errors can lead to interruptions and delays in scraping. These tools and measures, if not properly addressed, can complicate the process and increase operational costs.
- **Legality of data collection on pages:** With the introduction of strict data protection regulations, companies must ensure their scraping practices comply with applicable laws [55]. Non-compliance with these regulations can result in severe penalties, including hefty fines and damage to the company's reputation. Therefore, it involves navigating copyright issues, website terms of use, and personal data protection.
- **Ensuring the quality of collected data:** The quality of data collected via web scraping can vary significantly. Data may be incomplete, inaccurate, or outdated, which can harm the quality of competitive analyses [56]. Institutions must implement rigorous data cleaning and validation processes to ensure the reliability and usefulness of the data [57].
- **Costs of implementation and monitoring:** Large-scale web scraping can be costly in terms of computing resources and bandwidth [58], mainly due to the need to manage and process large amounts of data. This can result in high expenses for servers, storage of extracted data, and network request management, significantly increasing operational costs.
- **Constraints related to personal data protection:** The use of web scraping techniques also raises ethical concerns [59]. Companies must ensure their practices respect the rights of content owners and users. Adopting a responsible and transparent approach to data collection and use is essential for maintaining stakeholder trust and avoiding controversies [60]. Indeed, data protection policies[1] in this area are governed by laws such as the General Data Protection Regulation (GDPR) in Europe [61] and the California Consumer Privacy Act (CCPA) in the United States [62]. These laws impose strict rules on the collection and processing of personal data, requiring transparency, explicit consent, and data minimization. Companies risk severe sanctions for non-compliance. Moreover, laws like the Computer Fraud and Abuse Act (CFAA) [63] in the United States can penalize unauthorized access to computer systems. For example, in August 2023, international regulators emphasized the importance of protecting publicly accessible data against illegal scraping, urging companies to adopt an ethical approach [60]. In 2022, Meta was fined €265 million[2] for failing to protect its users' data from scraping.

While web scraping is a powerful technique for data collection, its limitations must be carefully considered. To overcome these challenges, it is crucial to adopt ethical practices, stay informed about site changes, and use tools that meet the project's specific

---

[1] https://www.williamfry.com/knowledge/data-scraping-personal-data-data-protection-rules-apply/.
[2] https://www.williamfry.com/knowledge/data-scraping-personal-data-data-protection-rules-apply/.

needs. Ultimately, a thoughtful and respectful approach to targeted sites is necessary to ensure effective and sustainable data extraction.

4 Case Study

4.1 System Architecture

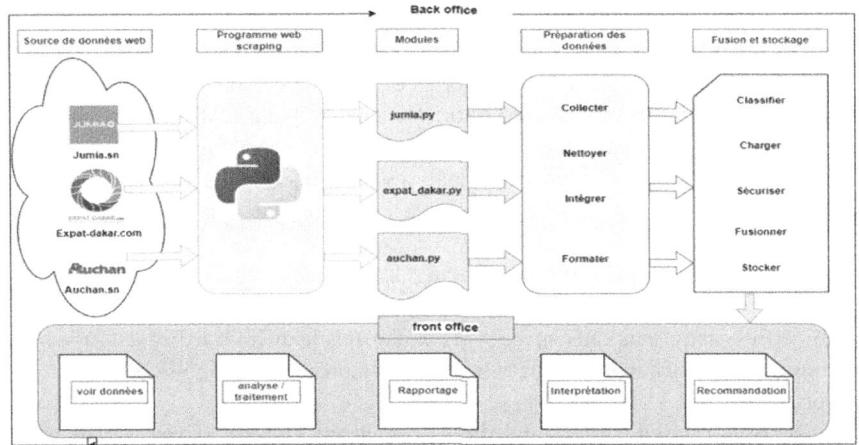

Fig. 1. System Architecture

This Fig. 1 shows the architecture of our system. It is composed of three main modules:

- **A Data Acquisition Module:** This module, based on intelligent web scraping, synchronously collects data from selected sources [64]. The Python library BeautifulSoup is utilized for this purpose.
- **A Preprocessing Module:** This module cleans, standardizes, and merges data into a CSV file [19]. Various Python modules are used to perform the necessary tasks.
- **An Analysis and Presentation Module:** This module provides real-time decision-making information through graphical representations. Power BI is chosen here as the tool for visualizing decision-making information.

Thus, our system takes a URL as input and sends it as bait to its target site via an HTTP GET request, awaiting a response. It then proceeds to analyze the HTML document. If errors are encountered during this step (e.g., issues with the request or the DOM), the system halts its execution. Otherwise, the script searches for a specific data pattern, which it subjects to processing, including the removal of duplicates, missing values, and erroneous data, as well as the categorization of the collected elements. Next, it extracts this data, converts it into a suitable format for its program (such as CSV, JSON, etc.), and stores it (see Fig. 2).

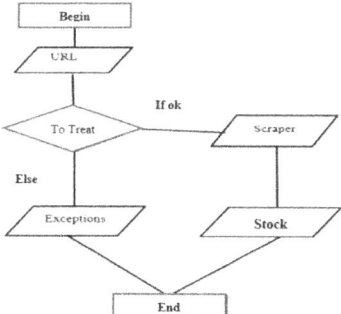

Fig. 2. System operation

4.2 Presentation of the Corpus

For this study, we selected a representative sample of online stores in Senegal, covering various sectors such as fashion, electronics, and consumer goods [36]. The selection criteria include the popularity of the sites, the diversity of products, and the availability of data. Additionally, we chose three sites as the main study samples: Jumia, Expat-Dakar, and Auchan. The selection criteria for these samples are based on their leading position in the Senegalese market and the diversity of their offerings. Jumia[3] is the largest e-commerce platform in Senegal, offering a wide range of products and attracting a high volume of visitors, making it a valuable source for analyzing consumption trends. Auchan[4], primarily a retail chain, has also adapted to e-commerce, attracting a diverse clientele with its selection of food and non-food items. Expat-Dakar[5], on the other hand, is characterized by its classified ads, providing a unique perspective on local consumer behavior. These platforms enable the collection of rich and representative data of the market, offering a broad range of products and services. Jumia and Auchan generate numerous interactions, providing opportunities to observe price fluctuations, promotions, and consumption trends. By incorporating Expat-Dakar, the research also covers classified ads, thereby providing a more nuanced and comprehensive analysis of purchasing behaviors and pricing strategies in Senegal.

Each of these online stores has unique features and data organization. The online store Jumia offers a wide range of products organized into categories such as electronics, with details on products, customer reviews, and delivery information (see Fig. 3).

---

[3] https://gaynako.com/e-commerce/top-35-sites-vente-ligne-senegal/#Jumia_jumiasn.
[4] https://gaynako.com/e-commerce/top-35-sites-vente-ligne-senegal/#Auchan_auchansn.
[5] https://gaynako.com/e-commerce/top-35-sites-vente-ligne-senegal/#Expat_dakar_expat-dakarcom.

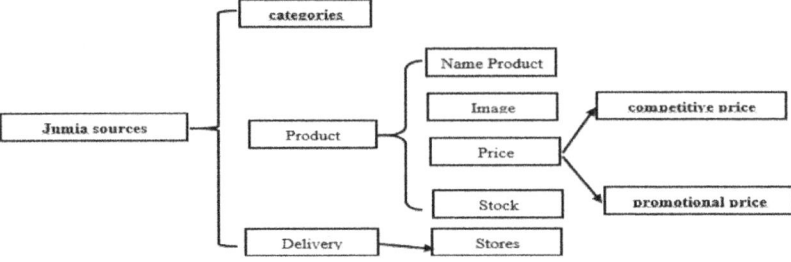

Fig. 3. Data Organization on JUMIA

The Auchan store (see Fig. 4), a leader in large-scale food distribution in Senegal, organizes its data by products, with details on prices, promotions, and specific categories. This approach allows us to capture a variety of relevant data for our case study on competitive intelligence in e-commerce in Senegal.

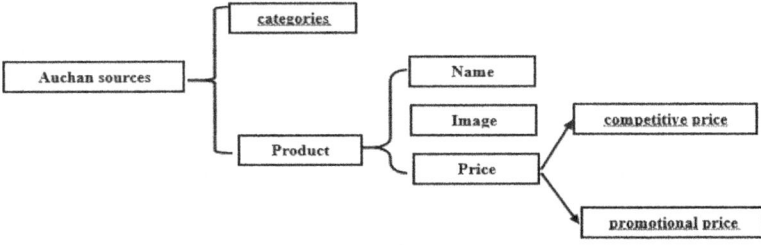

Fig. 4. Data Organization on AUCHAN

Regarding Expat-Dakar we explored its content as follows: category, owner, announcement (name, image, type, price).

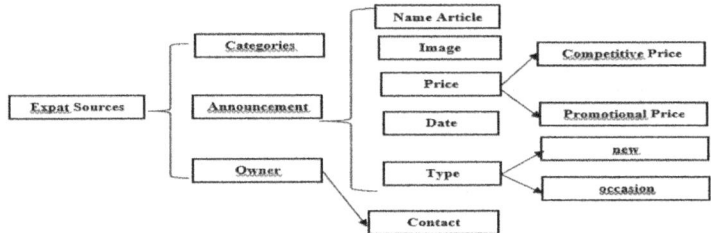

Fig. 5. Data Organization on Expat-Dakar

4.3 Data Acquisition

Implementing an effective web scraping system requires careful selection of existing technologies [65]. Our goal is to perform a mixed active competitive intelligence on the three sources [66]. Therefore, considering the structure of the sources, we opted for

DOM-based web scraping using the Python library BeautifulSoup as the collection tool. The process of collecting data from each site involves the following steps:

1. The module takes as input the main URL of the store, for example, https://www.jumia.sn/.
2. rom this base URL, we collect all the category URLs (see Figs. 3, 4 and 5) and store them in a file named `category.csv`. This category collection is done by scraping the HTML DOM (see Fig. 6). The URLs of subcategories generally follow the format `urlsite/SubCategory`, for example, https://www.jumia.sn/maison-bureau-electromenager.
   a. For each line in this file (corresponding to a category), we access and collect all the product data listed on that page using HTML DOM information (see Fig. 7).
   b. We continually update the index of the collected data to avoid re-collecting the same products in future scraping sessions. This process is repeated at regular intervals to ensure no new or updated data is missed (Fig. 8).

Fig. 6. Presence of Categories on Jumia's Homepage

Fig. 7. DOM Showing Category Tags and URLs on Jumia

Fig. 8. DOM Showing Product Data on Jumia

5 Data Preprocessing and Processing

The raw data extracted undergoes a preprocessing phase. This step ensures that the raw data collected is cleaned and organized to make it usable. It includes tasks such as removing duplicates, handling missing values, correcting errors, and normalizing formats. For example, the collected data may contain redundant or incorrect information, which, if not treated, can distort subsequent analyses [59].

The actual processing, on the other hand, involves extracting relevant information and converting it into structured formats (CSV, JSON, XML). The data is then categorized and, in our case, may undergo various manipulations to identify trends, make predictions, or generate strategic insights [67]. These steps result in data that is ready to be integrated into more complex analysis models, thus enhancing the effectiveness of competitive intelligence systems or other web scraping applications. To achieve this, a compliance table was established (see Table 3) to ensure the consistency of the collected data.

Table 3. Compliance table

Auchan	Jumia	Expat-Dakar	Final Data
Article	Produit	Announcement	Produit
Nom Article	Nom Produit	Name Article	Nom produit
Prix	Prix	Price	Prix
Flash	Promotions	--	Promotions
Notes et Commande	Notes	--	Avis Client
Livraison	Livraison	Contact	Livraison

From this table, the merged data will be stored in JSON format. Figure 9 shows the organization of the unified JSON file. The goal is to ensure optimal structuring for more in-depth analysis with cross-referenced data [59].

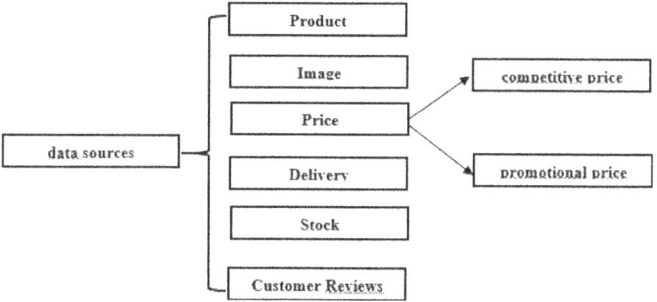

Fig. 9. Organization of Unified Data

6 Results & Discussions

We performed several types of analyses [58] based on the needs: descriptive analysis, predictive analysis, and prescriptive analysis. These analyses aim to produce robust knowledge to guide our decisions with a very low margin of error. The results allow us to identify, among other things, the categories dominating sales, the effect of promotions, customer reviews, and the cities with the highest purchases. Specifically, on Jumia, dominant categories in total sales include electronics and fashion products, which account for over 40% of sales. The majority of transactions (70%) were made on discounted products, highlighting consumers' marked sensitivity to prices and special offers. Customer reviews are largely positive, with an average satisfaction rating of 4.5 out of 5, reinforcing Jumia's favorable reputation. Finally, geographically, sales are concentrated in urban areas such as Dakar and Thiès, accounting for 60% of total sales.

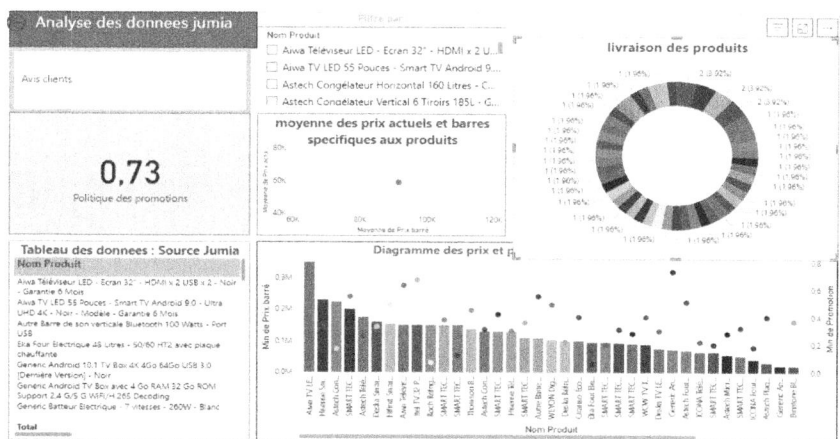

Fig. 10. Dashboard 1 for JUMIA

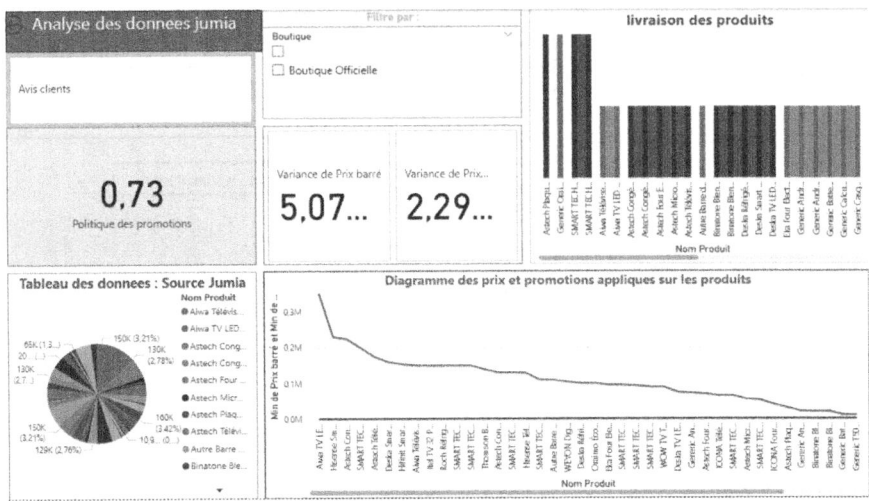

Fig. 11. Dashboard 2 for JUMIA

The same analysis is conducted for Auchan (see Figs. 10 and 11), albeit with different study variables at times. The analysis reveals that Auchan, as a key player in large-scale retail, places a greater emphasis on the in-store experience, complemented by an omnichannel strategy that integrates e-commerce. This approach includes competitive pricing and stock optimization to meet local demand effectively.

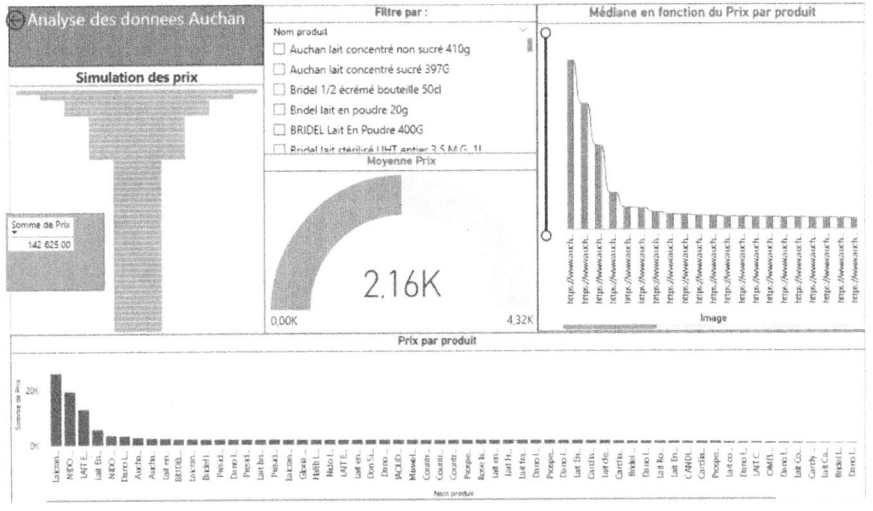

Fig. 12. Dashboard 1 for AUCHAN

Web Scraping for Competitive Intelligence   27

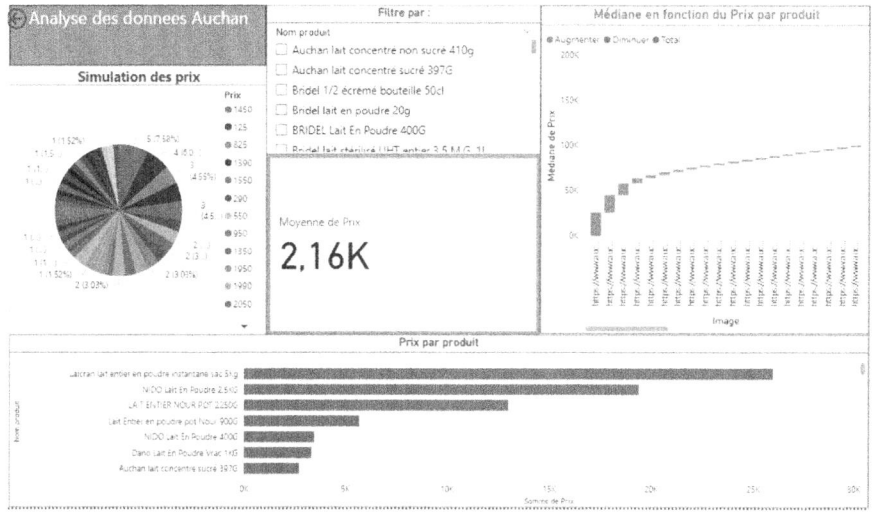

Fig. 13. Dashboard 2 for AUCHAN

The data also enabled us to perform a cross-analysis of the two sources, Auchan and Jumia (see Figs. 12 and 13). Additionally, Expat-Dakar, which focuses on small ads, adopts a community-driven approach by facilitating exchanges between individuals. Its model is based on ease of use and local proximity, although it does not offer logistical services (Figs. 14 and 15).

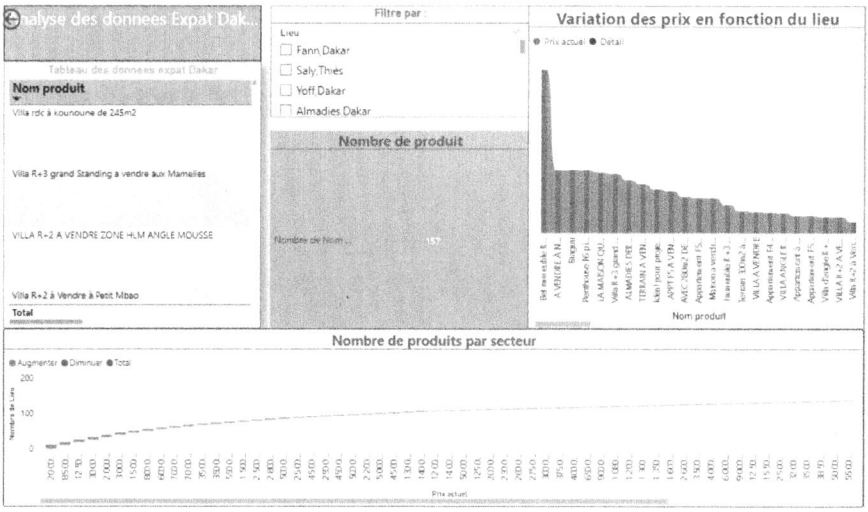

Fig. 14. Dashboard 1 for Expat

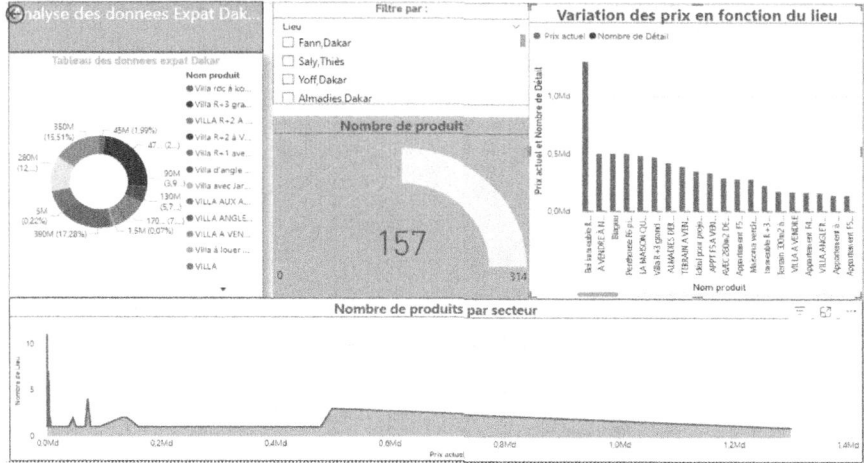

Fig. 15. Dashboard 2 for Expat

At Expat, we employed the following analytical parameters:

- **Number of Products per Location:** This enables us to identify the sectors where activities are more concentrated.
- **Maximum Price per Sector:** Offers tend to be more expensive in downtown Dakar.
- **Minimum Price per Sector:** Offers are generally less expensive in the Dakar suburbs.
- **Varieties of Products:** In pursuit of new products.
- **Total Number of Products:** Exceeding 300, with an average of 157 (Figs. 16 and 17).

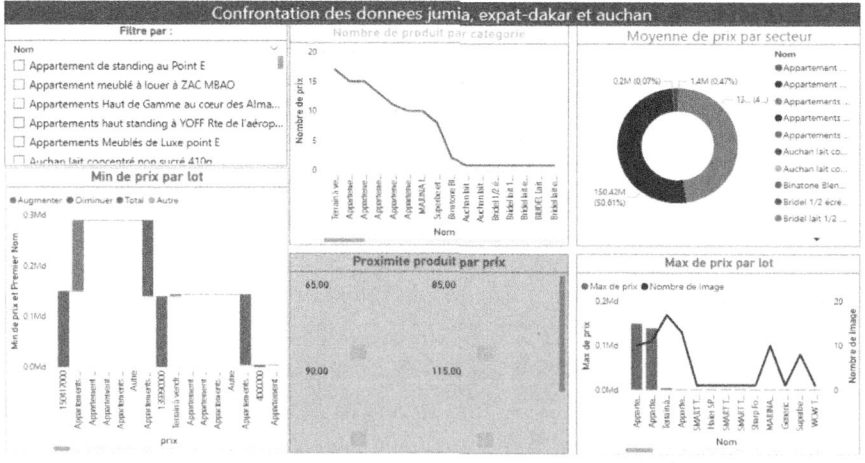

Fig. 16. Cross-Analysis Dashboard

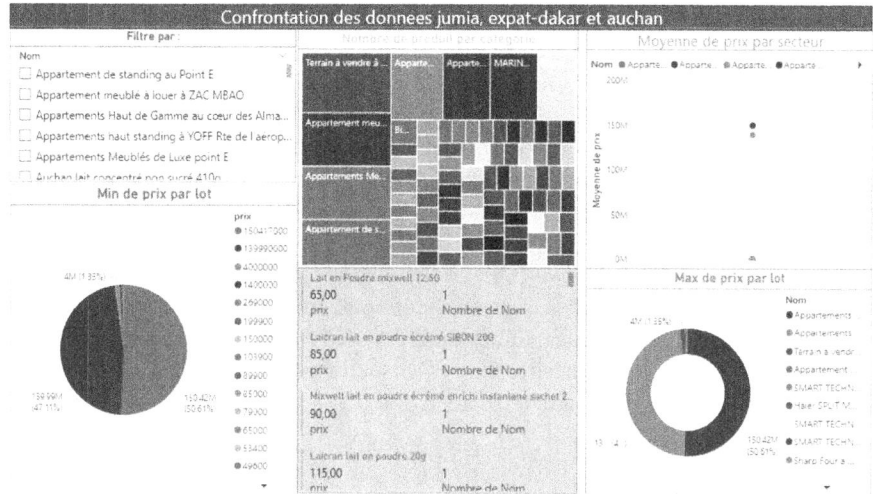

Fig. 17. Cross-Analysis Dashboard

In this way, companies can collect various types of data, including product specifications, price information, user reviews, and social media mentions. This comprehensive data collection provides a holistic view of market dynamics and competitor tactics. Therefore, ensuring the accuracy and quality of the collected data is crucial. Companies need to implement rigorous data quality control measures, validate the data, and consolidate the information to ensure its reliability. To maximize their chances of success, organizations must demonstrate flexibility and innovation in their information gathering by integrating advanced data acquisition systems such as Natural Language Processing (NLP) and web crawlers. These tools enable more targeted and efficient data collection, even amid the growing abundance of available data.

The integration of artificial intelligence and advanced machine learning techniques promises to further enhance these capabilities, allowing for more sophisticated analyses and more accurate market trend predictions. However, this technological evolution comes with significant challenges. In this context, web scraping will continue to play a central role in business strategies, helping companies navigate effectively in an increasingly complex and dynamic competitive environment.

Thus, to improve their position, Jumia should strengthen the empowerment of local merchants by providing analytical tools and solid return policies. Auchan could adopt a more eco-responsible strategy by promoting local products and enhancing its loyalty program. Expat-Dakar should integrate more efficient payment and delivery solutions while offering targeted advertising options to increase the visibility of listings. These recommendations are based on the analysis of purchasing behaviors, logistics, and the expectations of local consumers.

7 Conclusion

This study demonstrates the effectiveness of web scraping as a strategic tool for collecting and analyzing competitive data in the online commerce sector. Indeed, regardless of the approach or tool used, web scraping in competitive intelligence allows for the automation of large-scale data extraction. Tools such as frameworks are widely used for efficient data extraction and processing. By employing advanced web scraping techniques, we were able to effectively extract and analyze data from various online stores across sectors like electronics, fashion, and food. The results obtained allowed us to identify market trends, assess price competitiveness, and provide strategic recommendations to enhance companies' competitive positions. Future studies could focus on increasing the number of sources and integrating advanced technologies such as artificial intelligence to uncover more correlations in the data and make predictions.

References

1. Lesca, H., Schuler, M.: Veille stratégique: comment ne pas être noyé sous les informations. In: Colloque Vsst'95 (1998)
2. Métais, E.: Intention stratégique et transformation de l'environnement concurrentiel: enjeux d'une conception de la stratégie centrée sur les ressources de l'entreprise. Theses. Fr. Doctoral dissertation, Aix-Marseille 3 (1997)
3. Tahar Chaouche, B., Azeb, S.: La veille concurrentielle et la compétitivité de l'entreprise Cas de ATM Mobilis. Doctoral dissertation, Université Mouloud Mammeri (2023)
4. Depeyre, C.: Orchestrer les actifs pour rester concurrentiel: La trajectoire stratégique de Raytheon. In: Gérer et comprendre, no. 1, pp. 55–66 (2008)
5. Clements, D.W.G.: Flux d'informations, systèmes de contrôle et gestion d'entreprise. Manag. Int. Rev. **8**, 27–29 (1968)
6. Djiwadikusumah, F., Irawan, G.H., Al-Fadilah, R.H.: Web scraping situs e-commerce menggunakan teknik parsing dom. Jurnal Siliwangi Seri Sains dan Teknologi **7**(2), 52–57 (2021)
7. Leitzelman, M., Ereteo, G., Grohan, P., Herledan, F., Gandon, F., Buffa, M.: De l'utilité d'un outil de veille d'entreprise de seconde génération. In: Journées Francophones d'Ingénierie des Connaissances, vol. 20 (2009)
8. Dewi, L.C., Chandra, A.: Social media web scraping using social media developers API and regex. Procedia Comput. Sci. **157**, 444–449 (2019)
9. Maududie, A., Retnani, W.E.Y., Rohim, M.A.: An approach of web scraping on news website based on regular expression. In: 2018 2nd East Indonesia Conference on Computer and Information Technology (EIConCIT), pp. 203–207. IEEE, November 2018
10. Shin, Y., Gupta, M., Myers, S.: The nuts and bolts of a forum spam automator. In: 4th USENIX Workshop on Large-Scale Exploits and Emergent Threats (LEET 11) (2011)
11. Wasi, S., Shaikh, Z.A., Shamsi, J.: Contextual event information extractor for emails. Sindh Univ. Res. J. SURJ (Sci. Ser.) **43**(1 (a)) (2011)
12. Gunawan, R., Rahmatulloh, A., Darmawan, I., Firdaus, F.: Comparison of web scraping techniques: regular expression, HTML DOM and Xpath. In: 2018 International Conference on Industrial Enterprise and System Engineering (ICoIESE 2018), pp. 283–287. Atlantis Press, March 2019
13. Lotfi, C., Srinivasan, S., Ertz, M., Latrous, I.: Web Scraping Techniques and Applications: A Literature

14. Viikmaa, A.: Web Data Extraction for Content Aggregation from E-Commerce Websites. Doctoral dissertation, Dissertação (Mestrado)—University of Tartu (2016)
15. Rahmatullah, A., Gunawan, R.: Web scraping with HTML DOM method for data collection of scientific articles from google scholar. IJIS **2**(2), 95–104 (2020)
16. Glez-Peña, D., Lourenço, A., López-Fernández, H., Reboiro-Jato, M., Fdez-Riverola, F.: Technologies de scraping Web dans un monde d'API. Brief. Bioinform. **15**(5), 788–797 (2014)
17. Dongo, I., Cadinale, Y., Aguilera, A., Martínez, F., Quintero, Y., Barrios, S.: Web scraping versus API Twitter: une comparaison pour une analyse de crédibilité. In: Dans Actes de la 22e conférence internationale sur l'intégration de l'information et les applications et services Web, pp. 263–273, November 2020
18. Sirisuriya, S.D.S.: Importance of web scraping as a data source for machine learning algorithms-review. In: 2023 IEEE 17th International Conference on Industrial and Information Systems (ICIIS), pp. 134–139. IEEE, August 2023
19. Parikh, K., Singh, D., Yadav, D., Rathod, M.: Detection of web scraping using machine learning. Open Access Int. J. Sci. Eng. **3**(1), 114–118 (2018)
20. Zhao, B.: Web scraping. Encyclopedia of big data, 1 (2017)
21. Scarnò, M., Seid, Y.: Use of artificial intelligence and Web scraping methods to retrieve information from the World Wide Web. J. Eng. Res. Appl. **8** (2018)
22. Upshall, M.: Extracting Meaning from Web Content. eLucidate, 13(1) (2016)
23. Brossard, C.: Analyse par intelligence artificielle d'images de tomodensitométrie de patients traumatisés crâniens afin de prédire leur évolution neurologique. Doctoral dissertation, Université Grenoble Alpes [2020] (2022)
24. Cording, P.H., Lyngby, K.: Algorithmes pour le scraping Web (2011). http://www2.imm.dtu.dk/pubdb/views/publicationdetails.php
25. Mitchell, R.: Instant web scraping with Java. Packt Publishing, Birmingham, AL (2013)
26. Lawson, R.: Web Scraping with Python. Packt Publishing Ltd., Birmingham (2015)
27. Narang, Y., Rawat, S.S., Sati, D., Singh, A., Malik, A., Verma, S.: Web data extraction using DOM parsing for data collection and ontologies. In: Advancement of Intelligent Computational Methods and Technologies, pp. 156–161. CRC Press (2024)
28. Haralson, D.: Automating website crawling using web scraping techniques provided by PHP (2016)
29. Abiantoro, D., Kusumo, D.S.: Analyse des informations sur la qualité du contenu Web sur le site Web Koseeker à l'aide de la méthode d'audit du contenu Web et des outils ParseHub. In: 2020, 8e Conférence internationale sur les technologies de l'information et de la communication (ICoICT), pp. 1–6. IEEE, June 2020
30. Cording, P.H., Lyngby, K.: Algorithmes de web scraping. Lyngby: Université technique du Danemark. [Consultation: 14 juin 2017] (2011)
31. Mayaffre, D.: Corpus et web-corpus. Réflexion sur la corporalité numérique. Cahiers de praxématique (54–55), 233–248 (2010)
32. Schoch, P.: Intelligence stratégique localisée: Vers une gestion active et pertinente des réseaux d'influence. Editions Publibook (2018)
33. Tripier, M.: Concurrence et différence: les problèmes posés au syndicalisme ouvrier par les travailleurs immigrés. Sociologie du travail **14**(3), 331–347 (1972)
34. Le Roy, F.: L'affrontement dans la relation de concurrence. Rev. Fr. Gest. **1**, 179–193 (2004)
35. Viseur, R.: Éthique de la gestion du consentement au traitement de données personnelles: une analyse au prisme des dark patterns. In: INFORSID, pp. 133–148 (2023)
36. Diagne, O.: Web Scraping et veille concurrentielle: généralité, état de l'art et étude de cas sur les boutiques en ligne (2023)
37. Zinaoui, T.: Rôle de la veille concurrentielle dans la création de la richesse dans l'entreprise. Revue Marocaine de la Prospective en Sciences de Gestion, (3) (2020)

38. Cylia, B., Yanis, D.: La veille stratégique comme facteur de compétitivité et de performance dans les entreprises Le cas de L'ENIEM, Tizi-Ouzou. Doctoral dissertation, Université Mouloud Mammeri (2023)
39. Lesca, H., Lesca, E.: Veille stratégique. La méthode LE SCAning (1994)
40. Absil, G.: Analyse SWOT-Un outil d'analyse et d'aide à la décision (2011)
41. Seni, D.A.: Analyse stratégique et avantage concurrentiel. Puq (2013)
42. Lordon, A.: Etudes qualitatives et analyse concurrentielle. Doctoral dissertation, Aix-Marseille 3 (2006)
43. Rabahi, R.: La veille concurrentielle au sein de l'entreprise Cas du développement d'un plan marketing dans EURL SATI. Doctoral dissertation, Université Mouloud Mammeri (2023)
44. Aurier, P.: ÉDITORIAL: Concurrence et analyse concurrentielle: quelques clés d'entrée et challenges pour la discipline marketing. Recherche et Applications en Marketing, 1–8 (1999)
45. Abbey, G.A.: Révélée par l'analyse du prix. Tropicultura **15**(3), 153–158 (1997)
46. Rey, P., Tirole, J.: Analyse économique de la notion de prix de prédation. Revue française d'économie **12**(1), 3–32 (1997)
47. Arena, R.: Réflexions sur l'analyse sismondienne de la formation des prix. Revue économique, 132–149 (1982)
48. Jorge, O., Pons, A., Rius, J., Vintró, C., Mateo, J., Vilaplana, J.: Increasing online shop revenues with web scraping: a case study for the wine sector. Br. Food J. **122**(11), 3383–3401 (2020)
49. Lecocq, X., Demil, B., Warnier, V.: Le business model, un outil d'analyse stratégique. L'expansion management review **123**(4), 96–109 (2006)
50. Ramarotafika, L.L., Silem, A.: Les enjeux de la veille commerciale et mercatique. Défis et stratégies pour les économies émergentes, 175
51. Boegershausen, J., Datta, H., Borah, A., Stephen, A.T.: Fields of gold: scraping web data for marketing insights. J. Mark. **86**(5), 1–20 (2022)
52. Leitzelman, M.: Recherche de combinaisons de Web Services 2.0 pour outiller le veilleur. In: VSST'2010 Veille Strategique Scientifique & Technologique, October 2010
53. Haas, L., Kossmann, D., Wimmers, E., Yang, J.: Optimizing queries across diverse data sources (1997)
54. Rezzag, H., Bouaroura, S.: Extracteur de données web sur la comparaison de prix (2020). Doctoral dissertation, جامعة غرداية
55. Hayet, S., Souhila, Y.: Etude comparative de web scraping: Etude des outils scrapy et Apache-nutch. Doctoral dissertation, Université Mouloud Mammeri (2019)
56. Domken, A., Strowel, A.: Le RGPD: un modèle international en droit de la protection des données?. Faculté de droit et de criminologie, Université catholique de Louvain (2019)
57. Crépin, L., Vercouter, L., Demazeau, Y., Jacquenet, F., Boissier, O.: Les Systemes Multi-Agents Hippocratiques. Doctoral dissertation, Ph.D. thesis (2009)
58. Blouin, A., Beaudoux, O., Loiseau, S.: Un tour d'horizon des approches pour la manipulation des données du web. Document numérique **11**(1), 63–83 (2008)
59. Hasan, W.K.A.: Un aperçu des recherches actuelles sur le captcha. Int. J. Comput. Sci. Eng. Surv. (IJCSES) **7**(3), 141–157 (2016)
60. Cebeillac, A., Rey-Coyrehourcq, S.: Webscraping: enjeux techniques et éthiques. In: Données individuelles localisées: enjeux juridiques, éthiques et techniques à l'heure du RGPD, November 2019
61. Saerens, P., Charry, K.: La connaissance des consommateurs du règlement général sur la protection des données (RGPD) affecte-t-elle les sentiment d'impuissance, vulnérabilité des consommateurs face aux publicités en ligne personnalisées? Cette connaissance peut-elle avoir des effets sur la réactance des consommateurs face aux publicités en ligne personnalisées?
62. Baik, J.S.: Data privacy against innovation or against discrimination?: The case of the California Consumer Privacy Act (CCPA). Telemat. Inform. **52** (2020)

63. Jensen, S.: Abusing the computer fraud and abuse act: why broad interpretations of the CFAA fail. Hamline L. Rev. **36**, 81 (2013)
64. Eason, G., Noble, B., Sneddon, I.N.: On certain integrals of Lipschitz-Hankel type involving products of Bessel functions. Phil. Trans. Roy. Soc. London **A247**, 529–551 (1955)
65. Druey, G.: Étude, conception, collecte, curation et évaluation d'un scraping de sites web liés au transport maritime pour améliorer la prédiction du fret de matières premières (2020)
66. Kumar, V., Saboo, A.R., Agarwal, A., Kumar, B.: Generating competitive intelligence with limited information: a case of the multimedia industry. Prod. Oper. Manag. **29**(1), 192–213 (2020)
67. Bellalij, M.: Introduction à la notion de la transformation digitale. Revue Internationale du Chercheur **2**(2) (2021)

Financial Cost Sensitive Feature Selection Method Based on Association Rule Applied to Credit Scoring

Ghislain Dorian Tchuente Mondjo[1,3]([✉]) and Kely Maxime Motue Djoko[1,2,3]

[1] Université de Yaoundé I, Faculté des Sciences, Département d'Informatique,
Yaoundé 812, Cameroun
tchuente.mondjo@gmail.com, motuekely@gmail.com
[2] IRD, Sorbonne Université, UMMISCO, Bondy 93143, France
[3] Fondation pour la Recherche l'Ingénierie et l'Innovation (FR2I),
Yaoundé 14306, Cameroun

Abstract. Cost-sensitive machine learning techniques are frequently used by data mining researchers to improve their models. In banking credit scoring in particular, the financial cost of misclassification leads us to pay particular attention to cost-sensitive modelling. Knowing that feature selection is a crucial preprocessing step in machine learning because it greatly affects a model's capacity for prediction and generalization, it becomes important to propose financial cost-sensitive feature selection methods. In this paper, we propose Cost Sensitive Association Rules Feature Selection more Larger (ARFSL-CS), which is a two-phase feature selection algorithm based on Sequential Forward Selection (SFS). In the first phase, SFS selects the attributes according to a confidence threshold of the association rules sensitive to the financial cost whose consequent is the class of the loan and in which they are in the antecedent. In the second phase, SFS selects from the remaining features those which minimize the financial cost of misclassification of the model when applied to a dataset described only by each of the features. Experiments carried out on three datasets, using a cost-sensitive Gradient Boosting credit scoring model, show that ARFSL-CS selects the attribute subsets that most minimize the overall cost of financial misclassification for the banker with a gain of 8.7%, 21%, and 69.9% compared to the prediction model without feature selection in the three considered datasets.

Keywords: Cost-sensitive feature selection · Association rules · credit scoring · financial cost

1 Introduction

From 2023, the Basel III approach[1] encourages to revise credit risk framework in banking lending process. In fact, the recent financial crisis and regulation concern made credit scoring methods a major topic in the banking industry. Credit risk

---
[1] https://www.bis.org/bcbs/publ/d570_highlights.htm.

analysis will use datamining methods to extract useful knowledge from bank's data to identify potential bad loans. One piece of knowledge that could be useful to the bank is the set of lender attributes that helps better distinguish between paid and unpaid loans. To this end, the selection of the most relevant attributes has become a key theme in the process of building prediction models.

Because it greatly affects a model's capacity for prediction and generalization, attribute selection is a crucial preprocessing step in machine learning. A training set with a high dimensionality will provide a model that is hard to interpret, so attribute selection can be used to either create a model with greater prediction performance or a more interpretable model.

Large number of works have been done in the literature [18] on feature selection process. These methods can be classified into three main categories: Filter, Wrapper, and Embedded. A common wrapper-type method used is Sequential feature selection (SFS). SFS [5] is a greedy algorithm that iteratively adds or removes features from a dataset in order to improve the performance of a predictive model. SFS can be either forward selection or backward selection. The LASSO [3] and Ridge [4] regularization approaches are common embedded methods that tackle the limit of common approaches that is greater computational cost.

On the other hand, cost-sensitive learning is a subfield of machine learning that addresses classification problems where the misclassification costs are not equal [25]. It is common for data mining researchers to use cost-sensitive machine learning methods that incorporate the costs of classification error in their construction [26]. Cost-sensitive learning helps solve problems often related to the class imbalance problem and an important cost related to business criteria is the financial cost used by [22] which shows that cost-sensitive algorithms can better increase the retailer profits compared to cost-insensitive algorithms.

The purpose of this work is to know if it is possible to increase bank's profit by using a cost sensitive algorithm build from the most relevant attributes choosen also in a cost sensitive way. Cost-sensitive automatic classification techniques rely on data that usually contains redundancies or even irrelevant attributes to minimize financial losses. Removing redundancies or eliminating attributes that are irrelevant from a financial cost sensitivity perspective can be helpful in reducing the banker's losses and shortfalls.

In order to take in consideration the financial costs during the selection of attributes, this paper proposes a Cost Sensitive Association Rules Feature Selection more Large (ARFSL-CS) method that select attributes that minimize the banker's financial losses. The idea here is to integrated financial misclassification cost to compute the score attribute vector that classify the attributes according to their relevance. The objective of ARFSL-CS is to select the most significant subset of attributes for the bank and use it to construct a cost-sensitive algorithm that will reduce the banker's losses.

The remainder of this paper is arranged as follows: In Sect. 2, we present related work. The proposed methodology is presented in Sect. 3. The experimental results of the proposed model are presented in Sect. 4. Conclusion and suggestions for further research are discussed in Sect. 5.

2 Related Work

The related work of this paper will be divided in four parts: Feature selection, Association rule Feature selection method, cost sensitive feature selection methods and Financial cost sensitive method in datamining.

2.1 Feature Selection

Feature selection is the process of isolating the most consistent, non-redundant, and relevant features to use in model construction. As the quantity and diversity of datasets increase, it is crucial to gradually reduce their size. Reducing modeling's computational cost and enhancing predictive model performance are the primary objectives of feature selection. Considering that, large number of works have been done in the literature [18]. In general, these methods can be classified into three main categories: Filter, Wrapper, and Embedded.

Filter-type methods such as ReliefF [6] and MI (Mutual Information) [8] use variable ranking techniques as the main criteria for selecting variables [9]. The attributes are given a score based on a suitable ranking criterion, and attributes that are deemed unnecessary or uninformative below the threshold are removed.

Mutual Information

Let X be a variable and Y a target variable, the impact that X can have on another variable can be measured by the amount of mutual information (MI) exchanged between X and Y, such that the variable having the most mutual information with the target is the best. MI is mathematically defined as follows:

$$MI(X,Y) = \sum_{x \in X} \sum_{y \in Y} p_{(X,Y)}(x,y).log\left(\frac{p_{(X,Y)}(x,y)}{p_X(x)p_Y(y)}\right)$$

MI is zero when X and Y are statistically independent $(p_{(X,Y)}(x,y) = p_X(x)p_Y(y))$.

Relief. The impact of the variable X on the target Y can be measured in another way by measuring the degree of separation of the classes of Y by the instances of X: This is the Relief method proposed by Kira and Rendell in [6]. This method consists in finding the nearest neighbors X_{neighA} of the same class of X_i and X_{neighB} of a different class of X_i. And therefore, if the value of X_i is different from X_{neighA}, the attribute X separates two instances of the same class, which is not desirable, therefore, the weight of the attribute X will decrease. On the other hand, if X_i and X_{neighB} have different values, this means that X separates two instances of different classes, which is desirable, and therefore, the weight of X increases.

$$W_X = W_X - (X_i - X_{neighA})^2 - (X_i - X_{neighB})^2$$

On the other hand, wrapper methods such as SFS (Sequential Forward Selection) [5] and RFE-SVM (Support Vector Machine Recursive Feature Elimination) [10] use an iterative feature selection process based on prediction performance to find the best subset of features. Compared to a filter approach, this approach generally obtain better performances [7] but is significantly more expensive because it requires training and cross-validating the model for every feature subset combination.

Sequential Forward Selection. This method was proposed by [5] to select attribute subsets sequentially by taking into account the model's performance on these subsets. Let A be the set of attributes in the database and V_i be the subset of attributes of size i selected by SFS. Initially, all $V_i = \{\}$, $\forall i \in \{1, ..., |A|\}$. We calculate the prediction performance of each attribute of A and select the attribute A_j having obtained the best performance, hence $V = \{A_j\}$. Let $B = A - V_1$ to obtain V_2, we calculate the performance of the attribute subsets $V_1 \cup \{B_k\}$, $\forall i \in \{1, ..., |A|-1\}$. The subset with the best performance will be V_2 and so on for the other sizes.

Recursive Feature Elimination of Support Vector Machines (RFE-SVM). The RFE-SVM method was proposed by Guyon in [10]. This method like SFS selects attribute subsets depending on the prediction results of a model on these attribute subsets, whereas it initially starts with all attribute sets, uses SVM model to assign weights to attributes, and the attribute with the smallest weight will be removed from the attribute set. Let A be the set of attributes in the database and V_i be the subset of size 2 selected by RFE-SVM. Initially $V_{|A|} = A$, use SVM to assign weights to all attributes of $V_{|A|}$, choose the attribute with the smallest weight and remove this attribute to get $V_{|A|-1}$. This will be done recursively and sequentially, from the largest size to the smallest size.

Embedded feature selection methods integrate the feature selection machine learning algorithm as part of the learning algorithm, in which classification and feature selection are performed simultaneously. The features that will contribute the most to each iteration of the model training process are carefully extracted. Compared to the wrapper strategy, the Embedded feature selection methods results in lower computational costs than wrappers. The LASSO [3] and Ridge [4] regularization approaches are common embedded methods.

LASSO (L1-Regularization). Introduced by Robert Tibshirani in 1996 [3], LASSO is an efficient tool for regularization function selection (LASSO). The LASSO approach penalizes the number of absolute values of the machine learning algorithm parameters. Any coefficients are reduced to zero by the additional limit (regularization). During the feature selection process, features with non-zero coefficient after the removal step are selected for use in the model, while those with exactly zero coefficient are omitted.

$$Min\ J(W) = \sum_{i=1}^{n}(y_i - \hat{y}_i)^2 + \lambda \sum_{k=1}^{m}|W_k|$$

where $\hat{y}_i$ is the prediction for observation, y_i is the actual value for observation, W_k are the regression coefficients and λ is a hyperparameter that controls the intensity of the regularization.

Ridge (L2-Regularization). The Ridge method like LASSO is a method proposed by Arthur Hoerl and Robert Kennard in [4] with the aim of avoiding overlearning regression models by assigning a penalty based on L2 regularization. Ridge's penalty like Lasso's forces the regression coefficients to be smaller, thus avoiding having too large values and reducing the risk of overfitting. Except that compared to LASSO's penalty, Ridge's penalty shrinks the coefficients to values close to zero. The loss function used by Ridge is:

$$Min \ \ J(W) = \sum_{i=1}^{n}(y_i - \hat{y}_i)^2 + \lambda \sum_{k=1}^{m}(W_k)^2$$

where $\hat{y}_i$ is the prediction for observation, y_i is the actual value for observation, W_k are the regression coefficients and λ is a hyperparameter of regularization.

In 2024 Neetha in [28] proposes a feature selection method called adaptive manta ray foraging optimization (AMRFO), in a context of brain tumor classification with the aim of selecting irrelevant features which lead to a classification error.

2.2 Association Rule Feature Selection

Association rule learning is a rule-based machine learning method to discover interesting relationships between variables in large databases. It can be used to identify strong rules between attributes in the dataset.

In 2010, Chawla [12] proposed to use Association Rules Networks (ARN), where regression analysis [13] will be used to formally test the relationship between the extracted attributes after applying a minimal cut partition clustering algorithm to extract the pertinent attributes.

In 2017, Salma [11] proposes to select attributes using association rules based on constraints. The constraint on the association rules used here is that the before part of the rule must be a value of the target attribute, and the after part of the association rules must be of dimension one.

The association rule feature selection proposed by Qu in 2019 [14] will use the association rules to create a vector of attribute scores whose score for an attribute represents the highest confidence of the rules that are associated with that attribute. These association rules have the following constraints: the antecedent must be a modality of an attribute, and the consequent must be a class modality. Then, this vector will be arranged in descending order to position the attributes having a correlation with the class at the top of the list. This vector of scores will be used to select the best subset of attributes from the SFS strategy (Sequential Feature Selection). Initially, the attribute subset is empty, and an attribute from the attribute score vector is added into the attribute subset if adding it improves prediction performance.

2.3 Cost Sensitive Feature Selection

The selection of cost-sensitive characteristics makes it possible to take into account costs related to the context in the selection process to improve the quality of the results.

In 2012, He and Jason [21] proposes a dynamic feature selection algorithm that sequentially chooses features based on previously selected features and their values, and stops the selection process to make a prediction according to a user-specified accuracy-cost trade-off.

Later in 2017, Liu [18] proposes to explore the class imbalance issue of data by optimizing F-measures decomposed into a series of cost-sensitive classification problems. He investigate the cost-sensitive feature selection by generating and assigning different costs to each class with rigorous theory guidance.

In 2019, Zhao [20] suggests using the $l_{2,1}$ norm to create a cost-sensitive feature selection algorithm. In order to guarantee that every feature chosen is independent, it also suggests adding an orthogonal constraint term to reduce testing expenses and classification error costs at the same time. Huang [16] presents the concept of label meaning in cost-sensitive feature selection in the same year and suggests a feature selection method that bases testing cost on label meaning.

In 2021, Long [17] suggests using neighborhood granularity and label improvement in 2021 to choose cost-sensitive features on multi-label data. He takes into account both the process cost of gathering thematic qualities like money, time, and others, as well as the comparatively varied relevance of the labels associated with a given data instance.

The same year, Pes [2] did a comparative study on cost-sensitive learning strategies for high-dimensional and imbalanced data. He validate the advantageous effect of integrating cost-sensitive learning with feature selection, particularly when highly skewed data distributions are present. Reviewing Barrera [1] work in 2023 on feature selection problems helps us better understand the 161 articles published between 2019 and 2023 (20 April 2023), emphasizing the formulation of the problem and performance measures, and proposing classifications for objective functions and evaluation metrics.

It is evident that most of these works nest cost sensitivity into feature selection methods by assigning misclassification costs depending on the context.

2.4 Financial Cost in Datamining

In 2018 Metzler [22] proposes learning strategies based on cost-sensitive trees, applied in the context of highly imbalanced data. Initially, he suggested a cost-sensitive splitting criterion for decision trees that considers the transaction costs. He expands on this with a decision rule for classification with sets of trees. He then proposes a new cost-sensitive loss function by computing the gradient. Both methods have proven to be particularly relevant in the context of unbalanced data, particularly in the context of fraud detection. Experiments show that these cost-sensitive algorithms can increase retailer profits by 1.43% compared to non-cost-sensitive algorithms and that the gradient boosting approach outperforms all its competitors.

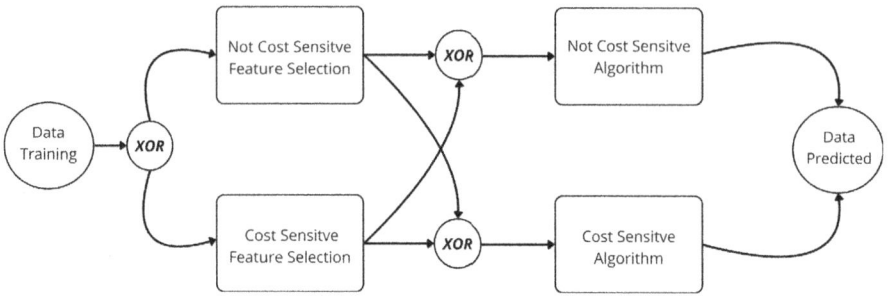

Fig. 1. General model representation.

This section allowed us to present four essential ideas (an aggregation of the principle, advantages and disadvantages has been presented in the Table 1) which are feature selection, cost-sensitive feature selection, feature selection based on association rules and financial cost in data mining. Using the SFS strategy on a vector of attribute scores obtained from association rules to select a better subset of attributes sensitive to a cost function proposed by Qu [14], assigning a cost to classes for each misclassification and taking into account these misclassification costs in a gradient boosting model proposed by Metzler in [22] and taking into account misclassification costs in attribute selection algorithms to have cost-sensitive attribute selection algorithms to take into account data imbalance in certain contexts, lead us to implement a cost-sensitive attribute selection method to reduce the banker's overall losses related to misclassification, based on association rules and dependent on a cost-sensitive Gradient Boosting classification model.

3 Methodology

Figure 1 presents the general model studied in this paper, as input we have training data, we will then go through one of the possibilities, that is to say: 1- Cost sensitive feature selection and cost sensitive algorithm, 2- Not Cost sensitive feature selection and not cost sensitive algorithm, 3-Cost sensitive feature selection and not cost sensitive algorithm, 4-Not Cost sensitive feature selection and cost sensitive algorithm.

As part of this paper we focus on the first possibility because prediction algorithms sensitive to financial costs have been proposed to better reduce financial losses compared to algorithms not sensitive to costs, which allows the algorithm to Cost-sensitive selection proposed in this paper to better reduce financial losses.

Table 1. *Comparison of different concepts related to the selection of attributes sensitive to financial costs.*

Concept	Principle	Benefits	Disadvantages
Feature Selection	These algorithms reduce the number of variables in a dataset while retaining the information most relevant to the learning task.	***Dimensionality Reduction*** (Fewer attributes means less model complexity), ***Performance Improvement*** (By removing redundant or irrelevant attributes, the model becomes more efficient and accurate), ***Overfitting Prevention*** (By reducing the number of attributes, the risk of overfitting is reduced), ***Computational Time Saving*** (Less data to process speeds up the training and inference processes).	***Potential loss of information*** (Risk of removing attributes that could be useful in some complex interactions), ***Computational cost*** (Methods like wrappers can be computationally expensive), ***Data dependency*** (Biased or noisy data can mislead the selection.)
Feature Selection from Association Rules	The most important feature is the one with the greatest correlation with the target or with other features.	***Better interpretability of results, generation of different feature ranking models from metrics like support, confidence*** (These models can be considered as base models to extract a better model.)	***High computational cost*** (Generating association rules from large datasets can be expensive in terms of computational time and memory, especially if the number of features or items is very high.), ***Parameter sensitivity*** (The choice of support and confidence thresholds can influence the results obtained.), ***Difficulty in processing real data*** (Association rule mining algorithms work well when the data is categorical.)
Cost-Sensitive Feature Selection	These are designed to take into account not only model performance (such as accuracy), but also the cost associated with prediction errors.	***Cost optimization*** (They allow minimizing overall costs by taking into account the financial impacts of errors and data costs.), ***More realistic decision*** (In environments where the cost of errors varies considerably, these algorithms allow us to better adapt models to economic realities), ***Improved contextual performance*** (These models can be more effective in situations where raw performance is not the only criterion of success.)	***Complexity*** (Considering costs makes algorithms more complex to design and implement.), ***Reliance on cost estimates*** (The success of these methods depends heavily on accurate cost estimates, which can be difficult to obtain or model in some contexts.), ***Loss of overall accuracy*** (By focusing on minimizing costs, the overall accuracy of the model can be reduced if priorities are too biased toward financial aspects or acquisition costs.)
Financial Cost-Sensitive in Data Mining	Not all errors are equally important in some contexts during model building. In the case of credential scoring, an error in not predicting a default can have a much higher cost than an error in classifying a repayable loan as non-repayable.	***Economic impact-based optimization*** (This approach prioritizes errors based on their true cost.), ***Better decision-making*** (By taking costs into account, decisions are more aligned with the company's strategic objectives.), ***Flexibility*** (These models allow for adjusting error weights as needed.), ***Risk reduction*** (Minimizing costly errors can help reduce financial losses.)	***Increased complexity*** (The costs of different types of errors need to be assessed and estimated, which is not always easy or intuitive.), ***Possible reduction in overall accuracy*** (By prioritizing certain errors based on costs, the overall accuracy of the model may decrease).

3.1 Decision System with Misclassification Cost Function

In data mining and machine learning [15], decision systems with misclassification costs are an important concept and are defined as follows. A DS decision system is a 5-tuple: $DS = (U, C, D, V, f)$ where:

1. U: A finite non-empty set of objects called a universe

2. C: A non-empty finite set of condition attributes
3. D: $D = \{d\}$ is a finite set of decision attributes
4. V: $V = \{V_a\}$ is a set of values for each attribute such that $a \in C \cup D$
5. f: $f = \{f_a\}$ is an information function for each attribute $a \in C \cup D$ ($f_a : U \times (C \cup D) \Rightarrow V_a$)

For example, Table 2 presents a decision system where $U = \{1,2,3,4,5,6\}$, $C = \{City, Occupation, Age, Amount, Interest\ rate\}$ and $D = \{Class\}$.

Table 2. Example Dataset

ID	City	Occupation	Age	Amount	Interest rate	Class
1	Yaoundé	0	30	500000	2	PAID
2	Yaoundé	1	45	120500	1.5	PAID
3	Douala	3	40	5000000	3	UNPAID
4	Yaoundé	0	25	500000	2	UNPAID
5	Yaoundé	0	42	3000000	1.5	PAID
6	Yaoundé	0	50	800000	2	PAID

A decision system with misclassification cost (MC-DS) can then be defined as a 6-tuple: MC-DS = (U, C, D, V, f, mc) where:

1. U, C, D, V, f have the same meanings as in the previous definition.
2. mc is a misclassification cost function ($C \cup D \Rightarrow \mathbf{R}^+ \cup \{0\}$)

In classification problems with two classes $y_i \in \{0,1\}$, the goal is to learn or predict which class $c_i \in \{0,1\}$ a given example i belongs according to its k characteristics $X_i = [x_i^1, x_i^2, ..., x_i^k]$. In this context, classification costs can be represented using a cost matrix 2×2, which introduces the costs associated with two types of correct classification, true positives (C_{TP_i}), true negatives (C_{TN_i}), and two types of classification errors, false positives (C_{FP_i}), false negatives (C_{FN_i}).

Let S be a set of N examples i, $N = |S|$, where each example is represented by the augmented feature vector $X_i^a = [X_i, mc_i]$ and labeled using the class label $y_i \in \{0,1\}$. According to the banker:

1. For a bad borrower announced as good, we lose the amount granted or at least part of it.
2. For a good borrower announced as bad, there is a deficit (sf).

Assuming this, we define a misclassification cost function cst as:

$$mc_i = \begin{cases} C_{FP_i} = X_i[amt] \times X_i[lgd] & if\ y_i = 0 \\ C_{FN_i} = sf = X_i[amt] \times X_i[rt] \times X_i[d] & else \end{cases} \quad (1)$$

where $X_i[amt]$, $X_i[rt]$, $X_i[d]$, $X_i[lgd]$ represent the amount, rate, duration, and loss given default of the given loan, respectively. The cost of a classification error for a set S is:

$$mc(S) = \sum_{i}^{|S|} mc_i \qquad (2)$$

A classifier f that generates the predicted label c_i for each element i is trained using the set S. The cost of using the classifier f on S is calculated by:

$$Cost(f(S)) = \sum_{i=1}^{N}[y_i(c_iC_{TP_i} + (1-c_i)C_{FN_i}) + \\ (1-y_i)(c_iC_{FP_i} + (1-c_i)C_{TN_i})] \qquad (3)$$

3.2 Cost Sensitive Gradient Boosting

Gradient Boosting. Unlike the well-known Adaboost algorithm [19], gradient boosting performs optimization in the function space rather than in the parameter space. At each iteration, a weak learner f_t is learned using the residuals (or errors) obtained by the linear combination of the previous models. The linear combination F_t at time t is defined as follows:

$$F_t = F_{t-1} + \alpha f_t \qquad (4)$$

where F_{t-1} is the linear combination of the first $t-1$ models and α_t is the weight given to the tth weak learner. The weak learners are trained on the residuals $r_i = y_i - F_{t-1}(x_i)$ of the current model. These residuals are given by the negative gradient $-g_t$, of the used loss function L with respect to the current prediction $F_{t-1}(x_i)$:

$$r_i = -g_t = -\left[\frac{\partial L(y, F_{t-1}(x_i))}{\partial F_{t-1}(x_i)}\right] \qquad (5)$$

Once the residuals r_i are computed, the following optimization problem is solved:

$$(f_t, \alpha_t) = \arg\min_{\alpha, f} \sum_{i=1}^{m}(r_i - \alpha f(x_i))^2 \qquad (6)$$

Cost Sensitive Loss for Gradient Boosting. Metzler in [22] suggests using the cost function L which derives from the equation (3). For $\hat{F}_i = F(x_i)$ we have:

$$L(y|\hat{F}_i) = \frac{1}{m}\sum_{i=1}^{m}(1-s_i)y_i e^{-\hat{F}_i} + (1-y_i)s_i e^{\hat{F}_i} \qquad (7)$$

To use it in a gradient boosting algorithm, it remains to compute the first and second order derivative of L for each instance i with respect to $\hat{F}_i$. They are given by:

$$\frac{\partial L}{\partial \hat{F}_i} = \xi_i[-(1-s_i)y_i e^{-\hat{F}_i} + (1-y_i)s_i e^{\hat{F}_i}] \qquad (8)$$

and
$$\frac{\partial L}{\partial \hat{F}_i^2} = \xi_i[(1-s_i)y_i e^{-\hat{F}_i} + (1-y_i)s_i e^{\hat{F}_i}] \tag{9}$$
where $\xi_i = C_{TN_i} - C_{FP_i} + C_{TP_i} - C_{FN_i}$,
$$s_i = \frac{C_{TN_i} - C_{FP_i}}{C_{TP_i} - C_{FN_i} + C_{TN_i} - C_{FP_i}}$$
and $\forall i \in \{1,...,m\}$ $C_{FN_i} < 0$, $C_{FP_i} < 0$, $C_{TP_i} > 0$ and $C_{TN_i} > 0$.

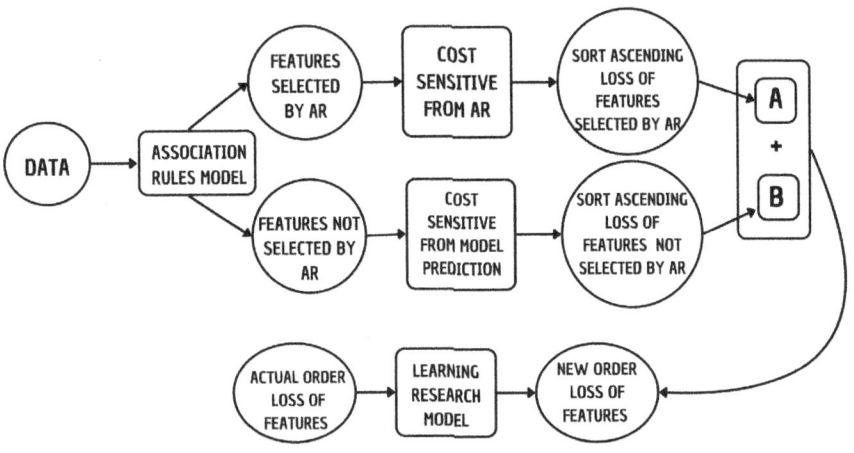

Fig. 2. Specific model representation.

Algorithm 1: L_2 Mining algorithm

Input: supp_min : support minimal seuil
Output: Conf : confiance des item sets fréquents de taille 2
Data: D : Ensemble de données

1 init P_2, $supp\_min$
2 $n \leftarrow count(P_2)$
3 **for** $i < n$ **do**
4      $supp_{P_{2_i}} \leftarrow support(P_{2_i})$ $//P_{2_i} = (X_i, Y)$
5   **if** $supp_{P_{2_i}} > supp\_min$ **then**
6          $L_2.add(P_{2_i})$
7          $conf_{2_i} \leftarrow \frac{count(L_{2_i})}{count(X_i)}$

8 **return** L_2.Conf

3.3 Cost Sensitive Association Rules Feature Selection More Large (ARFSL-CS)

We propose the specific model shown in Fig. 2, which uses association rules and cost sensitivity[2] to provide a financial loss-sensitive order of the features, and

---
[2] Cost sensitivity from association rules and from the prediction model.

Algorithm 2: Cost Sensitive Association Rules Feature Selection more Large (ARFSL-CS)

Input: sup_min : minimum support threshold, conf_min : minimum confidence threshold
Output: set_opt_loss : Best cost sensible features subset
Data: D : Dataset

1. $Init\ GB - CS\ //\ Cost\ Sensitive\ Grandient\ Boosting$
2. $T_2 \leftarrow Apriori(sup\_min, D)$
3. $R_2 \leftarrow Association\_Rules(T_2, conf\_min)$
4. $V_{select} \leftarrow MAX(R_2 \times mc(R_2))$
5. $V_{forget} \leftarrow Get\_feature\_forget(D, V_{select})$
6. $V_{forget} \leftarrow Get\_Feature\_Loss(GB - CS, D, V_{forget})$
7. $V_{select} \leftarrow Sort\_ascending(V_{select})$
8. $V_{forget} \leftarrow Sort\_ascending(V_{forget})$
9. $V_{loss} \leftarrow V_{select} + V_{forget}$
10. $d \leftarrow divide\_lenght$
11. $set\_opt\_loss \leftarrow GLRFSL - CS(V_{loss}, GB - CS, d)$
12. **return** set_opt_loss

---

then uses a learning research model to derive a new order of attributes, such that by extracting the subset of attributes based on their sizes using the k-best strategy, we will only have better subsets of attributes. The learning search model considers the order of attributes as a model. Adjusts this during the search and will provide a new model that represents a new order of attributes.

The ARFSL-CS proposed in this paper and presented in Algorithm 2 must first calculate the confidence of the set of frequent item sets of size 2 denoted L_2 between the attribute modalities and the category denoted $\{V = v, C = c\}$ from L_2 Mining Algorithm 1 of Qu [14] to the lines 2 and 3 in Algorithm 2.

Then, on line 4, we group together all the item sets whose attribute is V, then we associate with each association rule a cost equal to the confidence of this rule multiplied by the loss of rules which will be calculated using the cost function $mc(S)$ defined in the previous subsection. The loss of the rule will represent the sum of losses for which the rule is verified. We then select the maximum cost of this group of item set such that the rule is $\{V = v\} \Rightarrow \{C = c\}$, this score will represent the score of the attribute V. We will have a loss attribute vector called the selected attribute vector V_{select} by defining minimum support and minimum confidence. The confidence of a rule is used here to measure the correlation between attributes and categories.

The multiplication of loss and confidence in the ARFSL-CS algorithm is due to the fact that assuming that we have two association rules $R_1 : \{A = a\} \Rightarrow \{C = c_1\}$ and $R_2 : \{B = b\} \Rightarrow \{C = c_2\}$ with the same loss of p calculated from mc but a respective confidence of 1.0 and 0.8. By multiplying $p \times 1.0$ there is no change; on the other hand, by making $p \times 0.8$ the loss decreases. This is explained by the fact that if the attribute is strongly correlated to a class, it will not distinguish the other classes at best hence its loss does not decrease, on the other hand if the attribute is not strongly correlated to a class, it can have a correlation to another class distinguish at least two other classes hence its loss decreases.

Due to minimal support and minimal trust, some rules will be removed, which will result in some attributes being removed. The attributes thus deleted will be used to form the forgotten attribute vector V_{forget} to lines 5 and 6. The forgotten attribute vector V_{forget} will be constructed by extracting attributes that belong to the starting attribute set, but do not belong to the attribute set of the selected attribute vector. Then, calculate the financial loss of each forgotten attribute using the Ft-CS learning model. Then, the selected V_{select} and forgotten V_{forget} attribute vectors are arranged in ascending order on lines 7 and 8 and concatenated on line 9 to obtain the attribute score vector which will be passed to the GLRFSL-CS Algorithm 3. We can then search for the best subsets of attributes based on the size of the subset using the GLRFSL-CS (Cost Sensitive Global and local Research Feature Subset by Learning scored vector) search algorithm proposed in this paper in Algorithm 3. The idea of this algorithm is to leave the current attribute order to provide a new attribute order in such a way that it allows us to extract subsets of attributes that reduce the banking loss. $\eta_{cost}(f, D, GB - CS)$ returns the banker's loss for a training set D, on characteristics f using a model sensitive to financial costs $GB - CS$.

Algorithm 3: Cost Sensitive Global and Local Research of Feature Subset by Learning (GLRFSL-CS)

Input: V_{loss} : Scores vector of feature, GB-CS : Learning model, d : step
Output: opt : Best cost sensible features subset
Data: D : Dataset

1 $\beta \leftarrow |V_{loss}|$
2 $i \leftarrow 1$
3 **while** $valid == False$ **do**
4 $\quad z.add(V_{loss_d}^i)$
5 $\quad w.add(V_{loss_d}^i)$
6 $\quad opt[|z|] \leftarrow Min(\eta_{cost}(opt[|z|], D, GB - CS), \eta_{cost}(l, D, GB - CS))$
7 $\quad opt[|w|] \leftarrow Min(\eta_{cost}(opt[|w|], D, GB - CS), \eta_{cost}(g, D, GB - CS))$
8 $\quad f \leftarrow Min(\eta_{cost}(z, D, GB - CS), \eta_{cost}(w, D, GB - CS))$
9 $\quad$ **if** $\eta_{cost}(f, D, GB - CS) < \eta_{cost}(f_{cost}, D, GB - CS)$ **then**
10 $\quad\quad opt[|z|], f_{cost}, g \leftarrow f, f, f$
11 $\quad\quad$ update f_{cost} in V_{loss_d} with ascending order
12 $\quad$ **else**
13 $\quad\quad g.pop()$
14 $\quad$ SBS step on $opt[m]$ and update V_{loss} if needed
15 $\quad$ Test $[opt[m], V_{loss_d}^i]$ and update V_{loss} if needed
16 $\quad$ **if** $i > \beta$ **then**
17 $\quad\quad valid \leftarrow True$
18 $\quad i \leftarrow i + d$
19 **return** opt

Firstly, we add the characteristic V_{loss}^i to the vectors z and w in lines 4 and 5, then we adjust $opt[|z|]$ and $opt[|w|]$ locally on lines 6 and 7 if the loss on the subset of attributes z and w is, respectively, lower than the loss on the subset of attributes $opt[|z|]$ and $opt[|w|]$. Then put into f the attribute subset with the smallest loss (the line 8) and compare f to the current best attribute subset f_{cost}, adjust V_{loss} from f if f has a loss strictly lower than that of f_{cost}.

Table 3. Example of Data set

A	B	C	D	E	F	Target
y	5M	30	2	2	0	1
y	3M	45	2	1.5	1	1
d	500k	40	1	3	3	0
y	500k	25	1	2	0	0
y	120k	42	1	1.5	0	1
y	800k	50	2	2	0	1

Table 4. Rules obtained with a support of 0.33 and a confidence of 0.66.

Before	After	Conf	$Loss_1$	$Loss_2$
A=y	Target=1	0.8	26983	21586
D=2	Target=1	1.0	26833	26833
D=1	Target=0	0.66	2083	1374
E=2	Target=1	0.66	20166	13309
E=1.5	Target=1	1.0	7650	7650
F=0	Target=1	0.75	19483	14612

Table 5. Rules obtained with a support of 0.33 and a confidence of 0.8.

Before	After	Conf	$Loss_1$	$Loss_2$
A=y	Target=1	0.8	26983	21586
D=2	Target=1	1.0	26833	26833
E=1.5	Target=1	1.0	7650	7650

Then, on line 14, a step of the SBS (Sequential Backward Selection) strategy is used to have the best subset of reduced size among that selected by the SFS strategy. This idea was taken from the Sequential Floating Forward Selection (SFFS) algorithm of [23]. During this process, an adjustment to the attribute loss vector is made each time a new subset of attributes with minimal financial loss is discovered.

Test the new attribute subset at the line 15 in order to select better attribute subsets by concatenating $opt[m]$ to V_{loss}^i, during this process, adjustments to the score vector V_{loss} can be done in case of reduction of losses. ARFSL-CS can be used with all learning algorithms, whether cost-sensitive or not, for the purpose of selecting attributes that minimize losses. The mc of the equation (2) function can be adjusted depending on the context in which we find ourselves.

3.4 Application Example

The purpose of this example is to highlight the cost sensitivity in the ARFSL-CS algorithm presented in Algorithm 2 using association rules. Table 3 presents an example dataset. In this table, the features A="City", B="Amount", C="Age", D="Duration", E="Interest rate", F="Occupation".

Table 4 presents the association rules obtained from the support thresholds equal to 0.33 and the confidence equal to 0.66. In this table, the attribute **Before** represents the antecedent of the rule, **After** represents the consequent and **Conf** the confidence of an association rule. In addition, the attribute $Loss_{2_i} = Loss_{1_i} \times Conf_i$ represents the loss of confidence in a rule and $Loss_1$ (calculated using mc) the loss to be realized for this rule.

As explained in the previous subsection, the rules whose antecedent is an attribute modality and whose consequent is a modality of the target attribute are extracted. Subsequently, the rules whose antecedents are associated with the same attribute are grouped together (the colored boxes), and we assign the greatest confidence loss of each group of rules as the score of the attribute associated with this group of rules.

In Table 4, for example, a group of rules is the one in red, the attribute associated with this group is the attribute D which will have as score $max(26833, 1374) = 26833$. After assigning a score to each attribute, we will obtain the loss vector of the attributes selected by the association rules by arranging these attributes ($\{A, D, E, F\}$) in ascending order.

In the Table 4 the set of attributes that have not been selected by the association rules (second phase) is the set $\{B, C\}$, and the scores of these attributes B and C will be obtained by using the data related to each attribute to train a prediction model M_B and M_C, and therefore, the losses of each model M_B and M_C will represent the scores of attributes A and B respectively. After assigning the scores of attributes B and C, we obtain the attribute vector forgotten by the association rules by ranking these attributes in an increasing manner according to their scores.

The concatenation of the vector of attributes selected by the association rules and that of the attributes forgotten by the association rules will be passed to the search algorithm based on SFS and SBS. The same process will be performed for the rules in the Table 5 with a set of selected attributes $\{A, D, D\}$ and a set of forgotten attributes $\{B, C, F\}$.

4 Experiments

In this part, we compare the ARFSL-CS algorithm to the LASSO, Ridge, ReliefF and MI algorithms with the aim of observing the impact of taking into account cost sensitivity in the selection of attributes.

The data used in the experiment are: LDB, German Credit Data [24] and Credit Risk[3]. German and Australian datasets come from UCI Machine Learning Repository, LDB is a dataset from a local bank. This experiment was carried out on a 16 GB RAM using the Sklearn Python tool for learning models.

We used the xgboost python tool from sklearn, which implements boosting, for the construction of prediction models without cost sensitivity and with cost sensitivity[4].

4.1 Dataset

Table 6. Dataset

Dataset	Instances	Attributes	Class
LDB	28952	12	2
German	1000	20	2
Credit Risk	28638	12	2

We start by applying these algorithms on 3 different datasets as presented at the Table 6:

- LDB: This dataset of 28,952 instances gathers information from various individuals or individuals registered in a local bank where each individual has 17 attributes and one target attribute.
- German Credit Data [24]: This dataset classifies people described by a set of attributes as having good or bad credit risk. It has 20 attributes and one target attribute.

---
[3] https://www.kaggle.com/datasets/laotse/credit-risk-dataset/.
[4] https://github.com/dmlc/xgboost.

- Credit Risk Dataset[5] : This dataset contains 28,638 instances, 11 attributes and a target attribute.

4.2 Evaluation Metrics

We use the following metrics to compare the results of different models:

- Gain: Represents the Gain in losses of using attribute selection algorithms on a prediction model:

$$Gain(f, F, X) = \frac{f(X) - F(f, X)}{f(X)}$$

or f is model prediction, F is feature selection algorithm and X est Data set. The greater its value, the more the attribute selection algorithm reduces losses.
- Rank: Represents the rank of the selection algorithm in terms of gain loss[6]. The smaller the value, the better the selection algorithm has.
- NFS: Number of features selected. The smaller its value, the more the attribute selection algorithm selects fewer attributes.

We will then explore the results in terms of accuracy, precision, and recall of the cost-sensitive algorithm ARFSL-CS which obtains the banker's losses from $mc(CST)(2)$, in order to observe their deviations compared to the base algorithm without feature selection. In order to obtain statistically significant experimental results, a 5-fold cross-validation experiment was used.

4.3 Description of Results and Observations

In this subsection, we describe and comment on the results obtained from the experiments on credit scoring databases:

A - Description

GB represents the gradient boosting model. $GB - L$, $GB - LR$ and $GB - H$ respectively represent the gradient boosting model with the objective functions *binary logistic*, *binary logitraw* and *binary hinge*[7]. We also have $GB - CS$ which represents the gradient boosting model with the cost-sensitive objective function as proposed by Metzler in [22].

The Tables 10, 11 and 12 represent the results in terms of losses (Cst), accuracy (Acc), precision (Prec) and recall (Rec), feature selection algorithms ARFSL-CS, MI, ReliefF, Ridge and LASSO on gradient boosting GB models. The *Base* algorithm returns the results of prediction models without attribute selection.

The Tables 7, 8 and 9 represent the results in terms of percentage of gains, rank of algorithms in terms of gains and the number of features selected (NFS)

---

[5] https://www.kaggle.com/datasets/laotse/credit-risk-dataset/.
[6] If both ranks 1, then they rank all 1.5 [20].
[7] These models represent the models not sensitive to financial costs.

Table 7. Gain, Rank, and number of features selected results on LDB Dataset

Model	Metric	MI	ReliefF	LASSO	Ridge	ARFSL-CS
GB-L	Gain	1.42%	1.30%	1.30%	0%	**1.93%**
	Rank	2	3.5	3.5	5	**1**
	NFS	**8**	11	11	12	**8**
GB-LR	Gain	1.33%	2.65%	2.65%	0.11%	**8.19%**
	Rank	4	2.5	2.5	5	**1**
	NFS	8	11	11	11	**7**
GB-H	Gain	1.49%	0.59%	0.59%	2.31%	**15.01%**
	Rank	3	4.5	4.5	2	**1**
	NFS	**9**	11	11	**9**	**9**
GB-CS	Gain	8.33%	0%	0.30%	0.57%	**21.05%**
	Rank	2	5	4	3	**1**
	NFS	**5**	12	10	10	6
Means	Gain	3.14%	1.135%	1.21%	0.74%	**11.54%**
	Rank	2	4	3	5	**1**
	NFS	**7.5**	11.25	10.75	10.5	**7.5**

by the ARFSL-CS, MI, ReliefF, Ridge and LASSO algorithms. The gain in loss is obtained by calculating the difference in loss when there is selection of attributes and the loss when there is no selection of attributes (**Base**).

Table 8. Gain, Rank, and number of features selected results on German Dataset

Model	Metric	MI	ReliefF	LASSO	Ridge	ARFSL-CS
GB-L	Gain	14.28%	0%	8.65%	9.49%	**18.70%**
	Rank	2	5	4	3	**1**
	NFS	18	20	19	16	**15**
GB-LR	Gain	15.05%	0%	0%	3.47%	**24.18%**
	Rank	2	4.5	4.5	3	**1**
	NFS	15	20	20	16	**3**
GB-H	Gain	6.97%	0%	0%	8.47%	**20.19%**
	Rank	3	4.5	4.5	2	**1**
	NFS	**15**	20	20	16	**15**
GB-CS	Gain	69.53%	69.53%	58.35%	69.53%	**69.94%**
	Rank	3	3	5	3	**1**
	NFS	**1**	**1**	**1**	**1**	3
Means	Gain	26.45%	17.38%	16.75%	22.74%	**33.25%**
	Rank	2	4	5	3	**1**
	NFS	12.25	15.25	15	12.25	**9**

Table 9. Gain, Rank, and number of features selected results on Credit Risk Dataset

Model	Metric	MI	ReliefF	LASSO	Ridge	ARFSL-CS
GB-L	Gain	0%	3.17%	0%	5.92%	**15.43%**
	Rank	4.5	3	4.5	2	**1**
	NFS	11	10	11	10	**9**
GB-LR	Gain	9.17%	**10.86%**	0%	7.35%	9.17%
	Rank	2.5	**1**	5	2	2.5
	NFS	**10**	**10**	11	**10**	**10**
GB-H	Gain	0.59%	0%	0%	3.79%	**11.90%**
	Rank	3	4.5	4.5	2	**1**
	NFS	**9**	11	11	10	**9**
GB-CS	Gain	**8.76%**	4.29%	0%	2.95%	**8.76%**
	Rank	**1.5**	3	5	4	**1.5**
	NFS	**10**	**10**	11	**10**	**10**
Means	Gain	4.63%	4.58%	0%	5.0025%	**11.31%**
	Rank	3	4	5	2	**1**
	NFS	10	10.25	11	10	**9.5**

B - Best rank and gain in loss

The results of Tables 7, 8 and 9 show that ARFSL-CS is the best selection algorithm in terms of gain in losses. In the LDB and German datasets, ARFSL-CS obtained a rank of 1 on all gradient boosting prediction models as presented in Tables 7 and 8 which shows that ARFSL-CS mostly obtains better gains in loss compared to other state-of-the-art attribute selection algorithms such as MI, ReliefF, LASSO, Ridge. In contrast, in the results of the Credit Risk dataset presented in Table 9, ARFSL-CS obtains a rank of 1 on all gradient boosting prediction models except the gradient boosting model with a binary *logitraw* objective function denoted GB-LR, where the ReliefF algorithm was better with a gain in losses of 10.86%, which shows that in this specific case, the correlation selection strategy compared to the ReliefF target variable is better than the SFS strategy implemented by ARFSL-CS.

ARFSL-CS has a higher percentage of average gain in all datasets, as presented in Tables 7, 8 and 9, which shows that on average, ARFSL-CS generated better gains in terms of bank losses. These results also show that on average, ARFSL-CS scores better compared to other state-of-the-art feature selection algorithms. We also note that MI obtained the second rank in terms of loss gain on the LDB and German data sets as presented in Tables 7 and 8.

In the results of Table 7, from the LDB dataset, the ARFSL-CS model makes a banking loss gain of 21.05% with the cost-sensitive gradient-boosting prediction model noted GB-CS, which corresponds to 47,769,325 XAF (forty-seven million XAF). For the German and Credit Risk datasets, the results in Tables 8 and 9 show that ARFSL-CS made a respective bank loss gain of 69.94% and 15.43% using the GB-CS and GB-L models respectively. These results represent the best gains obtained on the three datasets LDB, German and Credit Risk, they were obtained from ARFSL-CS and two of these results are obtained using the GB-CS model (on LDB and German) which is a model sensitive to financial costs. These results also show that using a model without cost sensitivity could be interesting in reducing losses. These results do not include the comparison aspect between cost-sensitive and noncost-sensitive models in the context of minimizing bank losses overall and will be discussed in the subsection **Prediction results**.

C - Number of features selected

Concerning the number of selected attributes, the results presented in the Tables 7, 8 and 9, also show that ARFSL- CS obtained the best average number of selected attributes compared to other algorithms in the LDB, German and Credit Risk datasets, showing that in addition to having obtained better gains in bank losses, ARFSL -CS has a good ability to reduce the size of attributes. We also note that MI tied with ARSFSL-CS in terms of average of selected attributes on the LDB dataset.

In general, the results presented in Fig. 3 show that ARFSL-CS obtains the best gain in banking losses, the best rank among the state-of-the-art algorithms presented in this paper and the best in terms of the number of selected attributes. These results show that ARFSL-CS can select attributes that make it possible to properly classify data instances with high loss costs with a limited number of attributes.

Table 10. Prediction results on LDB dataset

Model	Metric	Base	MI	ReliefF	LASSO	Ridge	ARFSL-CS
GB-L	CST	231336549	228051124	228324888	228324888	231336549	**226871337**
	Acc	0.9880	0.9878	0.9879	0.9879	0.9880	**0.9882**
	Prec	0.9879	0.9878	0.9878	0.9878	0.9879	**0.9882**
	Rec	0.9880	0.9878	0.9879	0.9879	0.9880	**0.9882**
GB-LR	CST	222894760	219923868	216982374	216982374	222641461	**204638331**
	Acc	0.9871	0.9871	**0.9876**	**0.9876**	0.9871	0.9851
	Prec	0.9871	0.9871	**0.9877**	**0.9877**	0.9871	0.9852
	Rec	0.9871	0.9871	**0.9876**	**0.9876**	0.9871	0.9851
GB-H	CST	237195721	233645966	235784705	235784705	231699831	**201584553**
	Acc	**0.9884**	0.9877	0.9883	0.9883	0.9882	0.9875
	Prec	0.9884	0.9877	**0.9883**	**0.9883**	0.9882	0.9875
	Rec	**0.9884**	0.9877	0.9883	0.9883	0.9882	0.9875
GB-CS	CST	226856304	207943963	226856304	226162270	225543145	*179086979*
	Acc	0.9804	0.9805	0.9804	0.9793	0.9797	*0.9809*
	Prec	0.9812	0.9814	0.9812	0.9803	0.9806	*0.9818*
	Rec	0.9804	0.9805	0.9804	0.9793	0.9797	*0.9809*

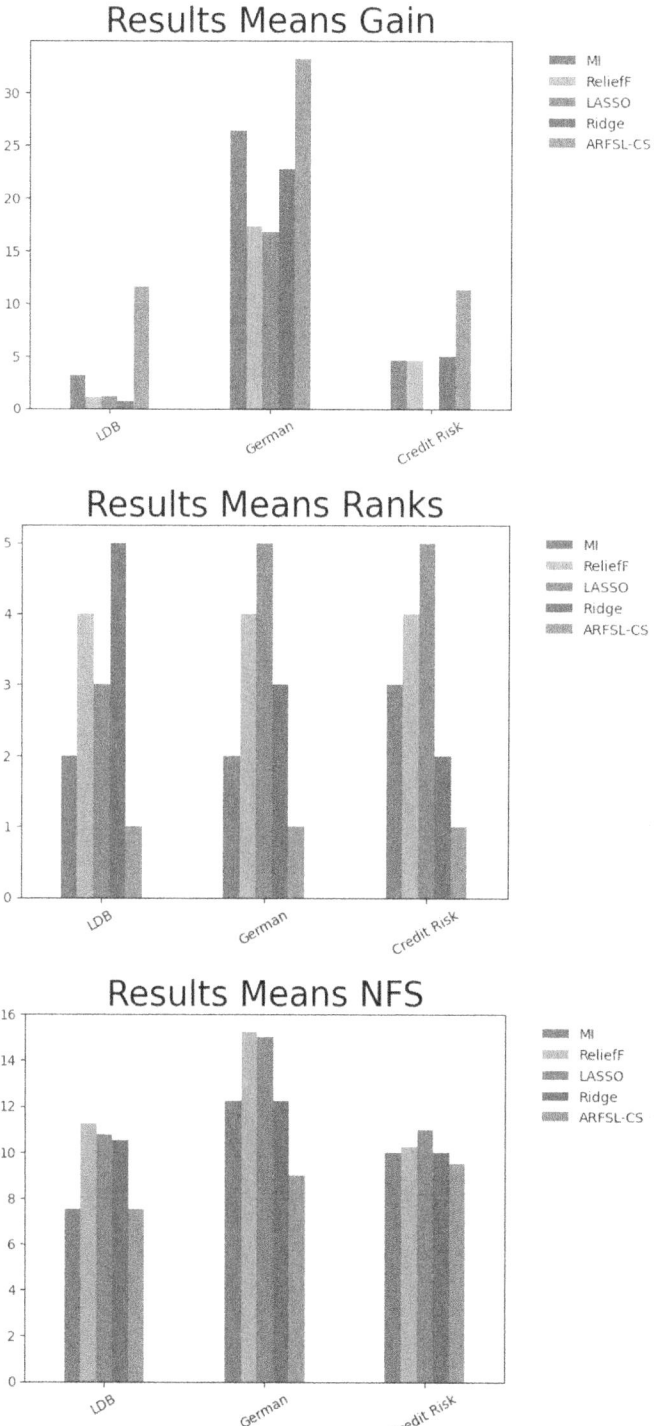

Fig. 3. Results in terms of average gain in losses, average ranks in gain and average number of selected features.

D - Prediction results

In terms of prediction results of the selection algorithms in Tables 10, 11 and 12, we observe that ARFSL-CS is the only algorithm among all attribute selection algorithms cited in this paper that always reduces the banking loss, regardless of the decision tree model in which it is applied.

These results also show that the attribute selection algorithms ARFSL-CS, MI, ReliefF, Ridge and LASSO very often make it possible to reduce losses by keeping prediction results in terms of accuracy, precision and recall more or less close to the basic results which shows that the use of a selection algorithm such as ARFSL-CS makes it possible to always reduce losses without degrading the prediction performance of the models in terms of accuracy, precision and recall.

The prediction results of the LDB, German, and Credit Risk datasets presented in Tables 10, 11, and 12 show that in terms of bank loss costs, the ARFSL-CS algorithm manages to obtain the smallest bank loss cost on all three datasets compared to MI, ReliefF, Lasso and Ridge algorithms. In the LDB data set we obtained $179,086,979$ XAF from the $GB-CS$ model, in the German data set we got $23,409$ from the $GB-CS$ model, and in the credit risk data set we got $302,927$ from the $GB-CS$ model. These results confirm the hypothesis that the combination of a cost-sensitive attribute selection algorithm and a cost-sensitive prediction algorithm would give very interesting results.

Table 11. Prediction results on German dataset

Model	Metric	Base	MI	ReliefF	LASSO	Ridge	ARFSL-CS
GB-L	CST	117631	100823	117631	107453	106460	**95631**
	Acc	0.748	0.758	0.748	0.735	0.744	**0.765**
	Prec	0.7373	0.7485	0.7373	0.7281	0.7368	**0.7618**
	Rec	0.748	0.758	0.748	0.735	0.744	**0.765**
GB-LR	CST	84924	72138	84924	84924	81977	**64381**
	Acc	**0.748**	0.756	0.74	0.74	**0.748**	0.675
	Prec	0.7445	0.7287	0.7654	0.7445	**0.7560**	0.7395
	Rec	**0.748**	0.756	0.7445	0.74	**0.748**	0.675
GB-H	CST	109625	101978	109625	109625	100329	**87483**
	Acc	0.738	0.735	0.738	0.738	**0.75**	0.73
	Prec	0.7356	0.7340	0.7356	0.7356	**0.7471**	0.7330
	Rec	0.738	0.735	0.738	0.738	**0.75**	0.73
GB-CS	CST	77898	23728	23728	32437	23728	*23409*
	Acc	**0.688**	0.3	0.3	0.317	0.3	*0.34*
	Prec	0.7459	0.0916	0.0916	0.5955	0.0916	*0.7756*
	Rec	**0.688**	0.3	0.3	0.317	0.3	*0.34*

We also observe that, in the prediction results of the LDB and German datasets presented in Tables 10 and 11, the results obtained by ARFSL-CS from

Table 12. Prediction results on Credit Risk dataset

Model	Metric	Base	MI	ReliefF	LASSO	Ridge	ARFSL-CS
GB-L	CST	552191	552191	534673	552191	519482	**466947**
	Acc	0.9347	0.9347	0.9353	0.9347	**0.9357**	0.9322
	Prec	0.9362	0.9362	0.9371	0.9362	0.9375	**0.9348**
	Rec	**0.9347**	**0.9347**	0.9353	**0.9347**	0.9357	0.9322
GB-LR	CST	384433	349145	**342659**	384433	356154	349145
	Acc	0.9342	0.9343	0.9349	0.9342	**0.9354**	0.9343
	Prec	0.9374	0.9374	0.9382	0.9374	**0.9386**	0.9374
	Rec	0.9342	0.9343	0.9349	0.9342	**0.9354**	0.9343
GB-H	CST	558141	554815	558141	558141	536971	**491721**
	Acc	0.9342	0.9319	0.9342	0.9342	**0.9345**	0.9301
	Prec	0.9361	0.9335	0.9361	0.9361	**0.9365**	0.9324
	Rec	0.9342	0.9319	0.9342	0.9342	**0.9345**	0.9301
GB-CS	CST	332012	*302927*	317767	332012	322192	*302927*
	Acc	0.9112	*0.9137*	**0.9177**	0.9112	0.9129	*0.9137*
	Prec	0.9193	*0.9218*	**0.9249**	0.9193	0.9209	*0.9218*
	Rec	0.9112	*0.9137*	**0.9177**	0.9112	0.9129	*0.9137*

the $GB-CS^8$ and $GB-L^9$ models are better in costs, accuracy, precision and recall compared to other attribute selection algorithms and even compared to the base prediction on this same model, which shows that ARFSL-CS can provide not only a subset of attributes that minimize banking losses, but also improves usual prediction results such as accuracy, precision, and recall. We also observe this in the German dataset, in the Table 11 with the $GB-CS$ model, but the precision, prediction, and recall results are not always better than those of *Base*, but these results are best compared to the results of other selection algorithms.

5 Conclusion

The objective of our work was to increase the overall profit of the bank by selecting features that reduce bank losses. The idea is to select a subset of attributes that will reduce bank losses during the process of predicting bank risk based on association rules. We propose to use the association rules and the prediction performance of the model to provide a vector of scores which will be used as a base model to provide a new model which allows extracting subsets of attributes which better reduce the banker's losses. The results show that on average ARFSL-CS is better in terms of reduction of bank losses, rank in gain of losses, number of

---
[8] Only LDB dataset for $GB-CS$.
[9] LDB and German datasets for $GB-L$.

attributes selection compared to state-of-the-art algorithms such as MI, ReliefF, LASSO, Ridge. It provides prediction results more or less close to results without attribute selection on recall, accuracy, and precision metrics. We observe that some state-of-the-art algorithms rank first in some cases, even though they are not cost sensitive. This is explained by the fact that these algorithms, by selecting attributes in order to improve precision, recall, or accuracy, could reduce losses because bank losses are due to bank classification errors. We also noticed that the classifier that produce better results with ARFSL-CS are cost sensitive classifiers. In future work, we will study the impact of taking cost sensitivity into account on the explainability properties of black box models.

References

1. Barrera-García, J., Cisternas-Caneo, F., Crawford, B., Gómez Sánchez, M., Soto, R.: Feature selection problem and metaheuristics: a systematic literature review about its formulation, evaluation and applications. Biomimetics Basel **9**(1), 9 (2023). https://doi.org/10.3390/biomimetics9010009
2. Pes, B., Lai, G.: Cost-sensitive learning strategies for high-dimensional and imbalanced data: a comparative study. PeerJ Comput Sci. **24**(7), e832 (2021). https://doi.org/10.7717/peerj-cs.832
3. Tibshirani, R.: Regression shrinkage and selection via the lasso. J. Roy. Stat. Soc. Ser. B Methodol. **58**(1), 267–288 (1996)
4. Hoerl, A.E., Kennard, R.W.: Ridge regression: biased estimation for nonorthogonal problems. Technometrics **12**(1), 55–67 (1970)
5. Raman, B., Ioerger, T.R.: Instance-based filter for feature selection. J. Mach. Learn. Res. **1**(3), 1–23 (2002)
6. Kononenko, I.: Estimating attributes: analysis and extensions of RELIEF. In: European Conference on Machine Learning, pp. 171–182. Springer, Berlin, Heidelberg. (1994)
7. Kohavi, R., John, G.H.: Wrappers for feature subset selection. Artif. Intell. **97**(1–2), 273–324 (1997)
8. Battiti, R.: Using mutual information for selecting features in supervised neural net learning. IEEE Trans. Neural Netw. **5**(4), 537–550 (1994)
9. Chandrashekar, G., Sahin, F.: A survey on feature selection methods. Comput. Electr. Eng. **40**(1), 16–28 (2014)
10. Guyon, I., Weston, J., Barnhill, S., Vapnik, V.: Gene selection for cancer classification using support vector machines. Mach. Learn. **46**(1), 389–422 (2002)
11. Salma, M.U., et al.: Reducing the feature space using constraint-governed association rule mining. J. Intell. Syst. **26**(1), 139–152 (2017)
12. Chawla, S.: Feature selection, association rules network and theory building. In: Feature Selection in Data Mining, pp. 14–21. PMLR (2010)
13. Pandey, G., Chawla, S., Poon, S., Arunasalam, B., Davis, J.G.: Association rules network: definition and applications. Stati. Anal. Data Min. ASA Data Sci. J. **1**(4), 260–279 (2009)
14. Qu, Y., Fang, Y., Yan, F.: Feature selection algorithm based on association rules. J. Phys. Conf. Ser. **1168**, 052012 (2019)
15. Zhao, H., Li, X.: A cost sensitive decision tree algorithm based on weighted class distribution with batch deleting attribute mechanism. Inf. Sci. **378**, 303–316 (2017). https://doi.org/10.1016/j.ins.2016.09.054

16. Huang, J., et al.: Cost-sensitive feature selection based on label significance and positive region. In: 2019 International Conference on Machine Learning and Cybernetics (ICMLC). IEEE (2019)
17. Long, X., et al.: Cost-sensitive feature selection on multi-label data via neighborhood granularity and label enhancement. Appl. Intell. **51**, 2210–2232 (2021)
18. Liu, M., et al.: Cost-sensitive feature selection by optimizing F-measures. IEEE Trans. Image Process. **27**(3), 1323–1335 (2017)
19. Freund, Y., Schapire, R.E.: A short introduction to boosting. In: Proceedings of the Sixteenth IJCAI, pp. 1401–1406. Morgan Kaufmann (1999)
20. Zhao, H., Shenglong, Yu.: Cost-sensitive feature selection via the $l_{2,1}$-norm. Int. J. Approximate Reasoning **104**, 25–37 (2019)
21. He, H., Daumé III, H., Eisner, J.: Cost-sensitive dynamic feature selection. In: ICML Inferning Workshop (2012)
22. Metzler, G., Badiche, X., Belkasmi, B., Fromont, E., Habrard, A., Sebban, M.: Tree-based cost sensitive methods for fraud detection in imbalanced data. In: Duivesteijn, W., Siebes, A., Ukkonen, A. (eds.) IDA 2018. LNCS, vol. 11191, pp. 213–224. Springer, Cham (2018). https://doi.org/10.1007/978-3-030-01768-2_18
23. Pudil, P., Novovičová, J., Kittler, J.: Floating search methods in feature selection. Pattern Recogn. Lett. **15**(11), 1119–1125 (1994)
24. Kaur, S., Cheema, S.S.: Big data and analysis of weather forecasting system. Int. J. Adv. Res. Comput. Sci. **8**(7), 176 (2017)
25. Fernández, A., García, S., Galar, M., Prati, R.C., Krawczyk, B., Herrera, F.: Learning from Imbalanced Data Sets. Springer, Cham (2018). https://doi.org/10.1007/978-3-319-98074-4
26. Bhapkar, Y.: Evaluation of K-NN and decision tree classifiers for classification of home loan customers using data mining classification technique (2022)
27. Tang, J., Alelyani, S., Liu, H.: Feature selection for classification: a review. In: Algorithms and Applications, Data Classification, p. 37 (2014)
28. Neetha, K.S., Narayan, D.L.: Feature selection using adaptive manta ray foraging optimization for brain tumor classification. Pattern Anal. Appl. **27**(2), 29 (2024)

Blockchain as an Alternative for Transparency and Optimal Handling of Microcredits in the Democratic Republic of Congo

Jonathan Kabemba Ntumbwa[1](✉)[iD], Robert Makila Beni[1][iD], and Patrick Mukala[2,3][iD]

[1] Université Nouveaux Horizons, Lubumbashi, Democratic Republic of the Congo
jonathan.kabemba@unhorizons.org.com, robert.makila@unhorizons.org
[2] University of Wollongong in Dubaï, Dubai, UAE
patrick.mukala@uowdubai.ac.ae
[3] Université Pédagogique Nationale, Kinshasa, Democratic Republic of the Congo

Abstract. Microfinance institutions frequently encounter substantial challenges in credit administration, a situation that can be viewed as a dual-faceted issue with the potential to either stimulate growth or precipitate decline. This paradox stems from their obligation to provide low-risk loans to applicants who often lack sufficient collateral. Effective risk management in this context demands a meticulous evaluation of several indicators, including a comprehensive review of the applicant's financial history. Research indicates that the digitization of microfinance operations has significantly advanced the sector. This study focuses on a model of data digitization designed to monitor all transactions associated with a credit or individual client, thereby improving transparency and optimizing credit processes within the Republic Democratic of Congo. The proposed model incorporates blockchain technology, which is acclaimed for its transformative and reliable capabilities, including the implementation of a Unique Loan Number and the enhancement of data security to improve operational efficiency.

Keywords: Blockchain · Smart Contract · Microfinance Institutions · Data Privacy · Transparency · Security

1 Introduction

Microcredits have significantly advanced financial inclusion by providing access to financial services for populations previously excluded due to the lack of collateral required by traditional banks [1]. Traditional banks generally offer loans only to individuals with property that can serve as collateral, as such assets provide security for the bank in case of default. Microfinance addresses the issue of financial exclusion among low-income populations through specialized institutions [2].

Supported by Université Nouveaux Horizons (UNH).

However, microfinance institutions (MFIs) face a substantial volume of loan applications. Ineffective credit management can undermine an MFI's operations, as their primary asset is capital. Without sufficient funds, an MFI cannot function effectively. This increasing demand for efficient credit management highlights the limitations of traditional management systems, which rely on centralized computer systems. These systems store credit information on servers accessible only to a limited number of personnel, posing significant risks such as information loss, unauthorized data manipulation, and challenges in information retrieval.

The microfinance sector, comprising multiple entities, requires the verification of credit information for customers or potential clients seeking loans. This information is centralized by a regulatory authority overseeing microfinance institutions.

In the Democratic Republic of Congo (DRC), MFIs are regulated by the Central Bank of Congo (CBC) and are linked to the CBC's Central Risk Bureau [3]. The CBC establishes policies for microcredit management and maintains comprehensive data on the credit status of clients. This data is managed through the ISYS-CERI credit management application, where MFIs input client data and request credit status checks. The process is as follows: 1) The MFI submits client identification information via the ISYS platform; 2) The CBC verifier reviews and returns the verification report to the MFI; 3) The MFI consults the report and incorporates it into the credit application process [4].

Centralizing this credit management data on a single server poses significant management challenges, particularly if the central server fails, which could disrupt the credit application process. A viable solution is to decentralize credit information, providing sector entities with transparent access to comprehensive customer data and facilitating the traceability of loan application processes. In response to these challenges, this article proposes a decentralized management system utilizing blockchain technology, known for its security, traceability, and trust-enhancing attributes [5].

The study is organized as follows: Sect. 2 reviews the current state of microfinance management using blockchain, outlining its operational landscape and challenges. Section 3 explains key blockchain technology concepts, focusing on security features relevant to microfinance. Section 4 proposes a blockchain-based architecture for microfinance management, detailing its design and security measures. Section 5 discusses potential challenges in implementing the proposed system, including technical and operational issues. Section 6 summarizes the findings and suggests directions for future research in blockchain applications for microfinance.

2 Related Work

Numerous studies have demonstrated the application of blockchain technology across various domains, including microfinance. According to [1], while farmers may lack conventional forms of collateral, such as financial assets, they typically possess alternative assets like livestock, land, and crops. Despite this, leveraging these assets as collateral remains challenging. The study explores how blockchain technology could facilitate the transfer of value from these assets, which are underutilized in the existing financial system. Additionally, blockchain technology is being employed to address critical issues in the social sector through social enterprises. A social enterprise utilizes its profits to enhance the welfare of communities in need. Research by [6] examines how blockchain can enhance the credibility, transparency, and auditability of social enterprise operations. The study addresses the challenges of developing digital currencies for social enterprises and the hurdles faced by stakeholders in adopting new technological infrastructures.

Further, [7] investigates how blockchain technology can improve accountability and transparency in managing waqf (Islamic endowments) within Islamic societies. Using institutional theory and Islamic institutional logic, the study identifies two key challenges in implementing blockchain solutions within the waqf management system: the issuance of incorrect receipts and difficulties in the distribution of waqf assets. Blockchain can address these issues by enhancing network and identification processes and providing a public ledger for waqf distribution, thus improving control and transparency. This research contributes to the understanding of Islamic institutions, specifically waqf organizations, and offers recommendations for leveraging blockchain technology to enhance accountability and transparency.

The rise of Islamic microfinance has seen the establishment of numerous organizations providing financial services in accordance with Islamic principles. Integrating blockchain and artificial intelligence offers a promising approach to improving Islamic microfinance services by enhancing transaction security and accessibility [8,9]. This framework aims to optimize transaction services and address challenges faced by Islamic finance.

Moreover, the exploration of Distributed Ledger Technology (DLT) in development contexts is gaining traction. [10] reviews the use of blockchain technology in governance and highlights issues with current DLT solutions, proposing improvements to accelerate progress toward the Sustainable Development Goals. Microfinance practices, which provide financial services to low-income individuals, draw from global experiences to present a framework that illustrates how emerging technologies like blockchain can drive digital transformation and sustainability [11]. Recent research by [12] suggests that blockchain technology holds transformative potential for microfinance management by reducing costs, enhancing transparency, and promoting financial inclusion among impoverished populations. Collectively, these studies underscore the advantages of blockchain technology for the transparent management of microcredits, as will be explored in this study.

3 Background

3.1 Blockchain

Blockchain is decentralized transactional database, which allows the management of validated and tamper-proof transactions on many participants in a network [13]. It is also defined as a distributed ledger that is structured in a linked list of blocks, where each block contains an ordered set of transactions. Blockchain solutions use cryptographic hashes to secure the link from a block to his predecessor. The blockchain as a decentralized book is a store of transactions in addition only, distributed on many machines, unlike traditional databases [14] which support Create, Read, Update, Delete (CRUD) operations. Managing a base centralized data is ensured by an administrator who holds all access rights and assigns access to users. Databases Centralized systems are based on the client/server model. Authenticated users can read or write to the database. They are fast but do not contain details of record history. Databases are not robust compared to blockchain [15].

Blockchains can be of different shapes. They can be public, private or further consortium [16]. Initially, Blockchain was only used in Finance and in transportation asset transfers via cryptocurrency and monetary transactions. As register, the Blockchain can serve as a recorder of tamper-proof data with full transparency. Public blockchains are large networks distributed that are executed via a token or native token. They are open to all and at all levels, and have open-source code, which their community keeps up to date. Private blockchains are smaller than those public and use tokens less or not at all. Their access is controlled. There blockchain consortium brings together several players who own rights. Most of stakeholders makes decisions. For example, ten financial institutions could agree and organize a blockchain in which a block should be approved by at least 8 of them to be valid. Blockchain can be used for several uses: asset transfer, blockchain as a register and smart contacts [17].

3.2 Smart Contract

A smart contract is a self-executing contract with the terms of the agreement directly written into code. It automatically enforces and executes the terms of the contract when predefined conditions are met, without the need for intermediaries. The execution of each contract statement is recorded as an immutable transaction stored in the blockchain. Smart contracts guarantee appropriate access control and contract enforcement [18,19].

In the management of microcredits utilizing blockchain technology, smart contracts are instrumental in verifying procedural clauses throughout the credit application process and ensuring compliance with operational protocols by all involved parties. These smart contracts not only verify the procedural requirements during credit processing but also ensure that the operational procedures are strictly adhered to by the participating agents. By automating and enforcing these procedures, smart contracts significantly enhance the efficiency, transparency, and trustworthiness of microcredit operations.

3.3 Cryptographic Primitives

Public Key Cryptography. Cryptography algorithms are key to safeguarding data, ensuring its authenticity, confidentiality, integrity, and non-repudiation. In our exploration, we've placed a particular emphasis on asymmetric cryptography, notably public key cryptography, given its pivotal role in modern information system security [20]. Public key cryptography employs distinct keys that are computationally feasible to generate, yet their mathematical functions possess computationally infeasible inverses. These cryptographic operations facilitate the creation of impervious digital signatures and mathematically fortified secrets. Within this realm, Elliptic Curve Cryptography (ECC) emerges as a variant of asymmetric cryptography, rooted in discrete logarithmic problems formulated through the addition and multiplication of points on an elliptic curve.

Encryption and Decryption. Data encryption is a method employed to obscure information, rendering it comprehensible only to authorized entities. Decryption serves as the means to recover encrypted data, revealing the original meaningful message, known as plaintext, which was transmitted by the sender before encryption or received by the receiver post-decryption [21]. The transformed, unintelligible data resulting from encryption is termed ciphertext. Within the realm of cryptography, two primary encryption methods exist: symmetric and asymmetric. Symmetric encryption entails the utilization of a shared private key between the sender and receiver for both encryption and decryption processes. Conversely, asymmetric encryption employs distinct private keys for encryption and decryption, necessitating mutual possession of each other's public keys by both parties. The proposed architecture adopts asymmetric encryption to ensure high levels of security and privacy in data transmission.

Hash Function and Digital Signature. A cryptographic hash function, denoted as h, operates as a mathematical algorithm designed to process input data of varying lengths, typically in the form of bit-strings, and generate a consistent-length output bit-string. This resultant output is commonly referred to as a message digest, hash value, or hash code [22]. When the hash value of a message is encrypted using a user's private key, it serves as their digital signature on that electronic document

Digital Signature. A digital signature employs mathematical methods to verify the genuineness and integrity of a message or digital document. It constitutes an electronically generated signature by a digital device to ascertain that both the sender's identity and the message's content remain unaltered throughout the transmission process [22].

Ellyptic Curve Cryptography. Elliptic Curve Cryptography (ECC) functions as a form of Asymmetric Key Cryptography, wherein every user is endowed with a distinct pair of keys: a private key and a corresponding public key. These keys serve as essential components for cryptographic operations within communication protocols. While the private key remains securely held by each user, the public key is disseminated to all users [23]. For public-key cryptography to operate effectively, all devices within the communication network may require access to predetermined constants.

Algorithm 1. Elliptic Curve Key Generation Algorithm [22]

1: Use an elliptic curve E over finite field F_p with p a prime number
2: Choose a point $P \in E(F_p)$ which generates a cyclic group of a prime order n
3: Choose a random integer d with $0 < d < n$
4: Compute $Q = dP$
5: **Public Key**: $K_{\text{pub}} = (p, n, Q, P)$
6: **Private Key**: $K_{\text{pr}} = d$

Algorithm 2. Signature Generation Algorithm [22]

Require: Message m, private key d, hash function h, base point P, and order n
Ensure: Signature (r, s)
1: Select a random or pseudorandom integer k, $0 < k < n$
2: Compute $B = kP = (x_B, y_B)$
3: Compute $r \equiv x_B \pmod{n}$
4: **if** $r = 0$ **then**
5:     Go to step 1
6: **end if**
7: Compute hash value of the message $h(m)$
8: Compute $s \equiv k^{-1}(h(m) + dr) \pmod{n}$
9: **if** $s = 0$ **then**
10:     Go to step 1
11: **end if**
12: The signature of m is (r, s)
13: Send the message m and the signature (r, s)

The primary challenge with Public Key Cryptography lies in the requirement for large key sizes to meet stringent security standards, leading to slower processes and increased bandwidth consumption. ECC addresses this challenge by employing smaller key sizes while maintaining robust security measures, thus offering a solution to the complexity inherent in traditional approaches.

Elliptic Curve Digital Signature Algorithm (ECDSA). The elliptic curve digital signature algorithm gained traction due to its shorter processing time and signature length compared to other methods, thanks to the shorter bit length of ECC. This led to its standardization by the American National Standards Institute (ANSI) in 1998.

The following protocol explains ECDSA, where Alex signs the message m and Bryan verifies Alex's signature [22]. The Algorithm 1 is used to generate the public and private key of the users after this, Algorithm 2 will be used by Alex to generate the signature for the message using the private key and hash function and then, Bryan will use the Algorithm 3 to accept or reject the message he receives using the public key and the hash function.

Algorithm 3. Signature Verification Algorithm [22]

Require: Message m, signature (r, s), public key $K_{\text{pub}} = (p, n, Q, P)$, and hash function h
Ensure: Accept or Reject
1: Verify that: $0 < r < n$ and $0 < s < n$
2: Compute hash value of the message m and convert this bit string $h(m)$ to an integer e
3: Compute $w \equiv s^{-1} \pmod{n}$
4: Compute $u1 \equiv (h(m)w) \pmod{n}$ and $u2 \equiv (rw) \pmod{n}$
5: Compute $A = u1P + u2Q = (x_A, y_A)$
6: **if** $x_A \equiv r \pmod{n}$ **then**
7:     **Accept** the signature
8: **else**
9:     **Reject** the signature
10: **end if**

---

4 Proposed Microfinance Management Architecture

4.1 Architecture

The proposed microfinance management architecture (Fig. 1) features distinct layers—business, network, blockchain, and application—carefully engineered to ensure the uninterrupted and secure tracking of credit processing within microfinance institutions, while protecting against disruptions and data manipulation.

This architecture functions as a detailed blueprint intended for replication by organizations joining the microcredit management consortium network. An additional blockchain layer will be introduced to enhance connectivity among these organizations, with institutional entities, rather than individuals, fulfilling central roles. This layer will adhere to the fundamental design principles of the core architecture.

Furthermore, to address critical security concerns, rigorous cybersecurity protocols will be embedded throughout the architecture, providing robust protection during its implementation.

Business Layer. The business layer constitutes the foundation for data processing within the proposed solution model. It delineates the sequence of credit processing activities, from the initial customer interaction to the final credit decision. This layer is integral to defining and managing the flow of credit operations.

Network Layer. The network layer is responsible for the permanent storage and management of data generated by participants in the credit processing chain. This layer ensures continuous connectivity among actors, enabling effective communication and maintaining the operability of the credit processing system. It handles the generation, recording, and storage of information, ensuring traceability within the private network.

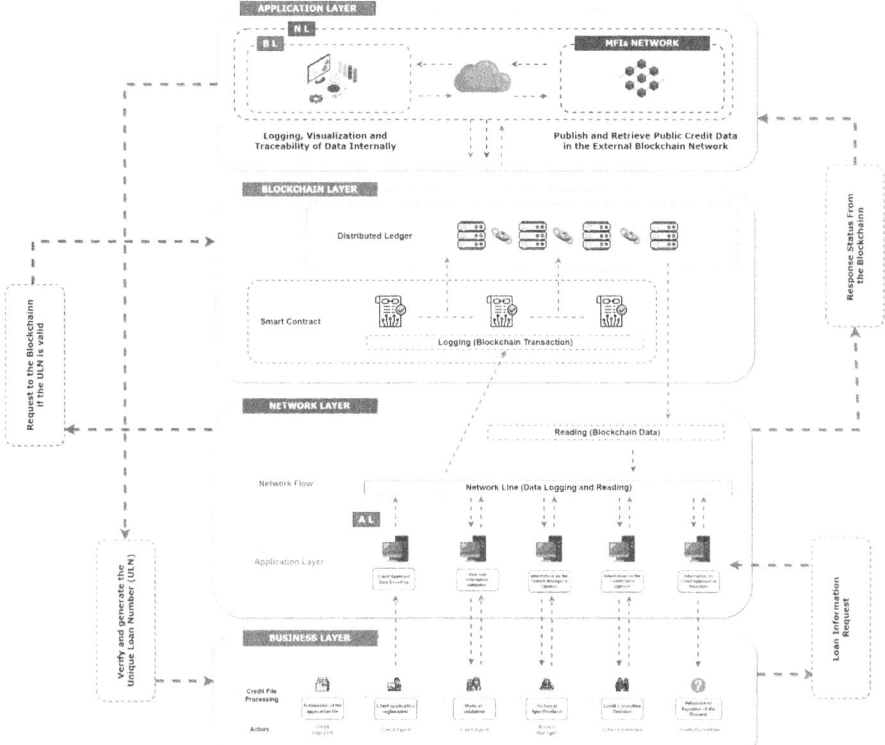

Fig. 1. Architecture diagram of the traceability system for microcredit management, illustrating the flow of information across various stages of the credit granting process.

Blockchain Layer. The blockchain layer is critical to the functionality of the proposed architecture. It guarantees data traceability throughout the credit processing chain. By leveraging immutable blockchain data, monitoring credit processing becomes more transparent and secure, as the data cannot be altered. The blockchain stores data as transactions, which are managed by smart contracts. These contracts facilitate the verification and execution of transactions, ensuring the integrity of the stored information [24].

In this model, smart contracts are employed to verify the ownership of the stored data, preventing unauthorized modifications by any actor in the credit processing chain.

Application Layer. The application layer ensures the permanent accessibility of data within the credit processing chain. It manages interactions between actors in the system and coordinates interactions between the private blockchain network and the consortium blockchain network. The architecture addresses both the technical and operational aspects of microfinance institutions (MFIs). Technically, the process involves: 1) Generating client data by inputting loan file information into the MFI's internal system; 2) Creating blocks at each stage of the file processing; 3) Validating and adding blocks to the blockchain through smart contracts; 4) Recording the finalized block chain in both the internal system of the MFI and the blockchain network for granted loans, while ungranted credits are only recorded internally.

Operationally, data is collected at each stage of the credit approval process, forming a blockchain ledger that provides network members with comprehensive loan history and financial information, thereby facilitating an overview of the borrower's repayment capacity.

4.2 Applied Information Security

Logical Access Control. Logical access control involves implementing mechanisms that restrict unauthorized access to assets or systems. The following access control models are applied:

- **Discretionary Access Control (DAC):** This model allows the owner of a resource to set access permissions for other users or processes. In the context of the information system, DAC is enforced to manage permissions for all subjects and objects, granting flexibility to resource owners in controlling access.
- **Mandatory Access Control (MAC):** Unlike DAC, MAC enforces access controls that are predetermined by the system and cannot be altered by end users. This model is applied across all subjects and objects within the information system boundary, ensuring a strict and uniform enforcement of security policies.
- **Role-Based Access Control (RBAC):** RBAC assigns permissions based on the roles of individuals within the system. Access rights for credit agents and other actors are determined by their assigned roles, ensuring that permissions align with their responsibilities and functions within the system.

Security Governance. Security (Fig. 2) encompasses a comprehensive framework within the information system, necessitating careful decision-making to ensure robust protection for the business. Effective security measures are essential for safeguarding data, maintaining system integrity, and mitigating potential threats.

Client Identification and Authentication. For risk avoidance and mitigation, a Unique Loan Number (ULN) is generated to identify clients and track their loan history based on personal information and fingerprint data. The process involves the following steps:

- **Verification and Generation of the Unique Loan Number (ULN):** The ULN is created and verified to ensure each client is uniquely identified.
- **Request for Loan Information:** Loan information is requested and associated with the ULN.

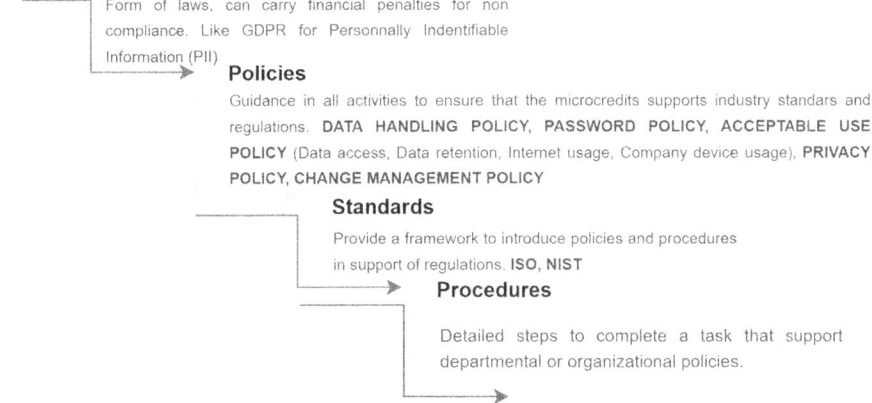

Fig. 2. Security Governance for the microcredit management architecture.

– **Blockchain Verification:** The system queries the blockchain to validate the ULN.
– **Blockchain Response:** The blockchain provides a response confirming the validity of the ULN.

This approach leverages the ULN and blockchain technology to enhance the accuracy of client identification and the integrity of loan information.

Web Application Firewall. A Web Application Firewall (WAF) filters and monitors HTTP traffic between a web application and the Internet, providing protection against common threats such as SQL injection, file inclusion, cross-site request forgery (CSRF), and cross-site scripting (XSS). By analyzing incoming and outgoing traffic, a WAF helps to prevent unauthorized access and mitigate potential vulnerabilities in web applications.

Operational Security and Insider Threat. In contemporary information systems, most security breaches are attributed to human factors, making insiders a significant vulnerability. Addressing operational security and insider threats involves several key strategies:

1. **User and Event Behavioral Analytics (UEBA):** UEBA tools analyze user behavior patterns on the network to detect anomalies that may indicate security threats. This is complemented by Security Information and Event Management (SIEM) systems, which aggregate and analyze log data to identify potential security issues and allocate resources effectively.
2. **Monitoring and Assessment:** Comprehensive surveillance of all inbound communication traffic and access attempts is essential. This includes using firewalls, gateways, remote authentication servers, intrusion detection and

prevention systems (IDS/IPS), SIEM solutions, and anti-malware tools to ensure robust security.
3. **Data Loss Prevention:** Measures must be taken to prevent data loss or leakage through various channels, including email content and attachments, copying data to portable media, file transfer protocols (FTP), posting data to web pages or websites, and interacting with applications or application programming interfaces (APIs).

These practices are vital for enhancing operational security and mitigating insider threats, ensuring a secure and resilient information system environment.

5 Implementation Challenges

Although the proposed architecture offers significant improvements in data security and operational efficiency, its implementation in microcredit management within the Democratic Republic of Congo presents several challenges:

– **Integration with Existing Systems:** One major challenge is integrating the blockchain system with the various legacy information systems used by microfinance institutions. Achieving seamless compatibility and communication between new blockchain technology and existing systems can be complex and resource-intensive. A robust network infrastructure, including reliable internet connectivity and appropriate hardware and software, is crucial for supporting blockchain operations effectively.
– **Training and Adaptation:** Effective implementation also requires substantial training for personnel to understand and utilize blockchain technology. This training must cover technical aspects as well as blockchain principles and processes to enable staff to manage and troubleshoot the system effectively. The adoption of blockchain technology will necessitate significant changes to established operational procedures, which may face resistance from staff accustomed to traditional methods. Additionally, ensuring compliance with local regulations and standards will require collaboration with regulatory authorities, which can be both intricate and time-consuming.

Overcoming these challenges is essential for the successful deployment of blockchain technology in microfinance institutions, thereby maximizing its potential benefits in terms of data security and operational efficiency.

6 Conclusion and Discussion

This paper presents an innovative network architecture that utilizes blockchain technology to overcome the complexities associated with microcredit management in diverse operational contexts. Through a comprehensive review of existing literature on microcredit systems and blockchain applications, this study proposes a model designed to significantly improve the operational efficiency of microfinance institutions, while simultaneously enhancing transparency and traceability in their processes.

The paper details the services offered by microfinance institutions and provides an in-depth analysis of their operational mechanics, which forms the basis for the proposed solution. The proposed architecture is a multi-layered network model, conceptualized based on established principles of computer network design. This architecture is intended for deployment within the blockchain networks of microfinance institutions, integrating seamlessly into their corporate infrastructures.

The research highlights that adopting a decentralized systems approach can substantially advance credit management practices and drive the evolution of microfinance organizations. This approach fosters increased trust among stakeholders and enhances the capability to monitor customer credit transactions. Nonetheless, the successful implementation of this model requires careful integration with the diverse information systems currently in use by microfinance institutions.

Acknowledgment. This work was supported by Université Nouveaux Horizons research funding.

References

1. Chinaka, M.: Blockchain technology–applications in improving financial inclusion in developing economies: case study for small scale agriculture in Africa. Massachusetts Institute of Technology (2016)
2. Labie, M., Montalieu, T.: Introduction. From microfinance to financial inclusion. Mondes En Développement **185**(1), 7–12 (2019)
3. Masangu, J-C.: Instruction No.5 to Credit Institutions relating to the Central Risk Office in the DRC. Official Instruction of Central Bank of the DRC (2013)
4. Bondo, D.: Insights on the process of credit acquisition from microfinance institution in DRC from Finca Agent. Personal interview by Jonathan Kabemba (2022)
5. Cherednichenko, S.: Designing a Blockchain architecture: types, use cases, and challenges (2020). https://medium.com/mobindustry/designinga-blockchain-architecture-types-use-cases-and-challenges9894fb7b58e
6. Mukkamala, R., Vatrapu, R., Ray, P., Sengupta, G., Halder, S.: Blockchain for social business: principles and applications. IEEE Eng. Manage. Rev. **46**, 94–99 (2018)
7. Mohaiyadin, N., Aman, A., Palil, M., Said, S.: Addressing accountability and transparency challenges In Waqf management using Blockchain technology. J. Islamic Monetary Econ. Finance **8**, 53–80 (2022)
8. Elasrag, H.: Blockchains for Islamic finance: obstacles challenges (2019)
9. Katterbauer, K., Syed, H., Kiev, L.: An innovative AI Blockchain framework for Islamic microfinancing. J. Islamic Fin. **11**, 67–80 (2022)
10. Seyedsayamdost, E., Vanderwal, P.: From good governance to governance for good: blockchain for social impact. J. Int. Dev. **32**, 943–960 (2020)

11. Pal, A., Dey, S., Nandy, A., Shahin, S., Singh, P.: Digital transformation in microfinance as a driver for sustainable development. In: Handbook of Sustainability Science in the Future: Policies. Technologies and Education by 2050, pp. 1–21. Springer (2021)
12. Mukala, P., Ntumbwa, J.K.: On the digital transformation of micro-finance institutions in the context of developing countries: a case from Democratic Republic of the Congo (2024)
13. Lynn, T., Mooney, J.G., Rosati, P., Cummins, M.: Disrupting finance: FinTech and strategy in the 21st century. Springer (2019)
14. Xiwei, X., Weber, I., Staples, M.: Architecture for Blockchain applications (2019). https://doi.org/10.1007/978-3-030-03035-3
15. Komalavalli, C., Saxena, D., Laroiya, C.: Overview of blockchain technology concepts. In: Handbook of Research on Blockchain Technology, pp. 349–371. Academic Press (2020)
16. Ghoggali, B.: Systeme Des Crédits Bancaires basé sur La Technologie Blockchain. Mémoire de Master, Université Mohamed Khider - Biskra (2020)
17. Ribeiro, A.: La Blockchain et ses potentielles applications. Université de Geneve (2016)
18. Górski, T.: Smart contract design pattern for processing logically coherent transaction types. Appl. Sci. **14**(6), 2224 (2024)
19. Zheng, Z., et al.: An overview on smart contracts: challenges, advances and platforms. Future Gener. Comput. Syst. **105**, 475–491 (2019). https://doi.org/10.1016/j.future.2019.12.019
20. Merlec, M.M., In, H.P.: DataMesh+: a Blockchain-powered peer-to-peer data exchange model for self-sovereign data marketplaces. Sensors **24**(6), 1896 (2024). https://doi.org/10.3390/s24061896
21. Islam, M.M., In, H.: A privacy-preserving transparent central bank digital currency system based on consortium Blockchain and unspent transaction outputs. IEEE Trans. Serv. Comput. **16**(4), 1–15 (2022)
22. Selikh, B.: On elliptic curves and application to cryptography (2023). https://doi.org/10.13140/RG.2.2.25775.10405
23. Shirale, V.R., Gawali, B.W., Desai, C.G.: A Study on Elliptic Curve Cryptosystem (2022)
24. Fauziah, Z., Latifah, H., Omar, X., Khoirunisa, A., Millah, S.: Application of blockchain technology in smart contracts: a systematic literature review. ATT **2**(2), 160–166 (2020)

Improving Smart Contract Security Using Sequential Models

Rosaire Senou[(✉)] and Jules Degila

Institut de Mathématiques et de Sciences Physique, African Center of Excellence in Applied Mathematics, Dangbo, Benin
{rosaire.senou,jules.degila}@imsp-uac.org

Abstract. Blockchain-enabled smart contracts execute without third-party involvement when specific conditions are met. This system significantly reduces the use of paper-based processes while managing substantial funds. As such, it has become the target of hackers. It has suffered several attacks, particularly the DAO (Decentralized Autonomous Organization) attack and the Parity multi-sig wallet hack, which had severe consequences. This has triggered the need for better security measures as the use of this technology has increased significantly in recent years. Several tools have been developed to tackle various problems while they still lack better achievements. As deep learning achieved better results in vulnerability detection domain, we proposed a deep-learning approach using bidirectional long-short term memory (BLSTM) to classify contract either vulnerable (detection of suicidal, prodigal and greedy contracts) or non-vulnerable. The aim was to propose a detection technique that might achieve better results so as to encourage the use of deep learning techniques. The experiment was conducted on a HPC (High-Performance Computing) cluster where each server has a processing power of 2.2 GHz and a RAM of 128G at least. We were able to achieve an accuracy and F1 score of 94%. This works also set a new benchmark to better smart contract detection while promoting future researches axes.

Keywords: Smart contract · security issues · blstm

1 Introduction

Smart contracts are programs which perform transactions automatically in the peer-to-peer network. Billions of dollars in cryptocurrency are at stake [1], rising the need of securing the assets involved. As smart contracts increase in number, several securities flaws are noticed leading to the possibility of exploiting them to steal or to block funds [2]. These security issues are severe threats used by attackers and they have caused stunning consequences so far. According to the statistics of SlowMist Hacked, more than 13 billions USD have been lost on blockchain platforms due to hacks [3].

The Ethereum blockchain is one of the most popular smart contract platforms with a market capitalization of more than 38 million USD [2, 4]. Thousands of smart contracts, have been deployed while several losses have been encountered. Blockchain properties such as irreversibility and immutability do not facilitate the loss recovery [5] as fixing the issues to get the funds back needs manual intervention which do not lead to automatic result, making the whole process cumbersome.

The occurrence of those incidents may demonstrate how negligent were developers with respect to security concern in smart contracts. Therefore, writing safe smart contracts become a serious issue. Though it might be a clumsy work to achieve it due to presence of underlying domain-specific language semantics [6], that can be identified through code inspection alone. Dynamic analysis checks an application when it is running or executing. It acts by inserting unsafe code into a program function to detect the presence of threats or not. It can outperform static analysis by detecting threats that were deemed negative in static analysis while getting exhausted or limited in threats coverage. As for Formal verification techniques, they make use of use of mathematical methods and theorem to prove parameters such as run-time, functional correctness, reliability etc. in a program code in order to ensure error-free code. They offer strong, mathematical guarantees while being complex and resource-intensive. Deep expertise in formal methods are required and becomes challenging when looking for accurate systems representations [23].

Other solutions based on deep learning techniques have been used to detect buggy contracts [2, 8, 9, 21] in order to improve the smart contract security ecosystem. These tools can be easily scaled, automated and can handle uncertain pattern with their evolving capability [8]. BLSTM has not been used so far as solutions approaches. We therefore proposed the use of BLSTM to detect faulty smart contract (suicidal, prodigal and greedy contracts).

In this study, our contributions are as follows:

- We proved that our model achieved detection test accuracy and F1 score of 94%
- We demonstrate that our proposed deep learning-based technique outperforms existing techniques
- We set a new benchmark related to the use deep learning methods to secure smart contracts by showing the efficiency achieve by BLSTM.

In the rest of the paper, problem statement is emphasized next, followed by the literature review section, the experimentation and results section and terminated by the conclusion and futures directives section.

2 Introduction

The occurrence of smart contract security breaches causes dramatic consequences as hundreds of millions of dollars were involved. This raise several concerns regarding how unsecure blockchain based smart contract can be. Distrust and disbelief gained people and therefore tarnished somehow the technology recognition worldwide [11].

According to [10, 16] most of the major tools uses static and dynamics analysis for security vulnerabilities detection. However, these solutions lack high precision and accuracy detection as they are logic-based rules tools which are effective for well-known vulnerabilities but struggle with new, complex, or subtle issues. Deep learning, by contrast, can adapt to detect these complex patterns. They tend to have higher accuracy due to their ability to learn from large amounts of data and detect non-obvious patterns [2].

To the best of our knowledge, LSTM was the first efficient machine learning technique used by [8] so far to tackle the parity's wallet bug. However, LSTM is far from being the best machine learning technique for this issue. Regarding the seriousness of the issue with all assets involved, it is very urgent to provide efficient security methods. Since deep learning techniques have evolved and have been applied in detecting other smart contract issues with high precision, it will be relevant to propose an improved version of the existing deep learning technique to better secure smart contracts.

3 Related Work

The fast evolution of blockchain technologies have led to its applications in several domains such as supply chain, health care system and insurance [13], Internet of things and financial system [2, 13]. Smart contracts are perceived at the very start as code is law [6]. Ethereum blockchain is one the most used smart contract platform and have suffered disastrous attacks [2, 8]. Several tools have been created to solve those issues. We will look at two different types of tools: tools without deep learning techniques and the one using deep learning techniques.

3.1 Tools Without Deep Learning Techniques

Studies have been conducted to produce robust and efficient tools to secure smart contracts. Static and dynamics analysis are the most used method by the tools [10, 16] which are logic-based rules. According to [2, 7] *Oyente* is part of the first static tools that makes use of symbolic execution for threats detections at bytecode level. These tools can tackle several threats such reentrancy, transaction ordering, exception handling, integer overflow/underflow and time manipulation [8]. *Slither* is a tool that makes use of static analysis framework for smart contract code. According to [10, 17] it exhibits fast and reliable security techniques to achieve automated vulnerability and optimization detection, code understanding and assisted code review. It can be used to detect Reentrancy, abuse of Tx origin, suicidal contract and time manipulation. *Securify* is another static analysis tool which checks security properties in smart contracts bytecode to detect vulnerable contracts. According to [20] the security properties are encoded as patterns in a particular language, and compared to contract's code for compliance or violation. It is capable of detecting reentrancy vulnerabilities, transaction ordering dependencies, exception handling problem, call stack depth limitation, no restricted wife, transfer and non-validated arguments [8]. *Maian* is a dynamic analysis tool that uses systematic techniques to detect trace properties violations in smart contract executions [8]. This tool tackle three types of vulnerabilities: greedy contracts (contracts that lock ether), suicidal contracts (contract that can be destroyed by an intruder) and prodigal contracts (contracts that can send funds to an arbitrary address) [15]. *Zeus* is proprietary tool that created by IBM that uses static analysis method to verify smart contract code correctness of smart for fairness validation. It showed better performance as compared to Oyente where less false positive rate and less analysis time are recorded [8] and can detect a wide range of vulnerabilities including as reentrancy, integer overflows, transaction order dependency, unhandled exceptions etc. Its operation is based on the high-level representation of the smart contract code written in Solidity instead of the bytecode [7, 8]. *ContactFuzzer* makes use of dynamic analysis to find vulnerabilities in smart contracts. Its operation is based on generating input for contracts using their Application Binary Interface and the use of instrumented EVM (Ethereum Virtual Machine) to run fuzzed contracts. A vast range of vulnerabilities such as reentrancy, locked Ether or unhandled exceptions can be detected. It demonstrated higher true positive rate as compared to Oyente and other static analysis tools [7] while showing [2]. *SmartCheck* detects threats by running the source code at high level and converting it to an intermediate state where uses XPaths patterns are considered for vulnerability checking. It is only suitable for detecting simple bugs such as redundant function, inadequate style guide and wrong compiler version [10]. *Vandal* is a static analysis that checks the EVM bytecode through two steps: decompilation and encoding. The bytecode is decompiled and the smart contract properties are encoded into Datalog which is easily extended to detect others vulnerabilities [19] including suicidal contract. With respect to suicidal smart contract detection, Oyente, Maian, slither Vandal and Zeus are able to perform it [2, 8]. However, as our objective is to use open-source tools that employ bytecode to extract the input opcode for our model, only Vandal and Maian can be considered [15, 19]. Oyente takes bytecode as input but allows only partial detection of suicidal contract [10]. Zeus and Slither tools require other intermediate process as they use solidity code as input which is converted first to bytecode before further processing [17, 18]. Besides Zeus is a proprietary tool developed by IBM which makes its availability restricted [18].

As smart contracts become more complex, the use of logic-based rules becomes limited as creating comprehensive rules that cover all potential vulnerabilities becomes increasingly difficult. Therefore, such tools can generate false positives (flagging safe code as vulnerable) and false negatives (missing actual vulnerabilities), leading to lower accuracy [8].

3.2 Tools Using Deep Learning Techniques

Deep learning techniques are proved to attain good results in program security. In blockchain field to the best of our knowledge, their application in smart contracts threats detection demonstrated better results. LSTM was proved to outperformed Maian in greedy, prodigal and suicidal contract detection [8]. BLSTM-ATT developed by [2] bettered securify, Oyente, Smartcheck and Mythril capabilities in reentrancy vulnerabilities detection. AWD-LSTM (Asynchronous Weight Drop – LSTM) was also used in tackling greedy, suicidal and prodigal contracts.

These results are therefore promising as to use deep-learnings techniques for tackling smarts contracts vulnerabilities. They are better suited for analyzing large volumes of smart contracts and can improve over time as they are exposed to more data allowing them to cope with changes with ease [8]. They therefore can get higher accuracy while detecting new complex patterns.

4 Methodology

Smart contract code can be available at opcode level or at high level programming code level. Our model is going to operate at the opcode level as the EVM that allows the contract execution talks in a much lower level: bytecode (a grouping of several opcodes) [8]. The Objective of this study is to propose a vulnerability detection technique that can automatically confirm whether a smart contract is suicidal, greedy, prodigal or not. Inspired by [2, 8], the following steps are adopted.

- First, smart contracts are extracted from Google Big query and etherscan in their bytecode level which is fed into the EVM to provide the corresponding opcode.
- Secondly, the opcode are run through Maian tool so as to provide the required label for threats classification.
- Third, the opcode of smart contract are processed (remove any unnecessary parts like spaces and punctuations, breaking down of source code into tokens, creation of fixed input sequences) and represented in the form of code vector with the help of an embedded matrix.
- Finally during experiments, the code vectors are fed into our BLSTM model for training it, to evaluate its performance using evaluation metrics (accuracy, F1 score, precision and recall). Based on the result, the model is adjusted till a best performance is obtained.

At the end, the model will allow smart contract classification where the contract will be either vulnerable or not.

The whole process is resumed in the figure below (Fig. 1).

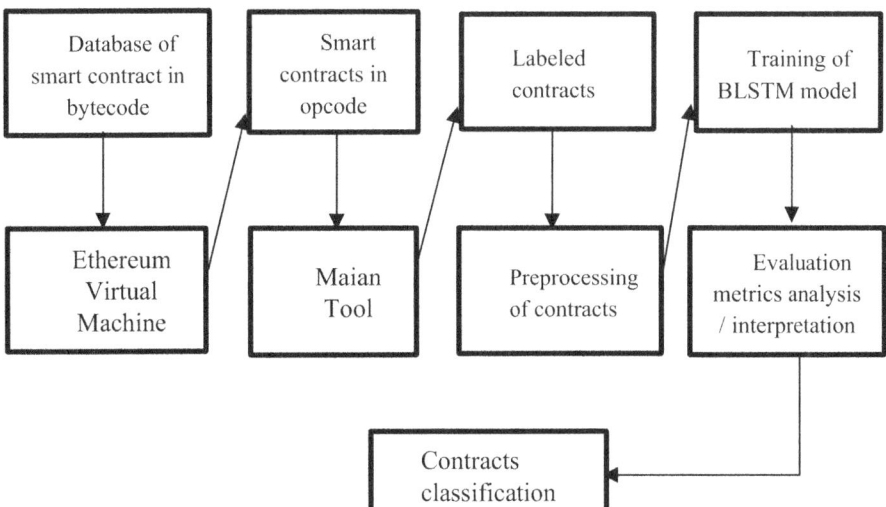

Fig. 1. Contract classification process

5 Experimentations and Results Interpretation

The experimentation was conducted on a HPC cluster where a single server has at least the following characteristics: Oracle server X7-2 with Intel Xeon Silver 4114 CPU @2.20 GHZ having a total core of 10 and a Memory ranging from 128 GB to 516 GB.

The Whole Cluster is consisted of 26 servers compounded together to give out the overall power to run complex script. The used data base is a public data base available at https://github.com/wesleyjtann/Safe-SmartContracts. The aim is to use the database to train both LSTM and BLSTM models in order to find out the performance of BLSTM over LSTM. The following parameters were considered for BLSTM and LSTM.

LSTM

Epochs = 10
Embedding dimension = 100
Batch size = 32
Dataset = 32.000
Optimizer = adam
Loss = binary_crossentropy

BLSTM

Epochs = 20
Embedding dimension = 100
Batch size = 32
Dataset = 32.000
Optimizer = adam
Loss = binary_crossentropy

The following graphs were obtained after training the models (Figs. 2 and 3).

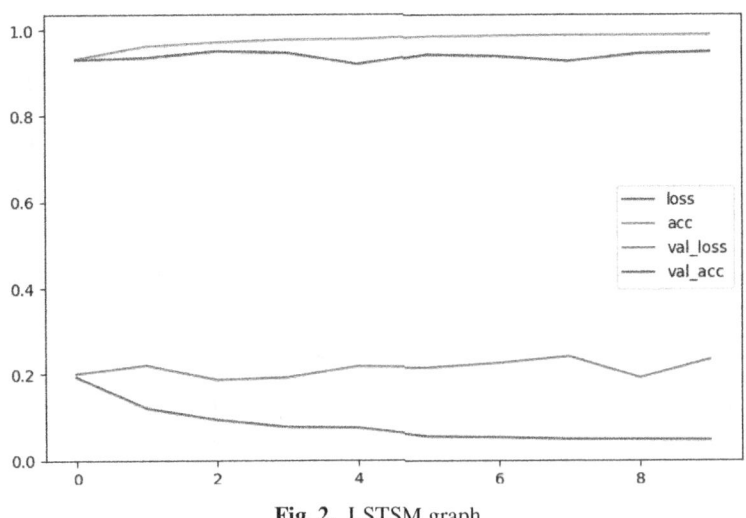

Fig. 2. LSTSM graph

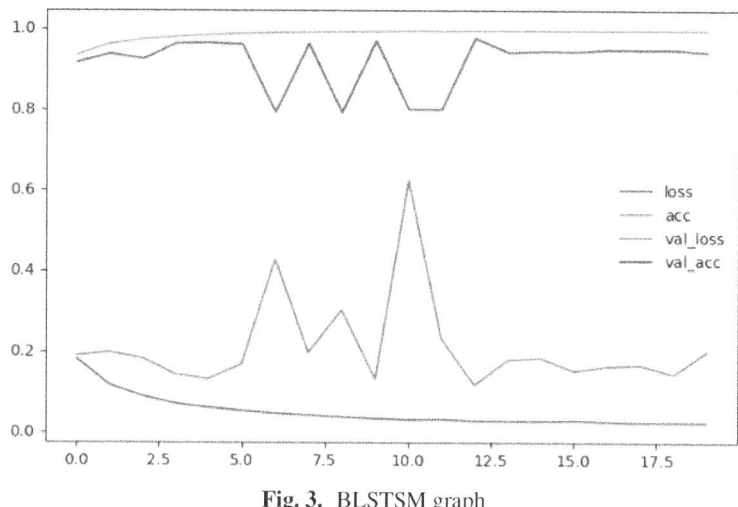

Fig. 3. BLSTSM graph

In the case of the LSTM, we can observe that the loss curves (loss and val_loss) seem to converge toward a stable value after a few epochs. This suggests that the model is learning and improving over time but reaches a plateau where it no longer progresses significantly. Looking at the accuracy curves (acc and val_acc), we see that they increase at the beginning of the training, then also stabilize. This confirms that the model reaches an optimal level of performance. Another important point to note is that the gap between the training and validation curves is not very significant, indicating that overfitting is not a major issue. In the case of the BLSTM, we notice that the loss and validation learning curves show peaks, indicating instability during training. However, the model managed to return to a trend toward a stable value, demonstrating that it can generalize well to new data (Tables 1, 2, and 3).

Table 1. Evaluation Parameters of LSTM and BLSTM.

Model	Evaluation Parameters			
	Precision	Recall	F1-score	Accuracy
LSTM	0,92	0,91	0,91	0,91
BLSTM	0,94	0,94	0,94	0,94

Table 2. Confusion Matrix of LSTM

		Prediction	
		V	NV
Actual Value	V	5971	941
	NV	254	6658

Table 3. Confusion Matrix of BLSTM

		Prediction	
		V	NV
Actual Value	V	6302	610
	NV	288	6624

The BLSTM achieves a percentage of 91% in terms of Accuracy, F1-score, recall and precision which are better than LSTM results. Indeed, BLSTM processes sequences in both directions (forward and backward). This allows the network to have access to both past and future context at each point in the sequence. The combination of forward and backward information helps the BLSTM capture more context, making it more effective at understanding dependencies that aren't strictly linear. This is not the case with LSTM where the context of work is limited to the flow of information in one direction [22].

We noticed that the BLSTM model considers fewer vulnerable contracts as non-vulnerable compared to the LSTM model. On the same sample sizes, 610 vulnerable contracts are considered vulnerable by the BLSTM while 941 contracts are considered as such by the LSTM. The BLSTM visibly makes fewer errors than the LSTM, which shows its superiority in terms of performance compared to the LSTM. This error of LSTM might be related to the processing information in only one direction in LSTM which might not capture all the dependencies in data. LSTMs might overfit to certain patterns in the sequence when they don't have the full context. All these limitations can lead to misinterpretations, resulting in false positives [22]. Our results are encouraging in the sense that they bring a new value in the literature compared to previous work [2, 21]. The existing tools stop at LSTM when detecting these types of bugs [8, 15] with the same dataset and BLSTM was used to tackle reentrancy bug with a different dataset bug but did not achieve such a result [2].

6 Conclusion and Perspectives

The security of smart contract is a serious concern as it implies funds and assets transactions which can be stolen if care are not taken. The achievements of deep learning method help in improving this aspect strengthening the trust and usage of the technology. Our result is a start point for improving upon previous work which would lead to new discovery in the long run. The limitations of our work are related to the increase of the number of epochs and data increase to improve upon the system training. Also, the comparison was limited to LSTM while it could be extended to other variant of deep learning models.

As future directives, we would look at how to tackle other types of security concerns (exceptions mishandling, buffer overflow, extra gaz consumption) using deep learning or reinforcement techniques. Some more tests could be performed with other literature review techniques (BLSTM with attention models or transformers) using same dataset in the same environment. We can also look for the use of machine learning techniques to tackle others issues related to smart contract security.

References

1. Destefanis, G., Marchesi, M., Ortu, M., Tonelli, R., Bracciali, A., Hierons R.M.: Smart contracts vulnerabilities: a call for blockchain software engineering? In: International Workshop on Blockchain Oriented Software Engineering (IWBOSE), pp. 19–25 (2018)
2. Qian, P., Liu, Z., He, Q., Zimmermann, R., Wang, X.: Towards automated reentrancy detection for smart contracts based on sequential models. IEEE Access **8**, 19685–19695 (2020)
3. Slowmist Hacked. https://hacked.slowmist.io/en/. Accessed 29 September 2023
4. Ethereum. https://en.wikipedia.org/wiki/Ethereum. Accessed 29 September 2023
5. Wang S., Yuan Y., Wang X., Li J., Qin R., Wang F.: An overview of smart contract: architecture, applications, and future trends. In: IEEE Intelligent Vehicles Symposium (IV), pp 108–113 (2018)
6. Parizi, R.M., Dehghantanha, A., Choo, K., Singh, A.: Empirical vulnerability analysis of automated smart contracts security testing on blockchains. In: Conference of the Centre for Advanced Studies on Collaborative Research (2018)
7. Perez, D., Livshits, B.: Smart Contract Vulnerabilities: Does Anyone Care? (2019). arXiv:1902.06710v2
8. Tann, W.J., Han, X.J., Gupta, S.S., Ong, Y.: Towards Safer Smart Contracts: A Sequence Learning Approach to Detecting Security Threats (2019). arXiv:1811.06632v2
9. Yuxin, W., Ting, C., Dabin, Z.: Hierarchical attention mechanism and bidirectional long short-term memory based neural network model for smart contract automatic classification. J. Comput. Appl. 1–9 (2019)
10. Sayeed, S., Marco-Gisbert, H., Caira, T.: Smart contract: attacks and protections. IEEE Access **8**, 24416–24427 (2020)
11. Bokhenek, A.: Parity Multisig Wallet Hacked, or How Come? https://cointelegraph.com/news/parity-multisig-wallet-hacked-or-how-come. Accessed 10 August 2023
12. Schroeder, S.: Wallet Bug Freezes More Than $150 Million Worth of Ethereum. https://mashable.com/2017/11/08/ethereum-parity-bug/?europe=true. Accessed 10 August 2023
13. Kumar, B., Panda, S., Jena, D.: An Overview of Smart Contract and Use cases in Blockchain Technology, 9th ICCCNT, IEEE, Bengaluru, India (2018)
14. Zheng, Z., et al.: Overview on Smart Contracts: Challenges, Advances and Platforms (2019). arXiv:1912.10370v1
15. Nikolic, I., Kolluri, A., Sergey, I., Saxena, P., Hobor A.: Finding the greedy, prodigal, and suicidal contracts at scale. In: Proceedings of the 34th Annual Computer Security Applications Conference, pp. 653–663 (2018)
16. Di Angelo, M., Salzer, G.: A survey of tools for analyzing ethereum smart contracts. In: IEEE, International Conference on Decentralized Applications and Infrastructures (DAPPCON), Newark, CA, USA, pp. 69–78 (2019). https://doi.org/10.1109/DAPPCON.2019.00018
17. Feist, J., Grieco, G., Groce, A.: Slither: a static analysis framework for smart contracts. In: IEEE/ACM 2nd International Workshop on Emerging Trends in Software Engineering for Blockchain (WETSEB), pp. 8–15 (2019)
18. Kalra, S., Goel, S., Dhawan, M., Sharma, S.: ZEUS: analyzing safety of smart contracts. In: Network and Distributed System Security Symposium, San Diego, CA, USA (2018)
19. Brent, L., et al.: Vandal: A Scalable Security Analysis Framework for Smart Contracts (2018). abs/1809.0398
20. Tsankov, P., Dan, A.M., Drachsler-Cohen, D., Gervais, A., Buenzli, F., Vechev, M.T.: Securify: Practical security analysis of smart contracts. In: Proceedings of the 2018 ACM SIGSAC Conference on Computer and Communications Security (2018)
21. Gogineni, A.K., Swayamjyoti, S., Sahoo, D., Sahu, K.K., Kishore, R.: Multi-class classification of vulnerabilities in smart contracts using AWD-LSTM, with pre-trained encoder inspired from natural language processing (2020). arXiv:2004.00362

22. Silva, D.G., Meneses, A.: Preliminary Studies: Comparing LSTM and BLSTM Deep Neural Networks for Power Consumption Prediction (2023). arXiv:2305.16546
23. Havelund, K., Pressburger, T.: Formal methods for software engineering: a survey. Softw. Eng. Notes **25**(4), 1–14 (2000)

The Limit of Direct Modulation in an FTTH/GPON Architecture

Zacharia Damoue[(✉)], Mamadou Alpha Barry, Abdourahmane Ndiaye, and Mamadou Moustapha Ndiaye

Ecole Supérieure Multinationale des Télécommunications (ESMT), Dakar, Senegal
{zacharia.damoue,alpha.barry,abdourahmane.ndiaye}@esmt.sn,
moustaphan1416@gmail.com

Abstract. Optical fiber has just made a remarkable entry into the access network where it is effectively replacing the twisted copper pair. As soon as GPON technology is installed, and faced with the exponential needs of customers in terms of bandwidth, it seems necessary to study this segment of the telecommunications network in order to better deal with this reality. In fact, increasing the speed of optical fibers will require to take account of phenomena in this part of network. Based on a functional FTTH/GPON network, the customer's optical line will be simulated using Optisystem software, trying to be as close as possible to the characteristics of real optical line. By increasing the data rate on the optical line thus constituted, the limit of direct modulation with NRZ coding could be found.

Keywords: direct modulation · factor of quality · Bit Error Rate

1 Introduction

The last few years have seen exceptional development in Information and Communication Technology (ICTs), including FTTx (Fiber To The x), mobile network technologies (4G and 5G) and IoT, which have made it possible to offer customers very high-speed broadband in the access network segment.

Indeed, the growing needs of customers for bandwidth-hungry services such as TVHD and home automation supported by the IoT mean that it is important to anticipate future requirements.

To this end, it is recommended to use the optical fiber support resulting from the deployment of GPON technology to study its behaviour by varying the bit rate progressively until the breaking point is reached.

The optical access network is the part of the optical telecommunications network that runs from the optical node (optical switch) to serve customers. It is the part of the network that relays the optical signal from the long-distance network via the metropolitan network. Access network infrastructures are either underground, with the implementation of very expensive civil engineering networks, and/or overhead [1].

This study is based on an FTTH/GPON network in operation in one of the areas of the city of Dakar, Senegal.

In this article, it is proposed to investigate the limit of direct modulation in the context of an FTTH/GPON network simulated by the Optisystem software.

To achieve this objective, the work is organised as follows:

- Section 2 deals with similar work carried out;
- The design of an FTTH/GPON network is proposed in Sect. 3;
- The simulation of an FTTH/GPON network is dealt with in Sect. 4;
- Section 5 deals with the performance obtained;
- Section 6 concludes.

2 Similar Work Carried Out

Zouhaira Abdellaoui and al [2] proposed the design, implementation and evaluation of an FTTH/GPON network for serving residential and business customers using Optisystem.

Rima Fitria Adiati and al [3] designed and analysed the performance of an FTTH/GPON network through an optical power budget and the rise time of the optical link in a residential area. The design satisfies the link power budget with the lowest power margin of 2.469dB/2.826dB uplink/downlink over the farthest distance. The highest rise time for the system is 0.2236 ns. The designed optical link was found to be compliant with the ITU-T GPON G.984.1 standard.

Arafat Abdallah Shabaneh and al [4] designed and analysed an FTTH/GPON network using a Bragg grating and an optical amplifier by Optisystem. The use of a FBG (Fiber Bragg Grating) component enabled interesting performances with an optimal evaluation of the power link budget. In addition to the power budget, the bit error rate (BER) and the quality factor (Q) were tested and obtained satisfactory results for various optical input power values, with a single-mode fiber length of 20 km and a line loss of 0.2 dB/km.

Fachri Maulana and al [5] built an FTTH/GPON network using Optisystem, relying on optical budget tests for feasibility and bit error rate (BER) tests to measure the performance of the optical network through attenuation.

W. Awalia and al [6] carried out work on an FTTH/GPON network simulated by Optisystem over a 17 km span. The performance of the simulation was analysed and found to be acceptable through an adequate bit error rate (BER).

Mustafa H. Ali and al [7] proposed the variation of input power and optical fiber length in an FTTH/GPON architecture using RZ and NRZ coding in order to analyse the performance for a 2.5 Gbit downstream data rate.

The RZ code is more resistant to fiber non-linearities and is able to reach 90 km for a power of 5 dBm at wavelengths of 1490 or 1557 nm, beyond which the bit error rate is greater than 10^{-9}. On the other hand, according to the results of the study carried out, the NRZ code makes it possible to achieve a range of 40 km for 1557 nm and 70 km for 1490 nm at a power of 5 dBm.

Faramarz E. Seraji and al studied in [8] the performance through the Optisystem simulated eye diagram of the RZ and NRZ codes on a single 10 Gbit/s channel and a 160 Gbit/s WDM channel in optical networks. The results showed that the RZ code performed better in tolerating non-linear effects and noisy environments. The NRZ code was shown to be a good choice for single-channel and long-haul networks.

Govind P. Agrawal argued in [10] that beyond 10Gbits/s, direct modulation could not be used because of the high chirp phenomenon caused by semiconductor lasers. Eight years later, in [11], the same author revised the data rate downwards to 5 Gbits/s as the limit for direct modulation. Faced with this situation, it seemed necessary to check the veracity of the results put forward by the author.

As a reminder, modulation enables the signal to be adapted to the transmission medium so that it can be transported under good conditions. There are two types of modulation:

- External modulation;
- Direct modulation.

In this article, focus will be on direct modulation.

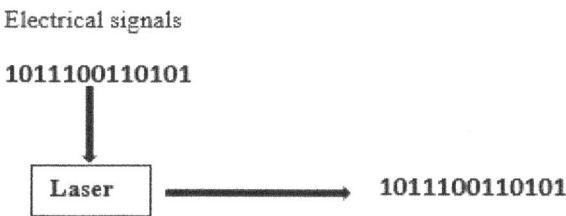

Fig. 1. Showing direct modulation

Figure 1 shows the digital signal that controls the laser, with bit "1" allowing illumination and bit "0" indicating the absence of light in the optical fiber.

Damoué and al [1] gave a special treatment to the engineering of an FTTH/GPON network, which will be used as a basis for the study that follows.

From the scientific literature consulted, the Optisystem software has been used to simulate FTTH/GPON networks and derive results to improve customer satisfaction.

3 Designing an FTTH/GPON Network

In this section, GPON technology will be presented, detailing all the constituent elements of the optical network, with particular emphasis on the technical concepts used.

The area covered by the study is residential and includes dwellings, small and medium-sized businesses, schools, clinics, etc. It seems necessary to give the essential characteristics of GPON technology in the following table.

The engineering rules in [1] were applied in the study area, namely:

- The infrastructure layer;
- The passive optical layer;
- The network layer.

This makes it possible to produce a network model that takes account of the objective realities in order to carry out simulations in conditions that are very close to the reality.

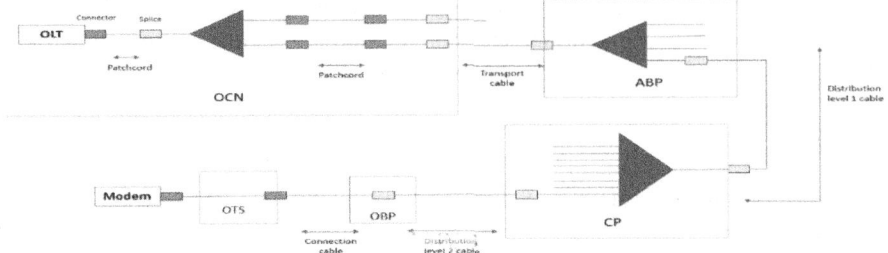

Fig. 2. Components of a customer's optical line

3.1 FTTH/GPON Network Components

The FTTH/GPON network is made up of the following elements:

- Optical fiber;
- Splices;
- Connectors;
- Passive splitters.

A brief study of these components is proposed, starting with the optical fiber, followed by splices, connectors and ending with passive splitters.

The choice of optical fiber used is G 657 version A2 (ITU-T standard) throughout the access network in the study area, as it is less sensitive to bending constraints.

The characteristics of this fiber are as follows:

- Maximum attenuation of 0.36 and 0.22 dB/km at wavelengths of 1310 and 1550 nm respectively;
- Maximum chromatic dispersion: 3.5 and 18ps / (nm x km) at wavelengths of 1310 and 1550 nm respectively;
- Permissible bending radius: up to 7.5 mm at wavelength 1550 nm for maximum induced attenuation of 0.4 dB;
- PMD coefficient of 0.6 ps/$\sqrt{km}$.

To connect the optical fibers, splices are made; fusion splicing is the best method of connecting two optical fibers and a loss value of 0.015 dB is applied.

Connectors are needed to connect fibers to equipments. The connectors used in the study area are SC/APC connectors. These connectors are available on the market with a maximum insertion loss of 0.2 dB.

A passive optical splitter is a piece of equipment that uses no energy to operate. In the downstream direction, the coupler splits the optical signal into several branches to serve customers. In the uplink direction, it will bring together the light streams coming from the customers and combine them on a single fiber.

Splitters introduce a significant loss likely to penalise the link budget. The loss is a function of the number of outputs and can be approximated by the following formula:

$$\alpha = 10\log_{10}(N) \quad (4)$$

where

- N is the number of outputs for a 1: N splitter

3.2 Theoretical and Technical Concepts

Theoretical and technical concepts are essential for FTTH/GPON network engineering and dimensioning. Among these concepts, the most significant are:

- Link budget;
- Bit error rate;
- The quality factor.

A study of these three points is proposed to better calibrate the network under analysis, starting with the link budget, the bit error rate and ending with the quality factor.

The balance for this link is calculated as shown in Fig. 2 as follows:

$$TL = \sum LOSSES = \alpha * L + Ns * Sl + Nc * Cl + Nsp * Spl \tag{1}$$

$$Rp = Tp - TL - SM \tag{2}$$

$$M = Rp - Rst \tag{3}$$

where:

- TL : Total Losses(dB)
- α : Linear loss(dB/km)
- L : Fiber Length(km)
- Ns : Number of splices
- Sl : splice loss(dB)
- Nc : Number of connectors
- Cl : Connector loss(dB)
- Nsp : Number of splitters
- Spl : Splitter loss(dB)
- Rp : Received power(dBm)
- Tp : TransmitterPower(dBm)
- SM : SecurityMargin(dB)
- Rst : Receiver sensitivity threshold(dBm)
- M : Margin(dB)

After link budget, it is time to introduce, the Bit Error Rate (BER). The bit error rate is a very important technical concept for measuring the quality of a digital transmission link. The BER represents the fraction of bits with errors in relation to the total number of bits sent in a digital transmission as shown by following formula.

$$\text{BER} = \frac{N_e}{N} \tag{5}$$

With:

- N_e the number of erroneous bits;
- N the total number of bits.

The bit error rate is an essential characteristic for digital transmission links. For the specific case of an optical telecommunications link, the acceptable BER, is a value between 10^{-9} and 10^{-12}. BER values below 10^{-12} are used for critical applications such as financial or healthcare.

Factors affecting BER include noise, interference, distortion, bit timing, attenuation, multipath fading, etc. [9].

In optical transmission systems, errors are assumed to be independent of each other, so the average bit error rate is equal to the probability Pe.

An error will occur if $V(t) > V_{\text{Threshold}}$ and bit "0" is sent, or conversely if $V(t) < V_{\text{threshold}}$ and bit "1" is sent. V(t) is the electrical voltage proportional to the optical energy received from the receiver and Pr(V) is the probability density resulting from V.

$$\mathbf{P_e} = \mathbf{P_r}(0)\mathbf{P_r}(V(t) > V_{\text{Threshold}}) + \mathbf{P_r}(1)\mathbf{P_r}(V(t) < V_{threshold}) \quad (6)$$

With:

- P_r ("1") and P_r ("0") are the emission probabilities of the symbols "1" and "0" respectively;
- $P_r(V(t) > V_{\text{Threshold}})$ and $P_r(V(t) < V_{threshold})$ are respectively the probabilities of detecting a "1" when a "0" is transmitted and conversely of detecting a "0" when a "1" is transmitted.

Assuming that the noise in optical transmission systems follows the statistics of Gaussian laws and the coding is balanced, then the bit error rate can be written as follows:

$$\mathbf{BER} = \mathbf{P_e} = \frac{1}{4}\left[erfc\left(\frac{\langle V_1 \rangle - V_{\text{Threshold}}}{\sigma_1\sqrt{2}}\right) + erfc\left(\frac{V_{\text{Threshold}} - \langle V_0 \rangle}{\sigma_0\sqrt{2}}\right)\right] \quad (7)$$

where:

- $\langle V_1 \rangle$ and $\langle V_0 \rangle$ are the average voltages of bits "1" and "0" respectively;
- σ_1 et σ_0 are the respective standard deviations of bits "1" and "0".

The complementary error function erfc is defined by:

$$\mathbf{erf}(x) = \frac{2}{\sqrt{\pi}} \int_x^\infty \exp(-t^2)dt \quad (8)$$

The minimum BER is defined for an optimum threshold voltage value equal to:

$$V_{\text{Threshold}}^{optimal} = \frac{\langle V_0 \rangle \sigma_0 + \langle V_1 \rangle \sigma_1}{\sigma_0 + \sigma_1} \quad (9)$$

Under this condition, the resulting BER is:

$$\mathbf{BER} = \frac{1}{2}erfc\left(\frac{\langle V_1 \rangle - \langle V_0 \rangle}{\sqrt{2}(\sigma_0 + \sigma_1)}\right) = \frac{1}{2}\left[erfc\left(\frac{Q}{\sqrt{2}}\right)\right] \quad (10)$$

Thus, the BER is a function of the quality factor.

The aim of theoretical and technical concepts is to achieve customer satisfaction, so it's important to analyze customer needs in an FTTH/GPON network architecture.

The study area is home to both residential and business customers. Since customers have different needs, it is necessary to assess the bandwidth requirements of each customer segment [2]. Tables 2 and 3 show the needs of each customer segment.

Table 1. Technical characteristics of the ITU-T G.984 standard

	GPON
Standard	ITU-T G.984
Downstream rate	155, 622 Mbits/s, 1.2, 2.5 Gbits/s
Upstream rate	155, 622 Mbits/s, 1.2, 2.5 Gbits/s
Downlink wavelength	1490 nm
Uplink wavelength	1310 nm
Protocol	Ethernet over ATM/IP or TDM
Maximum number of couplings	64
Transmitter power	OLT: ~ 0 to + 9 dBm, ONT: ~ -2 to + 4 dBm
Link report	~ 13dB (min) to 28dB (max) ~ 15dB (min) to 30dB (max) ~ 17dB (min) to 32dB (max)
Range	10, 20, 40, 60 km

Table 2. The needs of a residential customer at approximately 30 Mbps

SERVICES	BIT RATE
Very High-speed internet access	10 Mbits/s
TV HD	12 Mbits/s
VoIP	2 Mbits/s
On-line games	2 Mbits/s
Total	26 Mbits/s

Once an in-depth understanding of GPON technology and the elements that make up the optical access network has been acquired, and the technical and theorical constraints have been taken into account, it is appropriate to move on to the simulation of the optical access network.

Table 3. Approximate needs of a business customer at 40 Mbps

SERVICES	BIT RATE
Very High-speed internet access	10 Mbits/s
VoIP	2 Mbits/s
Videoconference	7 Mbits/s
Cloud	10 Mbits/s
FTP (File Transfert Protocol)	10 Mbits/s
Total	39 Mbits/s

4 Simulation of an FTTH/GPON Network

With the framework now defined, it's time to move on to the next stage in achieving our objectives, which is to use the software to produce a close-to-reality projection of an existing network. The modelling will therefore be based on the network presented in part III of the article (Fig. 2).

To model the network to be implemented in the study area on Optisystem, the rich component library will be used.

Taking into account the indications given in Fig. 2, the components that will be used in the modelling and their use are listed in Table 4:

The components in Table 4 were used to design the optical link shown in Fig. 2.

Section 4 summarises all the elements used to create the optical access network using Optisystem software.

Table 4. List of components used

Component	Symbol	Use
Pseudo-random bit generator (PRBS)		enerates random bits symbolising data streams
Pulse Generator NRZ coding		Generation of electrical pulses with non-return to 0 (NRZ) coding
Single-mode Laser		Generation of a single-mode laser, acting as a OLT
Bidirectional optical fiber		Representation of network fibers
APD photodiode		Optical receiver
Signal regenerator		Regeneration of the electrical signal
Bidirectional splice		Signal attenuator on bidirectional fibers
Bi-directional connector		Connector for bi-directional fibers
2x2 splitter		2x2 coupling
1x4 bidirectional splitter		1x4 coupling for bidirectional fibers
1x8 bidirectional splitter		1x8 coupling for bidirectional fibers
Display Eye diagram		Calculation and display of the electrical signal eye diagram

5 Results Obtained

The simulation results are shown in Fig. 3, which shows the quality factor Q as a function of the bit rate injected into the optical link in the downstream direction. The results are summarised in Table 5, showing the bit rate and the maximum quality factor and minimum bit error rate values.

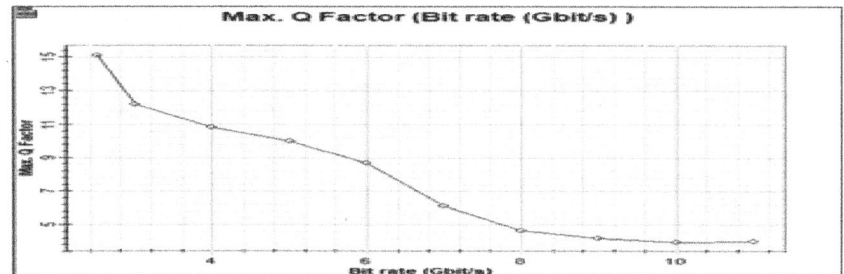

Fig. 3. Showing the quality factor as a function of bit rate in the downstream direction

Table 5. Showing bit rate, quality factor, and bit error rate in the downstream direction

	Bit rate	Max. Q	Min. BER
1	2.5	15.1	5.8e-052
2	3	12.2	2.06e-034
3	4	10.8	1.48e-027
4	5	9.98	8.97e-024
5	6	8.67	2.14e-018
6	7	6.12	4.46e-010
7	8	4.65	1.43e-006
8	9	4.2	1.13e-005
9	10	3.94	3.79e-005
10	11	4	3.09e-005

With a normal downlink bit rate of 2.5 Gbps corresponding to GPON technology, a quality factor Q of 15.1 with a comfortable bit error rate of 10^{-52} is observed. The BER deteriorates as the bit rate increases. With this in mind, for a transmission power of 9 dBm, a quality factor Q of 6.12 with a minimum error rate of 10^{-10} is obtained for a bit rate of 7 Gbits/s, marking the limit of the possibility of providing triple play (Voice, Internet and TV) to customers.

Above 7 Gbits/s, the BER degrades, making it impossible to transmit services such as TV that are sensitive to bit loss.

Carrying out the same exercise on the uplink channel, for a normal data rate of 1.25 Gbits/s, it is observed a quality factor Q of 9.68 corresponding to a bit error rate of 10^{-22}. At a data rate of 2.5 Gbits/s, the threshold bit error rate of 10^{-10} required for an optical telecommunications link (Fig. 4) is reached. This data rate enables audiovisual (video)

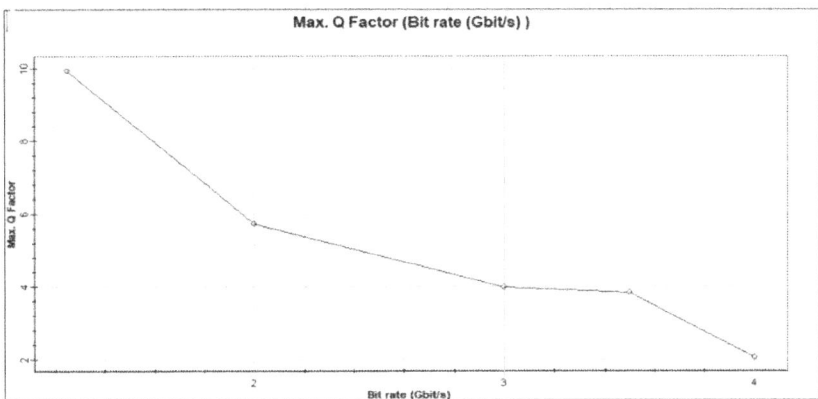

Fig. 4. Showing the quality factor as a function of bit rate in the uplink channel

Table 6. Showing bit rate, quality factor, and bit error rate in the uplink channel

	Bit rate	Max Q	Min. BER
1	1.25	9.68	1.74e-022
2	2	8.74	1.11e-018
3	2.5	6.18	3.19e-010
4	3	5.05	2.13e-007
5	3.5	4.61	2.04e-006
6	4	4.5	3.33e-006
7	4.5	3.33	0.000385
8	5	2.34	0.00906

streams of impeccable quality to be sent on the uplink channel (Table 6). For a data rate of 3 to 4 Gbits/s, the bit error rate is 10^{-6}, enabling voice services and Internet uplink traffic to be supported. It is necessary to specify that the best effort model is the default service model for internet.

In terms of analysing the results obtained, using GPON technology in the study area on the basis of an uplink rate of 1.25 Gbits/s and a downlink rate of 2.5 Gbits/s gives a bit error rate of 10^{-22} and 10^{-52} respectively. By maintaining the same architecture and gradually increasing the bit rate in both transmission directions, a deterioration in the bit error rate is noted (Table 6). This deterioration is mainly due to chromatic dispersion and modal polarisation, which are closely linked to the length of the link and the bit rate used.

6 Conclusion

FTTH/GPON networks are gradually replacing twisted-pair copper networks, providing comfortable speeds for telephony, TV with excellent picture quality and high-speed internet. Despite the quality of the services provided, customer demands are also growing. So, it became necessary to consider using the architecture of a functional FTTH/GPON network to establish the limit of direct modulation.

This required Optisystem to simulate an optical customer link, taking into account the quasi-real values of all its constituent elements. From the analysis of the results obtained from the simulations, direct modulation can reach 7 Gbits/s in the downstream direction with an excellent quality of service and 4 Gbits/s in the upstream direction with an acceptable quality of service for services such as voice and internet.

The result obtained of 7Gbits/s for the limit of direct modulation is closer to the value of 5 Gbits/s written in [11] than 10 Gbits/s found in [10].

References

1. Damoue, Z., Tamgno, J.K., Ndiaye, A., Bete, N.S.T.: Optimising the quantity of fiber in an FTTH/GPON network, In: ICECET, IEEE, 16–17 November 2023, Cape Town, South Africa (2023). https://doi.org/10.1109/ICECET58911.2023.10389435
2. Abdellaoui, Z., Meddeb, H., Dieudonne, Y.: Giga passive optical network GPON based upon fiber to the home FTTH, design, implementation and evaluation. In: Research Square, November 29th (2022)
3. Adiati, R.F., Kusumawardhani, A., Setijono, H.: Design and analysis of an FTTH-GPON in a residential area. JPFT **8**(2), 228–237 (2022)
4. Shabaneh, A.A., Melhem, M.L.: Execution simulation design of fiber-to-the-home (FTTH) device ingress networks using GPON with FBG based on optisystem. INTL J. Electron. Telecommun. **68**(4), 783–791 (2022). https://doi.org/10.24425/ijet.2022.143886
5. Maulana, F., Imansyah, F. Marpaung, J.: Attenuation analysis on fiber to the home (FTTH) network with Gigabit passive optical network (GPON) at oxygen home Pontianak. J3EIT **11**(2), 46–55 (2023). https://doi.org/10.26418/j3eit.v11i2.68551
6. Awalia, W., Pantjawati, AB.: Performance simulation of fiber to the home (FTTH) devices based on optisystem. In: International Symposium on Materials and Electrical Engineering (ISMEE) 2017 IOP Conference Series: Materials Science and Engineering, vol. 384, p.012051 (2018). https://doi.org/10.1088/1757-899X/384/1/012051
7. Ali, M.H., Abu-Alsaad, H.A., Almufti, A.M: Downstream performance analysis and optimization of 2.5 Gbits GPON-FTTx using NRZ and RZ modulation formats. J. Eng. Appl. Sci. **14**(21), 7951–7959 (2019)
8. Seraji, F.E., Kiaee, M.S.: Eye-diagram-based evaluation of RZ and NRZ modulation methods in a 10-Gb/s single-channel and a 160-Gb/s WDM optical networks. Int. J. Opt. Appl. **7**(2), 31–36 (2017). https://doi.org/10.5923/j.optics.20170702.01
9. Verma, S., Kakati, A., Bhulania, P.: Performance analysis of Q-factor and polarization for GPON network using optisystem. In: Information Technology (InCITe)-The Next Generation IT Summit on the Theme-Internet of Things, Connect your Worlds International Conference on 2016 Oct 6, pp. 134–141. IEEE (2016)
10. Agrawal, G.P.: Fiber–Optic Communication Systems, 3 edn., p. 122. Wiley (2002)
11. Agrawal, G.P.: Fiber–Optic Communication Systems, 4 edn., p. 106. Wiley (2010)

Artificial Intelligence (AI) and Machine Learning (ML) Applications

Impact of Climate in Modeling the Evolution of COVID-19 Cases in Côte d'Ivoire

Silué Donilèmin Jules(✉) and Ismaël Koné

UREN, Unité de Recherche et d'Expertise Numérique, Université Virtuelle de Côte d'Ivoire,
Abidjan, Côte d'Ivoire
{donilemin.silue,ismael21.kone}@uvci.edu.ci

Abstract. In order to prevent future pandemics or epidemics, our project involved studying the evolution of Covid-19 cases and the impact of climate on its spread. We used machine learning models to analyze and better predict the spread of COVID-19 in Côte d'Ivoire, based on Covid-19 cases and climate data from 11 March 2020 to 28 January 2022 for the city of Abidjan. As the data is temporal, we used time series analysis models such as ARIMA, Facebook Prophet with additive and multiplicative seasonality and the LSTM recurrent neural network. The root mean square error (RMSE) was used to study the performance of the models. Firstly, the study of cases without climate data showed that the ARIMA (2,1,3) model performed best (RMSE cross-validation: 66.35; RMSE test: 132.69). Secondly, the study with data showed that climate has an impact on the spread of the disease with the LSTM model (RMSE cross-validation: 2.94; RMSE test: 14.63) performing much better. On the other hand, we noted drawbacks in the use of the Prophet and ARIMA models in view of the high discrepancies between the validation and test scores. This study also shows that climate change can have an impact on the spread of a virus or disease. This is shown by the cold temperatures during holiday periods and festivities, when people are increasingly close to each other. So, it's important for the authorities and the medical community to take climatic factors into account when making decisions about epidemics.

Keywords: climate · COVID-19 · Côte d'Ivoire · time series · machine learning

1 Introduction

Covid-19 disease is a disease transmitted by SARS-Cov-2 (Severe Acute Respiratory Syndrome Coronavirus 2). It was discovered in the city of Wuhan in China on November 17, 2019 [1]. In Côte d'Ivoire, the first case of Covid-19 was recorded on March 11, 2020. Its symptoms are fever, feelings of fatigue and headaches, dry coughs and diarrhea. In addition, it is spread by the projection of droplets of saliva of an infected person who coughs when close to other people or when shaking their hand. Further-more, its spread has been very rapid and has negatively impacted the lives of populations around the world. Generally, and in particular in Côte d'Ivoire how has it evolved? Does the climate in Côte d'Ivoire have no impact on the spread of the disease? How could the scientific community prevent and control future pandemics or epidemics as data on Covid-19 cases are increasingly voluminous, and with climate change? We will study the impact of climate in modeling the evolution of Covid-19 cases Côte d'Ivoire using big data and Machine Learning analysis models. Thus, the objectives of our research are first to analyze the covid-19 data, then to predict future cases and finally to how the evolution of the pandemic so that it can help prevent and control possible pandemics or epidemics.

1.1 Literature Review

In the article [2], Cataud Marius Guédé carried out a study on the spread and persistence of Coronavirus disease. That study focused on the epidemiological situation of Covid-19 in Côte d'Ivoire and the spatial dynamics of virus transmission. To carry out that study, they used the Geographic Information System (GIS) to analyze data from March 11, 2020 to February 20, 2021. It appears that 96% of confirmed cases come from the two health districts Cocody-Bingerville and Treichville-Marcory of Le Grand Abidjan. Consequently, they proposed as control solutions, better patient care, mass screening, and a vast information campaign on barrier measures.

Kouamé KL et al. in their article [3], took stock of the Covid-19 pandemic in Côte d'Ivoire during the period from March to May 2020. They analyzed the spread of the pandemic, the mode of transmission of the pandemic and research into risk factors. The average control chart and the 5M model with the ISHIKAWA diagram were the means used for the study. The pandemic evolves randomly. This speed has several causes. To curb the pandemic, automation of hand washing devices in public places, regular spraying of places, compulsory wearing of masks, good protection of directly consumable foods is necessary to carry out.

In this article [4], the authors studied the spread of covid-19 by linking the pandemic to factors such as the number of confirmed cases, contact cases, meteorological data (temperature, rainfall, UV index, hygrometric degree, sunshine) and population density. When analyzing the data collected, the incidence (number of cases appearing per 1000 inhabitants in the given time interval) of covid-19 was the parameter used to understand the spread of the pandemic. The study being carried out on several areas in the world where climatological and meteorological data differ, we note that the incidence rate is very low when the temperature is very high in certain areas and in other areas, the rate of incidence decreases as temperature increases.

The evolutionary study of the Coronavirus epidemic in [5] was carried out on the one hand with the law of the logistic function model and on the other hand, with the gradient descent model in Machine Learning. During the study of the data, aspects such as the periods before, during and after the confinement in each of the countries were considered as parameters. Analyzes show that the number of cases of infection is strongly dependent on the number of tests carried out. They noticed noise in the data; which required data smoothing over seven (7) days to have better convergence of predictions.

Finally, Gergo Pinter and his collaborators [6] first showed the strengths and weaknesses of the SIR model. Then, to overcome the shortcomings of this method, they proposed two hybrid machine learning methods which are: the multi-layer imperialist perceptron competitive algorithm (MLP-ICA) and the fuzzy inference system based on an adaptive network (ANFIS) It appears that after training and validation of each of the MLP-ICA and ANFIS models, there is a better prediction which is made and which shows that the number of infected cases and the mortality rate would drop considerably. Finally, they noted that given the complexity of the COVID-19 pandemic and the small amount of data used for training, even more in-depth research would be needed to make Machine Learning models more efficient in order to validate and improve the quality of results and prediction.

1.2 Discussion on Literature Review

All this work shows that mathematical models are used extensively. Other studies have used machine learning algorithms to produce prediction results. Overall, these methods were able to predict the propagation of COVID 19 as a function of time. In light of this literature, our main objective is to show that climate may or may not have an impact on the modelling of the evolution of coronavirus infections. Our study could help the field of health and especially epidemiology in the treatment of the spread of a virus. In our study, we will:

- Study cases of covid-19 infection as time series,
- Show the impact of climatic factors on the evolution of Covid-19.
- Draw lessons from the findings of the study of the impact of climate on the spread of covid-19.

2 Methods and Materials

2.1 Data Acquisition

The data on COVID-19 were collected on one of the platforms of the Ivorian Ministry of Health and Public Hygiene [7] and are from the Greater Abidjan area. This platform linked to the coronavirus produces statistical data on the number of confirmed cases, per day. To these data, we associated the climatic data of the Greater Abidjan in the same period. Our data collected is from the period from March 11, 2020 to January 28, 2022.

Meteorological data are from the Greater Abidjan. The files are of the.csv type and contain daily data for each month.

The file on the number of cases of covid 19 is of type.csv and gives the number of cases recorded each day.

We concatenated the csv files into a single Excel file.

This gives us twenty-three (23) variables (Table 1):

Steps for merging CSV files

Table 1. List of variables

Variables	Types
DATE	Datetime
MAX_TEMPERATURE_C	Integer
MIN_TEMPERATURE_C	Integer
WINDSPEED_MAX_KMH	Integer
TEMPERATURE_MORNING_C	Integer
TEMPERATURE_NOON_C	Integer
TEMPERATURE_EVENING_C	Integer
PRECIP_TOTAL_DAY_MM	Float
HUMIDITY_MAX_PERCENT	Integer
VISIBILITY_AVG_KM	Float
PRESSURE_MAX_MB	Integer
CLOUDCOVER_AVG_PERCENT	Float
HEATINDEX_MAX_C	Integer
DEWPOINT_MAX_C	Integer
WINDTEMP_MAX_C	Integer
WEATHER_CODE_MORNING	Integer
WEATHER_CODE_NOON	Integer
WEATHER_CODE_EVENING	Integer
TOTAL_SNOW_MM	Integer
UV_INDEX	Float
SUNHOUR	Float
TEMPERATURE_NIGHT_C	Integer
NEW_CASES	Float

Step 1: Put all CSV files in the same folder.
Step 2: Create a new.txt file (text file) in the same folder as your.csv files.
Step 3: Open the file with Notepad.
Step 4: Paste the code: copy *.csv importfichier.csv, then save.
Step 5: Rename the.txt file to.bat and click on it.

And that's it, all your CSV files are merged.
We have 689 data samples in total.
As these data are chronological, we will use as methodology, time series analysis and prediction techniques (chronological).

Figure 1 shows the evolution of the number of Covid-19 cases from 11 March 2020 to 28 January 2022. It shows that the number of cases of covid 19 fluctuates between the periods of June–July 2020 with around 500 cases, March–April 2021 with around 700 cases, and increased exponentially to around 3000 cases between December 2021 and January 2022. These periods are school holidays and festive seasons in Côte d'Ivoire. There is a lot of movement of people.

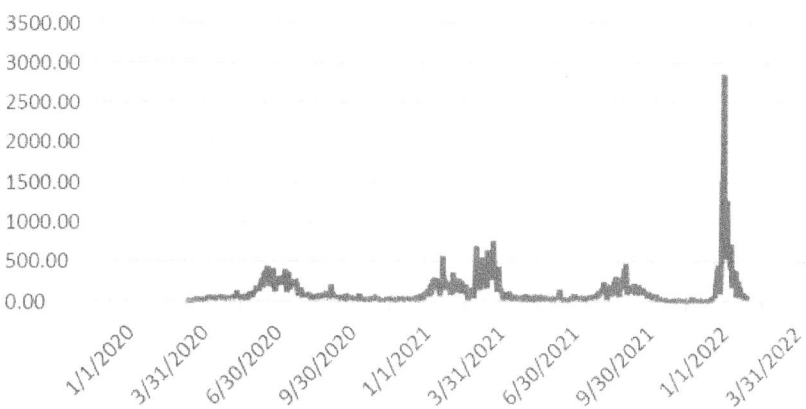

Fig. 1. Visualization of Covid19 cases

2.2 Time Series

A temporal or chronological series is a sequence of observations $x_1, x_2,...,x_n$ indexed by time t [8]. Time can be expressed in year, month, day, etc. There are two types: The univariate time series and the multivariate time series. The univariate time series presents a single variable observed over time and which is to be predicted and, as for the multivariate time series, it presents several observed variables and only one is to be predicted based on the others.

A time series has several descriptive indices and is made up of three main components. The components of a time series are the trend, the seasonality, the stationary (residual) component [8, 9].

The trend T_t: is a progressive ascending or descending change in the level of the series. The trend can be on the one hand local or global and on the other hand either linear or non-linear. We have for example [9]:

- The linear trend:

$$T_t = a + bt \qquad (1)$$

with a and b the coefficients of linear regression for:

$$a = \frac{\sum_{i=1}^{n}(t_i - \bar{t})(x_i - \bar{t})}{\sum_{i=1}^{n}(t_i - \bar{t})^2}. \qquad (2)$$

And

$$b = \bar{y} - a*\bar{t}. \tag{3}$$

- The quadratic trend:

$$T_t = a + bt - ct^2 \tag{4}$$

with a, b and c the coefficients of quadratic trend (form of non-linear regression).
- The logarithmic trend:

$$T_t = \log(t) \tag{5}$$

Seasonality S_t: it is the repetitive and predictable pattern that characterizes the values of a series. Series showing a seasonal cycle are considered to have seasonal effects. Seasonal patterns are useful for obtaining good fit and forecasts.

The stationary or residual component or error ε_t: is the remainder when the other components are removed. In addition, it makes it possible to predict the relative variation of new cases rather than the cumulative absolute value.

2.3 Prediction Methods

The analysis and prediction methods used in our research are: ARIMA, Facebook Prophet and LSTM. These are very useful methods in the processing of time series data and in the field of Big Data and Machine Learning.

Modeling Using the ARIMA Method

The ARIMA model is a model that refers to both the AR (Autoregressive), MA (Moving Average) and Integrated models. It is autoregressive of order p when its value at a time t depends linearly on the previous p values and is a moving average when the series presents fluctuations around an average value. We then consider that the best estimate is represented by the weighted average of a certain number of previous values. The ARIMA model has three components and three parameters p, d and q. The components are: trend, seasonality and noise.

The additive model of the time series X_t is defined by:

$$X_t = T_t + S_t + \varepsilon_t. \tag{6}$$

- X_t designates the data series of covid-19 cases collected.
- T_t is the trend corresponding to a long-term evolution of the series.
- S_t is seasonality linked to a periodic phenomenon of identified period.
- ε_t is the noise or error which is the random part of the series.

The AR, MA and ARMA models are as follows:

The Autoregressive (AR) model of order p: It is the number of shifts that must be considered for the AR model. It is also the use of past values in the regression equation for time series. If X_t an AR process of order p follows, then we have:

$$X_t = \varepsilon_t + \sum_{j=1}^{p} a_j X_{t-j} \tag{7}$$

where les ε_t is a white noise centered with variance σ^2 [10–12].

The moving average (MA) model of order q:

It is the use of the dependence between observed data and a residual error of a Moving Average model applied to shifted observations. If X_t an MA process of order q follows, then we have:

$$X_t = \varepsilon_t + \sum_{j=1}^{q} b_j \varepsilon_{t-j} \qquad (8)$$

with $b_0 = 1$ and ε_t is a white noise centered with variance σ^2 [10–12].

The ARMA model (autoregressive and moving average): The combination of the two AR and MA models allows us to obtain the ARMA model defined by [10–12]:

$$X_t = a_1 X_{t-1} + a_2 X_{t-2} + a_3 X_{t-3} + \ldots + a_p X_{t-p} + \varepsilon_t + b_1 \varepsilon_{t-1} + b_2 \varepsilon_{t-2} + \ldots + b_q \varepsilon_{t-q}. \qquad (9)$$

The ARMA method is used for stationary time series and has parameters p and q.

In order to deal with any form of stationary or non-stationary time series, it would be necessary to integrate the differentiation of order d into the ARMA.

Differentiation of order: is the number of times it is necessary to differentiate the observations of the time series in order to make it stationary. Differentiation is the subtraction of the current values of the series with its previous values. d must be equal to 0 in the case of an already stationary process [11–13].

From ARMA and differentiation, the ARIMA model can be established as follows:

- First order differentiation deals with linear trends and uses transformation

$$Y_t = X_t - X_{t-1}. \qquad (10)$$

- Second order differentiation deals with quadratic trends and uses a first order difference on a first order difference, which is:

$$Y_t = (X_t - X_{t-1}) - (X_{t-1} - X_{t-2}). \qquad (11)$$

- And so on.
- Y_t designates the transformation of the series of covid 19 cases into a stationary series at order n.

The ARIMA model therefore has parameters p, d and q and denoted ARIMA (p, d, q).

Modeling Using the Facebook Prophet Method

The Facebook Prophet model is a time series prediction model with multiple seasonality's. It is open source. There are two types of Facebook Prophet templates. These are the Facebook Prophet model with additive seasonality and the Facebook Prophet model with multiplicative seasonality.

The Facebook Prophet model with additive seasonality is an additive model with four components. [13–15].

It is defined by:

$$X_t = g(t) + s(t) + h(t) + \varepsilon_t. \qquad (12)$$

The function $g(t)$ is the growth function. It also presents the trend. It can be a linear growth function, a logistic growth function or in the form of a flat growth function (when there is no growth over time).

The seasonality function $s(t)$ is defined by:

$$s(t) = \sum_{n=1}^{N} \left(a_n coscos\left(\frac{2\pi nt}{p}\right) + b_n sinsin\left(\frac{2\pi nt}{p}\right) \right). \qquad (13)$$

The function $h(t)$ is the function exhibiting holiday effects. It allows you to adjust the forecasts when a vacation day or an event can influence the forecasts.

The function ε_t represents white noise. This is the error function.

After decomposing the time series using the Prophet model, we move on to the prediction stage. The forecast will contain a prediction for each historical value present in the dataset as well as additional forecasts for the number of periods in the past. Thus, a new database will be created. It contains several columns:

- ds containing the forecast timestamp entry,
- yhat containing the predicted value of the time series
- yhat _lower containing the bottom of the confidence interval for the forecast
- yhat _upper containing the bottom of the confidence interval for the forecast.

These data are used to construct the original data, the forecast and the confidence interval of the model.

Following this, it would be necessary to determine the hyperparameters to find the best forecast (prediction). These hyperparameters are: changepoint_prior_scala and n_changepoints.

Modeling Using the LSTM Neural Network Method

Neural networks are among the models of machine learning and more precisely Deep Learning. Among the types of neural networks, we have Recurrent Neural Networks (RNN). RNNs are widely used in sequential data management. We have three types of RNN including the LSTM RNN (Long Short Term Recurrent Neural Network) which will be used in our project. In LSTM neural networks, LSTM cells are used to learn to predict from sequences of varying lengths. Furthermore, LSTM is not only limited to time series. It can be used in processing other types of data [16].

Principle of LSTM

The principle of LSTM is to establish:

- A compact representation of the time series;
- A combination of a new entry with the series' past representation;
- The search for data from the series to forget;
- Displaying the prediction for the next time step.

How LSTM Works

An LSTM cell works using three operators called gates. They are the Forget Gate, the Input Gate and the Output Gate. It is also managed by a dynamic memory denoted C. this memory depends on the sequence of temporal data.

Taken from [17], Figs. 2, 3, 4, and 5 show in four (4) steps how an LSTM cell works to predict temporal data.

Step 1: Forget gate operation

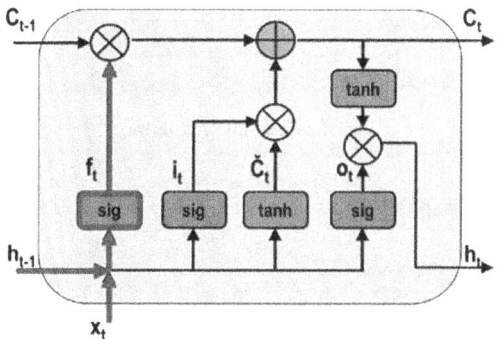

Fig. 2. Forget gate operation

Step 2: Input gate operation

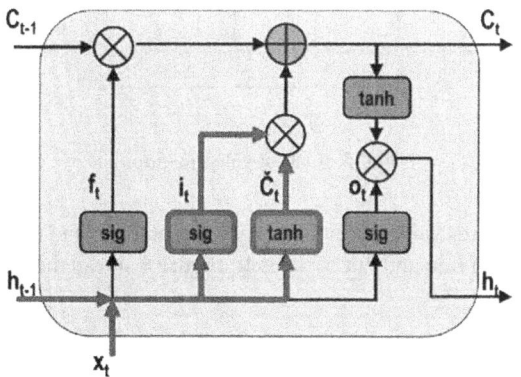

Fig. 3. Input gate operation

Step 3: cell state operation

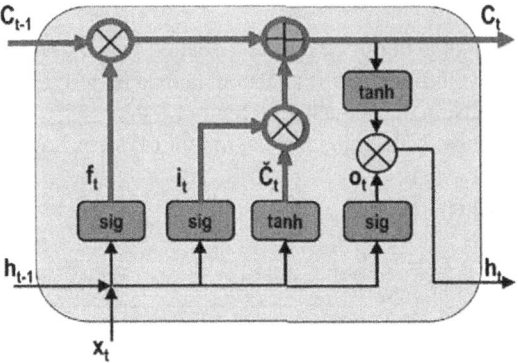

Fig. 4. Cell state operation

Step 4: Output gate operation

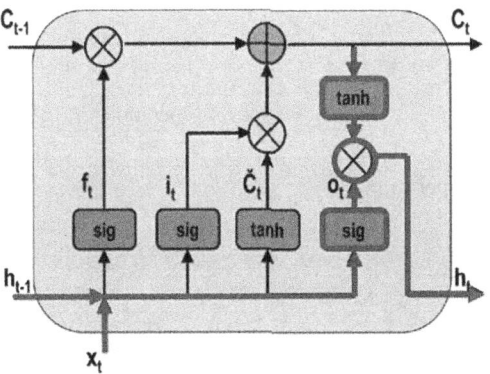

Fig. 5. Output gate operation

The LSTM cell stores values over arbitrary time intervals and the three gates regulate the flow of information into and out of the cell. Figure 6 shows the complete LSTM cell.

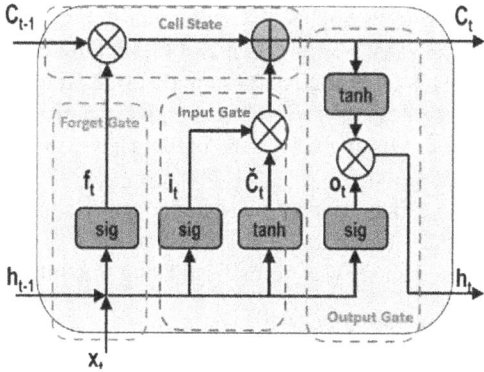

Fig. 6. Complete LSTM cell

2.4 Model Hyperparameters

The hyperparameters were obtained using the implementation of cross-validation in the implementation of each of our models (Table 2).

Table 2. Hyperparameters used for models

Models	Hyperparameters used for comparisons	
	Without climate data	With climate data
ARIMA	(2,1,3)	(4,1,4)
Facebook Prophet additive	Changepoint_prior_scale = 0.01 Seasonality_prior_scale = 0.1 n_changepoints = 3	Changepoint_prior_scale = 0.01 Seasonality_prior_scale = 1.0 n_changepoints = 3
Multiplicative Facebook Prophet	Changepoint_prior_scale = 0.1 Seasonality_prior_scale = 1.0 n_changepoints = 3	Changepoint_prior_scale = 0.01 Seasonality_prior_scale = 1.0 n_changepoints = 3
LSTM	Number of neurons = 4 Look_back = 3 Loss = MSE Dense (1) Function = tan Optimizer = adam	Number of neurons = 400 Look_back = 3 Loss = MSE Dense (1) Function = tan Optimizer = adam

3 Results and Discussion

3.1 Data Processing and Model Performance Metrics

Data processing

We have a data set of 689 samples. To implement the models, we used Notebook Jupiter from the ANACONDA 3 application and the Python language. The data used covers the period from 11 March 2020 to 28 January 2022. They include the number of confirmed cases of Covid-19 per day, and meteorological factors such as wind, UV index, sunshine, temperature, etc. Missing values and outliers have been treated to improve the analysis of the data by our models.

The python code data = data.dropna() was used to remove rows containing a missing value from the data set.

To avoid outliers, the data set was normalised using the following python code:

scaler = MinMaxScaler(feature_range=(0, 1))
data = scaler.fit_transform(data)

To implement each model, all the 689 days of data were divided into two subsets:

- the first subset containing the first 659 days of data was used for the cross-validation phase, and
- the second with the last 30 days, for the test phase.

Performance Metrics

The root mean square error (RMSE) is a measure used to determine the accuracy of a model's predictions. It uses the overall performance of the model from the actual and predicted values and is in the same unit as the variable being predicted. It is defined as follows:

$$RMSE = \sqrt{\frac{1}{n}\sum_{i=1}^{n}(x_i - \hat{x}_i)^2} \quad (14)$$

with x_i are the actual values and $\hat{x}_i$ are the predicted values.

The lower the RMSE, the better the model fits the data set. A lower RMSE indicates that the model's predictions are closer to the actual values. By using the RMSE, analysts and decision-makers can make informed choices about the reliability and performance of the forecasting models used.

The benefits: the RMSE is easily interpreted and is accurate. It is widely accepted and recognized as a measure of forecast accuracy. It is also sensitive to outliers.

The disadvantages are that the RMSE is insensitive to bias because it does not explicitly measure forecast errors. RMSE also lacks scale interpretation.

In our project, given that we are using the same number of data samples in our three forecasting models, the best model will be the one with the lowest RMSE. This will be the model with the best accuracy between our actual and predicted values.

3.2 Results

The implementation of the models was done in two main parts. The first part consisted of using a univariate data series where the number of cases is the only target variable to predict as a function of time. As for the second part, we used a multivariate time series where the variable to predict is the number of cases as a function of other variables which are climatic factors and time.

For each part, we first do the validation phase and then the test phase in the application of each model (Tables 3 and 4).

Table 3. Results in the case of univariate models

MODELS		RMSE
ARIMA (2,1,3)	VALIDATION	66.35
	TEST	132.69
ADDITIVE PROPHET	VALIDATION	141.04
	TEST	181.11
MULTIPLCATIVE PROPHET	VALIDATION	158.27
	TEST	321.43
LSTM	VALIDATION	81.02
	TEST	227.66

Table 4. Results in the case of multivariate models

MODELS		RMSE
ARIMA (4,1,4)	VALIDATION	71.70
	TEST	884.97
ADDITIVE PROPHET	VALIDATION	148.01
	TEST	287.33
MULTIPLCATIVE PROPHET	VALIDATION	162.89
	TEST	312.43
LSTM	VALIDATION	2.94
	TEST	14.63

3.3 Discussion

The results of the RMSE performance of the models used in the univariate case where the number of COVID cases is the only variable showed that the ARIMA (2,1,3) model had the best score in both the validation and test phases. In fact, its scores were the lowest compared with those of the other models. In the validation results, ARIMA gave a score of 66.35 and in the test phase, 132.69. This means that with the ARIMA model, the number of predicted cases varies by more or less 66 cases of covid-19 compared with the actual number of cases during the validation phase and varies by 132 cases during the test phase. The model giving the highest RMSE is the Prophet Multiplicative with 158.27 in training and 321.43 for the test. Here we see a large difference between the RMSEs in cross-validation and in test for the ARIMA, LSTM and Prophet multiplicative models.

This shows that these models are poor. This may be due to the fact that the number of cases used in the test phase is much smaller than in the validation phase. However, the Prophet additive model shows a smaller difference between its RMSEs scores (cross-validation: 141.04 and test: 181.11) but gives high RMSEs. It could be said that the additive Prophet model applied to the evolution of Covid-19 cases without climatic data could also be considered. However, it would produce very erroneous results.

In the case of the application of models with several independent variables, that is to say the climatic data and the target variable, that is to say the number of Covid-19 cases, we find that the LSTM model gives inferior results. The RMSEs were 2.94 for the training and 14.63 for the test. This means that with the LSTM model, the number of predicted cases varies by more or less 2 compared with the number of actual cases in the validation phase and varies by 14 in the test phase. The ARIMA test score (4,1,4) of 884.97 is the highest. Compared with its training score of 71.70, there is a significant difference between the two ARIMA scores. We can say that the ARIMA model was not a good model for analyzing and predicting our data. Furthermore, the Prophet models show a large gap between the validation and test RMSEs.

Therefore, by comparing the scores of the LSTM model in the univariate case and in the multivariate case, we can say that the climatic data significantly influenced our predictions. Climate data therefore has an impact on the propagation of COVID 19, and the best analysis and prediction model for our case study is the LSTM model.

Analysis of the predictive evolution of COVID-19 cases in our two experiments shows that the climate has an effect on the evolution of the number of confirmed cases. This is caused by shifts in wind and sunshine. What's more, the massive movement of populations during holiday and festive periods is very sunny or humid. It should also be mentioned that Covid-19 is a respiratory disease, and the temperatures at certain times of the year mean that people have to move closer together.

The following figures show the evolution of predicted and actual cases. Figure 7 shows the evolution of covid 19 cases and the predictions made using the LSTM model. The part of the curve in blue represents the curve for the actual covid-19 data, the curve in orange is that for the predictions during training and finally the curve in green is that for the predictions of the cases during testing. With the LSTM model, the predictions obtained are almost in agreement with the real covid-19 data (Fig. 8).

Figs. 9 and 10 show the y-curve for actual cases and the yhat curve for predicted cases in the cross-validation and test phases respectively. We can see that the curves show a large difference in evolution. The same is true for the multiplicative prophet model in Figs. 11 and 12.

Impact of Climate in Modeling the Evolution of COVID-19 Cases 109

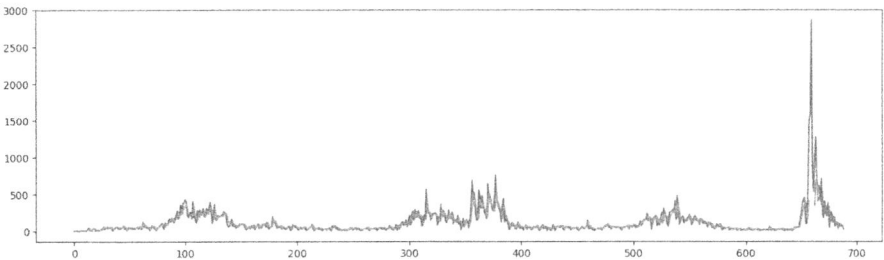

Fig. 7. The case prediction curve with the LSTM model with climatic data

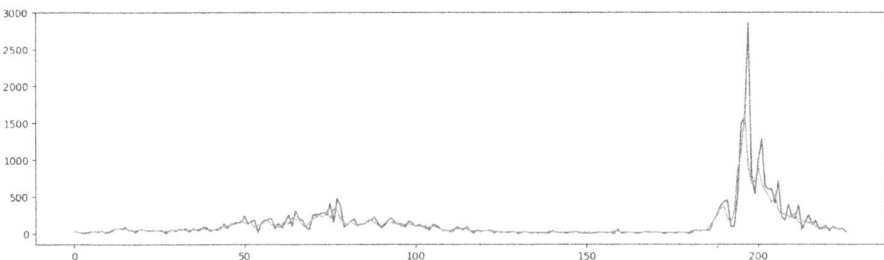

Fig. 8. LSTM univariate train and test

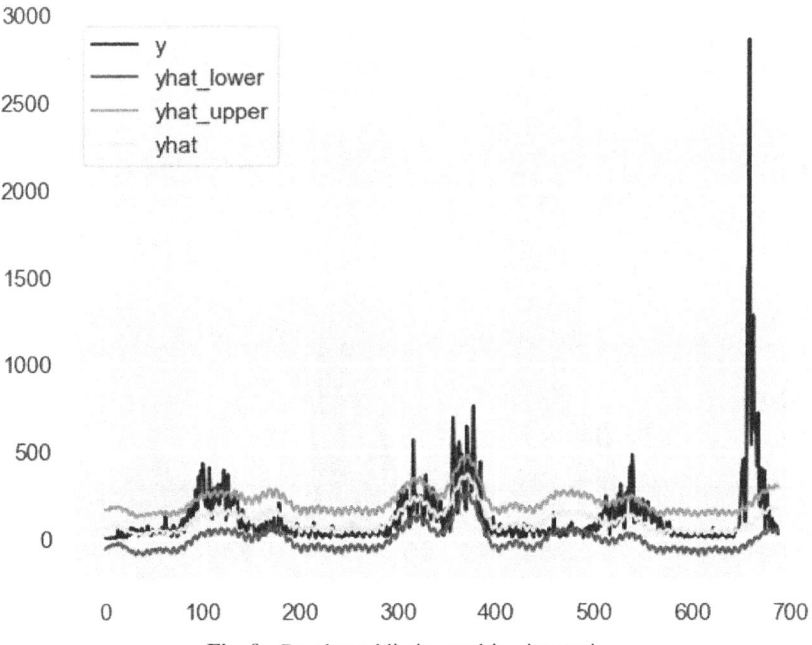

Fig. 9. Prophet addictive multivariate train

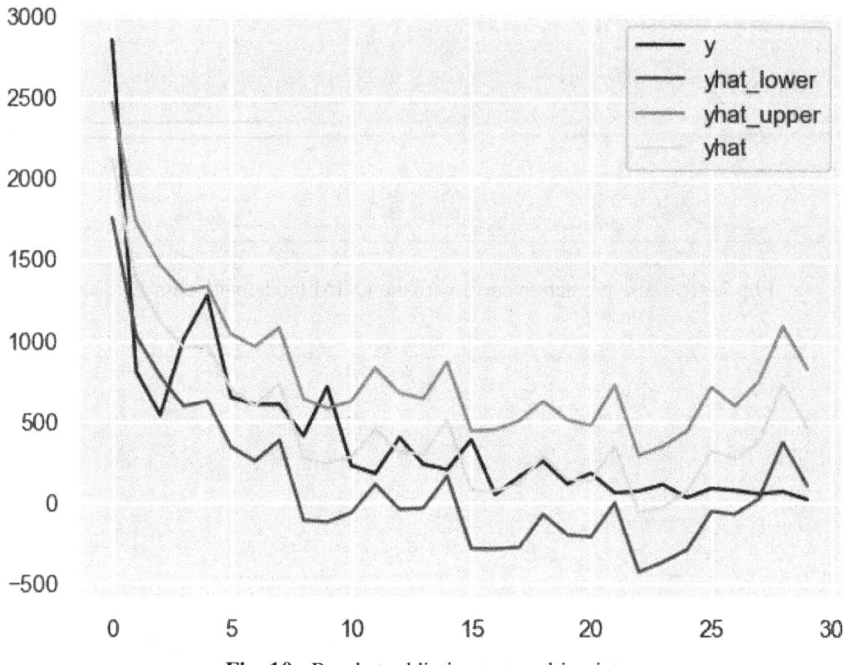

Fig. 10. Prophet addictive test multivariate

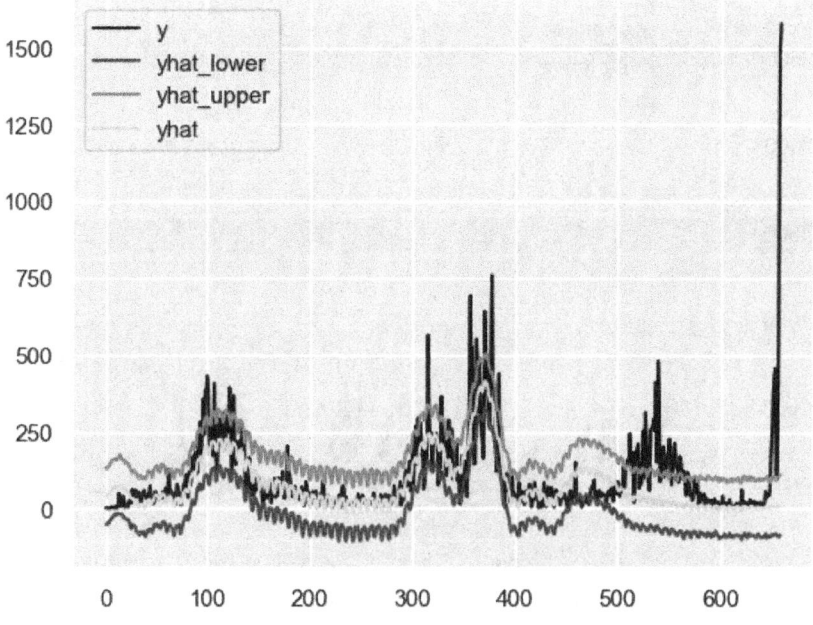

Fig. 11. Prophet train multiplicative multivariate

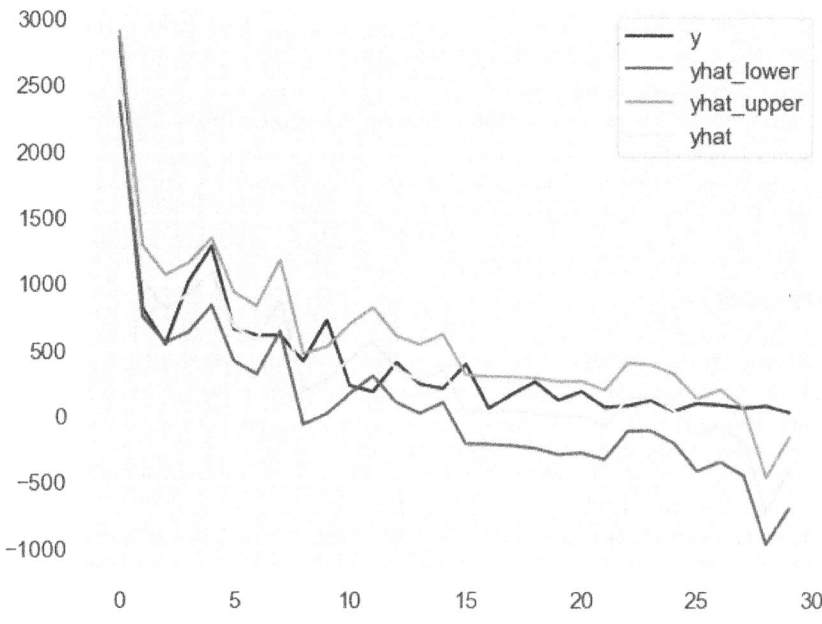

Fig. 12. Prophet test multiplicative multivariate

4 Conclusion

COVID-19 is a pandemic of global proportions. It has had a devastating impact not only on people's lives, but also on the operation of institutions and businesses. To combat this pandemic and prevent future pandemics in Côte d'Ivoire, and in order to take better measures, we have worked on the spread of COVID-19 in Côte d'Ivoire using data from Greater Abidjan. The aim is to make predictions capable of producing good results based on COVID-19 data and climatic factors over the period from 11 March 2020 to 28 January 2022.

To implement this project, we have developed machine learning models for univariate and multivariate time series. The models used are ARIMA, Facebook Prophet with additive seasonality, Facebook Prophet with multiplicative seasonality and LSTM recurrent neural networks.

After visualizing the data, the algorithms were implemented in Python using Anaconda's Jupiter Notebook. The results obtained showed that in the first stage of the analysis of cases without climate data, the ARIMA (2,1,3) model was the most effective (validation RMSE: 66.35; test RMSE: 132.69) and in the second stage of the study with climate data it was possible to understand that climate has an impact on the spread of the disease with the LSTM model (cross-validation RMSE: 2.94; test RMSE: 14.63) which was much more effective. Climatic data therefore has an influence on the spread of the Covid-19 virus. The climate is due to the hot and very cold temperature ^per period during the year Also, it to say that the results of the predictions were for certain models very far from reality and very large differences between the phases of validation and test. This is why political decision-makers and the medical community must now take climatic factors into account in their decision-making and in the fight against any other disease, especially when the disease is respiratory.

As far as perceptions are concerned, it is worth considering the use of deep learning techniques, which will make it possible to make better predictions with long-term data on the one hand, and to study the evolution of climate change before understanding its impact on the evolution of a disease on the other. In this way, Africa, and Côte d'Ivoire in particular, will be able to cope with major epidemics.

References

1. Dieudoné, B.-K.: General Communication on the Coronavirus: Learning Tool CAMES (2020)
2. Guédé, C.M., Koffi, B.A.F., Guélé, G.P.: Spatial and epidemiological analysis for decision support in the fight against Covid-19 in Ivory Coast. Eur. Sci. J. **17**(24), 28 (2021). https://doi.org/10.19044/esj.2021.v17n24p28
3. Kouamé, K.L., Yao, A.B., N'Dri, K.L.: State of play of the COVID-19 pandemic in Côte d'Ivoire. Rev. Mali. Infect. Microbiol. **16** (2021)
4. Julien, H., et al.: Evolutionary catastrophe, what could be the influence of weather conditions on the evolution of the CoViD-19 pandemic? Disaster Medicine – Urgences Collectives **4**(3), 175–180 (2020)
5. Rémond, J., Rémond, Y.: On simplified modeling of the 2020 Covid-19 epidemic: Part 1. Modeling and simulation of new cases in three countries: France, Italy and Spain. HAL Id: hal-02573159 (2020). https://hal.science/hal-02573159
6. Pinter, G., Felde, I., Mosavi, A., Ghamisi, P., Gloaguen, R.: COVID-19 pandemic prediction for Hungary: a hybrid machine learning approach. Mathematics **8**(6), 890 (2020). https://doi.org/10.3390/math8060890(2020)
7. http://coronavirustracking.ci/. Accessed 20 June 2022
8. Monbet, V.: Modeling of time series, course support (2011)
9. Goude, Y.: Introduction to time series, trend and seasonal component (2016)
10. Delignières, D.: Time series-ARIMA models (2000)
11. Avram, F.: Time series: regression, ARIMA modeling (p, d, q), course support (2012)
12. Goude, Y.: ARIMA process, course support, MAP-STA2: time series (2022)
13. ARIMA vs Prophet vs LSTM for time series prediction. https://neptune.ai/blog/arima-vs-prophet-vs-lstm. Accessed 20 June 2022
14. Time Series Analysis with Facebook Prophet: How it Works and how to use it. https://towardsdatascience.com/time-series-analysis-with-facebook-prophet-how-it-works-and-how-to-use-it-f15ecf2c0e3a. Accessed 20 June 2022
15. Prophet Model. https://otexts.com/fpp3/prophet.html. Accessed 20 June 2022
16. Recurrent neural networks for time series. https://metalblog.ctif.com/2021/09/06/les-reseaux-de-neurones-recurrents-pour-les-series-temporelles/. Accessed 04 July 2022
17. Stérin, T.: Recurrent neural networks and memory: application to music, internship report (2016)

Preventing Typosquatting with IDN Conversion: A Siamese Neural Network Approach

Evrard Cabrel Nguemeyou Tchouangang[(✉)], Idrissa Sarr, Alex Corenthin, and Bassirou Kassé

Université Cheikh Anta Diop, Dakar, Senegal
nguemeyou.evrard@gmail.com,
{idrissa.sarr,alex.corenthin,bassirou.kasse}@ucad.edu.sn
https://edmi.ucad.sn/

Abstract. This article focuses on the management of DNS system regarding to the introduction and promotion of Internationalized Domain Names (IDNs). In fact, Internationalized Domain Names (IDNs) allow users to use non-Latin characters to register domain names, enabling the inclusion of various languages. However IDN has triggered more potential DNS abuses. To address these additional risks of abuses initiatives have been developed focusing primarily on two types of attacks: semantic and homograph attacks. Nonetheless, the main drawbacks of these solutions are their complexity and resources consuming characteristics. The aim of this paper is to address these challenges by proposing an approach that is resource-efficient and easy to implement. Our approach is based on the calculation of visual similarity using Siamese neural networks to identify homographs that can be used for malicious purposes to deviate people from the correct domain. We defined and trained our model on 5000 domain names of the .SN ccTLD. The model is promising since it helps detecting potential risks of abuse at the domain name creation level, allowing possibilities to use mitigation mechanisms. Despite the various difficulties of Overfitting due to the size of the dataset and the length of the domain names, the model was able to achieve an accuracy of 98.7%.

Keywords: DNS · abused domains · siamese network · typosquatting · Internationalized Domain Names · Neural Network

1 Introduction

The Domain Name System (DNS) is one of the main components that makes the Internet work. It translates domain names that we can understand, such as 'example.com', into IP addresses that machines can understand. However, the DNS is often the target of malicious attacks or abuses. One simple method

---

Centre Universitaire de Recherche et de Formation aux Technologies de l'Internet for funding partially this work.

of attack is typosquatting. This involves registering variants of a popular domain, slipping in common, barely perceptible typing errors with the aim of diverting the user to another malicious site. For example, domains such as "Amazan.com" or "Gooogle.com" have been created to deviate users of Amazon.com and Google.com. To face these challenges, researchers have proposed several approaches, ranging from probabilistic techniques to Large language models (LLM).

In addition, Internationalised Domain Names (IDNs) allow users to use non-Latin characters to register domain names, enabling the inclusion of accentuated characters in the DNS [8]. Since 2009, the first ccTLD with IDNs appeared online following the approval of a fast-track process by l'ICANN [9]. Since then, the adoption of IDNs has grown strongly, as shown in Figs. 1 and 2 from the report by l'ICANN, illustrating the growing interest of TLDs in this technology, particularly within the Senegalese TLD. As a result, the domain names "fatick.sn" and "fàtick.sn" now become variants which, for the average Senegalese, are identical but structurally completely different. In other words, a malicious user can replace one character with another belonging to the authorised diacritical set, thus creating a domain name which, although resembling the reserved name, will not be detected as such and can be registered as valid. However, since IDNs were introduced by ccTLDs in 2010 [10,11], the spectrum of attacks has widened. ccTLDs must therefore be more alert and increase their level of vigilance to address abuse in the face of the growing adoption of IDNs by countries.

To mitigate the additional risks of abuse associated with the adoption of IDNs, initiatives have recently been developed focusing primarily on two types of abuses: semantic attacks [14], where deceptive domain names are created from ambiguous words, and homograph attacks [16,18,20], where visually similar characters from different scripts mimic legitimate domain names to deceive Internet users. One of the drawbacks of these solutions is their complexity and resource-intensive characteristics. In addition, they are mainly reactive rather than proactive, meaning they are more keen to react rather than to anticipate abuses.

The aim of this paper is to address these challenges by proposing a resource-efficient and easy-to-implement approch. Following the example of several previous works [15,19,22], the proposed method is based on the calculation of visual similarity using Siamese neural networks [5]. It allows the generation of domain name variants and the selection of the most relevant by visual similarity with a view to blocking them or requiring prior authorisation as stipulated in the naming charter of most of ccTLDs.

The remainder of this document is organised as follows. Section 2 reviews related work on IDNs and the management of associated abuse. Section 3 describes the problem and associated challenges. Section 4 presents our approach. Section 5 evaluates the results obtained while Sect. 6 concludes the paper by presenting research perspectives.

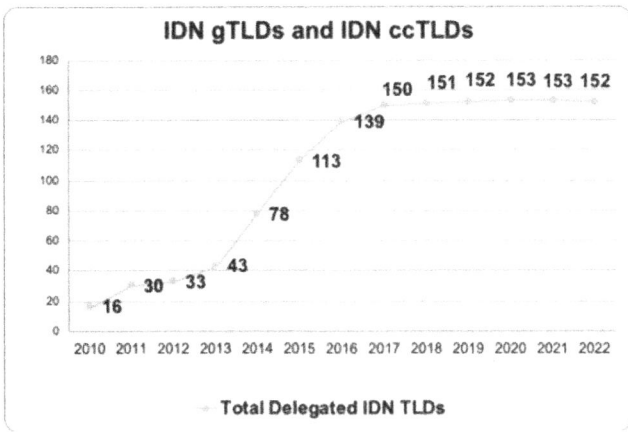

Fig. 1. Total Delegated IDN TLDs *source = idn-annual-report-2022* ICANN

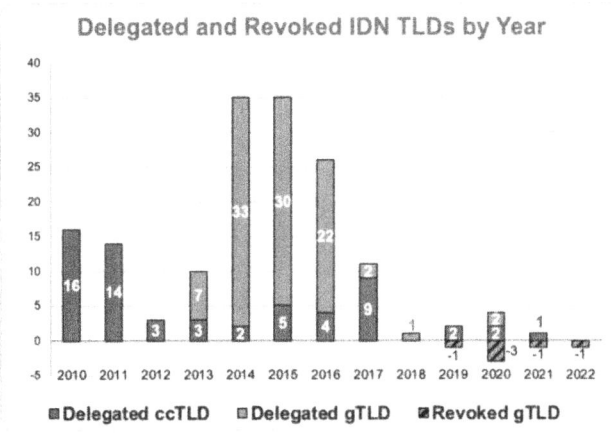

Fig. 2. Delegated ccTLD, gTLD and Revoked gTLD *source = idn-annual-report-2022* ICANN

2 Related Work

In fact, when we talk about abuse of IDNs in this paper, we refer to homograph attacks, as highlighted by the work of Gabrilovich and Gontmarker [7] in 2002. However, to date, there is a lack of studies on this topic due probably to the fact that many registries have not yet adopted IDNs. However, trends have recently changed according to the IDN World Report, which revealed the existence of 7.5 million IDNs registered at late December 2017 [18] and the observation of the first attacks like the Binance one in May 2018 [3].

With the growing adoption of IDNs, several web browsers (such as Chrome and Firefox) have made updates to display IDNs in the address bar. In these updates, the punycode form is used for domain names containing non-ASCII characters. For example, the domain name "facébook.com" will appear as "xn–facbook-dya.com" in the address bar. However, this representation does not solve the problem of homographs. As well as being difficult for users to read, the punycode cannot be used to determine whether a site is abusive, because all sites containing non-ASCII characters are converted in the same way.

In practice, Y. Zhang et al. [24] evaluated the use of IDNs in more than 800 TLDs and found that the homograph problem is universal, with around 12.32% of users facing this problem. A number of studies have been carried out into the problems of abuse induced by IDNs, such as the work of Chiba et al. [6] who analyse and propose countermeasures against misleading IDNs, or T. Shirakura et al. [17] who highlight the possible threats caused by erroneous IDN processing while proposing possible global solutions.

Several approaches are used to detect IDN abuses such as the use of DNS measurements [23], IDN characteristics [1] or artificial intelligence methods [2,21]. Some of these studies focus on homograph detection based on visual similarity. Others use the Levenshtein distance or one of its variants, but this often leads to a high rate of false positives [4,13]. More recent works exploit siamese neural networks [15,19,22]. Even though these networks offer very good accuracy, they are time-consuming due to the conversion of domain names into images [19] or the use of bidirectional deep learning [15].

Although these networks offer high precision, they are slowed down by the conversion of domain names into images [19] and by the use of complex architectures [15,19], which is often cited as a major limitation.

In conclusion, there are several methods that offer good performance in detecting homographs. However, they are often not designed to anticipate these attacks and require significant resources to be deployed. We therefore envision to propose a less costly approach, capable of generating relevant homographs at a low cost in terms of resources.

3 Problem Statement

The main aim of our study is to protect domain names in the context of IDNs, by anticipating the risks of typosquatting linked to homograph attacks. As mentioned in the literature, many homograph attacks have already targeted large companies. For example, Binance was the subject of such an attack, where attackers created several domain names imitating "binance" by subtly modifying the characters, including adding a colon under certain letters [3]. To fully understand this context, it is important to see how IDNs are applied, particularly for the ".SN" domain. This IDN implementation can be divided in two stages: before and after the introduction of IDNs. Before the arrival of IDNs, the domain name system used only ASCII characters. Then, universe of possibilities was represented by Γ_1 obtained from the alphabet Ω_1 such as:

$$\Omega_1 = \{-, 0, 1, ..., 9, a, ..., z\}$$

The rules for checking compliance with the naming framework for the ".SN" domain were based exclusively on the following rules. Let N be the set of domain names already registered with $N = \{n_1, ..., n_n\}$. Let R be the list of reserved terms defined as $R = \{r_1, ..., r_m\}$ and $Gen(r_i) = R - \{r_i\}$ the restriction release function on r_i and $Sim_{sp}(a, b)$ the similarity function that calculates the phonetic similarity between a and b. A new domain(n_i) can be registered according to the following rules:

- **Rule 1**: $n_i \in \Gamma_1$.
- **Rule 2**: $\forall r \in R, \forall n \in N, n_i \neq r \wedge n_i \neq n$.
- **Rule 3**: $\exists r \in R \mid r = n_i, Gen(r)$.
- **Rule 4**: $\forall r \in R, Sim_{sp}(\bar{n}_i, \bar{r}) > \epsilon$ with $0 < \epsilon < 1$

Basically, a domain name is accepted if the follwoing criteria are satisfied: (1) the domain name is not in reserved terms, (2) it is not yet registered, and (3) it is not too similar (phonetically and syntactically) to a reserved term. In case of the domain name is a reserved one or similar to a reserved term, an authorisation code is required to proceed with registration. These rule have given good performances in preventing some domain name abuses.

With the implementation of IDNs, the universe of possibilities became Γ_2 with the alphabet Ω_2 defined as follows :

$$\Omega_2 = \Omega_1 \cup \{\text{à, á, â, ã, ä, å, æ, ç, è, é, ê, ë, ì, í, î, ï, ñ, ò, ó, ô, õ, ö, œ, ß, ù, ú, û,} \\ \text{ü, ý, ÿ}\}$$

In short, the introduction of IDNs came with numerous variants of domain names that can be registered. Therefore, is essential to (1) generate homoglyphs of reserved terms to broaden the control base and (2) identify homoglyph variants of new domains on the fly when they are created in order to estimate the risks of typosquatting. To achieve this, we propose to generate relevant domain names using visual similarity. Such a new context leads to the following rule updates.

- **Rule 1**: $n_i \in \Gamma_2$.
- **Rule 2**: $\forall r \in R \cup R_I, \forall n \in N, n_i \neq r \wedge n_i \neq n$.
- **Rule 3**: $\exists r \in R \cup R_I, \mid r = n_i, Gen(r)$.
- **Rule 4**: $\forall r \in R \cup R_I, Sim_{sp}(\bar{n}_i, \bar{r}) > \epsilon$ avec $0 < \epsilon < 1$
- **Rule 5**: $\forall r \in R \cup R_I, Sim_{vis}(n_i, r) > \beta$ avec $0 < \beta < 1$

R_I designates terms that are not part of R but have strong visual similarities with terms in R. In other words, if we consider H as the set of potential homographs of the reserved terms (elements of R), then $\forall x \in H, x \in R_I \implies \exists y \in R$ such that $Sim_{vis}(x, y) < \beta$. As a reminder similarity Sim_{sp} is evaluated on a syntactic and phonetic basis whereas Sim_{vis} is based on the visual appearance between two domain names.

4 Proposed Approach

We propose a method based on homographs by generating new and potentially exploitable domain names. For each reserved domain name, we create variants by replacing each ASCII character with its diacritical equivalent in IDN. We then use a siamese neural network [5] to evaluate the similarity between these variants and the original domain name in order to determine the relevance of each new name generated.

4.1 Generation of IDN Domain Names

In this subsection, we explain the process of automatically generating domain names using diacritical and visual character variations. Specifically, we take a set of domain names and examine each character to see if there are any variations with accents or visually similar characters in the IDNs. For each character leading to some variants, we create a new version of the domain name by replacing that character with one of its variants. We repeat this process for each character in the initial domain name, which allows us to generate a set of domain names that could potentially be abused.

Diacritic Ensemble: This group includes the different variants of a letter obtained by adding diacritical marks, such as accents or umlauts. These signs change the pronunciation or meaning of a letter while maintaining visual proximity. For instance, the diacritical set of the letter "e" in the IDN alphabet Ω_2 includes é, è, ê and ë.

Visually Similar Characters: These are characters that can be easily confused because of their similar appearance. For example, 'o' and '0' are often confused, as are 'i' and 'l' in some fonts.

Taking into account the IDN alphabet Ω_2, the different diacritical sets and visually similar characters that will be considered are listed in the following table (Table 1).

Table 1. Diacritical sets taken into account

a	'a', 'à', 'á', 'â', 'ã', 'ä', 'å', 'æ'	b	'b', 'β'
c	'c', 'ç'	i	'i', 'ì', 'í', 'î', 'ï', 'l', '1'
n	'n', 'ñ'	o	'o', 'ò', 'ó', 'ô', 'õ', 'ö', 'œ'
s	's', 'ç'	u	'u', 'ù', 'ú', 'û', 'ü'
y	'y', 'ý', 'ÿ'	o	'0'

Generation Principle: As mentioned previously, for a given term, we need to generate a set of elements based on the diacritical variants of the characters. To do this, we use the Breadth-First Search(BFS) method to build a tree where the leaves represent the set of variants generated. At each iteration, a character from the initial word is selected, and the corresponding diacritical variants are identified. These variants are then distributed to the different nodes at the next level of the tree. In this way, as we progress through the tree, we gradually cover all the possible combinations of diacritical characters, as illustrated in Fig. 3.

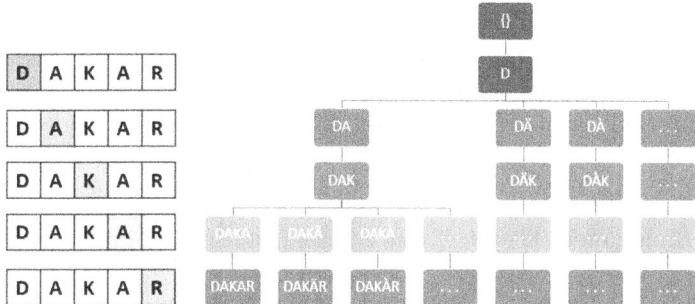

Fig. 3. Example of generation for the reserved term DAKAR

After generating the different variants of terms, we often obtain a large number of results where some are not enough relevants. It is therefore crucial to set a filter for holding only the most valuables ones, which are the terms that are most likely to be used by others for abuse purposes. It is obsious that finding the valuable domain among several others might be a tough game and requires human interventions or a very well trained model. This is why, we rely on neural networks to ease that task.

4.2 Selection of Potentially Exploitable Terms

In this sub-section, we describe the selection of domain names generated in order to retain only the most relevant ones. We assume that the more diacritical or visual changes a domain name undergoes, the more likely it is to attract the attention of the human eye. So we start by filtering the domain names to keep only those that have undergone a single variation from the base domain name. We then use a visual similarity calculation, using a Siamese neural network coupled with a character embedding model. This approach helps us to identify the terms most likely to be misused.

Definition of Visual Similarity: The visual similarity between two words assesses how similar they are in appearance. In our approach, we calculate this visual similarity using Siamese neural networks, as illustrated in Fig. 4.

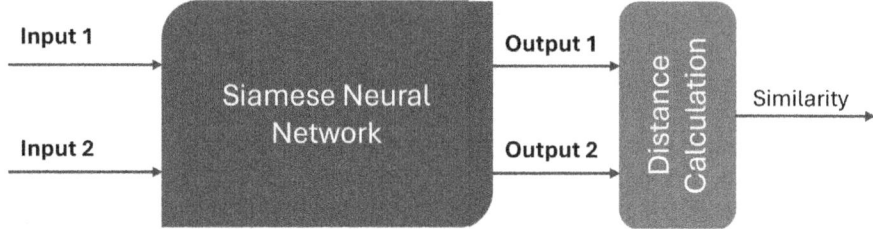

Fig. 4. Architecture of the Siamese neural network

Description of the Siamese Neural Network: These networks are based on a neural architecture and are specially designed to compare pairs of inputs and determine their similarity, as shown in Fig. 4. For our case, we developed a Siamese network where each branch consists of a convolutional neural network, as illustrated in Fig. 5. The main layers of this network are as follows:

- **Embeddings layer:** This layer converts character indices into dense vectors, enabling character embeddings to be calculated.
- **Convolutional Layers:** These layers extract local features from character sequences by applying filters of different sizes. Several convolution layers are used with filters of various sizes, and the ReLU activation function is used to introduce non-linearity.
- **Max Pooling:** This layer reduces dimensionality while retaining the most relevant information, i.e. the maximum values of the features extracted by the convolutions.
- **Concatenation:** This step combines the features extracted by the filters of different sizes to form an overall feature vector, summarising the information extracted.
- **Fully Connected Layer:** Finally, this layer applies a linear transformation to obtain the model's final outputs.
- **Distance between embeddings:** The output vectors of the model's sub-networks are then compared using a distance function. In our case, we will use the Euclidean distance. The result of this distance is used to measure the similarity between the two inputs.

After defining the model, let us evaluate it in the next section where we describe used parameters used to run the algorithm.

5 Approach Assessement

To evaluate the approach, we consider a dataset made of IDN domain names generated from a single diacritic variation, compared with reserved terms. We recall that the model goal is to identify most relevant variant of a given domain name. Basically, we begin with the configuration of the hyperparameters, then the training dataset description and end with the obtained results.

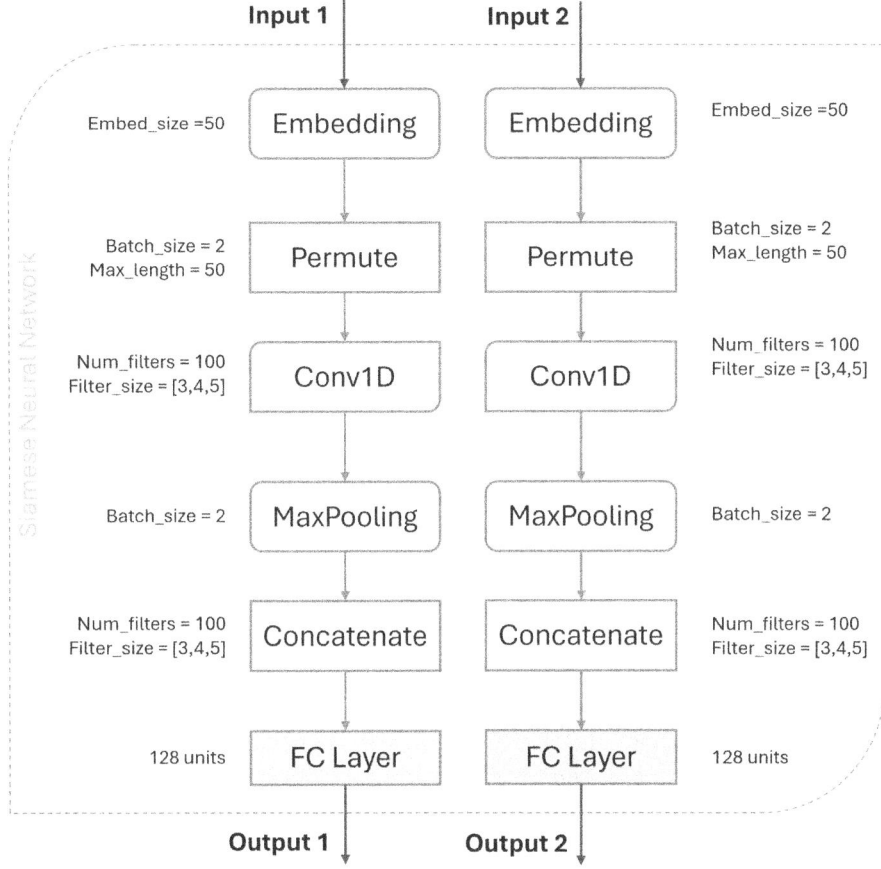

Fig. 5. Detailed Architecture of our Siamese neural network

5.1 Definition of Hyperparameters

To define the hyperparameters, we carried out a series of tests to identify the best combination of values offering optimum results. Finally, the parameter values selected are presented in Table 2. The list of hyperparameters to be defined is as follows:

- **vocab_size:** Vocabulary size (total number of unique characters).
- **embed_size:** Dimension of embedding vectors for each character.
- **num_filters:** Number of filters used for each filter size.
- **filter_sizes:** Size filters to extract patterns of different lengths.
- **max_length:** Maximum length of input sequences.

Table 2. Hyperparameter values for model training

Parameter	Value	Parameter	Value
vocab_size	26	embed_size	50
num_filters	50	filter_sizes	100
max_length	50		

5.2 Assessment Measures and Functions

To calculate the accuracy of the model, we use the accuracy formula given by the Eq. 1. This accuracy is associated with a classification threshold α which we will define.

$$Accuracy = \frac{Number of correct predictions}{Total number of predictions} \quad (1)$$

To refine a model, we also need a loss function. Generally, for Siamese neural networks, this is the contrastive loss function, the formula for which is given in Eq. 2.

$$L(y, D_w) = y \cdot \frac{1}{2} \cdot D_w^2 + (1-y) \cdot \frac{1}{2} \cdot \max(0, m - D_w)^2 \quad (2)$$

where:

- $L(y, D_w)$ is the contrastive loss function,
- y is the binary label indicating similarity (1 for similar, 0 for dissimilar),
- D_w is the distance between the representations of the two inputs,
- m is the margin that defines the distance beyond which dissimilar pairs no longer contribute to the loss.

To calculate the similarity of the two model outputs, we need a distance or similarity function. In our case, the most suitable function with vectors as output is the Euclidean distance, the formula for which is given by the Eq. 3.

$$d(A, B) = \sqrt{(x_1 - y_1)^2 + (x_2 - y_2)^2 + \cdots + (x_n - y_n)^2} \quad (3)$$

5.3 Building the Datasets

In terms of datasets, we use a dataset generated from reserved terms with unitary diacritical variation. We have selected a random sample of 500 domain names from the ".SN" reserved terms and generate their diacritical variations to form high similarity pairs. To create pairs with very low similarity, we use non-unitary diacritical variations, i.e. variations of several characters. We assume that when there are several diacritical variations, they are easily detectable by the human eye. This variation gave us a dataset of around 5000 elements for the training dataset. For the evaluation dataset, we proceeded in the same way for 150 other domain names present in the database of reserved terms, which gave us around 3,000 elements.

5.4 Presentation and Interpretation of Results

In this section, we present the results obtained after configuring, training, and evaluating our Siamese model. We describe the performance of the model in terms of precision and other relevant metrics listed in Subsect. 5.2.

The model was trained over 10 epochs. After the training phases, the model has displayed a loss function value of **0.0031** with a fixed learning rate value (**lr = 0.0001**).

To assess the contrastive accuracy of Siamese models, it is crucial to choose a α classification threshold between 0 and 1. In our case, this means identifying the threshold that maximises accuracy. To do so, we have varied the threshold from 0.4 to 0.9 and selected the one with the best accuracy. We obtained afterwards the curve in Fig. 6 and then plotted the ROC curve for each threshold (see Fig. 7).

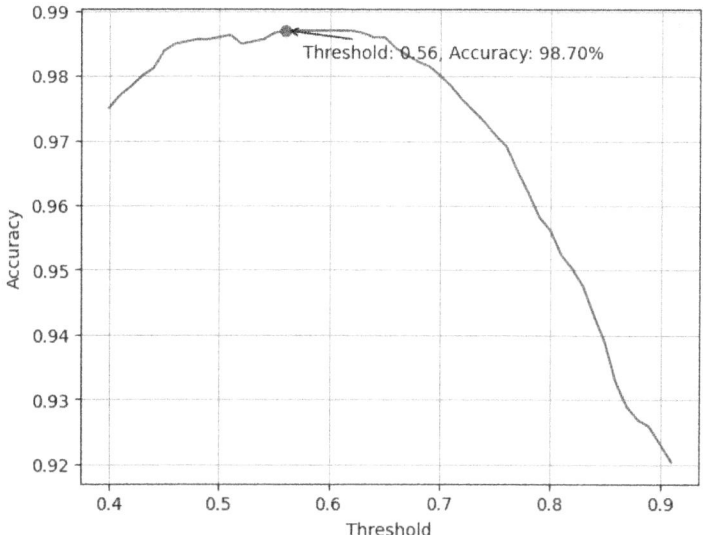

Fig. 6. accuracy variation by threshold

The analysis of results depicted by Fig. 6 let appear that the best accuracy is obtained with the threshold **0.58**. In fact, this threshold valued leads our model to its best accuracy **98.70%**. Furthermore, with the ROC curve in Fig. 7, we have the associated Area Under Curve(AUC) scored to **98%** confirming the accuracy of the model in terms of classification. As a reminder, the ROC is used to identify the threshold above which a model performs best.

As mentioned in the Sect. 2, work that converts domain names into images makes computational cost a limitation as well as the complexity of the Deep Learning architecture to be used [15]. In addition to these limits which are exceeded in our solution, it is important to position our solution using the ROC-AUC index as done in several articles [15,19].

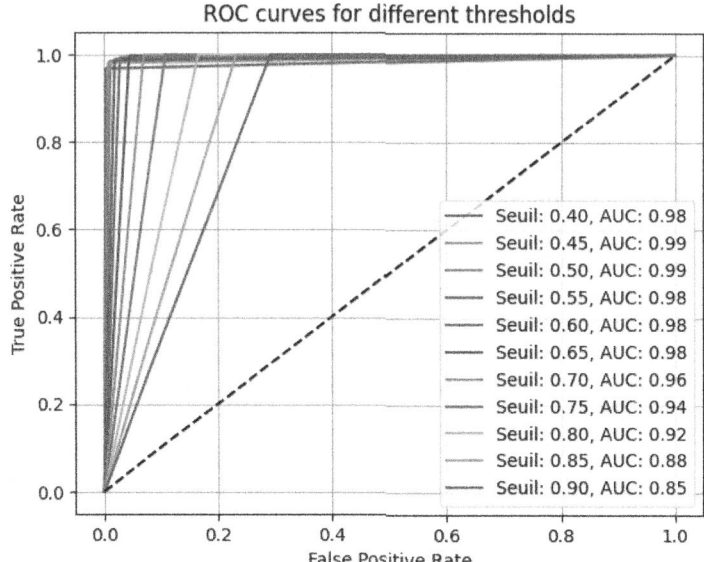

Fig. 7. ROC curve for thresholds

Table 3. Performance of the model

Methods	ROC-AUC
Edit Distance [22]	0.81
Percent Edit Distance [22]	0.86
Visual Edit Distance [22]	0.89
Siamese-CNN [12]	0.93
Siamese-GRU [15]	0.97
Siamese-LSTM [15]	0.97
Siamese-Char (Proposed Solution)	**0.98**

In addition to the complexity limitations mentioned above, the Table 3 highlights that our solution has a higher value of the ROC-AUC index, indicating better performance compared to the other methods compared.

5.5 Use Cases

To demonstrate our solution impact, we applied it through two cases of domain name generation. The first case is related to the **orange.sn**, which generates homographs such as **0range.sn, orangè.sn, orangë.sn, orañge.sn, ōrange.sn**, and **örange.sn** with a threshold set to 0.99. When the threshold is lowered to 0.98, other variations such as **oränge.sn, orangé.sn**, and **oránge.sn** are also included were added. The second case is linked to the domain name **gouv.sn**, which generates variants such as **goúv.sn**, **gõuv.sn**, **gôuv.sn**, **goüv.sn**, **gòuv.sn**, **göuv.sn**, and **g0uv.sn** with a threshold set at 0.98. Intuitively, we can see that the generated variants are so closed to the initial domain names and can be used by abusers to deviate people. This is the reason we have added **Rule 5** to make sure that reserved terms are more protected. Moreover, in case of the domain name is not a restricted one, generated variants are presetend to costumers as potental risks they can prevent by taking appropriate actions at the registration time.

In addition to the generated elements mentioned above, certain terms such as "órangé" or "göùv" are also produced, but these are considered to be model generation errors, as they deviate from the assumptions defined in the constitution of the dataset in Sect. 5.3.

6 Conclusion and Perspectives

In this article, we propose a preventive solution to counter typosquatting attacks using homographs. Unlike previous work, which is often complex, resource-intensive and reactive, our approach is more simple to implement, lightweight and capable of generating relevant domain names that could be used for typosquatting.

Our method is based on two main aspects: the generation of unitary diacritical variations of terms, and the calculation of similarity using a Siamese neural network associated with a Euclidean distance. The results obtained are very promising, with an accuracy of **98.70%** and an AUC score of **98%**, for a similarity threshold of 0.56. Ongoing works are conducted to apply this approach to the ".SN" registry, in order to strengthen the domain names security and to define a recommandation system based on the user pofiles at the registration time. We envision also, to assess our work with more AI algorithms in order to improve its performance and relevance.

References

1. Almarzooqi, A., Mahmoud, J., Alzaabi, B., Ghebremichael, A., Aldwairi, M.: Detecting malicious domains using statistical internationalized domain name features in top level domains. In: 2022 14th Annual Undergraduate Research Conference on Applied Computing (URC), pp. 1–6 (2022). https://doi.org/10.1109/URC58160.2022.10054226
2. Almuhaideb, A.M., et al.: Homoglyph attack detection model using machine learning and hash function. J. Sensor Actuator Networks **11**(3) (2022). ISSN 2224-2708. https://doi.org/10.3390/jsan11030054. https://www.mdpi.com/2224-2708/11/3/54
3. BINANCE. Summary of the phishing and attempted stealing incident on binance. https://www.icann.org/en/announcements/details/icann-bringing-the-languages-of-the-world-to-the-global-internet--fast-track-process-for-internationalized-domain-names-launches-nov-16-30-10-2009-en. Accessed 11 Nov 2024
4. Black, P.E.: Compute visual similarity of top-level domains (2008)

5. Bromley, J., Guyon, I., LeCun, Y., Säckinger, E., Shah, R.: Signature verification using a "Siamese" time delay neural network. In: Advances in Neural Information Processing Systems, vol. 6 (1993)
6. Chiba, D., Hasegawa, A.A., Koide, T., Sawabe, Y., Goto, S., Akiyama, M.: Domain-scouter: analyzing the risks of deceptive internationalized domain names. IEICE Trans. Inf. Syst. **103**(7), 1493–1511 (2020)
7. Gabrilovich, E., Gontmakher, A.: The homograph attack. Commun. ACM **45**(2), 128 (2002)
8. ICANN. Guidelines for the Implementation of Internationalized Domain Names — Version 1.0 - ICANN. https://www.icann.org/resources/pages/idn-guidelines-2003-06-20-en
9. ICANN. Icann bringing the languages of the world to the global internet — fast track process for internationalized domain names launches nov 16. https://www.icann.org/en/announcements/details/icann-bringing-the-languages-of-the-world-to-the-global-internet--fast-track-process-for-internationalized-domain-names-launches-nov-16-30-10-2009-en. Accessed 11 Nov 2024
10. IDN ccTLD - ICANNWiki. https://icannwiki.org/IDN_ccTLD
11. IDN CCTLD fast track process. https://icannwiki.org/IDN_ccTLD_Fast_Track_Process
12. LeCun, Y., Bengio, Y., Hinton, G.: Deep learning. Nature **521**(7553), 436–444 (2015)
13. Linari, A., Mitchell, F., Duce, D., Morris, S.: The curse"of popularity, Typo-squatting (2009)
14. Liu, B., et al.: A reexamination of internationalized domain names: the good, the bad and the ugly. In: DSN, pp. 654–665 (2018)
15. Ravi, V., Alazab, M., Srinivasan, S., Arunachalam, A., Soman, K.P.: Adversarial defense: DGA-based botnets and DNS homographs detection through integrated deep learning. IEEE Trans. Eng. Manag. **70**(1), 249–266 (2021)
16. Sern, L.J., David, Y.G.P., Hao, C.J.: PhishGAN: data augmentation and identification of homoglyph attacks. In: 2020 International Conference on Communications, Computing, Cybersecurity, and Informatics (CCCI), pp. 1–6. IEEE (2020)
17. Shirakura, T., Hasegawa, H., Yamaguchi, Y., Shimada, H.: Potential security risks of internationalized domain name processing for hyperlink. In: 2021 IEEE 45th Annual Computers, Software, and Applications Conference (COMPSAC), pp. 1092–1098 (2021). https://doi.org/10.1109/COMPSAC51774.2021.00149
18. Suzuki, H., Chiba, D., Yoneya, Y., Mori, T., Goto, S.: Shamfinder: an automated framework for detecting IDN homographs. In: Proceedings of the Internet Measurement Conference, pp. 449–462 (2019)
19. Vinayakumar, R., Soman, K.P.: Siamese neural network architecture for homoglyph attacks detection. ICT Express **6**(1), 16–19 (2020)
20. Wang, M., Zang, X., Cao, J., Zhang, B., Li, S.: Phishhunter: Detecting camouflaged IDN-based phishing attacks via Siamese neural network. Comput. Secur. **138**, 103668 (2024)
21. Wang, M., Zang, X., Cao, J., Zhang, B., Li, S.: Phishhunter: detecting camouflaged IDN-based phishing attacks via Siamese neural network. Comput. Secur. **138**, 103668 (2024). ISSN 0167-4048. https://doi.org/10.1016/j.cose.2023.103668. https://www.sciencedirect.com/science/article/pii/S0167404823005783
22. Woodbridge, J., Anderson, H.S., Ahuja, A., Grant, D.: Detecting homoglyph attacks with a Siamese neural network. In: 2018 IEEE Security and Privacy Workshops (SPW), pp. 22–28. IEEE (2018)

23. Yazdani, R., van der Toorn, O., Sperotto, A.: A case of identity: detection of suspicious IDN homograph domains using active DNS measurements. In: 2020 IEEE European Symposium on Security and Privacy Workshops (EuroS&PW), pp. 559–564 (2020). https://doi.org/10.1109/EuroSPW51379.2020.00082
24. Zhang, Y., et al.: Understanding and characterizing the adoption of internationalized domain names in practice. IEEE Trans. Depend. Secure Comput. 1–15 (2024). https://doi.org/10.1109/TDSC.2024.3386905

Enhancing LoRaWAN Network Performance with Reinforcement Learning: Mitigating Collisions and Reducing Energy Consumption

Pape Abdoulaye Fam[(✉)], Ibrahima Faye, Papa Silly Traore, and Mamadou Lamine Ndiaye

Université Cheikh Anta Diop, Ecole Supérieure Polytechnique, Dakar, Senegal
papeabdoulaye.fam@ucad.edu.sn
https://esp.sn/

Abstract. LPWAN technologies like LoRaWAN connect objects to the Internet using a base station or gateway. These networks must meet several requirements: low deployment costs, low energy consumption, high capacity, and data security. They often use simple communication protocols like ALOHA to reduce traffic, which can lead to increased packet collisions as the number of connected devices grows. Recent advancements propose using reinforcement learning techniques to improve LoRaWAN network performance. For instance, decentralized learning at the device level can optimize radio parameters for each packet transmission, reducing interference and enhancing reliability. Algorithms like the Multi-Armed Bandit and Upper Confidence Bound (UCB) have shown promise in reducing collisions and extending device battery life with minimal processing and memory overhead. This article further explores reinforcement learning for ultra-dense LoRaWAN networks to mitigate radio collisions and minimize energy consumption. The study demonstrates that these techniques can effectively enhance network performance.

Keywords: multi-armed bandits · ressource allocation · LoRaWAN

1 Introduction

The Internet of Things (IoT) is one of the most popular and multidisciplinary topics in information and communication technologies (ICT). It connects various objects that can collect relevant data and transmit it to different platforms [1]. Vendors often advertise objects or devices as "connected" or "smart" objects. This interaction between objects, people and platforms leads to a wide range of innovative applications in various sectors: intelligent transport, smart cities, healthcare, well-being, agriculture, energy management, asset tracking, and more. The connectivity of all these smart objects relies on various technologies, each responding to different criteria such as the frequency bands used (licensed or unlicensed), radio coverage, deployment costs, throughput, energy consumption, quality of service, etc.

Low Power Wide Area Networks (LPWAN) [2,3], including LoRaWAN [2], are emerging communication technologies designed for the Internet of Things (IoT). The primary goal of these technologies is to connect various objects to the Internet through a base station known as a "gateway". LPWAN networks must satisfy several key requirements [3]: they should have low deployment costs for operators, consume minimal energy for connected devices, support a high capacity of devices, and ensure the security and confidentiality of the data transmitted over the network. To meet these requirements, technologies are primarily based on simple or non-existent communication protocols with extremely low levels of signaling, such as ALOHA [4], to reduce and control traffic on these networks. Due to this simple Medium Access Control (MAC) protocol, the increase in the packet collision rate due to the considerable number of connected devices is a critical factor limiting the network performance [4].

The scientific community focused on the Internet of Things (IoT) has recently shown interest in applying reinforcement learning techniques to enhance network performance in LoRaWAN networks [5–11]. One noteworthy approach is using decentralized learning for resource allocation at the LoRaWAN device level [9,10]. Researchers [9,10] have demonstrated that by utilizing Multi-Armed Bandit (MAB) algorithms, devices can adjust radio parameters for each packet transmission, thereby optimizing interference reduction and reliability performance. Authors in [10] presented the first implementation of learning algorithms on devices within a LoRaWAN network to reduce collisions among devices operating in the ISM band. They introduced learning algorithms, including the upper confidence bound (UCB) for selecting frequency channels on a LoRa device. Additionally, the authors in [8–10] demonstrate through experiments that the device's battery life can be extended with minimal processing and memory requirements, achieving better results than the traditional random selection method. The proposed algorithms are cost-effective, and the research can be further developed to address denser networks.

Therefore, inspired by related work [5–11], this paper aims to further investigate the application of reinforcement learning techniques in ultra-dense LoRaWAN networks. Our focus is on mitigating radio collisions while minimizing network energy consumption. We demonstrate that these reinforcement learning techniques effectively decrease packet collisions and energy usage.

This paper is organized as follows: Sect. 2 introduces LoRaWAN and its system architecture. Section 3 outlines the system model. Section 4 defines the performance metrics used for evaluation. Section 5 discusses the problem and presents the proposed solution. Section 6, presents the results of computer simulations. Finally, Sect. 7 concludes the paper.

2 LoRa and LoRaWAN Technologies [2]

As shown in Fig. 1, LoRaWAN is an end-to-end network architecture that offers a low-power, long range, cost-effective connectivity solution for network operators, whether public or private, across various Internet of Things (IoT) applications

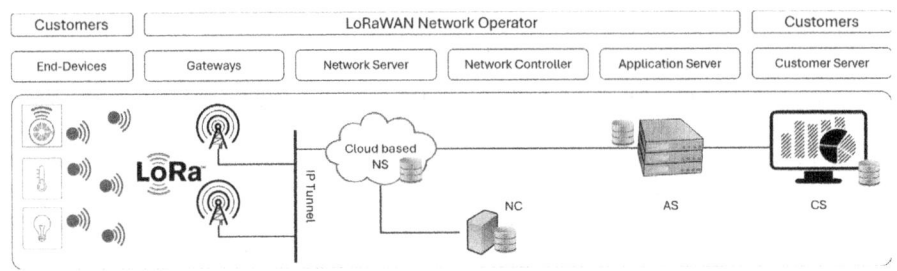

Fig. 1. LoRaWAN Network Architecture [2].

[2]. The LoRaWAN system architecture, developed by the LoRa Alliance, is built on the LoRa (Long Range) wireless communication system and defines various protocols that work together to establish an end-to-end system. As a result, a LoRaWAN system is typically divided into two separate layers: the LoRa physical layer, which employs a spread spectrum modulation technique, and the LoRaWAN Medium Access Control (MAC) layer protocol stack.

2.1 LoRa Physical Layer

Semtech developed the LoRa physical layer technology, which enables long-range, low-power, low-speed communications. The modulation technique is proprietary and exclusive to Semtech [2,13,15,16]. Depending on the deployment region, it operates on frequency channels of 433 MHz, 868 MHz or 915 MHz. LoRa modulation utilizes a variant of spread spectrum known as Chirp Spread Spectrum to encode information. A chirp is a sinusoidal signal whose frequency either increases (up chirp) or decreases (down chirp) over time [16]. This modulation technique is resilient against various types of interference, including narrowband, broadband, and multipath fading. Spectrum spreading is accomplished by generating a linear chirp signal, where the frequency changes continuously according to the spreading factor (SF) [20].

$$SF = \log_2 \left(\frac{R_c}{R_s} \right). \tag{1}$$

Equation (1) presents the expression for the spreading factor (SF), where R_c represents the bit rate of the transmitted message (Chirp) and R_s denotes the bit rate of the symbol to be transmitted. The payload for each transmission can range from 2 to 255 bytes, with a potential data rate of up to 50 Kbps depending on the SF [2,15].

LoRa modulation encodes a symbol using 2^{SF} chirps. Semtech documentation details the relationship between modulation rate R_b, spreading factor SF, bandwidth BW, and the performance of the error correction coding rate CR as [20]:

$$R_b = SF \times CR \times \left(\frac{BW}{2^{SF}} \right) \; bits/sec. \tag{2}$$

The range of LoRa communications is influenced by its bandwidth (BW), the signal's transmission power, and the spreading factor (SF). Increasing the spreading factor can extend the signal's range. However, this also leads to longer transmission times, which decrease throughput, increase power consumption, and ultimately reduce battery life.

2.2 LoRaWAN MAC Layer

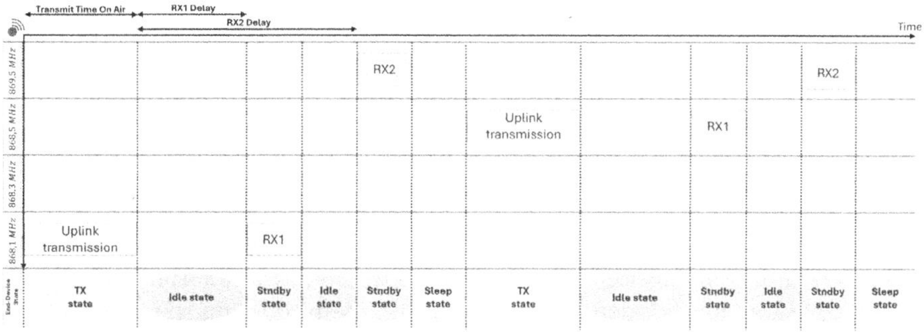

Fig. 2. LoRaWAN MAC class A for end-devices.

LoRaWAN specifies a media access control mechanism that enables end devices to communicate with a gateway through the LoRa modulation technique. While the LoRa modulation itself is proprietary, the LoRaWAN MAC layer is an open standard developed and supported by the LoRa Alliance. As illustrated in Fig. 1, LoRaWAN networks are structured using a star-of-stars topology. This means multiple nearby gateways can receive the data transmitted by an end device, and there is no fixed connection between end devices and gateways. As a result, handovers from one gateway to another are unnecessary, even for mobile end devices. The gateways forward data packets between the devices and a cloud-based network server through various backhaul options, such as satellite, cellular, Ethernet, or Wi-Fi. The network server then routes these packets to the appropriate application or customer server and vice versa.

Pure ALOHA. The LoRaWAN MAC layer is built upon pure ALOHA protocol [4]. End devices can transmit data over any available channel at any time, provided they follow specific rules. Specifically, for each radio transmission, end devices must randomly select a frequency channel from a predefined list of channel frequencies. Additionally, they must adhere to the maximum transmit duty cycle and duration (or dwell time) and comply with local regulations.

End devices in a LoRaWAN network operate asynchronously, transmitting data only when they have information to send. This functionality is ideal for cost-effective devices as it helps save energy. When an end device has data, it wakes up and sends it without checking the channel status or synchronizing with the gateway. As a result, these devices can be prone to collisions and interferences.

Collisions occur when two end devices attempt to transmit data simultaneously, using the same transmission parameters, without waiting to check if the radio channel is available. Essentially, the end devices are unaware of the current state of the radio channel, which prevents them from considering channel state information before transmitting.

When a collision occurs, the affected end device must retransmit the same data. Suppose it does not receive an acknowledgment of receipt within a predefined delay. In that case, the device will resend the same packet using the same transmission parameters but randomly select a back-off period before doing so. The process fails if an acknowledgment is not received after three retransmission attempts. This not only degrades the quality of service but also increases energy consumption.

Listen Before Talk (LBT). The previous section explains that the LoRaWAN network operates based on pure ALOHA standards. However, the LoRaWAN specification also allows for Listen-Before-Talk (LBT) mechanisms, which help reduce collisions in high-density environments. Despite this advantage, the frequency channel sensing required by LBT techniques increases the end device's energy consumption. As a result, LBT may not be suitable for low-power, battery-operated end devices.

LoRaWAN Device Classes. The LoRaWAN specification defines three types of end devices: Class A, Class B, and Class C. Each end device must operate in one of these three classes.

Class A: Bidirectional Devices. [15] LoRaWAN devices implement at least the operating mode described by class A (see Fig. 2). This is a bidirectional communication process. After an uplink transmission, the end device allows two short time slots to receive downlink messages from the gateway.

Once the device transmits data, it waits for the downlink reception time delay. It first opens the RX1 window on the same frequency used for transmission, lasting long enough to detect the preamble. The RX2 window follows, opening after a duration equal to twice the RX1 reception time. RX2 operates on a different subband, which is agreed upon with the Network Server (NS) and can be adjusted using MAC commands.

The device cannot send another uplink message until RX2 is closed. This LoRaWAN Class A device is energy-efficient and ideal for applications with low downlink traffic and latency constraints. All parameters are region-specific as defined in the LoRaWAN Regional Parameters specification.

Class B: Bidirectional Devices with Scheduled Receive Slots [15]. Class B definesbi-directional end devices that utilize scheduled reception slots and two random windows. The gateway manages scheduling through synchronization beacons. Unlike Class A, where the server must wait for an uplink to send messages, Class B allows immediate communication with critical applications by synchronizing end devices to receive downlink messages.

Class C: Bidirectional Devices with Continuous Receive Slots [15]. This class refers to devices that nearly continuously receive data, only pausing when transmitting. These devices constantly listen for downlink messages, making this mode ideal for providing minimal latency for communication from the server to the end device.

3 System Model

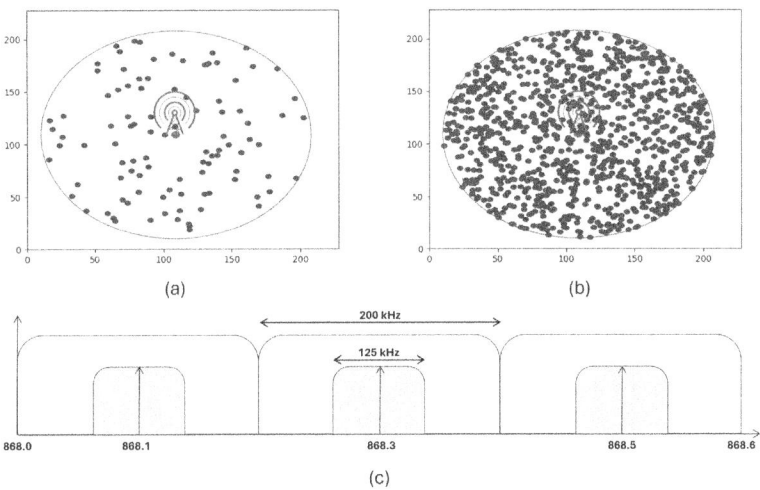

Fig. 3. System model. (a) The LoRaWAN network architecture with $N = 100$ end devices. (b) The LoRaWAN network architecture with $N = 1000$ end devices. (c) Illustration of the mandatory LoRaWAN frequency channels in region EU870.

Figure 3 presents the proposed LoRaWAN system discussed in this paper. As shown in Fig. 3, a set $\mathcal{N}$ of N LoRaWAN end devices is randomly distributed within a network area, with one gateway at the center receiving messages from these end devices. In this area, $K = 3$ frequency channels are available, denoted as $\mathcal{K}$.

The end devices operate in Class A mode and generate data traffic according to a Poisson process, where the interarrival time is characterized by the parameter λ. This parameter reflects the average time for sending data packets and indicates the type of application, such as temperature sensors or gas meters. Each end device adheres to its duty cycle, transmitting uplink packets for a fixed duration before sending the next packet.

When the gateway receives data on one channel, it sends an acknowledgment response back to the corresponding end device on the same channel after a fixed delay (See Fig. 2). Because these communications operate on unlicensed ISM bands, they are susceptible to interference from other end devices within the network and from uncoordinated neighboring networks. This uncontrolled interference can be unevenly distributed across the K different channels.

When multiple end devices transmit packets simultaneously using the same frequency channel, the gateway receives overlapping packets. Whether the gateway can successfully decode these packets depends on several factors. These factors are known as "collision behavior," which the authors discuss in detail in reference [15,16]. These considerations are integrated into the proposed system model.

Several studies [12,14,16,17] indicate that the likelihood of collisions in a network rises with an increasing number of end devices. This increase can lead to a reduction in the quality of service. Additionally, when end devices do not receive an acknowledgment response, they often retransmit the same data multiple times, contributing to higher power consumption. According to the authors in reference [16], the performance of the network declines further in the absence of adaptive mechanisms for adjusting transmission parameters, mainly due to issues such as interference.

4 Performance Metrics

To assess the scalability and performance of the proposed solution, we will utilize two performance indicators as defined in [12–16]: the Data Extraction Rate (DER) and the Network Energy Consumption (NEC).

4.1 Data Extraction Rate (DER) or Quality of Service Metric

As defined in [12,16], the Data Extraction Rate (DER) of the network is given by:

$$DER = \frac{1}{N} \sum_{n=1}^{N} \frac{R_p^n}{N_p^n} \quad (3)$$

In this context, N represents the maximum number of end devices, R_p^n indicates the number of successfully received packets, and N_p^n denotes the number of packets transmitted by end device n.

As stated in [15,16], the Delivery Ratio (DER) is defined as the ratio of the number of messages successfully received to the number of messages transmitted over a specified period. The DER is a valuable metric for assessing the scalability of a deployed LoRaWAN network.

The value of the DER is influenced by several factors, including the location and number of end devices and various physical layer parameters. The DER ranges from 0 to 1, with values closer to 1 indicating a more effective LoRa deployment. In an ideal scenario, one would anticipate a DER of 1.

4.2 Network Energy Consumption (NEC) Metric

As end devices are expected to be deployed in various scenarios using batteries with a lifespan of at least ten years, it is crucial to evaluate the energy consumption during transmissions thoroughly. As shown by authors in [14,15,18,19]. Network Energy Consumption (NEC) refers to the energy the network uses when transmitting and receiving packets from all end devices.

$$NEC = \sum_{n=1}^{N} \sum_{i=1}^{N_p^n} Ec_i^n. \qquad (4)$$

In this context, N represents the maximum number of end devices, while N_p^n denotes the number of packets transmitted by end device n. Additionally, Ec_i^n refers to the energy consumption associated with packet i sent by end device n. It is important to note that a lower value of the NEC metric indicates a more efficient deployment of the LoRaWAN network, as it leads to longer battery life.

As demonstrated in [15], the general formula for Network Energy Consumption (NEC), represented by (4), varies under different scenarios. In this paper, we will examine the following scenario.

NEC Calculation with End Device States and ACK received in the First Reception Window (RX1). This scenario is based on scenario 0 from [15], where we incorporate the various states of the end device. We assume that an acknowledgment for the packet is received during the first downlink reception window (RX1) after transmitting an uplink packet. This results in:

$$Ec_i^n = Etx_i^n + Eidle_i^n + Estb_i^n + Esleep_i^n + Erx1_i^n \qquad (5)$$

$Eidle$, $Estb$, and $Esleep$ represent the energies consumed during idle, standby, and sleep states. $Erx1$ refers to the energy consumed for packet reception during the RX1 reception window, which varies based on the duration of downlink packet reception. This scenario is illustrated in the simulation section under the "Confirmed frame."

5 Problem Formulation and Proposed Solution

As discussed in Sect. 3, collisions may occur if multiple devices attempt to use the same channel and radio parameters simultaneously when end devices communicate with the gateway over a designated frequency channel. Given the potential for many end devices (as illustrated in Fig. 3), the likelihood of collisions and packet losses increases, negatively impacting network performance.

Collisions and packet losses lead to numerous retransmissions, resulting in higher power consumption and reduced battery life for the end devices. Literature reviews indicate that packet loss is a significant challenge for IoT networks [5–11,16,17]. It has been shown that low-complexity reinforcement learning algorithms can help reduce packet losses and enhance network performance.

Inspired by the authors in [5–11,16,17], we propose to evaluate the performance of a LoRaWAN network that utilizes reinforcement learning for selecting frequency channels using the Multi-Armed Bandit (MAB) algorithm.

5.1 Problem Formulation

Selecting the optimal transmission parameters for an end device is a complex challenge. This issue can be framed as follows: Identify the best policy π that maximizes the number of successfully transmitted packets over time. In this context, a policy π determines the frequency channel each end device uses for its transmissions. Additionally, a collection of policies Π is defined as the set $\mathcal{K}$, encompassing the available frequency channels within the LoRaWAN network. Formally, our problem is formulated as follows:

$$\pi^*(t) = \arg\max_{\pi \in \Pi} S(t), \tag{6}$$

where $S(t)$ is a vector representing the number of available frequency channels K. This vector models the state of the radio environment affecting the successful transmission of packets by an end device.

5.2 Reinforcement Learning Techniques as a Solution

In a given set of frequency channels, denoted as $\mathcal{K}$, an end device must select a frequency channel k, which corresponds to a specific policy π. The end devices are unaware of the conditions of the frequency channels, allowing them to choose any channel from the set $\mathcal{K}$.

At each packet arrival time t, each end device selects a frequency channel (policy) that yields a reward $r_{\pi(t)}$, where $r_{\pi(t)}$ can be either 0 or 1. When the end devices make their selection, they can transmit their packets over one specific frequency channel $k \in \mathcal{K}$. This transmission can either be successful or unsuccessful. If the packet is received successfully, the end device will receive an acknowledgment from the network.

This scenario is analogous to the Multi-Armed Bandit (MAB) problem, where the frequency channel can be considered an arm or action, and the outcome of the transmission (success or failure) can be viewed as the reward. If the end device receives an acknowledgment, it can be said that the reward $r_{\pi(t)} = 1$; otherwise, if no acknowledgment is received, then $r_{\pi(t)} = 0$.

To address the problem discussed in the previous section, we utilize Multi-Armed Bandit (MAB) algorithms on the end-device side to manage the uncertainties of the wireless environment.

In this context, we focus on selecting the frequency channel in LoRaWAN networks using a distributed learning algorithm. In this approach, end devices rely solely on locally available information, such as the received acknowledgment responses, to determine the best frequency channel that minimizes collisions. Therefore, this method assumes that the end device is an "intelligent" IoT device.

The literature [8–10] demonstrates that the naive approach, which selects the frequency channel with the highest estimated mean probability of success, can lead to significant failures. This "greedy" policy heavily relies on the outcomes of the initial draws. For example, if the first transmission on one channel fails while the first transmission on another channel succeeds, the end device may permanently abandon the first channel. This is problematic because, even if it has the potential for the best average performance over time, it will never be used again based on just that initial failure. In such a situation, literature has shown that the upper confidence bound (UCB) algorithm gives better performances.

5.3 Upper Confidence Bound Algorithm

The upper confidence bound (UCB) algorithm [5,7–11] follows the principle of *"optimism in face of uncertainty"* by employing a confidence interval for the unknown average reward of each arm. This approach can be viewed as adding an exploration "bonus" to the estimated mean probability of success. UCB starts by selecting each arm once, allowing it to calculate the upper confidence interval for each arm. During each round, UCB chooses the arm with the largest upper confidence interval and then updates that arm's confidence interval based on the observed outcomes. The key concept of UCB is to enhance the cost function $S(t)$ (or average reward) by incorporating a bias factor. Different bias factors result in various versions of the UCB algorithm. For instance, if the bias factor is set to 2, we obtain UCB1 [5]. Alternatively, if the bias factor is chosen as the empirical variance, it leads to UCB-Tuned [5].

At each end-device n, the index of the proposed UCB policy selection frequency channel (arm) is given as

$$S_k(t) = X_k(t) + B_k(t) \tag{7}$$

where the empirical mean reward of frequency channel k, denoted as $X_k(t)$, is used to predict the exploitation, while $B_k(t)$ refers to the exploration bonus that addresses the exploration-exploitation dilemma. The expression for $X_k(t)$ can be formulated as:

$$X_k(t) = \frac{1}{T_k(t)} \sum_{i=1}^{N_p^n} r_{\pi(t)} \mathbb{1}_{\pi(t)=k} \tag{8}$$

where $T_k(t) = \sum_{i=1}^{N_p^n} \mathbb{1}_{\pi(t)=k}$ is the number of times the frequency channel k is chosen up to packet index N_p^n of end-device n.

The exploration "bonus" $B_k(t)$ is given as

$$B_k(t) = \sqrt{\frac{2 \log(N_p^n)}{T_k(t)}}. \tag{9}$$

Hence, this refers to the UCB1 algorithm. For each end-device, the variable t represents the total number of packets transmitted since the beginning. Since time is not divided into slots, this index t is unique to each end device and is not shared among them. As detailed in this section, each end device operates its own UCB1 algorithm independently, as detailed in this section.

6 Simulation Results

6.1 Simulation Parameters

The LoRaSim simulator emulates the behavior of a LoRaWAN network, as shown in Fig. 2, and provides simulation results. Developed with Python's SimPy package, LoRaSim is a discrete-event simulator that implements a radio propagation model based on the well-known log-distance path loss model. It allows calculating a radio transceiver's sensitivity at room temperature for various LoRa spreading factors and bandwidth (BW) settings.

The LoRaSim simulator is useful for simulating collisions in LoRa networks and analyzing their scalability. We have enhanced the simulator to integrate the LoRaWAN "confirmed" type frame and the MAB UCB algorithm and to provide a more accurate evaluation of energy consumption.

The updated version of the LoRaSim simulator developed for this project is available on our GitHub page at https://github.com/paafam/LoRaSim/.

Our simulation focuses on a LoRaWAN network with a single application, such as gas metering or a weather station with an air quality indicator. Additionally, we utilize the system model presented in the previous section for the simulation, with the relevant parameters summarized in Table 1.

6.2 Simulation Results

To analyze the performance of the UCB_1 algorithm, we compare the behavior of a "normal" end device that uses random frequency channel selection with that of an "intelligent" end device, which utilizes reinforcement learning techniques to select the best frequency channel intelligently. The results are presented regarding data extraction rate, probability of success, and network energy consumption.

Table 1. Simulation system parameter

Parameters	Values
Modulation technique	LoRa
Spreading Factor (SF)	12
Coding Rate (CR)	4/5
Bandwith (BW)	125 kHz
Transmission Power	14 dBm
Number of freq. channels K	3
Center frequency	$\{868.1, 868.3, 868.5\}$ MHz
Number of end-devices	from 10 to 1000
Average packet transmission rate λ	180000 (approx. 3 mn time interval)
Packet payload size	20 bytes
Simulation time	1 day

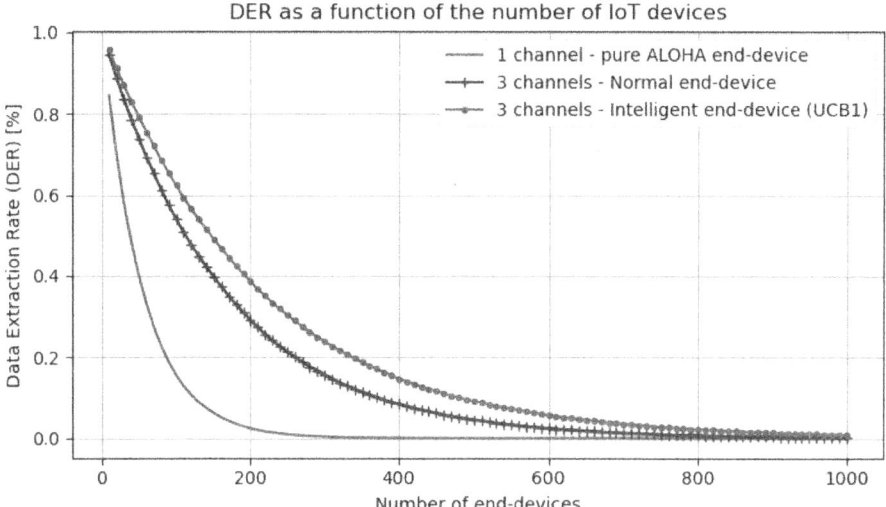

Fig. 4. Data Extraction Rate (DER) or success probability as a function of the number of end-devices in the network. Results are presented for the single channel end-device in pure ALOHA (red curve), the "normal" (blue curve) and "intelligent" (green curve) type of end-devices. (Color figure online)

Data Extraction Rate (DER) Improvement. Figure 4 illustrates the evolution of the Data Extraction Rate (DER), or the probability of success, as a function of the number of end devices in the network. Each data point represents a Monte Carlo simulation run lasting approximately one day, with each simulation repeated 100 times.

The results are displayed for two types of end devices: "normal" (blue curve) and "intelligent" (green curve). As a reference, Fig. 4 also includes the results of a single-channel end device (red curve), which aligns with the well-known ALOHA success probability equation [4].

As the number of end devices in the LoRaWAN network increases, the Data Extraction Rate (DER) decreases exponentially for both types of end devices. Notably, the "intelligent" end devices yield better DER results than the "normal" devices, with a significant difference.

For applications requiring a DER greater than 0.6 to function effectively, it is possible to support 108 "intelligent" end devices, while only 82 "normal" end devices can be accommodated. This shows that learning techniques are instrumental in selecting the optimal frequency channel to maximize the data extraction rate or success probability.

This improvement can be attributed to the learning algorithm's ability to dynamically identify and adjust to the optimal policy, which provides the best settings for each transmission.

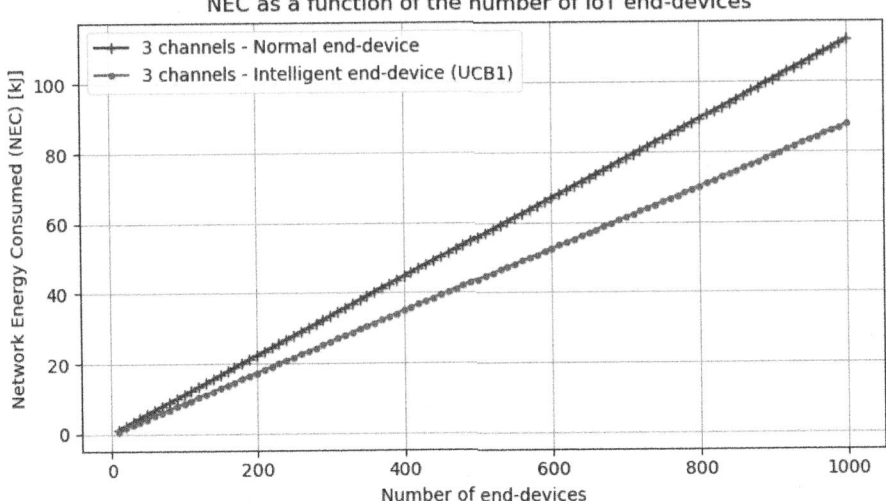

Fig. 5. Network Energy Consumption (NEC) as a function of the number of end-devices in the network. Results are presented for the "normal" (blue curve) and "intelligent" (green curve) type of end-devices. (Color figure online)

Network Energy Consumption (NEC) Improvement. Figure 5 illustrates the effects of learning techniques on Network Energy Consumption (NEC). The results are presented for two types of end devices: "normal" (represented by the blue curve) and "intelligent" (represented by the green curve).

As the number of end devices increases, the NEC rises linearly for both devices. However, the "intelligent" end devices are more energy-efficient than the "normal" ones. The reduction in NEC is significant, especially with many devices in the network. For instance, when there are $N = 1000$ end devices, energy consumption decreases by 23%.

Consequently, employing learning techniques reduces the network's overall energy consumption. This ultimately results in longer battery life and improved autonomy for end devices.

7 Conclusion

In this paper, we evaluated the performance of ultra-dense LoRaWAN networks composed of "intelligent" end devices that utilize reinforcement learning to mitigate radio collisions and reduce energy consumption. To assess the performance of the UCB1 algorithm, we employed an extended version of the LoRaSim simulator to emulate the behavior of a LoRaWAN network featuring these "intelligent" end devices. Our computer simulation demonstrated that these "intelligent" end devices achieved significantly better results than "normal" end devices. These findings indicate that learning techniques are crucial in selecting the optimal frequency channel, maximizing the Data Error Rate (DER), and reducing overall network energy consumption. This leads to longer battery life and increased autonomy for the end devices.

References

1. Barro, P., Degila, J., Zennaro, M., Wamba, S.: Towards smart and sustainable future cities based on Internet of Things for developing countries: what approach for Africa? EAI Endorsed Trans. Internet Things **4**(13) (2018)
2. Sornin, N., Luis, M., Eirich, T., Kramp, T., Hersent, O.: LoRaWAN Specification, LoRa Alliance, Inc. (2016)
3. Usman, R., Parag, K., Mahesh, S.: Low Power wide area networks: an overview. IEEE Commun. Surv. Tutor. **19**(Secondquarter), 855–873 (2017)
4. Abramson, N.: The aloha system: another alternative for computer communications. In: chez Proceedings of the November 17-19, 1970, Fall Joint Computer Conference, AFIPS, New York, NY, USA (1970)
5. Askhedkar, A.R., Chaudhari, B.S.: Multi-armed bandit algorithm policy for LoRa network performance enhancement. J. Sen. Actuator Networks **12**(3) (2023). Art. no. 3
6. Valach, A., Macko, D.: Optimization of LoRa networks using multi-armed bandit algorithms. In: Pandit, M., Gaur, M.K., Rana, P.S., Tiwari, A. (eds.) Artificial Intelligence and Sustainable Computing, pp. 371–389. Springer Nature, Singapore (2022)
7. Bonnefoi, R., Besson, L., Manco-Vasquez, J., Moy, C.: Upper-confidence bound for channel selection in LPWA networks with retransmissions. In: 2019 IEEE Wireless Communications and Networking Conference Workshop (WCNCW), pp. 1–7 (2019)
8. Abdelghany, A., Uguen, B., Moy, C., Lemur, D.: Decentralized adaptive spectrum learning in wireless IoT networks based on channel quality information. IEEE Internet Things J. **9**(20), 19660–19669 (2022)
9. Moy, C., Besson, L.: Decentralized spectrum learning for IoT wireless networks collision mitigation. In: 2019 15th International Conference on Distributed Computing in Sensor Systems (DCOSS), May 2019, pp. 644–651 (2019)
10. Moy, C.: IoTligent: first world-wide implementation of decentralized spectrum learning for IoT wireless networks. In: 2019 URSI Asia-Pacific Radio Science Conference (AP-RASC), pp. 1–4 (2019)
11. Besson, L., Bonnefoi, R., Moy, C.: GNU radio implementation of MALIN: 'multi-armed bandits learning for internet-of-things networks'. In: 2019 IEEE Wireless Communications and Networking Conference (WCNC), pp. 1–6 (2019)
12. Fam, P.A., Faye, I.: Towards more energy efficient MAC protocols for LoRaWAN networks. In: 2020 XXXIIIrd General Assembly and Scientific Symposium of the International Union of Radio Science, pp. 1–4 (2020)
13. Faye, I., Fam, P.A., Traoré, P.S., Ndiaye, M.L.: LoRaWAN networks: a more Precise assessment of the energy consumption. In: 2021 XXXIVth General Assembly and Scientific Symposium of the International Union of Radio Science (URSI GASS), pp. 1–3 (2021)
14. Marini, R., Mikhaylov, K., Pasolini, G., Buratti, C.: LoRaWANSim: a flexible simulator for LoRaWAN networks. Sensors (Basel) **21**(3), 695 (2021)

15. Faye, I., Fam, P.A., Ndiaye, M.L.: Energy consumption of IoT devices: an accurate evaluation to better predict battery lifetime. Radio Sci. **57**(12), e2021RS007423 (2022)
16. Bor, M.C., Roedig, U., Voigt, T., Alonso, J.M.: Do LoRa low-power wide-area networks scale? In: Proceedings of the 19th ACM International Conference on Modeling, Analysis and Simulation of Wireless and Mobile Systems, Malta Malta, pp. 59–67. ACM (2016)
17. Abdelghany, A., Uguen, B., Moy, C., Lemur, D.: Modelling of the packet delivery rate in an actual LoRaWAN network. Electron. Lett. **57**(11), 460–462 (2021)
18. Rajab, H., Cinkler, T., Bouguera, T.: Evaluation of Energy Consumption of LPWAN Technologies (2021)
19. Bouguera, T., Diouris, J.-F., Chaillout, J.-J., Jaouadi, R., Andrieux, G.: Energy consumption model for sensor nodes based on LoRa and LoRaWAN. Sensors **18**(7) (2018). Art. no. 7
20. Semtech Corporation. AN1200.22: LoRa Modulation Basics. Semtech Application Note, Revision 2 (2015)

Detection and Treatment of Various Rice Diseases in Benin Using AI: From Bibliometric Analysis to Survey

Alfred Adinsi(✉) and Pélagie Houngue

Institut de Mathématiques et de Sciences Physiques, Université d'Abomey-Calavi – IMSP, Dangbo, Bénin
{alfred.adinsi,pelagie.houngue}@imsp-uac.org,
fredadinsi@gmail.com

Abstract. Rice diseases represent a major challenge to global food security. The use of Artificial Intelligence (AI) in the detection and treatment of these diseases offers innovative perspectives to improve crop productivity and resilience. This study presents a bibliometric analysis of current research on the application of AI in the field of rice crop health from 2019 to June 2024. The data used in this study comes from the Scopus database and is presented using Biblioshiny software and visualization technologies. From January 2019 to June 2024, the literature in this field grew at an average rate of 46.14%. From the analysis of the 543 collected documents, India is the most productive country, accounting for 58% of total publications and 23% of total citations. The Chitkara University Institute of Engineering and Technology is the most productive research institute, with 29 publications. Geographically, most of this research is conducted in India, China, Bangladesh, Malaysia, USA, Saudi Arabia, Thailand, Ethiopia, Australia, and Indonesia. We also examined the main bibliometric reviews on precision agriculture with Artificial Intelligence (AI), highlighting existing gaps and future research opportunities. This study contributes to the understanding of the field's evolution and proposes insights to guide future research efforts in this crucial area of agriculture of precision.

Keywords: Bibliometric analysis · Artificial Intelligence · IoT · Rice Disease · Machine Learning · Convolutional Neural Networks · Precision Agriculture · Ouest-Africa · Benin

1 Introduction

The cultivation of rice is crucial for global food security, particularly in developing regions like Benin, where it serves as a fundamental food source. However, the production of rice is constantly threatened by various diseases that can severely reduce yields and jeopardize food security. In response to these challenges, Artificial Intelligence (AI) is emerging as an innovative solution to improve the detection and treatment of rice diseases.

Smart agriculture replaces conventional farming systems by using advanced technologies such as the Internet of Things (IoT), AI, and machine learning (ML) to ensure higher productivity and precise agricultural management to meet the growing food demand. Researchers' interest in smart agriculture has increased in recent years, with several bibliometric studies examining this theme. However, it is important to note that there are few bibliometric studies specifically focused on the application of AI in the detection and treatment of rice diseases, especially in context like Benin, where the local specificities of diseases have not yet been sufficiently explored.

Researchers such as Liu et al. (2023) [1] demonstrated the effectiveness of convolutional neural networks for detecting rice diseases from images, while Shah et al. (2016) [2] used deep learning techniques to classify different rice diseases with high accuracy. These studies highlight AI's potential to transform agricultural disease management, but they do not consider the direct impact on food security in Benin or the importance of a contextual approach. Additionally, Siddarajamma et al. (2022) [3] provided a review of machine learning approaches for rice disease detection, emphasizing the growing importance of these technologies in agriculture.

This study aims at exploring recent advances in the use of AI to detect and treat rice diseases, focusing on the potential impact of these technologies on disease management and food security in Benin. Through a comprehensive bibliometric analysis, we will examine research trends and identify key scientific contributions in this field.

We focus on the following research questions:

- What is the current volume of literature published on the use of AI to detect and treat rice diseases, and how has it evolved over time?
- Who are the leading authors and relevant journals that have published the most cited articles on this topic, and what are their characteristics?
- What are the main concepts studied regarding the application of AI in rice disease management, and how are they interconnected?

The remainder of this paper is organized as follows. First of all, materials and methods are presented in Sect. 2. Then, Sect. 3 outlines the bibliometric study results. Subsequently, Sect. 4 provides previous studies and survey on the topic. Finally, conclusion and future research directions are discussed in Sect. 5.

2 Materials and Methods

To achieve the first objective of this work, which is to understand the evolution of research on the detection and treatment of rice diseases using Artificial Intelligence technologies, we conducted a bibliometric analysis based on data extracted from the Scopus database on June 29, 2024, using the following search string:

("Rice disease" OR "Rice pathology" OR "Rice infection" OR "Rice ailment" OR "Rice affliction" OR "Rice disorder" OR "Rice health issue" OR "Rice crop disease" OR "Rice plant disease" OR "Rice malady" OR "Rice pestilence" OR "Rice anomaly" OR "Rice bacterial disease" OR "Rice viral disease" OR "Rice leaf disease" OR "Rice seed disease" OR "Rice deficiency" OR "Rice crop pathology" OR "Rice contamination" OR "Rice foliar diseases") AND ("AI" OR "Machine learning" OR "Deep learning"

OR "Computational intelligence" OR "Intelligent systems" OR "Neural networks" OR "Self-learning systems" OR "Cognitive computing" OR "Intelligent agents" OR "Smart technology" OR "Expert systems" OR "Predictive analytics" OR "Cognitive systems").

Bibliometric analysis is the statistical study of bibliographic data, primarily from scientific and technical literature. It measures scientific activity in a particular category: journal, country, or other areas of interest [4].

As for our analysis, the collected data, consisting of 543 documents, including 233 scientific articles, were exported in BibTex format to enable in-depth analysis. The data were analyzed using biblioshiny, the interface of the bibliometric software bibliometrix. This analysis allowed us to visualize publication trends, authors collaborations, the most influential journals, and the most studied research topics.

To produce clear visualizations, the tables and graphs from the bibliometric analysis were processed in Microsoft Excel. Then, several published articles were selected and thoroughly reviewed to highlight the various technological approaches used in the detection and treatment of rice diseases. Figure 1 shows the methodology used for the bibliometric analysis.

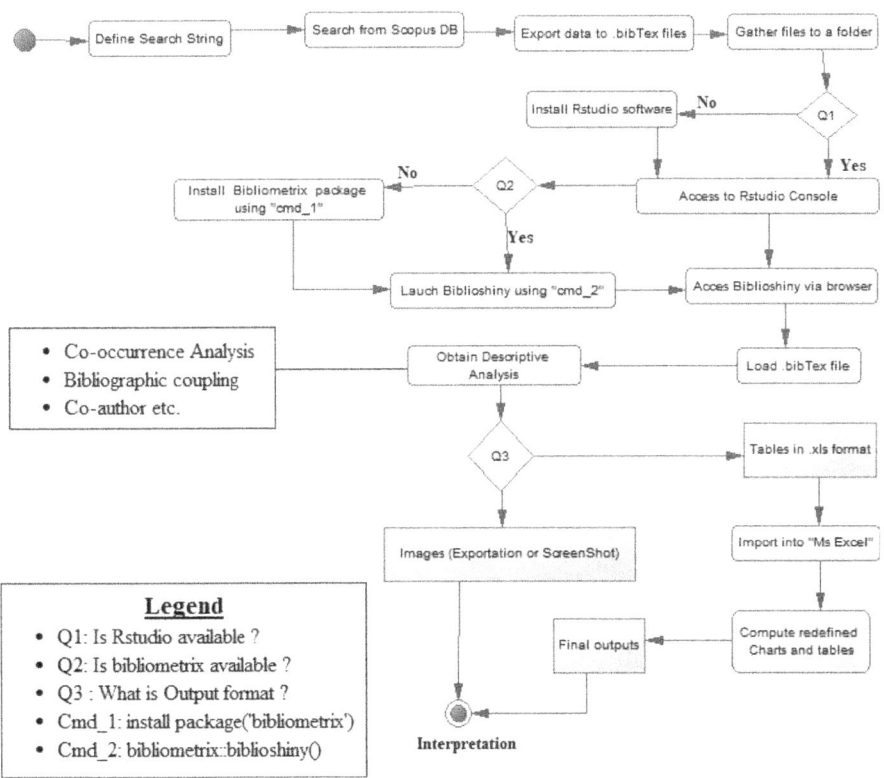

Fig. 1. Research Methodology

Figure 1 illustrates the methodology used to analyze and interpret data during the writing process. The steps are detailed as follows:

- **Define Search String:** This initial step involves defining the search terms for the bibliometric study, serving as the foundation of the process before initiating the database search.
- **Search from Scopus DB**: Once the search terms are defined, a search is conducted in the Scopus database to retrieve relevant publications.
- **Export data to .bibTex files:** The search results are exported in .bibTex format, which is commonly used for managing bibliographic references.
- **Gather files to a folder:** The .bibTex files are collected into a specific folder for further processing.
- **Install RStudio software:** The RStudio software is installed to enable bibliometric analysis.
- **Access to RStudio Console:** Access to the RStudio console is required to execute commands related to the Bibliometrix package.
- **Install Bibliometrix package using "cmd_1":** A question (Q1) verifies whether the Bibliometrix package is already available. If not, the command install.packages("bibliometrix") (cmd_1) must be executed.
- **Launch Biblioshiny using "cmd_2":** If the package is installed, the command biblioshiny() (cmd_2) is used to launch the interactive Biblioshiny interface.
- **Access Biblioshiny via browser:** Once Biblioshiny is launched, it can be accessed via a web browser for interactive use.
- **Load .bibTex file:** The collected .bibTex files are loaded into Biblioshiny for bibliometric analysis.
- **Obtain Descriptive Analysis:** A descriptive analysis is performed, including methods such as co-occurrence analysis, bibliographic coupling, and others. A question (Q3) asks for the desired output format.
- **Tables in.xls format:** The analysis results can be exported as tables in.xls format, which is compatible with Excel.
- **Import into MS Excel:** These files are then imported into Microsoft Excel for adjustments or complementary analyses.
- **Compute redefined charts and tables:** Enhanced charts and tables are created in Excel to obtain more precise and explicit results.
- **Images Outputs (exportation or screenshot**): Images or screenshots of the results can be generated for better visualization.
- **Final outputs:** The final results are ready for interpretation after completing all these steps.
- **Interpretation:** Finally, the results are interpreted to draw relevant scientific conclusions.

3 Results of Bibliometric Study

This section provides an in-depth analysis of the results from our bibliometric study, involving a detailed examination of scientific publications related to the detection and treatment of various diseases affecting rice using artificial intelligence. The findings offer valuable insights into the current state of research in this field, highlighting emerging trends and areas for future exploration. These results are critical in order to guide future research directions and policy decisions in the field of rice disease detection and treatment using AI.

3.1 Main Information: Overview

Table 1 below presents an overview of the preliminary information on the datasets extracted from the Scopus database from 2019 to 2024. The analysis reveals a diverse distribution of document types. From 543 documents examined, 232 are articles, 247 are conference proceedings, and the others include book chapters, reviews, data documents, editorials, and retracted articles. These documents come from 323 different sources, reflecting a significant diversity of scientific contributions in the field of detection and treatment of rice diseases using Artificial Intelligence (AI). The authors of these documents number 1,610, of whom only 12 have written publications alone. On average, each document is co-authored by about 3.83 authors, with an international collaboration rate of 12.34%, highlighting the importance of global cooperation in this research area. The keywords associated with these documents include 1,824 Plus keywords (ID) and 974 author keywords (DE), indicating a rich variety of subjects and concepts explored. The annual growth rate of publications is 46.14%, illustrating a growing and sustained interest in this topic. The average citation duration of the documents is 1.63 years, with an average of 11.69 citations per document. This information highlights the growing enthusiasm among researchers for the detection and treatment of rice diseases using AI, emphasizing emerging trends and areas for future exploration in this crucial field for agriculture and food security.

Table 1. Main information on published documents in the Scopus database

Description	Results
MAIN INFORMATION ABOUT DATA	
Timespan	2019:2024
Sources (Journals, Books, etc.)	323
Documents	543
Annual Growth Rate %	46,14
Document Average Age	1,63
Average citations per doc	11,69
References	0

(continued)

Table 1. (*continued*)

Description	Results
DOCUMENT CONTENTS	
Keywords Plus (ID)	1824
Author's Keywords (DE)	974
AUTHORS	
Authors	1610
Authors of single-authored docs	12
AUTHORS COLLABORATION	
Single-authored docs	46
Co-Authors per Doc	3,83
International co-authorships %	12,34
DOCUMENT TYPES	
Article	232
Article article	1
Article conference paper	1
Book chapter	10
Conference paper	247
Conference paper article	1
Conference paper conference paper	1
Conference review	34
Conference review conference paper	1
Data paper	2
Editorial	1
Retracted	1
Review	11

3.2 Annual Scientific Production and Production of Key Sources

The analysis of annual scientific production on the detection and treatment of various rice diseases using artificial intelligence, based on data from the Scopus database, reveals significant trends according to Fig. 2. Publications in this field have seen a notable increase over the years. In 2019, 12 articles were published. This number more than doubled in 2020, reaching 30 articles. The year 2021 saw a strong increase, with 80 articles published. In 2022, this trend continued with 126 articles. The year 2023 was particularly prolific, with 215 articles published, marking a peak in scientific production on this subject. By May 2024, 80 articles had already been published, demonstrating a continued and significant contribution to research in this field. Then, Fig. 2 indicates a growing interest in research on the detection and treatment of rice diseases using artificial intelligence. This increase in scientific production could be attributed to a rise in international collaborations and investments in this area. In summary, the analysis of Scopus data shows a growth trend in scientific production on the detection and treatment of various rice diseases using artificial intelligence. This trend reflects the increasing importance placed on research in this field and its potential impact on agriculture and global food security.

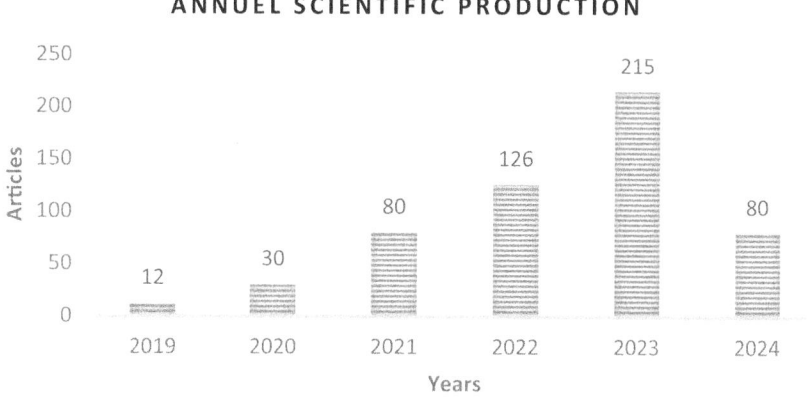

Fig. 2. Annual Scientific Production in Scopus

What about the most relevant sources for the detection and treatment of various rice diseases using artificial intelligence? Fig. 3 helps us focus on this question by displaying the top 10 sources that have produced the highest number of articles on this topic in the Scopus database. The ranking is based on the total number of articles published by each source.

From this figure, we can see that the top three positions are held by "Lecture Notes in Networks and Systems" with 23 articles, "Frontiers in Plant Science" with 13 articles, and "Communications in Computer and Information Science" with 12 articles. This helps us to determine that these sources are the most relevant in the literature regarding the detection and treatment of rice diseases using artificial intelligence.

It is interesting to note that these results highlight the diversity of research sources in this field, ranging from specialized agriculture journals like "Frontiers in Plant Science" to more generalist journals like "Multimedia Tools and Applications," which cover a wide range of topics related to artificial intelligence.

In summary, the analysis of the most relevant sources highlights the variety of publications in the literature on the detection and treatment of rice diseases using artificial intelligence. These results provide valuable insights for researchers and professionals seeking access to the most influential and relevant works in this field.

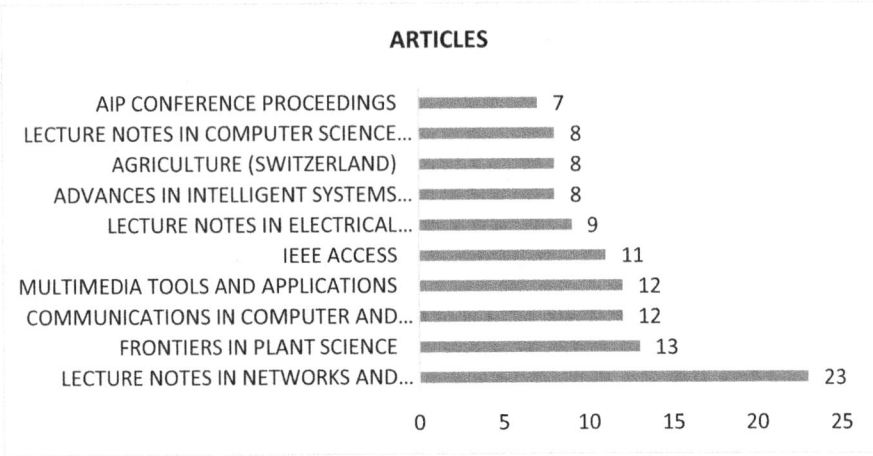

Fig. 3. Top 10 Most Relevant Sources in Scopus

3.3 Dynamics of the Sources

When examining Table 2, which relates to data on the growth of publications in the top five sources, we notice a significant increase over the years. In 2024, "Lecture Notes in Networks and Systems" published 19 papers, "Frontiers in Plant Science" published 13, "Multimedia Tools and Applications" published 12, "IEEE Access" published 11, and "Communications in Computer and Information Science" published 10 papers. This constant growth indicates the increasing importance of these sources in publishing research on the detection and treatment of rice diseases using artificial intelligence.

It is also interesting to note that these five sources began publishing papers on this topic at different times. For example, "Lecture Notes in Networks and Systems" and "Frontiers in Plant Science" both published their first paper in 2020. Since then, there has been a continuous increase in the number of publications each year, suggesting that interest in this research field has grown over time.

In 2019, none of these sources had published papers on this subject yet. In 2020, "Lecture Notes in Networks and Systems" and "Frontiers in Plant Science" each published 1 paper, while "Communications in Computer and Information Science" published 2. In 2021, the number of publications increased, with "Lecture Notes in Networks and Systems" and "Multimedia Tools and Applications" each publishing 1 paper, "Frontiers in Plant Science" publishing 3 papers, "Communications in Computer and Information Science" publishing 4 papers, and "IEEE Access" publishing 2 papers.

The most significant growth occurred in 2023, when "Lecture Notes in Networks and Systems" published 18 papers, "Frontiers in Plant Science" and "Communications in Computer and Information Science" published 13 and 9 papers respectively, "Multimedia Tools and Applications" published 6 papers, and "IEEE Access" published 8 papers. In 2024, this growth trend continued, further consolidating the role of these sources as key players in disseminating research on the application of artificial intelligence to fight rice diseases.

Table 2. Dynamics of the Sources in Scopus.

Year	Lecture notes in networks and systems	Frontiers in plant science	Communications in computer and information science	Multimedia tools and applications	IEEE Access
2019	0	0	0	0	0
2020	1	1	2	0	0
2021	1	3	4	1	2
2022	3	9	9	1	5
2023	18	13	9	6	8
2024	19	13	10	12	11

3.4 Top 10 Authors by Number of Documents

When examining the most prolific authors based on Fig. 4 from our database, we note that KUKREJA V stands out with 18 papers, followed by SHARMA R with 10 papers and ZHANG H with 8 papers. The authors DANIYA T, KUMAR S, and LU Y each published 7 papers. AGGARWAL M, GOYAL N, KHULLAR V, and KUMAR A complete the top 10 with each having published 6 papers.

This distribution of publications highlights the diversity of contributors in this field, with significant contributions from several researchers. It is interesting to note that many of the most prolific authors appear to be from Asia, which may reflect the increasing importance of this region in the field of rice and artificial intelligence research.

Fig. 4. Top 10 Most Relevant Authors in Scopus

3.5 Top 10 Most Cited Documents

In this section, we examine the 10 most cited documents in the field of detection and treatment of various rice diseases using artificial intelligence. Figure 5 below presents these documents along with their total number of citations.

The most cited document is that of Rahman et al. (2020) [5], published in 2020 in Biosystems Engineering, with a total of 317 citations. Next, we have the document by Jiang et al. (2020) [6], published in 2020 in Computers and Electronics in Agriculture, which received 232 citations. The document by Liang et al. (2019) [7], published in 2019 in Scientific Reports, ranks third with 188 citations.

Following these documents, the one by Li et al. (2020) [8], published in 2020 in Sensors, accumulated 172 citations. The document by Chen et al. (2020) [9], published in 2020 in the Journal of the Science of Food and Agriculture, obtained 168 citations. Ahmed et al. (2019) [10], with a publication in 2019 at the International Conference on Sustainable Technologies, received 163 citations.

The document by Shrivastava et Pradhan (2021) [11], published in 2021 in the Journal of Plant Pathology, obtained 162 citations. Krishnamoorthy et al. (2021) [12], with a publication in 2021 in Environmental Research, has 156 citations. Another document by Shrivastava (Shrivastava et al., 2019) [13], published in 2019 in the ISPRS Archives of Photogrammetry, Remote Sensing and Spatial Information Sciences, also has 156 citations. Finally, the document by Wang et al. (2021) [14], published in 2021 in Expert Systems with Applications, received 149 citations.

Analyzing this data, it is clear that these documents have had a significant impact in the field of detection and treatment of rice diseases.

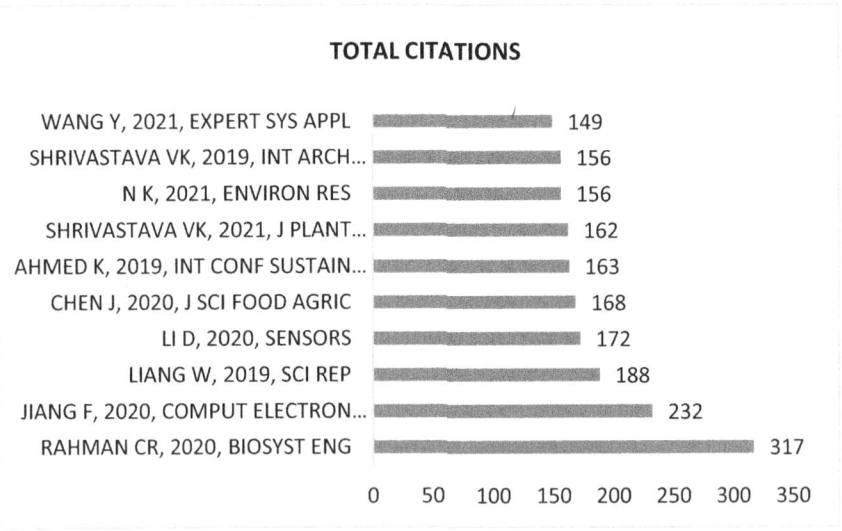

Fig. 5. Top 10 Most Cited Documents in Scopus

3.6 Top 10 Most Productive Universities

The scientific output of universities in the field of detection and treatment of rice diseases using artificial intelligence reveals significant contributions from several academic institutions, as illustrated in Table 3. Chitkara University Institute of Engineering and Technology stands out as the leader with a total of 29 publications. This institution has made significant contributions to research, demonstrating a notable commitment to this field. Annamalai University and Zhejiang University follow with 16 publications each. These universities are also very active in research, illustrating their commitment to advancing knowledge in this crucial area.

Graphic Era Hill University has 13 publications, while the SRM Institute of Science and Technology has contributed with 12 publications. These institutions also make significant contributions to research in this field. Graphic Era Deemed to be University, Chitkara University, Heilongjiang Bayi Agricultural University, Kasetsart University, and Nanjing Agricultural University have each published 9 documents. Although slightly less prolific, these universities play an important role in advancing research on rice diseases.

Table 3. Most Productive Universities

Affiliation	Articles
Chitkara University Institute of Engineering and Technology	29
Annamalai University	16
Zhejiang University	16
Graphic Era Hill University	13
Srm Institute of Science and Technology	12
Graphic Era Deemed to be University	10
Chitkara University	9
Heilongjiang Bayi Agricultural University	9
Kasetsart University	9
Nanjing Agricultural University	9

3.7 Top 10 of Scientifically Productive Countries and Most Cited Countries

Figure 6 and Table 4 present the top 10 most productive and most cited countries for the subject addressed. The data clearly show that India leads in scientific production in the field of detection and treatment of rice diseases using artificial intelligence, with an impressive total of 608 publications. China ranks second with 232 publications, closely followed by Bangladesh with 52 publications.

Indonesia, Saudi Arabia, the United States, Pakistan, Thailand, Egypt, and the Philippines complete the top 10 with respective contributions of 42, 26, 21, 20, 19, 15, and 12 publications. Although these countries do not produce as much as India or China, their involvement in research on this topic is noteworthy.

This geographical distribution of publications highlights the global interest in rice health research and underscores the international efforts to improve the detection and treatment of rice diseases through artificial intelligence.

Table 4. Top 10 Scientific Producing Countries

Region	Frequence
INDIA	608
CHINA	232
BANGLADESH	52
INDONESIA	42
SAUDI ARABIA	26
USA	21
PAKISTAN	20
THAILAND	19
EGYPT	15
PHILIPPINES	12

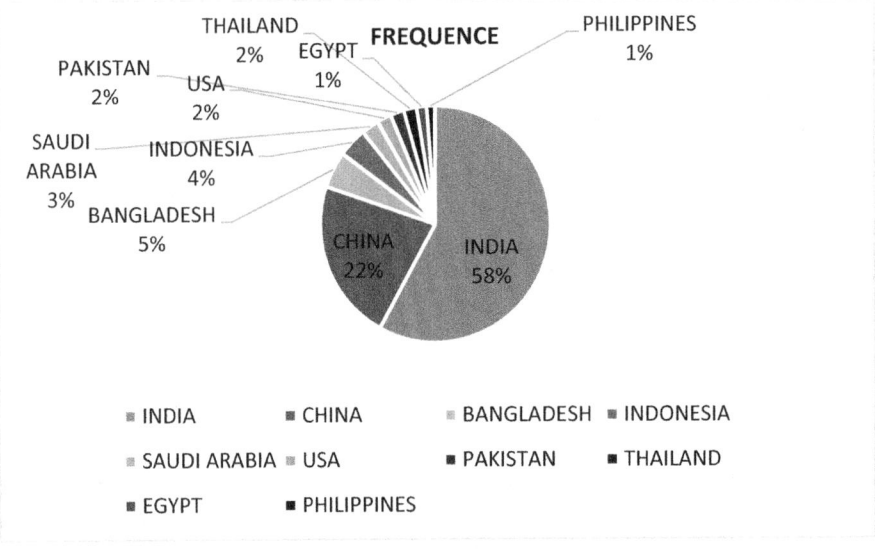

Fig. 6. Top 10 Most Cited Countries

Table 5 also shows that the two most cited countries in our database are India and China. Furthermore, it is noteworthy that compared to the list of the most productive countries, some countries like Bangladesh, Malaysia, the USA, Saudi Arabia, Thailand, Ethiopia, Australia, and Indonesia are among the top 10 most cited countries.

Table 5. Top 10 Most Cited Countries

Rank	Country	Number of Citations	Average Citations
1	INDIA 1927		10,50
2	CHINA	1758	20,4
3	BANGLADESH	474	26,30
4	MALAYSIA	238	39,7
5	USA	180	60,00
6	SAUDI ARABIA	105	21
7	THAILAND	99	14,10
8	ETHIOPIA	41	20,5
9	AUSTRALIA	32	10,70
10	INDONESIA	23	2,3

4 Discussion

This section reviews previous bibliometrics reviews and scientific articles on the topic and their limitations in order to identify future directions for our research.

4.1 State of the Art

In the Scopus database, few bibliometric articles on smart agriculture have been written in Africa, especially on cultivation of rice. Different categories of study have been identified from the literature review.

Digital Agriculture in West Africa

The study conducted by Degila et al. (2023) [15] focused on the bibliometric analysis of digital agriculture in five West African countries: Benin, Burkina Faso, Côte d'Ivoire, Ghana, and Nigeria. The main objective of this research was to examine the impact of digital technologies on agricultural practices. The findings highlighted the growing adoption of technologies such as artificial intelligence (AI), the Internet of Things (IoT), and blockchain in these countries. This trend has been particularly evident since 2014, a period during which significant interest in these technologies was observed. These digital tools are progressively transforming agricultural methods by providing innovative solutions to address challenges related to production.

Plant Disease Detection

Bonkra et al. (2023) [16] conducted a bibliometric analysis on the use of deep learning for diagnosing apple leaf diseases. The findings revealed a significant increase in the number of publications on this topic since 2017, reflecting a growing interest in disease detection algorithms. These algorithms leverage deep learning techniques to enhance the accuracy and efficiency of identifying diseases affecting apple leaves, highlighting the potential of advanced artificial intelligence methods in agricultural disease management.

Drone Technologies in Agriculture

The study performed by Slimani et al. (2024) [17] explores the use of drones equipped with artificial intelligence (AI) for precision agriculture. These drones are employed in various applications, including crop monitoring, precision irrigation, and environmental detection. The findings highlight the transformative potential of this technology in revolutionizing agricultural practices. By providing real-time data and improving decision-making processes, AI-powered drones offer innovative solutions to enhance productivity, optimize resource use, and address environmental challenges in the agricultural sector.

IoT and AI Convergence in Agriculture

The study done by Soni et al. (2023) [18] examines the impact of the Internet of Things (IoT) and artificial intelligence (AI) across various sectors, including agriculture. The findings emphasize that the integration of AI facilitates deep data analysis and accurate predictions, enabling significant improvements in agricultural practices. By leveraging these technologies, farmers can make informed decisions about crop management, resource allocation, and disease prevention, ultimately enhancing productivity and sustainability in the agricultural sector.

Artificial Intelligence in Agriculture

Karmaoui (2023) in [19] focuses on mapping academic contributions to the applications of artificial intelligence (AI) in agriculture. The findings reveal steady research growth in this field since 1979, with a notable peak in 2020. The dominant areas of focus include machine learning, the Internet of Things (IoT), and big data, highlighting their pivotal roles in advancing agricultural practices. These technologies have been instrumental in addressing key challenges such as optimizing resource use, enhancing productivity, and improving decision-making processes in the agricultural sector.

Table 6 summarizes key information on the state of the art.

Table 6. State of the Art

Main Theme	Key Studies	Technologies or Methodologies	Key Findings
Digital Agriculture in Africa	Degila et al. (2023) [15]	Bibliometric study, AI, IoT, Blockchain	Growth since 2014, increasing adoption of advanced technologies
Plant Disease Detection	Bonkra et al. (2023) [16]	Deep Learning, Detection Algorithms	Effective algorithms for diagnosing plant diseases, rising research since 2017

(*continued*)

Table 6. (*continued*)

Main Theme	Key Studies	Technologies or Methodologies	Key Findings
Drones in Agriculture	Slimani et al. (2024) [17]	Drones, AI, Precision Agriculture	Enhanced agricultural management and environmental monitoring
IoT and AI Convergence	Soni et al. (2023) [18]	IoT, AI, Machine Learning (ML)	Optimization of agricultural practices through predictive analytics
AI in Agriculture	Karmaoui (2023) [19]	Bibliometric study, Machine Learning, Big Data	Exploration of dominant trends since 1979, with a peak in 2020

4.2 Detection and Treatment of Plant Disease: A Survey

Numerous scientific articles have been written over the years on the use of AI in agriculture. Here, we will present a few of them along with their limitations, which we will supplement with a literature review in future work.

Support Vector Machine (SVM) Based Approaches

(Hamdy, Walid., 2023) [20] presents a model for detecting rice leaf diseases (Oryza sativa L.) using a Support Vector Machine (SVM) classifier, optimized by the particle swarm optimization (PSO) algorithm. The proposed model achieves an impressive 98.89% accuracy in detecting rice leaf diseases. The model has demonstrated its effectiveness in classifying three rice leaf diseases: brown spot, leaf smut, and bacterial leaf blight. It is a powerful tool for managing rice diseases, with strong potential for application in agriculture. The model requires advanced technological infrastructures and high-quality data, which may be challenging in regions like sub-Saharan Africa where access to modern equipment and reliable connectivity is limited. The article does not sufficiently discuss the integration of this model into mobile applications or decision support systems for farmers.

Convolutional Neural Networks (CNNs) Based Approaches

The model proposed by Alford & Tuba, (2024) [21] is based on transfer learning and Convolutional Neural Networks (CNNs). The authors tested and compared several pre-trained models, including ResNet101V2, ResNet50V2, EfficientNetB2, VGG16, VGG19, and MobileNet2, and selected VGG19 as the base model, which was then fine-tuned for cassava disease classification. The final model achieved 99.31% accuracy during training and 80.27% accuracy during testing over 50 epochs.

The model outperformed previous studies, making a notable contribution to the field of automated cassava disease detection, particularly by leveraging transfer learning for small, imbalanced datasets. The drop in accuracy from training (99.31%) to testing (80.27%) suggests some overfitting to the training data, indicating room for improvement, especially with test data.

The study could benefit from a deeper discussion on the practical application of this model in real agricultural environments, including challenges such as detecting diseases under varying lighting conditions, integrating the model into portable devices or mobile applications for local farmers, and improving robustness in diverse agricultural contexts.

The study performed by Tanaka, Yu, (2023) [22] presents an innovative approach based on deep learning to instantaneously estimate rice yields (Oryza sativa L.) using red-green-blue (RGB) color images captured from the ground. A Convolutional Neural Network (CNN) is used to predict yield variations from images taken 0.8 to 0.9 m above the rice canopy in harvest plots. The model predicted 68% of yield variation with a relative mean squared error of 0.22. It detected genotypic differences and assessed the impact of agronomic interventions on yields in an independent dataset. The model was robust against different shooting angles (up to 30° from perpendicular), varying light conditions, and shooting dates during late maturation. Even with reduced image resolution (from 0.2 to 3.2 cm pixel − 1), it predicted 57% of yield variation, suggesting the approach could be extended to the use of unmanned aerial vehicles (UAVs). The article does not sufficiently discuss the practical challenges of applying this model in real agricultural environments, especially concerning ground data collection and UAV integration. The impact of terrain variations, such as soil texture or planting density, is not explored in depth, which could affect the model's performance. Furthermore, the effectiveness of this method in diverse agricultural contexts or regions with limited infrastructure is not fully addressed.

The article proposed by Akinlolu et al., (2023) [23] presents the use of convolutional neural networks (CNN) in developing an intelligent mobile system for diagnosing yam diseases. The system is integrated with a graphical user interface (GUI) developed using JAVA/XML, allowing users to detect three yam disease categories: yam anthracnose, yam mosaic virus, and healthy plants. The CNN model achieved an overall accuracy of 81.7% on test data. The mobile system aims to address the significant drop in yam productivity in West Africa, providing a useful tool for farmers to improve their yields and diagnose diseases quickly. The system's accessible design through a mobile platform is key in tackling the urgent issue of declining yam production, particularly in Nigeria. While the 81.7% accuracy is promising, it raises concerns about the model's robustness in real-world conditions, such as variations in cultivation and environmental factors. A comparison with other approaches, like machine learning models or different neural network architectures, would have added value. The study does not address potential limitations, such as the need for an internet connection or technical infrastructure that some farmers may lack. It would have been beneficial to gather feedback from potential users on the app's usability and functionality to better understand its practical impact on farmers' work.

Spatiotemporal Survey

The study by Barro et al., (2021) [24] focuses on spatiotemporal surveys to assess the variations in rice diseases caused by viral, bacterial, and fungal pathogens across different cropping systems in West Africa. The study spans four years and compares rice diseases in irrigated areas and rainfed lowlands using robust observational techniques. Significant differences in rice disease incidence were observed between the two cropping systems, with higher infection rates in irrigated areas, especially for diseases like bacterial leaf streak and leaf blast. In irrigated zones, practices such as rice transplantation and double cropping are common, while other practices like the use of registered cultivars and fertilizer application vary depending on the farming context. Diseases such as brown spot and yellow mottle disease have clear geographical patterns, highlighting the need for understanding ecological interactions for better disease management. The study's methodological approach could be improved by exploring the environmental and socio-economic factors that influence disease incidence and farmers' practices in more detail. The coexistence of multiple diseases in the same field or on the same plant requires further investigation, as it could impact integrated disease management strategies. While the study provides valuable insights into a specific region, the generalizability of the findings to other areas in West Africa should be explored to increase the applicability of the research recommendations.

5 Conclusion and Future Work

The primary objective of this study was to provide an overview of the current level of research on the use of Artificial Intelligence (AI) for the detection and treatment of rice diseases. By employing a bibliometric analysis of data sets extracted from the Scopus database, we were able to derive valuable information such as annual scientific production, the most prolific sources, countries, as well as the most-cited documents and authors.

The results show that India and China are the two most productive countries in terms of scientific publications in this field. This dominance indicates a strong interest and significant investments by researchers from these countries in applying AI to rice disease management.

On the other hand, it is crucial for research conducted in less developed countries to address the existing gap by providing more information on the specific challenges faced by these regions. The four most prolific sources identified are "Lecture Notes in Networks and Systems," "Frontiers in Plant Science," "Multimedia Tools and Applications," and "IEEE Access." This highlights the importance of these journals in disseminating advancements in the detection and treatment of rice diseases.

In future work, we will complement this analysis with a more comprehensive literature review on the topic and identify various AI technologies and models suitable for the detection and treatment of rice diseases. Furthermore, it would be beneficial to further explore the integration of these technologies to develop more effective and resilient crop management systems, thereby enabling rapid and precise intervention for managing rice diseases in Benin.

References

1. Liu, H., Cui, Y., Wang, J., Yu, H.: Analysis and research on rice disease identification method based on deep learning. Sustainability **15**(12), 9321 (2023). https://doi.org/10.3390/su15129321
2. Shah, J.P., Prajapati, H.B., Dabhi, V.K.: A survey on detection and classification of rice plant diseases. In: 2016 IEEE International Conference on Current Trends in Advanced Computing (ICCTAC), pp. 1–8 (2016). https://doi.org/10.1109/ICCTAC.2016.7567333
3. Siddarajamma, B., Praveen Kumar, M.S., Sivaprasad, N., Boranna, R.: Machine learning-based approach to detect and classify rice blast disease. In: 2022 IEEE 2nd Mysore Sub Section International Conference (MysuruCon), pp. 1–6 (2022). https://doi.org/10.1109/MysuruCon55714.2022.9972605
4. Liu, Y., Li, M.: Bibe: a web-based tool for bibliometric analysis in scientific. PeerJ PrePrints (2016). https://doi.org/10.7287/peerj.preprints.1879v1
5. Rahman, C.R., et al.: Identification and recognition of rice diseases and pests using convolutional neural networks. Biosyst. Eng. **194**, 112–120 (2020). https://doi.org/10.1016/j.biosystemseng.2020.03.020
6. Jiang, F., Lu, Y., Chen, Y., Cai, D., Li, G.: Image recognition of four rice leaf diseases based on deep learning and support vector machine. Comput. Electron. Agric. **179**, 105824 (2020). https://doi.org/10.1016/j.compag.2020.105824
7. Liang, W., Zhang, H., Zhang, G., Cao, H.: Rice blast disease recognition using a deep convolutional neural network. Sci. Rep. **9**(1) (2019). https://doi.org/10.1038/s41598-019-38966-0
8. Li, D., et al.: A recognition method for rice plant diseases and pests video detection based on deep convolutional neural network. Sensors **20**(3), 578 (2020). https://doi.org/10.3390/s20030578
9. Chen, J., Zhang, D., Nanehkaran, Y.A., Li, D.: Detection of rice plant diseases based on deep transfer learning. J. Sci. Food Agric. **100**(7), 3246–3256 (2020). https://doi.org/10.1002/jsfa.10365
10. Ahmed, K., Shahidi, T.R., Irfanul Alam, S.Md., Momen, S.: Rice Leaf disease detection using machine learning techniques. In: 2019 International Conference on Sustainable Technologies for Industry 4.0 (STI), pp. 1–5 (2019). https://doi.org/10.1109/STI47673.2019.9068096
11. Shrivastava, V.K., Pradhan, M.K.: Rice plant disease classification using color features: a machine learning paradigm. J. Plant Pathol. **103**(1), 17–26 (2021). https://doi.org/10.1007/s42161-020-00683-3
12. Krishnamoorthy, N., Narasimha Prasad, L.V., Pavan Kumar, C.S., Subedi, B., Abraha, H.B., Sathish Kumar, V.E.: Rice leaf diseases prediction using deep neural networks with transfer learning. Environ. Res. **198**, 111275 (2021). https://doi.org/10.1016/j.envres.2021.111275
13. Shrivastava, V.K., Pradhan, M.K., Minz, S., Thakur, M.P.: Rice plant disease classification using transfer learning of deep convolution neural network. Int. Arch. Photogram. Remote Sens. Spatial Inf. Sci. **XLII-3/W6**, 631–635 (2019). https://doi.org/10.5194/isprs-archives-XLII-3-W6-631-2019
14. Wang, Y., Wang, H., Peng, Z.: Rice diseases detection and classification using attention based neural network and Bayesian optimization. Expert Syst. Appl. **178**, 114770 (2021). https://doi.org/10.1016/j.eswa.2021.114770
15. Degila, J., et al.: A survey on digital agriculture in five west African countries. Agriculture **13**(5), 1067 (2023). https://doi.org/10.3390/agriculture13051067
16. Bonkra, A., Bhatt, P.K., Kaur, A., Kamboj, S.: Scientific landscape and the road ahead for deep learning: apple leaves disease detection. In: 2023 International Conference on Artificial Intelligence and Smart Communication (AISC), pp. 869–873 (2023). https://doi.org/10.1109/AISC56616.2023.10085221

17. Slimani, H., El Mhamdi, J., Jilbab, A.: Assessing the advancement of artificial intelligence and drones' integration in agriculture through a bibliometric study. Int. J. Electr. Comput. Eng. **14**(1), 878 (2024). https://doi.org/10.11591/ijece.v14i1.pp878-890
18. Soni, T., Gupta, D., Uppal, M., Gupta, G.: Mapping the scientific landscape of internet of things and artificial intelligence using VOSViewer. In: 2023 International Conference on IoT, Communication and Automation Technology (ICICAT), pp. 1–4 (2023). https://doi.org/10.1109/ICICAT57735.2023.10263692
19. Karmaoui, A.: The Future of Artificial Intelligence in Agricultural Field, pp. 71–94 (2023). https://doi.org/10.4018/978-1-6684-4649-2.ch003
20. Hamdy, W., Ismail, A., Awad, W.A., Ibrahim, A.H., Hassanien, A.E.: A support vector machine model for rice (Oryza sativa L.) leaf diseases based on particle swarm optimization. Stud. Comput. Intell. **1000**, 45–54 (2023). https://doi.org/10.1007/978-3-031-13702-0_4
21. Alford, J., Tuba, E.: Cassava plant disease detection using transfer learning with convolutional neural networks. In Varol, A., Karabatak, M., Varol, C., Tuba, E. (eds.) 12th International Symposium on Digital Forensics and Security, ISDFS 2024. Institute of Electrical and Electronics Engineers Inc. (2024). https://doi.org/10.1109/ISDFS60797.2024.10527320
22. Tanaka, Y., et al.: Deep learning enables instant and versatile estimation of rice yield using ground-based RGB images. Plant Phenomics **5** (2023). https://doi.org/10.34133/PLANTPHENOMICS.0073
23. Akinlolu, A.O., Odejobi, O.A., Ajayi, F.O., Jimoh, E.R.: Mobile-based deep learning for yam disease diagnosis. In: 2023 International Conference on Science, Engineering and Business for Sustainable Development Goals, SEB-SDG 2023 (2023). https://doi.org/10.1109/SEB-SDG57117.2023.10124483
24. Barro, M., et al.: Spatiotemporal survey of multiple rice diseases in irrigated areas compared to rainfed lowlands in the western burkina Faso. Plant Dis. **105**(12), 3889 (2021). https://doi.org/10.1094/PDIS-03-21-0579-RE

An Edge-AI-Based Monitoring of Rift Valley Fever Vectors Using Deep Learning

Aboubacry Hamat Ba[1], Dame Diongue[1(✉)], Maissa Mbaye[1], Ousmane Dieng[2], Nicolas Djighnoum Diouf[3], Mariama Sene-Wade[3], Ndeye Mery Dia Badiane[4], Mamadou Ciss[5], and Assane G. Fall[5]

[1] Laboratoire d'Analyse Numerique et Informatique/LANI, CEA-MITIC, Gaston Berger University, Saint-Louis 234, Senegal
{dame.diongue,maissa.mbaye}@ugb.edu.sn

[2] Power-management and Real-Time Systems Lab, University of Pittsburgh, Pittsburgh, PA 15260, USA
oud5@pitt.edu

[3] Department of Animal Husbandry and Livestock, Animal Health and Feeding, Faculty of Agronomic Sciences, Aquaculture and Food Technologies, Gaston Berger University, Saint-Louis, Senegal
{nicolas-djighnoum.diouf,ndeye-mery.dia}@ugb.edu.sn

[4] UFR Santé, Université Gaston Berger, Saint-Louis, Senegal
ndeye-mery.dia@ugb.edu.sn

[5] Laboratoire National de l'Elevage et de Recherches Vétérinaires, Institut Sénégalais de Recherches Agricoles (ISRA), Dakar-Hann 2057, Senegal

Abstract. Rift Valley Fever (among other zoonosis) have been worth to monitor from different bodies (Research, Governments, WHO, FAO, WOAH, etc.). However, traditional monitoring system based on the public health system lacks efficiency for different reasons (amount of data collected and their real-time nature). Several solutions based on AI/ML and Deep Learning (DL) have been proposed recently (sample processing, detection of environmental factors, vector monitoring, etc.). However, providing large data collections (in real time if possible) and reliable for these DL based solutions is a big challenge. In this paper we address and propose to monitor RVF vectors (*Aedes*, *Anopheles* and *Culex*) using an Edge-AI Framework for Citizen science. It mainly consists of a mobile application deployed on the smartphone of breeders, citizens, volunteers and clinicians. The mobile application embeds a customized DL model for RVF vector classification. The main outcomes of this paper are: *i)* design of an Edge-AI framework for data collection and vector monitoring; *ii)* a deep learning model for mosquito species classification to facilitate citizen science and *iii)* a mobile application embedding the ML Model. Efficientnet0, MobileNetV2 and Resnet50 has been tested for vector classification and we achieved an accuracy of 95.56% with a tuned and modified version of MobileNetV2 with the benefit of being mobile app friendly with a lighter size and faster.

Keywords: Mosquito vector classification and monitoring · Rift Valley Fever · Artificial Intelligence · Edge-AI · Deep Learning · Mobile Application · Zoonosis surveillance · One Health

1 Introduction

Rift Valley Fever (RVF) is one of the zoonoses closely monitored by international organizations, including the World Health Organization (WHO), the World Organization of Animal Health (WOAH), and the Food and Agriculture Organization (FAO). RVF is an acute disease affecting wild and domestic ruminants as well as humans, caused by a *Phlebovirus* virus transmitted by mosquito vectors or through direct contact with organs or fluids of infected animals.

The disease has been observed in parts of the African continent, Madagascar, various other islands in the Indian Ocean, and the Arabian Peninsula. Major outbreaks of Rift Valley fever occurred in Egypt (1977–78 and 1993), Mauritania (1987), Madagascar (199091), and Kenya and Somalia (1997) [33]. RVF was recognised for the first time outside of the African continent in 2000, with reported outbreaks in Saudi Arabia and Yemen [3,4]. Recent outbreaks were reported in Botswana, Mauritania and Mozambique in 2014, and in Comoros and Saudi Arabia in 2015 (and previous years). There are a few other African countries which reporter not suspected cases of RVF. More recent outbreaks occurred in countries such as Mauritania in 2020 [2]. According to the WHO, the virus has been present in the sub-region since 2020 [33].

The traditional surveillance system is based on the public health system with sampling campaigns and case reports after validation. This method is certainly very reliable but it lacks efficiency because of the costs that limit the amount of data collected, requires a lot of time to be spent on site, concentration of technical staff in urban areas in countries like Senegal. Moreover, vectors distribution, climate change, and land use dynamics can alter the temporal and spatial distribution of cases.

To address this problem, artificial intelligence seems to be a very promising solution. Several solutions based on artificial intelligence have been proposed. They range from diagnostic assistance to analyze samples, detection of favorable environmental factors, vector monitoring

However, the main difficulty is the collection of data continuously and over a sufficiently long period to detect important signals early enough. Efficient and low-cost data collection systems and shared databases can make it possible to consider the production of effective solutions.

In this paper, we propose a solution for monitoring RVF by vectors using a framework that uses the concept of Edge-AI to implement a collection system based on Citizen science. It mainly consists of a mobile application that is deployed on the smartphone of breeders, citizens and technicians for data collection. The application embeds a machine learning model based on MobileNetV2 customized for the classification and recognition of mosquito species

The contributions of this paper are threefold:

- The first contribution is an EDGE-AI architecture allowing the collection and processing of data at three levels: the collection level, the Edge level and the cloud level. Each level contains a more or less complex AI model to process the data. The objective is to allow the participation of non-expert people in the collection without having to delve into the technical aspects.
- The second contribution is the development of an AI/ML model for the classification of species of Rift Valley fever vectors. The aim of this model is to allow collectors to not need to recognize the species and to directly send information on mosquitoes by sending photos of the mosquitoes observed. The model that was developed to an accuracy of 95.56
- Finally a mobile application on which the AI / ML model is embedded to allow the collection of mosquito images and at the same time the identification of species. The goal is to be able to detect the presence of species at different locations.

2 Problem Statement: Vector Based Epidemiological Monitoring for RVF

2.1 Rational

Rift Valley fever is a disease that can have severe symptoms in both humans and small ruminants. The modes of transmission to humans and animals differ. In humans, the infection is transmitted through two main pathways: direct contact with blood or organs of infected animals, particularly during slaughter, or ingestion of contaminated meat or unpasteurized milk from infected animals [2].

In animals, infection is primarily transmitted through mosquito bites (*Aedes* spp. and *Culex* spp.) [4] and results in significant mortality among young ruminants and induces abortion in pregnant animals [25]. Detection of Rift Valley fever cases, as part of epidemiological monitoring, involves identifying both suspected and confirmed cases in animals or humans in the field. Clinical suspicion in humans is primarily based on the clinical presentation of the disease (axiliary temperature $\leq 37.5°$ C as well as hemorrhagic and neurological symptoms). Suspected cases in animals may be raised by observing abortions or deaths in young ruminants less than two months old during periods of the year favorable to Rift Valley Fever (August-December) [2].

For the final confirmation of Rift Valley fever cases, laboratory diagnosis through serology or genomic detection methods is required, which necessitates the collection of blood samples. additionally, mosquitoes are captured and analyzed to facilitate the identification of vector species and their virulence [2].

This approach to data collection of epidemiological monitoring of Rift Valley fever under these conditions presents several efficiency challenges.

First, Early detection of an epidemic is challenging due the slow confirmation of cases, which can result to the loss of early warning signals. The significant distances between the epidemic hotspots and laboratories can exacerbate disease spread. Consequently, vaccination may no longer be advised.

Second, sampling requirements hinder the collection of large-scale data due to lack of resources in the affected regions. Often, epidemic confirmation occurs only once the outbreak is already well underway. This data collection is more useful for retrospective of the disease's mechanisms.

Third, real-time detection of changes is highly challenging, including fluctuations in vector population, their movements, or the emergence of new species.

Fourth, data collection is frequently conducted through campaigns, which means it is neither continuous nor geographically widespread. This data insufficiency often necessitates extrapolations, leading to potential information loss.

Effective strategies exist for detecting early signals of an epidemic and issuing timely warnings:

- Real-time detection of suspected cases and their cross-referencing with relevant data;
- Tracking environmental conditions favorable to vector-borne disease development;
- Monitoring vectors dynamics among hematophagous insects - insects that suck human blood.

We propose engaging end-users and citizen volunteers in northern Senegal Fig. 1 to continuously and in real-time collect early signals of an epidemic outbreak, including suspected cases and vector monitoring. The system is based on an Edge AI architecture, integrating a mobile application for data collection with machine learning models for mosquito species identification. Federating machine learning models from Edge nodes enables the development of alert-triggering models.

2.2 Mosquito Species Classification

Mosquitoes are among the vectors responsible for the spread of arbovisus diseases (Zika, Dengue, Chikungunya, Yellow Fever, Rift Valley Fever), which significantly impact human health [11,27]. Traditional epidemiology systems encounter difficulties in maintaining effective surveillance, primarily due challenge of data collection and validation. Citizen science initiatives and platforms have been established to address these challenges, with most notable being Global Mosquito Alert [10]. Citizen Science involves of enlisting volunteer participants, with or without prior training, and communities interested in mosquito-related issues to collaborate with experts and scientists (epidemiologists, entomologists, public health, ecologists, etc.) in the collection and validation of mosquito surveillance data across various scales [7].

Regarding technological platforms, participants have access to mobile applications for uploading various types of data, such as forms, reports, photos, audio, and web applications for expert or trained citizen validation. Depending on the initiative, the validation process may involve all data or a representative sample, with or without the use of artificial intelligence for species recognition and population quantification [38].

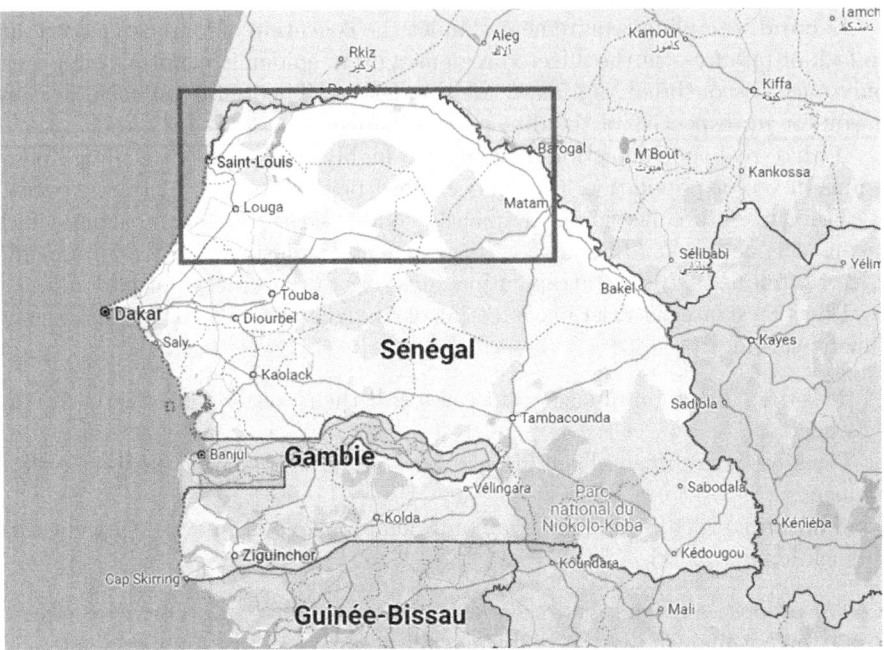

Fig. 1. Region of study: Northern Senegal, West Africa.

The collected data may concern monitoring the mosquito populations, including the number of adults and their location; assessing biodiversity, including genetic and species diversity; ecological data, such as the census of habitats favorable to larval development and breeding sites; and identifying the intensity of mosquito biting activity or noise nuisances (e.g. wing beats) on humans and animals. Example of projects include Zanzamapp [5], Mugguen Radar [35], Muekenatlas [37], and the Invasive Mosquito Project [16]. This approach provides several advantages: It enables data collection at multiple scales (local, national, global) and includes access to private data or data previously inaccessible to the research community such as in-home counting; It also reduces of costs associated with collection campaigns and allows for the establishment of a global mosquito monitoring system.

The applications of such platform can be broadly categorized into four areas.

- The establishment of early warning systems;
- Raising awareness and issuing warnings to populations and communities;
- Real-time monitoring of vectors;
- Education and research.

3 Related Work

According to the WHO [30], vector-borne diseases account for around 17% of all infectious diseases, causing over 700,000 deaths a year. These diseases are transmitted via bacteria, parasites or viruses. In this study, we focus on the vectors of viral diseases [8,13] such as chikungunya fever, Zika virus fever, yellow fever, West Nile fever, Japanese encephalitis; all caused by mosquitoes. As a result, mosquito surveillance is attracting increasing interest as part of global health initiatives. A number of works in the literature have addressed this issue, using a variety of approaches [13]:

3.1 Traditional Mosquito Monitoring

Traditional surveillance which generally involves placing traps [6,20–24,32] in habitats to capture mosquitoes. These range from basic traps to those using biochemical attractants to attract more mosquitoes. The species captured are then identified and classified by an entomologist. This approach appears to be very reliable, providing not only an estimate of the mosquito population but also the identification of species in a given area. However, there is a considerable time lag between setting the traps, collection and identification, which could allow the development of certain species such as *Aedes*, which can generally reach maturity after three days, depending on environmental conditions. So, in this paper, we give more attention to technological solutions using machine learning.

3.2 Modern ICT Oriented Monitoring

In recent years, the monitoring of mosquitoes to combat vector-borne diseases has attracted an increasing number of researchers using machine learning methods [9,14,18] such as convolutional neural networks (CNN, RNN, LSTM, etc.), decision trees and so on. This monitoring approach consists of collecting data (images, habitats, sound recordings of wing beats, etc.) and then processing them using machine learning to identify species and attempt to estimate population dynamics. Work on technological tools often focuses on the analysis of images (eggs, larvae or adult) or simply mosquito wing beats. Authors in [12] present a synthesis of new technological surveillance methods based on acoustic or optical wing beats data and those using intelligent traps.

Audio Data Approaches: In [36] Toledo et al. propose a classification of mosquito genera using a deep learning model (LSTM) to extract time-frequency characteristics from the wing-beat sound of three mosquito genera (*Aedes*, *Culex* and *Anopheles*). Khalighifar et al. [19] propose to record wing beats and then perform classification using TensorFlow embedded in a mobile application. They propose community-Science-Based surveillance to detect vector presence using a mobile application to identify the presence of vectors and also detect novel species.

Visual Data Approaches : Several studies in the literature try to tacle vector proliferation by capturing image of mosquito's eggs for identification and/or quantification.

- **methods using mosquito eggs:** Javed et al. in [17] developed EggCountAI to identify *Aedes* aegypti eggs. Their solution uses RCNN to detect and count eggs. This permit to identify favorable habitat for mosquito reproduction and gives an idea of mosquito fecondity by counting the number eggs laid by female *Aedes*. In [9] Pedro Saint Clair Garcia et al. use ovitrap coupled with a camera for trapping *Aedes* aegypti mosquito. Captured images are then classified using CNN to detect and count eggs laid by female *Aedes*. Their study was done in a close environment (Laboratory area).
- **methods using mosquito larvae:** As part of the surveillance of Dengue fever cases in Malaysia, Asmai et al. [1] use 4 deep learning models (VGG16, VGG19, ResNet50 and InceptionV3) to identify the larvae of the *Aedes* mosquito. As a result of their work, the RestNet50 model offers better performance, particularly in terms of size, and proves suitable for deployment on a mobile application. In the same vein, Sanchez-Ortiz et al. [34] propose a CNN-based identification with two classes of larvae based on the 8th segment of *Aedes* images. In Brazil, a study on Dengue fever led Martins et al. [28] to take action against the proliferation of *Aedes* aegypti, *Aedes* albopictus and *Culex* egg-laying sites. In their work, they propose to develop a Deep Learning model to detect the incriminating species using larval images. To do this, they compare several Deep Learning models based on cell phone images.
- **methods using adult images:** Similar to the work presented in this paper, Huang et al. propose in [15] a method for classifying disease-vector mosquitoes by combining Edge Computing and deep learning, with the difference that they work on the basis of *Aedes* and *Culex* images captured with a trap embedding a smart camera. Their solution consists of an intelligent trap called Smart Mosquito Zapper (SMZ) to capture and film mosquitoes (*Aedes* and *Culex*). The recordings obtained from SMZ are then processed through a convolutional neural network (CNN) for mosquito classification. However, the concern with this work is that it is difficult to reproduce in a natural environment, as the dataset is made up of only 2 classes (*Aedes* and *Culex*) and this can add a biases on the model's performance, with many false positives. In the similar vein, Okayasu et al. [29] propose a mosquito classification solution working with a dataset of 14,400 images made up of 3 species. To achieve this, they use two classification methods: a conventional method based on handcrafted features and a deep learning method based on convolutional neural networks. The conventional method relies on SVM to detect the main characteristics of each species from images, while the deep learning method uses convolutional neural networks to classify the species studied (*Aedes*, *Culex* and *Anopheles*). In their study [39], Zhao et al. take a broader view, proposing a transformer-based Swin MSI covering the identification of 17 mosquito species. Compared with other works in the literature, Swin MSI goes into

greater detail on identification, as it can identify mosquito subspecies with very acceptable performance.

4 Edge AI Framework for Vector Monitoring

4.1 General Architecture

Our proposal for a mosquito population monitoring system framework, vectors, is based on a three-level architecture: collection layer, Edge AI layer and cloud-Fog layer. These three levels allow, via the monitoring of vectors that are mosquitoes, to have an indirect assessment of the risk of emergence of an episode of Rift Valley fever epidemic. The main interest of these sofas is to have progressive treatment levels, from the most localized to the most global.

The Collection Layer represents the surveillance area or are deployed in the field (mosquito capture cages) and mobile devices embedding an application provided to breeders and volunteers participating in the citizen collection. The types of data are mainly geographic data (geolocation) in order to locate the collection area, images of mosquitoes (to identify the species present in the area and the size and dynamics of the vector population), and finally recordings of mosquito wing beats (when it is sufficiently audible). The devices embed a Deep Learning model for the automatic recognition of mosquito species, allowing efforts to be focused on collection rather than validation. These are nano models for making fairly simple AI predictions such as species recognition and possibly counting the number of individuals observed. The deployed smart mosquito traps are equipped with a trap camera that monitors the presence and number of specimens. A microcontroller will be used to take photos and extract data (geolocation, species and number of individuals, possibly weather). This device can temporarily store data when the network is not available or while waiting for manual collection by a technician and it will allow technicians to count the number of trips to the traps while monitoring larger areas. The data on vectors is also collected through the deployment of smartphones embedding an application and a Machine Learning model for species recognition and reporting of suspected cases. The owners of these smartphones are breeders and volunteer citizens from the northern part of Senegal.

The collection frequency can be less than 10 images per day and the transmission can be done via a mobile network, Lora, WiFi or bluetooth to transfer it to another manual collection device (Fig. 2).

The Second Level is the Edge-AI level. These are servers and small computers that are between 20 and 100 milliseconds away from the collection area. Each Edge-AI server is responsible for specific areas, making the models produced very specific and geographically located. This responsibility consists of creating data sets made up of data sent back (images, suspicious case reports) by devices (mobile and traps) in the collection area concerned, as well as updating the model deployed as the size of the data set increases. This is therefore the back-end of the embedded applications deployed in the field. The models created in the different areas are combined via Federated Learning in order to do

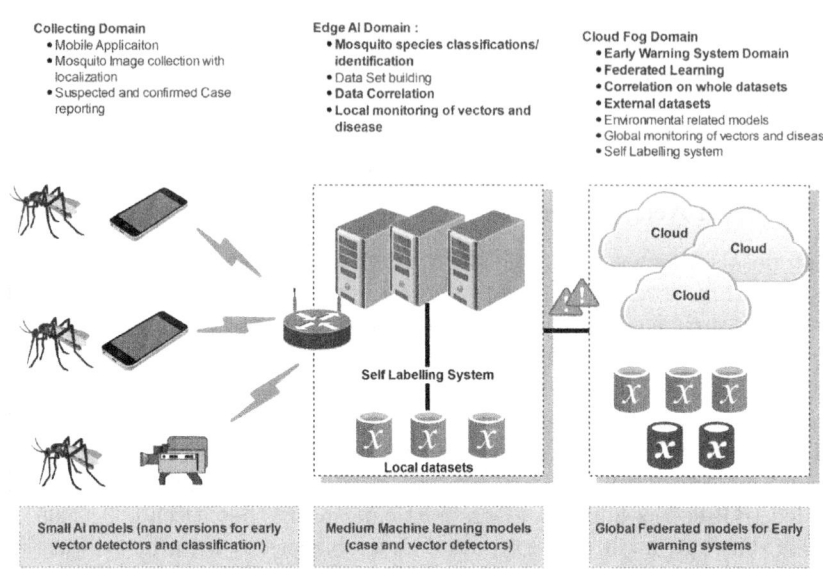

Fig. 2. Edge AI Vector Monitoring architecture.

more complex AI processing such as self-labeling of images, detection of progressive changes, global phenomena (mosquito population displacement, invasive species, overpopulation, etc.) and global correlations (suspicion of a species being a vector). For processing and storage capacities depending on the life cycle of mosquitoes, it is necessary to count between 1 and 5 images per day maximum per collector and over one-year cycles.

Finally, the Third Level is the Cloud. The framework uses the cloud to be able to do processing that requires greater computing or storage power than what is available on the Edge, to do the federation of machine learning models on a larger scale to be able to have global trends and a global early warning system. The cloud level can, for example, allow us to see changes in the territory of mosquitoes and their movements in different areas over time, then to detect correlations between the presence of certain species and the number of cases, but also to direct sampling on the animal and human population of public health services.

5 Methodology of Data Collection and Processing

The methodology about data is done via a pipeline depicted in Fig. 3 .

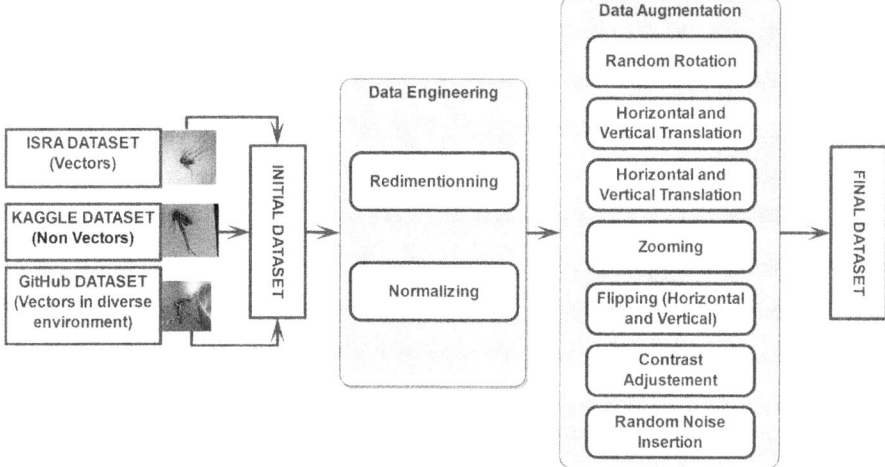

Fig. 3. Data Processing and

5.1 Data Collection

We built a mosquito image dataset using three main sources: 1. from ISRA (for images taken in a controlled environment) and 2. from GitHub to diversify the quality and background of the images and one from Kaggle to have some non vectors mosquitoes. So the main image dataset for detection comes from ISRA (Senegalese Institute of Agricultural Research) which provided us with a substantial amount high quality of data collected in controlled laboratory environments. The ISRA data is taken from a mosquito farm which is a controlled environment. Then, these images were rigorously labeled and classified by experts, which ensures reliability.

Finnaly, the initial dataset consists of 3200 raw mosquito images with a distribution according to the sources of 2000 images on Kaggle, 300 images on GitHub and 900 with ISRA.

In terms of classes, the images are divided into the following proportions into four distinct categories: 800 images of *Aedes*, 800 images of *Anopheles*, 800 images of *Culex*, and 800 images of non-vector mosquito species. In addition, the balance of proportions between categories aims to reduce the probability of overfitting.

Non-vector mosquito species include various other varieties of mosquitoes that are not associated with the three main vectors of Rift Valley fever (*Aedes*, *Anopheles*, and *Culex*). This distinction is essential because it improves the robustness of the model against false positives. The images in this class come mainly from the Kaggle the other two sources do not offer them.

Figure 4 illustrate sample of the dataset mainly from ISRA.

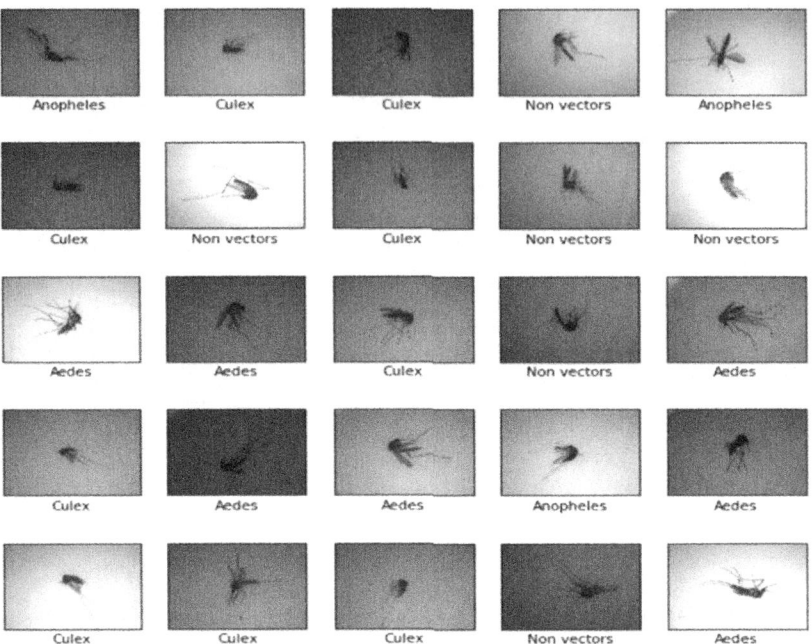

Fig. 4. Sample of Images of the resulting dataset. These shown images are mainly from ISRA.

5.2 Data Engineering and Processing

Data preprocessing is an essential step to ensure the quality and consistency of the images before using them for model training.

In this work, we performed various preprocessing operations on mosquito images, in order to improve and harmonize the dataset to prevent problems during model development.

Here we present the processing steps that were performed on the data. Here is a detailed overview of the preprocessing steps performed:

- **Image Resizing:** To ensure the consistency of the input data, all images were resized to a uniform size of 2592 × 1944 pixels. This size was chosen because it maintains a balance between sufficient resolution to identify important details of mosquitoes and the management of computing resources for processing and training the model.
- **Zooming in on Low Resolution Images:** Some of the images collected were of low resolution, making mosquitoes difficult to see. To improve the visibility of these mosquitoes, a central zoom was applied. This central zoom, with a factor of 0.8, was chosen to keep a large part of the image while focusing on the central region where mosquitoes are usually found.
- **Image Normalization:** The images were normalized in order to stabilize and speed up the training process. Normalization consists of adjusting the

pixel values so that they are between 0 and 1, which helps to avoid too large oscillations during training. This normalization is standard in image processing for CNN models.

5.3 Data Augmentation

Insufficient data can lead to overfitting, where the model performs well on the training data but fails on new data. To address this issue, we use data augmentation techniques, which not only improve the model performance but also reduce the risk of overfitting. Data augmentation generates new images from existing images by applying various transformations such as random rotation, shift, zoom, noise, lighting, contrast, and vertical and horizontal flips. However, these transformations were only applied to a portion of our dataset, precisely 140 images per category, for a total of 560 images, in order to maintain an appropriate balance and representativeness of the original data. Limiting the number of images to be augmented allows us to:

- Preserve the integrity of the original data: By limiting the data augmentation, we ensure that the model also learns from the unmodified images, which is essential to maintain the representativeness of the original data.
- Balance the dataset: Applying augmentations to all images could unbalance the dataset, making some transformations more frequent than others and potentially biasing the model.
- Ensure training efficiency: By focusing on a subset of the dataset, we can test the effectiveness of augmentations without overloading the model with excessive augmented data, which could unnecessarily extend training time.

Since deep learning requires large volumes of data, we have applied data augmentation by combining several techniques such as: random rotation, translation, zooming and flipping. We also added noise to the data, and played around with the contrast and brightness adjustments.

6 Deep Learning Model Development

6.1 Baseline Models for Transfer Learning

In the design of our deep learning model for mosquito image classification, we adopted a transfer learning approach. Transfer learning leverages models already trained on large datasets to improve the performance of a new model on a specific task. Transfer learning is based on the idea that the features extracted by a pre-trained model, which has already learned to identify generic patterns in images, can be reused for a new classification task, even if the categories of this task are different from those of the original dataset. The main advantages are to reuse rich and generalized representations learned by the pre-trained model, and the reduction of the need for large amounts of data specific to the new task and accelerating the model convergence process.

The baseline models we will use EfficientNetLite0, ResNet50, and MobileNetV2 are the potential candidates. These choices are supported by various scientific papers that highlight the effectiveness of these models in various image classification tasks. For example, [26] shows that ResNet50, EfficientNet, and MobileNetV2 achieve high accuracy in medical image classification, proving their applicability to other domains such as our case of mosquito image classification. Furthermore, [31] demonstrates that ensemble methods combining EfficientNet, MobileNet, and ResNet significantly improve classification performance, which reinforces the relevance of our model selection.

To identify the best model in this list, we will evaluate the performance of each of these models on our dataset in terms of accuracy.

Once we have identified the most efficient model, we will apply fine-tuning techniques to optimize it for mosquito classification.

6.2 Dataset Splitting Strategy

To evaluate the performance of the different models, we initially run the tests with the dataset of 6000 images, divided into training, testing and validation data according to several repartitions. In the initial configuration, we will assign 70% of the images to training, 20% to testing, and keep the remaining 10% for validation. To perform a comprehensive comparison, we will apply a full fine-tuning to the models at different stages. Full fine-tuning consists of adjusting all the parameters of the pre-trained model on a new dataset, in order to specialize the model to the specificities of the target task. Unlike a simple adjustment of the final layers, full fine-tuning optimizes all the layers of the network, thus allowing the model to be fully adapted to the new data.

We will start with a distribution where 70% of the images will be used for training, 20% for testing, and 10% for validation. Next, we will adjust the size of the sets by reducing the proportion allocated to training by 10%, while increasing the proportion dedicated to testing by 10%. This process will be repeated, gradually decreasing the size of the training set until 40% of the data is reserved for training and 50

We will then apply this process to the three selected baseline models: EfficientNetLite0, ResNet50, and MobileNetV2. The results obtained will be comprehensively reported and analyzed, allowing for a precise comparison of the performance of each model in different training and testing data configurations.

7 Results and Discussion

7.1 Baseline Model Selection for Transfer Learning

Table 1 presents a summary of the overall results of the different dataset compositions depending on the chosen model.

The results obtained from the three baseline models, EfficientNetLite0, ResNet50 and MobileNetV2, in the first dataset configuration (70% for training and 20% for testing) without fine tuning are relatively poor with respectively

Table 1. Comparison results of the precision of different models according to the dataset splitting

	Split config 1 (70% train/20% test)	Split config 2 (60% train/30% test)	Split config 3 (50% train/40% test)	Split config 4 (40% train/50% test)
EfficientNet0 (Base)	84.51%	83.76%	83.05%	82.95%
EfficientNet0 (Fine tuned)	94.37%	95.34%	95.13%	95.33%
RestNet50 (Base)	84.98%	84.53%	84.83%	84.05%
RestNet50 (Fine tuned)	96.01%	95.84%	95.18%	94.83%
MobileNetV2 (Base)	86.62%	85.67%	85.01%	84.73%
MobileNetV2 (Fine tuned)	93.31%	94.58%	94.03%	93.42%

84.51%, 84.98% and 86.62% as precision. We then fine-tuned, i.e. optimizing the hyperparameters, this boosted the respective precisions to 94.36%, 96.01% and 95.31%.

On the other hand, by gradually changing the size of the training set and increasing that of the test set, we observed that the accuracy of the models remained high despite the increase in the test data. This result indicates that the models do not suffer from overfitting and maintain their generalization ability, even when the number of training data is reduced. Furthermore, it was found that the larger the amount of training data, the higher the model accuracy. This relationship highlights the importance of having sufficient training data to maximize model performance. However, beyond accuracy performance, several other factors are crucial in the context of integrating these models into a mobile application, including prediction time and model size (Table 2).

Table 2. Comparison of models output for mobile application integration

Model	Accuracy	Prediction time on test data (s)	Prediction time on a single image (s)	Size (MByte)
EfficientNetLite0	94.36%	24	0.09	4
RestNet50	96.01%	34	0.11	25
MobileNetV2	95.31%	21	0.07	3.5

For a mobile application on Android or iOS, the size and efficiency of machine learning models are essential. Although ResNet50 achieves the highest accuracy of 96.01%, it has significant limitations for mobile devices. Its size of 25

MB and a prediction time of 34 s on the test dataset, as well as a time of 0.11 s per frame, make it too large and slow for effective use on mobile. On the other hand, MobileNetV2 and EfficientNetLite0 offer much more optimized alternatives. MobileNetV2, designed for mobile applications, shows an accuracy of 95.31%, a prediction time on the test data of 21 s, and a time of 0.07 s per frame. With a size of only 3.5 MB, it combines high accuracy with fast performance, making it an ideal option for mobile applications. EfficientNetLite0, on the other hand, achieves an accuracy of 94.36%, with a prediction time of 24 s on test data and 0.09 s per frame. Its 4 MB size also makes it suitable for mobile environments, although slightly less efficient than MobileNetV2 in terms of prediction time and accuracy. Thus, despite the slightly lower accuracy of EfficientNetLite0, MobileNetV2 emerges as the most balanced choice for a mobile application, offering an optimal combination of accuracy (95.31%), speed (21 s on test data, 0.07 s per frame), and lightness (3.5 MB). ResNet50, with its 96.01% accuracy, is more suitable for contexts where storage capacity and speed are not major constraints.

7.2 Optimization and Customization of MobileNetv2

Following the comparative study, it was found that MobileNetV2 had almost equivalent performances than ResNet50 but has a smaller size which is an advantage to be deployed on a mobile application.

To reduce the impact of this compromise we optimized the parameters of MobileNetV2 and improved its structure in order to have a higher precision.

To optimize the hyperparameters of our classification model, three main methods have to be explored: Random Search, Grid Search and Bayesian Optimization. The hyperparameter optimization calculations output the optimal hyperparameters and the layers that correspond to this for the model architecture. The result of this processing allows to reach a maximum accuracy of **95.56%** with the following output configuration:

- Learning rate (learning_rate): 0.00001
- Dropout rate for dense layers (dropout_rate_dense): 0.35
- Batch size (batch_size): 128
- Number of units in each dense layer (units_dense_layer): 256
- Number of dense layers (num_dense_layers): 5
- L2 regularization rate for dense layers (l2_reg_dense): 0.0001
- Dropout rate for convolution layers (dropout_rate_conv): 0.3
- Optimizer (optimizer): Adam
- Fine-tuning of the base model layers (fine_tuning): Enabled
- Data preprocessing (preprocessing): 'rescale'
- Number of epochs (epochs): 150
- Weight initialization (initializer): He_normal
- Layer activation function (activation): ReLU
- Loss function (loss): 'categorical_crossentropy'

As for improving the model by adding additional layers we have this new architecture of the model,

1. MobileNetv2()
2. Dense Laye 1 (256 Neurons, activation ReLU, dropout 0.35)
3. Dense Laye 2 (256 Neurons, activation ReLU, dropout 0.35)
4. Dense Laye 3 (256 Neurons, activation ReLU, dropout 0.35)
5. Dense Laye 4 (256 Neurons, activation ReLU, dropout 0.35)
6. Dense Laye 5 (256 Neurons, activation ReLU, dropout 0.35)
7. Convolutional Dropout Layer (dropout rate 0.3)
8. Global Averate Pooling (Last hidden layer with the average)
9. Output Laye (4 nodes for 4 classes, activation SoftMax)
10. Optimization Function(Adam, Learning Rate: 0.00001)

Five dense layers have been added, each composed of 256 neurons and using the ReLU activation function. For each dense layer, we will add a regularization layer with a dropout rate of 0.35. This rate means that 35% of the nodes in each dense layer are randomly deactivated at each training step, which helps prevent overfitting by forcing the model not to rely too much on certain nodes.

As for the convolution layers, we will apply a dropout rate of 0.3. This additional regularization in the convolution layers also helps prevent overfitting and improve the robustness of the model. Additionally, a Global Average Pooling layer is added in the last hidden layer. This layer calculates the average of the values for each feature map, thus reducing the dimensionality and making it easier to feed the values to the Dense output layer. This allows capturing the global characteristics of the image while reducing the number of parameters and the risk of overfitting. The output layer of the model has four nodes, corresponding to the four classes of the problem to be solved. We used the SoftMax activation function for this layer, which allows converting the outputs into probabilities, thus facilitating the interpretation of the results as category classifications.

To optimize our model, we use the Adam optimizer, known for its efficiency and its ability to dynamically adapt to learning rates. The Learning rate is set to 0.00001, a relatively low value that allows fine and precise adjustments of the model weights. The loss function used is the categorical_crossentropy, suitable for multi-class classification problems. In terms of training configuration, the batch size was set to 128, which balances well the stability of gradients and memory usage. The model was trained for 150 epochs, providing enough cycles to allow the model to converge while avoiding overfitting.

Finally, to avoid overfitting, we add L2 regularization with a coefficient of 0.0001 to the dense layers. L2 regularization penalizes large weights by adding a sum of squared weights in the loss function, helping to keep the model weights relatively small. We also enable fine-tuning, allowing to retrain the base model layers to optimize overall performance.

7.3 Mobile Application Deployment

We have developed a mobile application that uses the mosquito classification model for vector tracking for Rift Valley fever outbreak surveillance and reporting of key information on this fever.

The application aims to achieve several key objectives:

- Mosquito Identification: The application allows users to capture images of mosquitoes directly from their mobile device. These images are then analyzed by the classification model that we have developed. This model, based on advanced machine learning techniques, is able to identify different mosquito species with high accuracy, thus facilitating the surveillance of pest and disease vector species.
- Storage and Geolocation: The captured images and classification results are automatically stored in a cloud database. Each record includes the GPS coordinates of the location where the photo was taken, which makes it possible to track the geographical distribution of different mosquito species. This functionality is crucial for mosquito-borne disease surveillance and control efforts. These images will enrich the dataset.

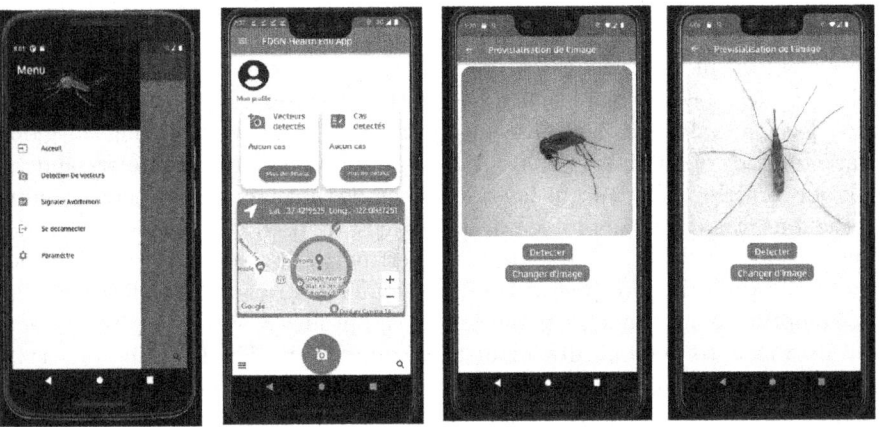

Fig. 5. Mobile Application Screenshots case alert and mosquito detection.

The model in the mobile app has been tested to ensure that it works properly when users choose images from their gallery or take photos with their device. This testing includes evaluating the prediction and the app works properly for the tests we have performed (Fig. 5).

8 Conclusion

In this work we developed a solution for the management and prevention of Rift Valley Fever (RVF), a zoonotic viral disease transmitted mainly by mosquitoes.

By combining the capabilities of artificial intelligence (AI) with the portability of mobile applications, we designed a powerful tool that allows the rapid and efficient detection of potential mosquito vectors of the RVF virus. The AI model, based on the MobileNet architecture, was successfully trained to analyze mosquito images and identify those likely to transmit the RVFV virus, achieving a validation accuracy of 95.56%. This model was integrated into a mobile application that allows users to capture images with their camera or select images from their gallery. The automated analysis process provides real-time classification results, making vector detection more accessible and immediate for livestock farmers and residents of risk areas.

References

1. Asmai, S.A.: Aedes mosquito larvae recognition with a mobile app. Int. J. Adv. Trends Comput. Sci. Eng. **9**(4), 5059–5065 (2020)
2. Barry, Y., et al.: Rift Valley fever, Mauritania, 2020: lessons from a one health approach. One Health **15**, 100413 (2022)
3. Bird, B.H., Ksiazek, T.G., Nichol, S.T., MacLachlan, N.J.: Rift Valley fever virus. J. Am. Vet. Med. Assoc. **234**(7), 883–893 (2009)
4. Bird, B.H., McElroy, A.K.: Rift Valley fever virus: unanswered questions. Antiviral Res. **132**, 274–280 (2016)
5. Caputo, B., et al.: ZanzaMapp: a scalable citizen science tool to monitor perception of mosquito abundance and nuisance in Italy and beyond. Int. J. Environ. Res. Public Health **17**(21), 7872 (2020)
6. Codeço, C.T., et al.: Surveillance of Aedes aegypti: comparison of house index with four alternative traps. PLoS Neglected Trop. Dis. **9**(2), e0003475 (2015)
7. Global Mosquito Alert Consortium. Citizen Scientist Roles and Motivations, Real-Time Targeted Vector Mosquito Monitoring (2020)
8. Ellis, B.R., Wilcox, B.A.: The ecological dimensions of vector-borne disease research and control. Cad. Saude Publica **25**, S155–S167 (2009)
9. Garcia, P.S.C., Martins, R., Coelho, G.L.L.M., Cámara-Chávez, G.: Acquisition of digital images and identification of Aedes aegypti mosquito eggs using classification and deep learning. In: 2019 32nd SIBGRAPI Conference on Graphics, Patterns and Images (SIBGRAPI), pp. 47–53. IEEE (2019)
10. Mosquito Alert Global: A new citizen science initiative that is leveraging networks of scientists and volunteers for the global surveillance and control of disease-vector mosquitoes
11. Goddard, J.: Mosquito-borne diseases. In: Infectious Diseases and Arthropods. ID, pp. 39–89. Springer, Cham (2018). https://doi.org/10.1007/978-3-319-75874-9_3
12. González, M.I., Encarnação, J., Aranda, C., Osório, H., Montalvo, T., Talavera, S.: The use of artificial intelligence and automatic remote monitoring for mosquito surveillance. In: Gutiérrez-López, R., Logan, J.G., Martínez-de la Puente, J. (eds.) Ecology of Diseases Transmitted by Mosquitoes to Wildlife, pp. 211–223. Brill, Wageningen Academic (2022)
13. González Pérez, M.: Novel approaches to improve mosquito surveillance, PhD thesis, Universitat Autònoma de Barcelona (2023)
14. González-Pérez, M.I., et al.: Field evaluation of an automated mosquito surveillance system which classifies Aedes and Culex mosquitoes by genus and sex. Parasites Vectors **17**(1), 97 (2024)

15. Huang, L.P., Hong, M.H., Luo, C.H., Mahajan, S., Chen, L.J.: A vector mosquitoes classification system based on edge computing and deep learning. In: 2018 Conference on Technologies and Applications of Artificial Intelligence (TAAI), Taichung, pp. 24–27. IEEE (2018)
16. Invasive Mosquito Project (2024). http://www.citizenscience.us/imp/
17. Javed, N., López-Denman, A.J., Paradkar, P.N., Bhatti, A.: EggCountAI: a convolutional neural network-based software for counting of Aedes aegypti mosquito eggs. Parasites Vectors **16**(1), 341 (2023)
18. Joshi, A., Miller, C.: Review of machine learning techniques for mosquito control in urban environments. Eco. Inform. **61**, 101241 (2021)
19. Khalighifar, A., et al.: Application of deep learning to community-science-based mosquito monitoring and detection of novel species. J. Med. Entomol. **59**(1), 355–362 (2021)
20. Kline, D.L.: Traps and trapping techniques for adult mosquito control. J. Am. Mosq. Control Assoc. **22**(3), 490–496 (2006)
21. Kröckel, U., Rose, A., Eiras, A.E., Geier, M.: New tools for surveillance of adult yellow fever mosquitoes: comparison of trap catches with human landing rates in an urban environment. J. Am. Mosq. Control Assoc. **22**(2), 229–238 (2006)
22. L'Ambert, G., Ferré, J.-B., Schaffner, F., Fontenille, D.: Comparison of different trapping methods for surveillance of mosquito vectors of West Nile virus in Rhône Delta, France. J. Vector Ecol. **37**(2), 269–275 (2012)
23. Lee, H.S., Noh, B.E., Kim, S.Y., Kim, H., Lee, H.I.: The comparative field evaluation of four different traps for mosquito surveillance in the Republic of Korea. Insects **15**(7), 531 (2024)
24. Li, Y., et al.: Comparative evaluation of the efficiency of the BG-Sentinel trap, CDC light trap and mosquito-oviposition trap for the surveillance of vector mosquitoes. Parasites Vectors **9**(1), 446 (2016)
25. Linthicum, K.J., Britch, S.C., Anyamba, A.: Rift Valley fever: an emerging mosquito-borne disease. Ann. Rev. Entomol. **61**(1), 395–415 (2016). https://doi.org/10.1146/annurev-ento-010715-023819
26. Ifunanya Umeaduma, L.: Survey of image classification models for transfer learning. WJARR **21**(01), 373–383 (2023). https://doi.org/10.30574/wjarr.2024.21.1.0006 https://doi.org/10.30574/wjarr.2024.21.1.0006 https://doi.org/10.30574/wjarr.2024.21.1.0006 https://doi.org/10.30574/wjarr.2024.21.1.0006
27. Manikandan, S., Mathivanan, A., Bora, B., Hemaladkshmi, P., Abhisubesh, V., Poopathi, S.: A review on vector borne disease transmission: current strategies of mosquito vector control. Indian J. Entomol., 503–513 (2023)
28. Martins, R.M., et al.: Development of a deep learning model for the classification of mosquito larvae images. In: Naldi, M.C., Bianchi, R.A.C. (eds.) Intelligent Systems. LNCS, vol. 14197, pp. 129–145. Springer, Cham (2023)
29. Okayasu, K., Yoshida, K., Fuchida, M., Nakamura, A.: Vision-based classification of mosquito species: comparison of conventional and deep learning methods. Appl. Sci. **9**(18), 3935 (2019)
30. World Health Organization: Vector-borne diseases (2020)
31. Pathan, S., Siddalingaswamy, P.C., Ali, T.: Automated detection of COVID-19 from chest X-ray scans using an optimized CNN architecture. Appl. Soft Comput. **104**, 107238 (2021)
32. Pezzin, A., et al.: Comparative study on the effectiveness of different mosquito traps in arbovirus surveillance with a focus on WNV detection. Acta Tropica **153**, 93–100 (2016)

33. Sah, R., Singh, P., Mohanty, A., Bora, I., Padhi, B.K., Head, M.G.: Multiple Rift Valley Fever outbreaks in Uganda: should there be global concern? J. Infect. Public Health **15**(12), 1376–1377 (2022)
34. Sanchez-Ortiz, A., et al.: Mosquito larva classification method based on convolutional neural networks. In: 2017 International Conference on Electronics, Communications and Computers (CONIELECOMP), pp. 1–6. IEEE (2017)
35. The Netherlands Nature Today. Nature Today, Muggenradar (2024)
36. Toledo, E., et al.: LSTM-based mosquito genus classification using their wingbeat sound. In: New Trends in Intelligent Software Methodologies, Tools and Techniques, pp. 293–302. IOS Press (2021)
37. Walther, D., Kampen, H.: The citizen science project 'Mueckenatlas' helps monitor the distribution and spread of invasive mosquito species in Germany. J. Med. Entomol. **54**(6), 1790–1794 (2017)
38. Yujia, H.E., Tyson, E.: Survey results complexities & overlaps in existing citizen science mosquito projects, Technical report, Mosquito Task Force Group (2017)
39. Zhao, D., et al.: A Swin transformer-based model for mosquito species identification. Sci. Rep. **12**(1), 18664 (2022)

Detection of Malicious Android Applications Based on Verification of Indicators of Compromise and Machine Learning Techniques

Theodore Dama[1(✉)], Aminata Sabane[1,2], Abdoul Kader Kabore[2], and Tegawendé F. Bissyande[1,2]

[1] Université Joseph KI-ZERBO (UJKZ), Ouagadougou, Burkina Faso
damatheo8@gmail.com
[2] Centre d'Excellence Interdisciplinaire en Intelligence Artificielle pour le Développement (CITADEL), Ouagadougou, Burkina Faso
{abdoulkader.kabore,tegawende.bissyande}@citadel.bf

Abstract. Android is the operating system with the largest share of the global smartphone market. The system's popularity makes it an attractive target for malware because of its users' data. Despite the security measures used by Google and certain researchers to combat malicious applications, some still slip through the net. In this article, we propose a new approach to detecting malware on Android. This approach combines indicators of compromise, external APK analysis services, and machine learning. We start by compiling a database of indicators of compromise in Android applications. Then, the first step is to exploit this database and the static analysis of Android applications to identify and extract indicators of compromise. The second step uses a machine learning technique to predict whether a given application is malware or not, using a vector of its permissions. This vector is composed of 0 if permission is absent and 1 if it is present. Detection based on indicators of compromise and the external APK analysis service detected 20 malicious applications among 100 benign applications on Androzoo. In addition, the machine learning model trained on a dataset consisting of 2,935 malicious applications and 2,897 benign applications gave a malicious application detection accuracy of 94%. This demonstrates the effectiveness of our approach in predicting malicious applications based on permissions.

Keywords: Android Security · APK · Reverse engineering · Indicator of compromise · machine learning

---

Supported by Centre d'Excellence Interdisciplinaire en Intelligence Artificielle pour le Développement (CITADEL), Burkina Faso.

1 Introduction

By the end of June 2024, 5.68 billion people were using mobile phones, meaning that 70% of the world's population is now considered to be mobile users[1]. According to Statista[2], the number of smart mobile devices (smartphones) will reach 6.2 billion users by 2029. The evolution of mobile devices and mobile applications has virtually metamorphosed the way we engage in our daily lives. The storage and exchange of personal data, online banking, e-commerce, social networking, and e-learning are all examples of services available directly on our mobile devices. Android, Google's OS (Operating System), is one of the main platforms adopted by the smartphone industry. According to Statista, the Android operating system has a global market share of 84.1%, compared with 15.9% for Apple's iOS system. Unfortunately, the system's popularity makes it an attractive target for malware. The Flubot attack at the end of 2021 affected Android users the most, extracting dex files, cloning email applications and stealing sensitive data from banking applications [1]. Android is the most popular target and the most vulnerable to various malicious attacks. These threats are becoming increasingly dangerous, as there is still a lack of appropriate security tools to effectively protect users. However, when organizations start to integrate these systems into their enterprise solutions, they face several configuration and security issues. Ransomware flourished by 72% during the COVID-19 pandemic, and mobile vulnerabilities increased by 50%[3].

Despite the security measures put in place by Google to combat malicious applications on its Play Store, some still manage to slip through the cracks. It's in this quest to secure Android that antivirus applications are emerging. Some of these antivirus applications, which are supposed to ensure security, are real digital killers, stealthy and life-destroying. These antivirus applications are viruses that spy on users. A case in point is SharkBot [3] a new-generation banking Trojan found in antivirus software distributed on the Google Play Store. It was discovered in late October 2021 on Cleafy telemetry. As a result, most cell phone users are susceptible to damage. There is still room for improvement in terms of detecting malicious Android applications.

Our contribution is an approach that enables the detection of malicious applications based on Indicators of Compromise and Machine Learning Techniques. In this proposal, we make the following contributions:

- An e?cacious approach for detecting malicious Android applications that extract indicators of compromise.
- An excellent combination of Compromise Indicators and Machine Learning in the detection of malicious Android apps.
- A visualization of Android application permissions weights according to certain categories.

---

[1] https://wearesocial.com/us/blog/2024/07/digital-2024-july-global-statshot-report/.
[2] https://fr.statista.com/.
[3] https://www.futura-sciences.com/tech/actualites.

We have organized our article as follows: We start with an introduction in Sect. 1. In Sect. 2, we present our Methodology, including some literature reviews and descriptions of our approach. We show the results of the implementation of our approach and a discussion in Sect. 3. The last section concludes the article.

2 Methodology

2.1 Vulnerabilities

According to ANSSI[4], a vulnerability is a malicious or clumsy error in the specification, design, production, installation, or configuration of a system, or in the way it is used. Not all vulnerabilities lead to a cyber attack. Most of them are made public and corrected. They are said to be dealt with through full disclosure. Software publishers and manufacturers of IT components may notice a malfunction and report it to the Security Operations Centre (SOC)[5]. Furthermore, zero-day vulnerabilities are the subject of a market in which the purchasers may be governments or criminal organizations (Fig. 1).

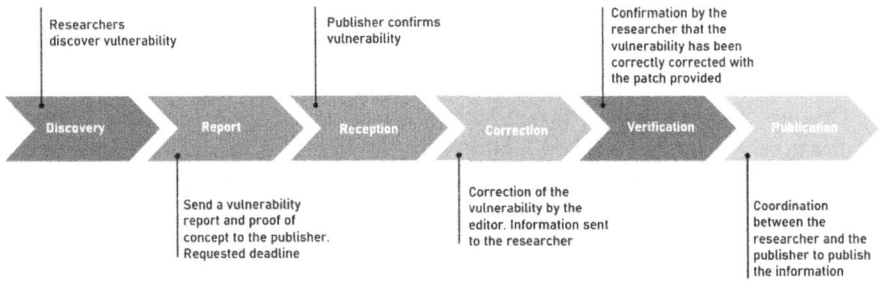

Fig. 1. Full disclosure timeline, CERT Orange Cyberdefense, Vulnerability Intelligence Watch department, 2019. (Color figure online)

Impact of Vulnerabilities. Vulnerabilities can have a wide range of consequences, from the simple malfunction of a piece of equipment to the destruction of a production line. It all depends on the nature of the infrastructure and the solution being targeted. As soon as the technical details of the threat are available, specialist developers will create demonstrators or exploits. The exploit can be integrated into a framework containing a multitude of tools to make the hacker's job easier.

---

[4] https://www.ssi.gouv.fr/particulier/glossaire.
[5] https://www.orangecyberdefense.com.

Directory of Vulnerabilities. Once discovered, vulnerabilities can be the subject of an identification called CVE for Common Vulnerabilities and Exposures. The Massachusetts Institute of Technology Research Establishment (MITRE) at the request of researchers issues CVEs. This organization can also delegate its identification powers to a company or research center. The latter then becomes a CNA (CVE Numbering Authority).

Other Vulnerabilities. In addition to the software vulnerabilities mentioned above, other vulnerabilities are not necessarily linked to an application. It is estimated that 75% of computer attacks are caused by inexperienced users who are not aware of good computer security practices[6]. This vulnerability is exploited by phishing attacks. Unreliable application markets are the source of infected applications. This is a way of passing off one application as another to unwary users. If the phone is lost or forgotten, the lack of a lock or a lock that is too weak constitutes a vulnerability. This can give a third party time to access sensitive information or perform critical actions.

2.2 Indicator of Compromise

According to Haber et al. [4], an indicator of compromise (IoC) is an object or activity that, when observed on a network or device, indicates a high probability of unauthorized access to the system. These indicators are used to detect malicious activity in its early stages and to prevent known threats. These digital traces are likely to reveal not only that an attack has taken place, but also more often than not which tools were used in the attack and who was behind it. IoCs can be used to determine the extent to which a compromise has affected an organization or to learn lessons from an attack, to help protect the system against future attacks. Indicators are usually collected from anti-malware and anti-virus software, but other artificial intelligence cybersecurity tools can combine and organize indicators when responding to an incident.

Use of Indicators of Compromise. Threat analysis helps to reveal the factors associated with a specific threat. If cyber intelligence detects new malware, it flags up IoCs such as file hashes, server addresses, and so on. Later, these indicators of compromise will be exploited to eradicate threats in an organization's infrastructure. An IoC detected on a system indicates that the system is probably the victim of a cyber attack, requiring certain countermeasures. Indicators of compromise are also added to the databases of passive monitoring tools and antivirus software, which can block intrusion attempts. For example, a security solution can use malware signatures to recognize malicious software and prevent it from running on a device.

The data made available describes the technical elements needed to identify any traces of compromise. (See Table 1)

---

[6] https://www.vademecum-patrimoine.com.

Table 1. Example of IoC data typology.

Indicator types	Descriptions
comment	Comment: this can be any other information that reveals the infrastructure used. Example: infrastructure used by the Lockean cybercriminal group
domain	Domain name: the domain names used for malicious activities are listed and can be found on compromised systems. Example: site_name.domain_name
email-src	Sender's e-mail address: an e-mail address is likely to be the source of malicious content. Example: admin@belpay.by
filename	File name: some compromised files can be identified by their name in the file system. Example: /bin/backup
ip-dst	Public destination IP address: the presence of a target IP address indicates a deployed compromise that has become capable of establishing communication with the threat. Detection of such traffic as authorized means that urgent action must be taken. Example: 104.168.174.32
ip-src	Public destination IP address: the presence of a target IP address indicates a deployed compromise that has become capable of establishing communication with the threat. Detection of such traffic as authorized means that urgent action must be taken. Example: 104.168.174.32
md5	MD5 fingerprint: MD5 fingerprint is applied to a file to identify compromised files within a file system. Example: 84837778682450cdca43d1397afd2310
sha1	sha1 fingerprint: The sha1 fingerprint is applied to a file to identify compromised files within a file system. Example: 1348d76072280a489cc8d6a15aeb3617b59585ba
sha256	sha256 fingerprint: The sha256 fingerprint is applied to a file to identify compromised files within a file system. Example: 6362084f61fa6a41b8b01b7c62215ad41a2623b69572ce558c33bffaa21f0af9
size-inbytes	File size: the file size indication is used to identify compromised files. Example: 1032192
text	Character string: the character string indication is used for various purposes. It is used to identify a specific character string or one that follows a regular expression.
url	Website address: the link to certain sites is known to be malicious. These links can be used to install exploits on a target.

2.3 Android App Analysis Methods

There are several analysis methods for detecting malware. Here are just a few of them:

- **Meta-information analysis**: such as ADROIT [5] and Manilyzer [6], systems that train machine-learning algorithms with a set of features collected from the AndroidManifest.xml file. System permissions are meta-information that is one of the most relevant features for detecting Android malware.
- **Clone analysis**: clones are made by copying the original applications and then distributing them free of charge while inserting malicious code. CodeMatch [7] proposes a two-stage approach that focuses first on identifying and deleting data, and then on the code in the clone library.
- **Network traffic analysis**: It is a pain to manually install and run Android applications to generate network traffic. As a result, AndroGenerator [8], an automatic network traffic generation system on Android, reproduces network traffic based on traffic characteristics. Once the network has been generated, it can be analyzed. This is the case of Q. Wang and al.'s work [9].
- **Analysis using API calls**: API calls are one of the most widely used functionalities, in the same way as Android permissions. They are used to model the behavior of an application and to characterize the actions it can take. Zhang and al. proposed DroidSIFT [10], a semantic-based classifier that uses API dependency graphs to form a Naive Bayes classifier.

2.4 Android Application Analysis Approaches

The various methods of analyzing the Android system can be static or dynamic.

The static analysis uses reverse engineering techniques to analyze the source code of the Android application. It relies on semantic signatures and focuses on analyzing code extracts without executing them. Arthur FOURNIER [11] has carried out work on malicious application detection using 151 Android system authorizations and machine learning.

Dynamic analysis examines the software's operating behavior during execution. It is impossible with static analysis to follow the actual behavior of a sample when it is executed. CopperDroid [12] uses a dynamic analysis approach based on a virtual machine, the aim of which is to reconstruct the behavior of malicious Android applications uniformly and automatically.

The hybrid analysis approach is the coexistence of static and dynamic analysis within the same approach. GroddDroid [13] proposes a hybrid method for improving the execution of malicious code from unknown malware. It particularly targets malware with trigger protections.

2.5 Machine Learning Approaches

Machine learning is a field of study in artificial intelligence. It is based on mathematical and statistical approaches to give computers the ability to "learn" from data. Statistics from articles on Android malware detection based on machine learning show static analysis taking pride of place from 2016 to 2020 [14]. F. Akbar and al. [15], proposed a permission-based detection of malicious Android applications using machine learning. They used a binary value to indicate presence or absence, with values of 1 or 0 respectively.

2.6 Our Approach

Our approach is divided into three main parts: APK extraction, data implementation and malware detection. Figure 2 gives an overview of the approach.

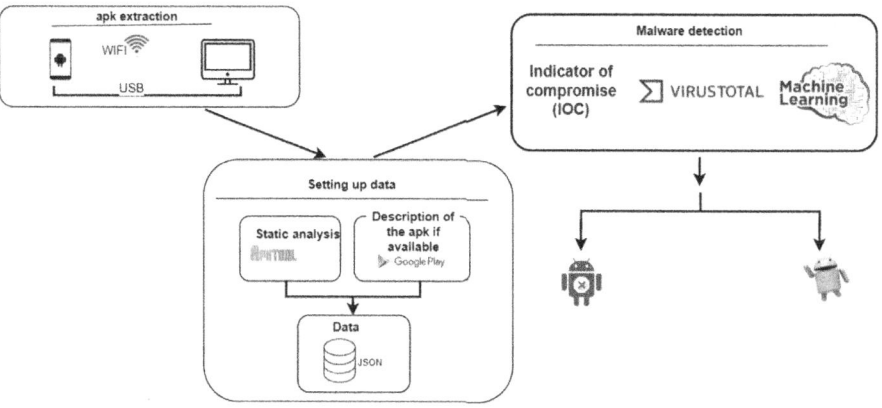

Fig. 2. Architecture of the proposed detection framework.

Step 1: Extraction of the APK. This stage of our approach involves making Android applications available. These applications are accessible thanks to files called APK (Android Package Kit). This contains all the relevant information and elements needed to install applications on an Android phone. The benign or malicious state of the applications on a phone says a lot about the state of that phone.

Step 2: Setting up the Data. This will involve pooling information relating to a given application. This involves reverse engineering, the point of entry for setting up APK data through static analysis. Decompressing the APK gives an idea of the structure of the folders and files. In this way, a certain amount of relevant information can be collected for a given application.

Step 3: Detection of Malicious Applications. Detection is carried out from several angles, including one based on indicators of compromise. The data pooled through a search for a certain amount of information helps to make a good analysis of the nature of a malicious application. The one based on machine learning uses the permissions of the Android system. Fahad Akabar et al. al. [15] use an Android permissions table with values of 1 or 0 depending on whether the application uses the permission or not.

3 Results and Discussion

3.1 Extracting the APK

We extract the Android packages installed on the phone using MVT(Mobile Verification Toolkit)[7], a toolkit for iOS and Android forensics. We use a USB cable with ADB, which requires USB debugging to be enabled. All we have to do is plug the Android phone into our computer to extract the APKs using the following command: *mvt-android check-adb –output /path/to/results*, */path/to/results* is the path of the folder that will receive the APKs. MVT also offers APK extraction via WIFI, the wireless connection. We have also developed an APK download tool. This tool takes as input an object containing the package names of the Android applications associated with each category selected(COMMUNICATION, DATING, SOCIAL, SPORTS,...).

3.2 Setting up Data

Reverse-Engineering the APK. We reverse-engineer the Android compressed file and the .apk application installation file. This gives us a well-structured set of folders and files. The APK can be reverse-engineered using dedicated software. In Fig. 3, we have used Apktool, but not all the tools provide a clear view of the application's resources after reverse engineering.

Information Research. The "re" module of the Python language was used to search for information within the resources of the decompressed APK. It can be used to define rules for combining strings and numbers. For each piece of information, we will explain how such information can be extracted from a decompressed APK. Description of the application: collected using web scraping by Beautiful Soup 4[8], on the Play Store website.

Pooling Information. This involves consolidating all the information sought on a given application. Some of the information collected is in the form of tables, such as permissions, URLs, and so on. We have therefore opted for the JSON (JavaScript Object Notation) format. The data is presented in the form of keys/values. The keys are the labels and the values are our information. Together they form an object variable, which is stored in JSON format (see Fig. 4).

---

[7] Mobile Verification Toolkit, https://docs.mvt.re/.
[8] https://www.crummy.com/software/BeautifulSoup/bs4/.

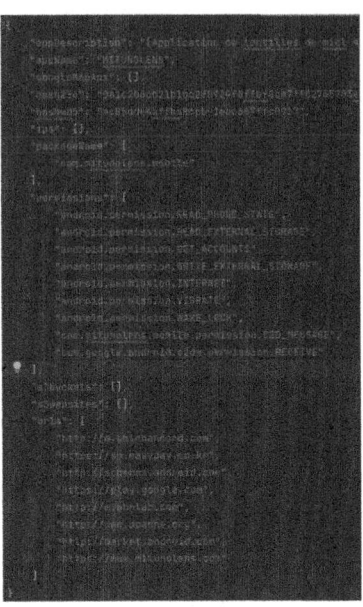

Fig. 3. Reverse engineering an APK with Apktool (AndroidManifest.xml).   **Fig. 4.** Pooling information in JSON format.

3.3 Malware Detection

Detector Based on Static Analysis. This detection includes the use of indicators of compromise and the total virus analysis report. We use consolidated information from applications in the data implementation section.

We have a database of indicators of compromise. This database is maintained by Julien Voisin and Tek on behalf of the Echap Association. We compare the IP address, domain name, and package name of an application with those in the IoC database. If an element of an application is identified in the IoC database, the application is considered to be malicious.

We submit the application's hash256 to the VirusTotal API to form another JSON file of this information linked to each application. This JSON file includes entries such as the md5 hash, the file size, the result of the 72 antivirus scan, and much more. We say that an application is malicious once it has been detected as malicious by one of the 72 antivirus scanners.

Detector Based on Machine Learning. Geiger et al. [15] state that AndroZoo is an ongoing effort to gather executable Android applications from as many sources as possible and make them available for analysis. Our machine-learning approach is based on the permissions requested by an application. We set up a permissions dataset of 5,832 applications, divided into 2,935 malicious and 2,897 benign applications. Training data accounted for 80%, with the remaining 20%

reserved for model testing. This dataset contained 2620 distinct permissions, many of these permissions do not influence whether the application is malicious [18]. We thus reduced the data characteristics to the top 100(see Fig. 8) and 150 (see Fig. 9) permissions determining malicious applications. Our dataset translates the permission information into a binary dataset where "0" indicates the absence and "1" is the presence of the permission in the application, as in the work of Fahad Akbar et Al [16]. The Scikit-learn machine learning library in Python facilitates the use of supervised and unsupervised learning models [19]. This library served as the basis for our models. The Fig. 5 illustrates the models and parameters used, and the detection of malicious or benign applications leads to binary classification.

```
# SVC with probability enabled, rbf kernel (default)
svc_model = SVC(probability=True, random_state=42)
svc_model.fit(X_train, y_train)

# KNN
knn_model = KNeighborsClassifier(n_neighbors=5)
knn_model.fit(X_train, y_train)

# GaussianNB
gaus_model = GaussianNB()
gaus_model.fit(X_train, y_train)

# SVM, SVC with probability enabled, linear kernel
svm_model = SVC(probability=True,kernel = 'linear', C = 1)
svm_model.fit(X_train, y_train)

# dtree
dtree_model = DecisionTreeClassifier(max_depth=2, random_state=42)
dtree_model.fit(X_train, y_train)
```

Fig. 5. Models and parameters.

3.4 Discussions

Effectiveness of APK File Compromise Indicators in Detecting Malicious Android Applications: Detection based on static analysis through the IoCs and VirusTotal, therefore, enabled 20 out of 100 benign applications on Androzoo [21] to be detected as malicious (see Fig. 6). These applications, which appear to be benign, have been identified because they hide compromised URLs, or their SHA256s have been classified as malicious by at least two VirusTotal antivirus engines.

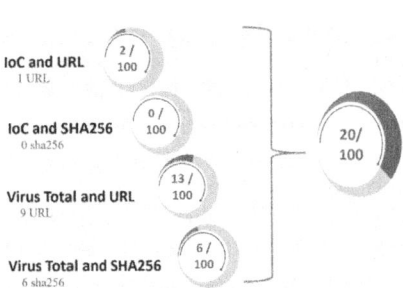

Fig. 6. Summary of IoC detections.

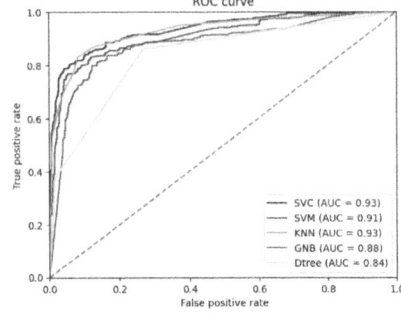

Fig. 7. ROC and AUC without reduction.

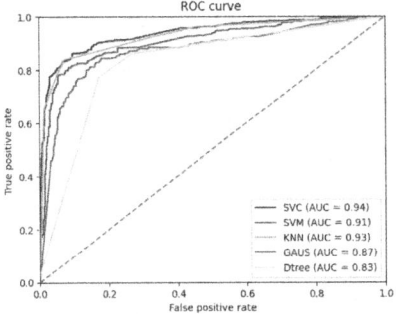

Fig. 8. ROC and AUC with top 100.

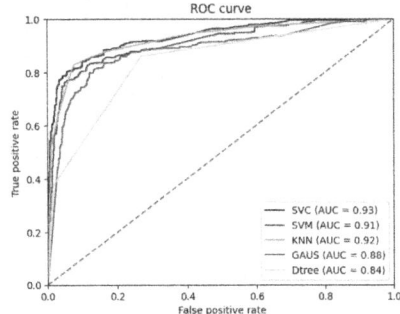

Fig. 9. ROC and AUC with top 150.

Effectiveness of Machine Learning in Detecting Malicious Android Applications: Our permissions dataset is made up of 2,935 malicious applications and 2,897 benign applications. Figures 7, 8, and 9 respectively show the performance (ROC and AUC) of models without permissions reductions, with the top 100 and top 150 most influential permissions of malicious APKs. DecisionTreeClassifier, Gaussian Naive Bayes (GaussianNB), SVM (Support Vector Machine) with the "linear" kernel remained unaffected by non-reduction to a reduction that only retains the top 150 permissions characterizing malicious APKs. Their best performances (0.84, 0.88, 0.91) are reduced before that of the SVC (Support Vector Classifier) algorithm with the "rbf" kernel, which is at its minimum of 0.93. In Fig. 8, the reduction of features up to the top 100 that determine malicious APKs enables the SVM (Support Vector Machine) algorithm with the "rbf" kernel to achieve the best accuracy of 0.94.

Our approach retains the reduction of the 100 significant permissions, with the SVC model having an AUC of 0.94. It is more efficient than the work of J. Li et al. [20] who retained only 20 significant permissions with a performance of 0.93.

Performance for a Toolkit Combining Static Analysis, Indicators of Compromise, and Machine Learning to Detect Malicious Android Applications: The results of Sects. 3.5 and 3.6 show that malicious applications escape detection using the permissions of the machine learning approach. These are likely to be detected by static analysis techniques, either by the URLs or by the application's signature. Combining such techniques enables a detection tool to be effective. An application is considered malicious if detected by one of the following means: the automatic learning model, based on permissions, or the presence of indicators of compromise within the application.

Permissions Required by an Android Application Depend on its Classification in the Application Markets: Our download tool allows us to group applications into categories. For now, we have only selected categories with more than ten (10) applications in them. According to this criterion, we have based our permissions study on these twenty (20) categories. The first column shows the categories and the other columns show the names of the permissions and the probability of requests per category. Each vector has a permissions weighting specific to a category. After this stage, we can establish the permissions database per APK, taking into account the weight of permissions for the category. The weight(value range between 0 and 1) of each permission is the probability of the permission's existence among a set of APKs in that category. This database is made up of 20 application categories and 313 Android permissions. Figure 10 zooms in on some of the permissions. We can see that the weights of the permissions differ by category. Consequently, the permissions requested by an Android application depend on its classification in the application markets. By analyzing the weights in Fig. 10, all applications in the SOCIAL category use the WRITE_EXTERNAL_STORAGE, WAKE_LOCK, and CAMERA permissions, which translates into weights for these permissions of 1. We can affirm

	categories	android.permission.WRITE_EXTERNAL_STORAGE	android.permission.WAKE_LOCK	android.permission.CAMERA
2	COMMUNICATION	0.54	1.0	0.62
3	FAMILY_EDUCATION	0.18	0.73	0
4	FAMILY_CREATE	0.77	0.92	0.31
5	TRAVEL_AND_LOCAL	0.56	1.0	0.38
6	ART_AND_DESIGN	0.83	0.92	0.25
7	GAME	0.33	1.0	0
8	FAMILY_ACTION	0.69	0.88	0.44
9	GAME_CASINO	0.75	1.0	0
10	GAME_ARCADE	0.3	0.8	0
11	GAME_MUSIC	0.41	1.0	0.06
12	FAMILY	0.55	0.82	0.18
13	GAME_EDUCATIONAL	0.5	0.83	0
14	GAME_PUZZLE	0	0.8	0
15	FAMILY_PRETEND	0	1.0	0
16	FOOD_AND_DRINK	0.5	0.92	0.58
17	DATING	1.0	1.0	1.0
18	VIDEO_PLAYERS	1.0	1.0	0
19	SPORTS	0.25	1.0	0.12
20	SOCIAL	1.0	1.0	1.0
21	BOOKS_AND_REFERENCE	0.5	0.94	0.44

Fig. 10. Vector view of permission weights by category.

that FAMILY_EDUCATION applications do not necessarily use CAMERA. This study will enable us to deepen and improve permission-based detection. It will take into account the application category when judging the permissions used. For if an application claiming to play music requests access to CAMERA, it is suspect.

3.5 Difficulties

We were faced with a lack of APK datasets organized into categories. This justifies the limitation of our study to the 20 categories out of 63 in total [22]. In the absence of a dataset of the permissions used by each category, we were therefore obliged to establish our dataset consisting of the weights of the permissions used by the 20 categories.

4 Conclusion

This document discusses the implementation of an approach for detecting malicious Android applications based on the verification of indicators of compromise and machine learning techniques. These steps are APK extraction, information pooling, and detection. The novelty of our approach lies in step 3. Instead of detection, which is based on a method for detecting malicious Android applications, we opted for a consolidation of static analysis via the identification of IoCs and submission to VirusTotal, and the contribution of machine learning based on the permissions requested by an application. Our SVC model obtained an AUC of 94% when we retained only the top 100 most decisive permissions of malicious applications. Consolidating these strengths enables us to detect applications that would otherwise escape the radar of machine learning and be detected by static analysis, and vice versa. We contributed to the implementation of a category-based application dataset in the Android application market. This allowed weights to be assigned to each permission, taking into account the frequency of the permission within a set of apps in the same category. As future work, we plan to take into account all Play Store applications categories, to study the demand for permissions according to each category.

References

1. Salsabila, H., Mardhiyah, S., Hadiprakoso, R.B.: Flubot malware hybrid analysis on android operating system. In: 2022 International Conference on Computing, Multimedia, Cyberspace and Information Systems (ICIMCIS), Jakarta, Indonésie, pp. 202–206 (2022). https://doi.org/10.1109/ICIMCIS56303.2022.10017486
2. SECURELIST by Kaspersky, IT threat evolution in Q1 2024. Mobile statistics CHECK POINT RESEARCH. https://securelist.com/it-threat-evolution-q1-2024-mobile-statistics/112750/. Accessed 14 April 2024
3. CLEAFY SharkBot: a new generation of Android Trojans is targeting banks in Europe. https://www.cleafy.com/cleafy-labs/sharkbot-a-new-generation-of-android-trojan-is-targeting-banks-in-europe. Accessed 02 Jan 2023

4. Haber, M.J., Rolls, D.: Indicators of compromise. In: Identity Attack Vectors. Apress, Berkeley, CA (2020). https://doi.org/10.1007/978-1-4842-5165-2_9
5. Martín, A., Calleja, A., Menéndez, H.D., Tapiador, J., Camacho, D.: ADROIT: Android malware detection using meta-information. In: IEEE Symposium Series on Computational Intelligence (SSCI), pp. 1–8. Athens, Greece 2016 (2016). https://doi.org/10.1109/SSCI.2016.7849904
6. Feldman, S., Stadther, D., Wang, B.: Manilyzer: automated android malware detection through manifest analysis. In: 2014 IEEE 11th International Conference on Mobile Ad Hoc and Sensor Systems, pp. 767–772, Philadelphia, PA, USA (2014). https://doi.org/10.1109/MASS.2014.65
7. Glanz, L., et al.: CodeMatch: obfuscation won't conceal your repackaged app. In: Proceedings of the 2017 11th Joint Meeting on Foundations of Software Engineering (ESEC/FSE 2017). Association for Computing Machinery, New York, NY, USA, pp. 638–648 (2017). https://doi.org/10.1145/3106237.3106305
8. Su, X., Zhang, D., Li, W., Wang, X.: AndroGenerator: an automated and configurable android app network traffic generation system. Secur. Comm. Netw. **8**, 4273–4288 (2015). https://doi.org/10.1002/sec.1341
9. Wang, Q., Yahyavi, A., Kemme, B., He, W.: I know what you did on your smartphone: inferring app usage over encrypted data traffic. In: 2015 IEEE Conference on Communications and Network Security (CNS), Florence, Italy, 2015, pp. 433–441 (2015). https://doi.org/10.1109/CNS.2015.7346855
10. Zhang, M., Duan, Y., Yin, H., Zhao, Z.: Semantics-aware android malware classification using weighted contextual API dependency graphs. In: Proceedings of the 2014 ACM SIGSAC Conference on Computer and Communications Security (CCS '14). Association for Computing Machinery, New York, NY, USA, pp. 1105–1116 (2014). https://doi.org/10.1145/2660267.2660359
11. Fournier, A.: Détection de Programmes Malveillants dédiée Aux Appareils mobiles, École Polytechnique de Montréal (2019). https://publications.polymtl.ca/3700/
12. Tam, K., Khan, S.J., Fattori, A., Cavallaro, L.: CopperDroid: automatic reconstruction of android malware behaviors. In: NDSS Symposium 2015, pp. 1–15 (2015). https://doi.org/10.14722/ndss.2015.23145
13. Abraham, A., Andriatsimandefitra, R., Brunelat, A., Lalande, J., Tong, V.V.T.: GroddDroid : a Gorilla for triggering malicious behaviors. In: 2015 10th International Conference on Malicious and Unwanted Software (MALWARE), Fajardo, PR, USA, 2015, pp. 119–127 (2015). https://doi.org/10.1109/MALWARE.2015.7413692
14. Wu, Q., Zhu, X., Liu, B.: A Survey of android malware static detection technology based on machine learning. Mob. Inf. Syst., 1–18 (2021). https://doi.org/10.1155/2021/8896013
15. Geiger, F.X., Malavolta, I.: Datasets of android applications: a literature. arXiv preprint arXiv:1809.10069 (2018)
16. Akbar, F., Hussain, M., Mumtaz, R., Riaz, Q., Wahab, A.W.A., Jung, K.-H.: Permissions-based detection of android malware using machine learning. Symmetry **14**, 718 (2022). https://doi.org/10.3390/sym14040718
17. Allix, K., Jérome, Q., Bissyandé, T.F., Klein, J., State, R., Le Traon, Y.: A forensic analysis of android malware–how is malware written and how it could be detected?. In: IEEE 38th Annual Computer Software and Applications Conference. Vasteras, Sweden 2014, pp. 384–393 (2014). https://doi.org/10.1109/COMPSAC.2014.61
18. Bassolé, D., Koala, G., Traoré, Y., Sié, O.: Vulnerability analysis in mobile banking and payment applications on android in African countries. In: Thorn, J.P.R.,

Gueye, A., Hejnowicz, A.P. (eds.) InterSol 2020. LNICST, vol. 321, pp. 164–175. Springer, Cham (2020). https://doi.org/10.1007/978-3-030-51051-0_12

19. Pedregosa, F., et al.: Scikit-learn: machine learning in Python. J. Mach. Learn. Res. (2011). https://hal.inria.fr/hal-00650905
20. Li, J., Sun, L., Yan, Q., Li, Z., Srisa-An, W., Ye, H.: Significant permission identification for machine-learning-based android malware detection. IEEE Trans. Industr. Inf. **14**(7), 3216–3225 (2018). https://doi.org/10.1109/tii.2017.2789219
21. Allix, K., Bissyandé, T.F., Klein, J., Traon, Y.L.: AndroZoo: collecting millions of Android apps for the research community. In: Proceedings of the 13th International Conference on Mining Software Repositories (MSR '16). Association for Computing Machinery, New York, NY, USA, pp. 468–471 (2016). https://doi.org/10.1145/2901739.2903508
22. Latif, R.M.A., Abdullah, M.T., Shah, S.U.A., Farhan, M., Ijaz, F., Karim, A.: Data scraping from Google Play store and visualization of its content for analytics. In: 2019 2nd International Conference on Computing, Mathematics and Engineering Technologies (iCoMET), Sukkur, Pakistan, pp. 1–8 (2019). https://doi.org/10.1109/ICOMET.2019.8673523

Two Phases Feature Selection Method for Classification Problems Based on Association Rules

Ghislain Dorian Tchuente Mondjo[1,3(✉)] and Kely Maxime Motue Djoko[1,2,3]

[1] Université de Yaoundé I, Faculté des Sciences, Département d'Informatique, 812 Yaoundé, Cameroun
tchuente.mondjo@gmail.com, motuekely@gmail.com
[2] IRD, Sorbonne Université, UMMISCO, 93143 Bondy, France
[3] Fondation pour la Recherche l'Ingénierie et l'Innovation (FR2I), 14306 Yaoundé, Cameroun

Abstract. Feature selection has become a key issue in data mining because the quality of the selected attributes affects the performance and generalization capabilities of classifiers. The challenge is to reduce the number of features without reducing prediction performance. The ARFS (Association Rules Feature Selection) algorithm will select an ordered vector of features from the association rules and will then use the sequential feature selection (SFS) method on this vector, to select a best subset. However, ARFS cannot consider all features when selecting attributes, it is not applicable on real data and the feature subset selected by ARFS does not depend on the size of the subset. We propose Association Rules Feature Selection larger (ARFSL) which is a two-phase algorithm based on ARFS. In a first phase, SFS selects the attributes according to a confidence threshold of the association rules whose consequent is the class and in which they are found in the antecedent. In the second phase, SFS selects from the remaining features those that optimize the prediction performance of the model when applied to a dataset described only by each of the features. Experimental results show that the proposed algorithm achieves average gains of 3.02%, 3.64% and 5.24% in terms of accuracy, f1, precision respectively, and selects on average fewer attributes compared to state-of-the-art algorithms such as: ReliefF, MI, SFS, RFE-SVM, RIDGE and LASSO.

Keywords: Feature selection · Two-phase algorithms · Association rules · Data mining

1 Introduction

Automatic classification problems typically rely on data that often contains redundancies or even attributes that are irrelevant to classification. Removing redundancies or eliminating attributes that are irrelevant can be very helpful in improving the effectiveness of classification models, and even their generalization performance.

To this end, the selection of the most relevant attributes has become a key theme in the process of building prediction models. The following question therefore arises: How to reduce the size of the attributes of the training input data and improve the efficiency of the algorithm without reducing the performance of the model ? For a given classification task, attribute selection involves selecting an interesting subset of attributes and removing the uninteresting or even redundant subset of attributes for a better performance of that classification task. Therefore, the classification models established from the selected subset of attributes are more explainable or interpretable [1].

The main reasons behind using attribute selection are: reducing the execution time of model training and reducing the storage score of the model obtained after training, thus avoiding the curse of dimensionality, a potential overfitting problem, which results in better generalization of the model and an increase in the possibility of achieving better performance. In the context of credit risk prediction, attribute selection consists of selecting the attributes that have the greatest impact on the performance of this task. This will avoid losses in banks and have a reduced set of attributes on which in-depth analyzes will be carried out. In the state-of-the-art, we have three approaches to attribute selection in the context of classification:

- Filters: [2] They perform a selection of attributes without involving any prediction algorithm, and rely on the existing relationships between certain attributes of the training data and the target class. Filter methods have smaller complexity compared to wrapper methods. Example: ReliefF, MI.
- Wrappers: [3] Compared to filter-type methods that do not take into account dependencies between certain attributes during selection, wapper methods take into account these dependencies by using a learning algorithm to compare the impact of pooling a subset of particular attributes, which makes it expensive in terms of execution time. Example: SFS, RFE-SVM.
- Embedded: [4] In these methods, attribute selection is performed and optimized during the classification process, which allows less computation compared to wrapper methods. Example: CART uses the Gini indicator as an attribute selection metric, LASSO, RIDGE.

In order to reduce the size of the feature subset and improve the efficiency of the feature selection algorithm without reducing the accuracy, [5] proposes ARFS. ARFS uses association rules to provide a vector of scores that represents the correlation between an attribute and the target. It then uses the descending order of this vector of scores to search for a subset of attributes with the best accuracy prediction performance from the SFS strategy (Sequential Feature Selection). After using the association rules to provide a vector of scores, it may happen that some features are removed due to minimum support and minimum confidence. This will not allow us to search for all the characteristics. Other disadvantages of ARFS are that it is not suitable for real-type data and it does not select attributes based on size.

To overcome these drawbacks, we propose ARFSL (Association Rules Feature Selection more Large) which is a two-phase algorithm which will construct a vector of attributes forgotten by the association rules, on which the second phase of searching for the subsets of attributes. During the search phase, the concatenation of the selected and forgotten attribute score vectors will be considered as an adjustable model.

Experimental results show that ARFSL achieves on average prediction performance gains of 3.02%, 3.64% and 5.24%, (obtained by averaging the gains over all state-of-the-art methods) in terms of precision, f1, recall respectively and selects on average the least attributes compared to state-of-the-art methods such as: MI, Releif, SFS, RFE-SVM, LASSO and RIDGE.

The rest of this work will be divided as follows: In Sect. 2, we will present the technical background and the related work, then, we will present the methodology where we will talk about the proposed ARFSL algorithm in Sect. 3. Finally, in Sect. 4 we will present the experiments and the limits of the proposed model.

2 Technical Background and Related Work

2.1 Technical Background

A - Association rules

The model used in this work uses association rules to find the set of frequent item sets of size 2 of attribute and category modalities.

A.1 - Item set

Association rule is an unsupervised machine learning method used to discover interesting correlation relationships between items in a database. Let $I = i_1, i_2, ..., i_m$ be the set of m items in the database D. The subsets T of I are item sets. In the database $D = \{T_1, T_2, ..., T_{|D|}\}$, each item set T_k is a transaction to which we associate a unique identifier denoted TID.

A.2 - Definition: Association rule

The association rule R is an implication of the form:

$$X \Rightarrow Y$$

where $X \subset I$ is the antecedent of rule R, $Y \subset I$ is the consequent of rule R and $X \cap Y = \emptyset$. The intuition is that, if the item set X appears in some transactions, there is a probability P that the item set Y is also present in these same transactions.

Support

The support of the association rule $R: X \Rightarrow Y$ is the proportion for which the item set $X \cup Y$ appears in some transactions of the database D. Let $count(X \cup Y)$ be the frequency of occurrence of the item set $X \cup Y$ in the database D, with $X \subset I$ and $Y \subset I$. Formally, the support of the association rule R is:

$$support(X \Rightarrow Y) = \frac{count(X \cup Y)}{|D|}$$

The minimum support, denoted sup_min represents the minimum filtering standard from which an association rule is considered frequent. Therefore, the item sets L_m whose support (equal to the support of its rule) is greater than or equal to sup_min are called frequent item sets of size m.

Confidence

The confidence of an association rule $R: X \Rightarrow Y$ is the proportion for which the association rule $X \Rightarrow Y$ is realized compared to the rules whose antecedent is X. Formally the confidence of R is defined as follows:

$$Confidence(X \Rightarrow Y) = \frac{support(X \Rightarrow Y)}{support(X)} \quad (1)$$

The minimum confidence, denoted $conf\_min$ is the confidence threshold set to filter out rules that are not strongly correlated.

B - L_2 exploration algorithm

In the ARFS proposed in the paper [5], we first need to find L_2 greater than or equal to sup_min between feature attributes and categories in D, and then calculate the confidence of these frequent 2-item sets. The Apriori-based frequent 2-item set mining algorithm presented in [5] is described in Algorithm 1.

Algorithm 1: Algorithm for exploring frequent item sets of size 2 denoted L_2

Input: sup_min : minimum support threshold
Output: Conf : confidence of frequent item sets of size 2
Data: D : Dataset

1 $init\ T_2,\ sup\_min$
2 $n \leftarrow count(T_2)$
3 **for** $j\ ¡\ n$ **do**
4      $sup_{T_{2_j}} \leftarrow support(T_{2_j}) \quad //T_{2_j} = (X_j, Y)$
5   **if** $sup_{T_{2_j}} > sup\_min$ **then**
6          $L_2.add(T_{2_j})$
7          $conf_{2_j} \leftarrow \frac{count(L_{2_j})}{count(X_j)}$
8 **return** L_2.Conf

2.2 Related Work

The related work of this paper will be divided in two parts: Feature selection, Association rule feature selection method.

A - Feature selection

Feature selection is a very important pre-processing task in machine learning because it has a great impact on the prediction performance and generalizability of a model. Attribute selection can be used for two purposes, either to have a model with better prediction performance, or to have an interpretable model, because a training set with high dimensionality will provide a model that is difficult to interpret. For classification problems, attribute selection methods are divided into three approaches: Filter, Wrapper, and Integrated approaches.

A.1 - Filtering methods

Filter-type methods assign weights to attributes by using ranking techniques to select attributes in order. A ranking criterion is defined to assign a score to attributes and a threshold is used to filter out some attributes that are considered less important. An example of a classification criterion is entropy, which is a measure that quantifies uncertainty and diversity in a dataset. The speed of Filter methods makes them more suitable for large datasets. On the other hand, since relationships between independent attributes are not taken into account, it is possible to choose redundant attributes. The following subsections present two well-known filtering methods.

Mutual information (MI)

Let X and Y be two random variables, Mutual information quantifies the quantity of data that is shared between a target attribute Y and an attribute X. The feature X contains the most information about the target if it is best able to distinguish data of one class y_c from data of another class $y_u (y_c \neq y_u)$. The mutual information of X relative to Y is defined as :

$$MI(X,Y) = \sum_{i=1; j=1}^{A,B} P(x_i, y_j).log\left(\frac{P(x_i, y_j)}{P(x_i)P(y_i)}\right) \quad (2)$$

where $X = (x_1, x_2, ..., x_A)$ and $Y = (y_1, y_2, ..., y_A)$.

Relief

Another approach to calculating the impact of a variable on a target called Relief would assign a score to each feature based on its ability to distinguish instances of different classes. This approach was proposed by Kira and Rendell in [9]. Let X be a variable, we select two instances close to X_i, one denoted X_{neighE} belonging to the same class as X_i and the other denoted X_{neighD} not having the same class as X_i. If X_i and X_{neighE} have a different value, the weight W_X of the attribute X will decrease because it separates two instances of the same class. On the other hand, if X_i and X_{neighD} have a different value, the weight

W_X of the attribute X will have to increase, because X separates two attributes of different classes. The weight W_X of the attribute X is calculated as follows:

$$W_X = W_X - (X_i - X_{neighE})^2 - (X_i - X_{neighD})^2 \qquad (3)$$

The first version of Relief is applicable to binary classification problems, an extended version was proposed in [18] to solve the redundancy problem and another version proposed in [19] to take into account multi-classes.

A.2 - Wapper methods

The specificity of wapper methods is that they are dependent on the results of the prediction model built from scratch to evaluate the subsets generated during the search. [10]. Using prediction models during attribute selection allows Wapper-like methods to generally achieve better prediction performance compared to filter methods, however, they become expensive in terms of resources and execution time. Many wrapper methods have been proposed in the literature, including RFE-SVM [13] and SFS [8]. In the following, we will focus on these two most widely used wrapper methods.

Recursive Feature Elimination of Support Vector Machines (RFE-SVM)

SVM-RFE is an attribute selection method proposed by Guyon in [13]. SVM-RFE produces a subset of attributes by backward elimination of an attribute based on the SVM ranking criteria. Let $X = (x_1, x_2, ..., x_n)$ be an attribute from an arbitrary database, Y be a target attribute and S be the subset of attributes produced by SVM-RFE. Initially $S = X$, then, we remove the ith attribute s_i having the smallest score $r_i = (w_i)^2$, where w_i corresponds to the weight of the ith attribute calculated from SVM. This procedure is repeated until the desired number of attributes is reached, or the performance can no longer be improved.

Sequential Forward Selection (SFS)

The SFS search strategy is a feature selection approach proposed by [8]. Let $X = (x_1, x_2, ..., x_n)$ be a set of n attributes and Y be a set of target attributes. Initially, we have an empty subset of attributes $S = \{\}$, then we calculate the prediction performance of each attribute in order to select the attribute with the best performance and add it to S. We then add in S an attribute a belonging to $X - S$ which, combined with S gives a better prediction performance compared to the other attributes belonging to $X - S - \{a\}$ and so on. We will therefore have $S = S \cup \{\arg\max_{u \in X-S}(J(S \cup \{u\}))\}$. In this method, once an attribute is added to an attribute subset, it cannot be removed, which does not achieve an optimal result.

A.3 - Embedded Methods

This approach takes into account the dependencies between attributes by including the attribute selection process during the attribute selection phase. This reduces the computational cost compared to wappers methods. The following subsections introduce the built-in methods LASSO and Ridge.

LASSO (L1-Regularization)

Lasso is an attribute selection method proposed by Tibshirani in [6], which imposes a constraint on the weights of the attributes in order to regularize them so that the attributes that have no impact in the implementation of a regression model have zero weights by using a penalization according to which the sum of the values of the coefficients of the regression model is less than an upper bound m. Let X be a data set and Y the associated target variable. $\hat{y}_i = f(X_i)$ is the prediction obtained from the model when the observation i^{th} is passed to the model f. The loss attributed to LASSO during model training is as follows:

$$Minimize \ F(W) = \sum_{i=1}^{n}(y_i - \hat{y}_i)^2 + \lambda \sum_{j=1}^{k}|w_j| \quad (4)$$

with

$$\sum_{j=1}^{k}|w_j| < m \quad (5)$$

where m is the upper limit of the sum of the coefficients, $\hat{y}_i$ is the prediction for observation, y_i is the actual value for observation, W_k are the regression coefficients and λ is a hyperparameter that controls the intensity of the regularization and if $\lambda \geq 0$, the regularization parameter that controls the amount of weight removal.

RIDGE (L2-Régularisation)

Ridge proposed by Arthur Hoerl and Robert Kennard in [7], is a method for selecting attributes by regularizing the attribute weights of a data set, by penalizing the loss function in such a way that the sum of the squared values of the regression model coefficients is less than an upper bound m. Unlike LASSO, Ridge does not assign zero weights to attributes, it assigns values close to zero. Let X be a data set and Y the associated target variable. $\hat{y}_i = f(X_i)$ is the prediction obtained from the model when the observation i^{th} is passed to the model f. The loss attributed to LASSO during model training is as follows:

$$Minimize \ F(W) = \sum_{i=1}^{n}(y_i - \hat{y}_i)^2 + \lambda \sum_{j=1}^{k}(w_j)^2 \quad (6)$$

with

$$\sum_{j=1}^{k}(w_j)^2 < m \quad (7)$$

where m is the upper limit of the sum of the coefficients, $\hat{y}_i$ is the prediction for observation, y_i is the actual value for observation, W_k are the regression coefficients and λ is a hyperparameter that controls the intensity of the regularization.

B - Association rule Feature Selection

Association rule learning is a rule-based machine learning method to discover interesting relationships between variables in large databases. It can be used to identify strong rules between attributes in the dataset.

In 2010, Chawla [15] proposed to use Association Rules Networks[1] (ARN) where regression analysis will be used to formally test the relationship between extracted attributes after a min-cut partitioning clustering algorithm is applied to extract the pertinent attributes.

In 2017, Salma [14] proposed to select attributes using association rules based on constraints. The constraint on the association rules used here is that the before part of the rule must be a value of the target attribute, and the after part of the association rules must be of dimension one.

Association Rules Feature Selection proposed by Qu in 2019 [5] will use the association rules to create a vector of attribute scores whose score for an attribute represents the highest confidence of the rules that are associated with that attribute. These association rules have the following constraints: the antecedent must be a modality of an attribute and the consequent must be a class modality. Then, this vector will be arranged in descending order to position the attributes having a correlation with the class at the top of the list. This vector of scores will be used to select the best subset of attributes from the SFS strategy. Initially, the attribute subset is empty, added an attribute from the attribute score vector into the attribute subset if adding it improves prediction performance.

From this section, we can observe some drawbacks of state-of-the-art attribute selection methods such as, not checking if there exists a subset of attributes from the set of attributes. Attributes selected by the filter methods which is better in terms of performance, the fact that we can no longer delete a characteristic when it has been added to the subset in the SFS method and a great difficulty in interpreting the attribute scores returned by different methods such as Lasso and Ridge. Which leads us to focus on the ARFS (Association Rules Feature Selection) method proposed by [5] which is an attribute selection method based on association rules and which uses the SFS strategy to select the best subset of attributes. The choice of ARFS is due to the fact that the association rules constitute a much more interpretable model.

The [5] ARFS will use the association rules to create a vector of attribute scores, where the score of an attribute represents the highest confidence of the rules that are associated with that attribute. These association rules have the following constraints: the antecedent must be a modality of an attribute and the consequent must be a class modality. Then, this vector will be arranged in descending order to position the attributes having a correlation with the class at the top of the list. This vector of scores will be used to select the best subset of attributes from the SFS strategy. Initially, the attribute subset is empty, added an attribute from the attribute score vector into the attribute subset if adding it improves prediction performance. The disadvantage of this method is that, by using minimum support and minimum confidence on the association rules,

---

[1] Use all existing connections between association rules to select attributes.

Table 1. Comparison of different state-of-the-art feature selection methods.

Approach	Principle	Benefits	Disadvantages
MI	The most important feature is the one that provided the most information about the target.	Captures nonlinear information between features and the target variable.	It does not take into account interactions and may be biased towards discrete features.
Relief	The most important feature is the one whose value differs for nearby instances that belong to different classes.	It can handle interactions and is efficient for data that has noise.	Sensitive to redundant features and does not perform well for correlative features.
SFS	Selection starts with an empty set of features and sequentially adds features based on model performance.	Can use any learning model.	Computationally expensive when the number of features is large; after adding a feature, it cannot be removed.
RFE-SVM	It starts with all features and sequentially eliminates them based on their importances calculated from the SVM model.	Effective for selecting the most discriminating features.	Very high computational costs for very large data.
LASSO	It penalizes the sum of the absolute values of the coefficients of the characteristics. It forces certain coefficients to become zero.	Naturally selects characteristics.	May be unstable when features are highly correlated.
Ridge	It penalizes the sum of the squares of the coefficients. Unlike Lasso, Ridge does not make the coefficients tend towards zero, but rather reduces their amplitude.	Useful to avoid overfitting.	Does not make a selection of natural characteristics.
ARFS	Uses association rules to assign scores to selected attributes based on support and confidence thresholds. Check if there is a subset of attributes (from the SFS strategy) that perform better than the attributes selected by the thresholds with prediction performance as criteria.	Can be used regardless of the learning model and is less time-consuming. It generates different rankings of attributes according to a confidence and support threshold value, which can provide a better result.	Does not take into account all features during selection, is not adapted to real data; after adding a feature, it cannot be removed. It does not select attributes based on their sizes.

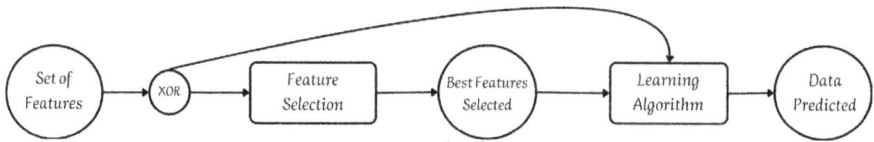

Fig. 1. General model representation

some rules will be removed and therefore, the attributes associated with these rules will not appear in the score vector attributes. And therefore, the search for the best subset of attributes will not be done on these attributes which have been forgotten. On the other hand, the ARFS method is not appropriate on real type data and does not provide the best subset of data depending on its size. The Table 1 is a summary of the idea, advantages and disadvantages of the state-of-the-art algorithms studied. To overcome these drawbacks, we propose the ARFSL (Association Rules Feature Selection more Large) algorithm which will be presented in the following section.

3 Methodology

The Fig. 1 presents the general model studied in this paper, as input, we have a set of attributes, we will then go through one of the possibilities, that is to say: 1- The non-feature selection, 2- Feature selection. For the purposes of this paper, we focus on the second possibility, because attribute selection can be used to improve model performance without attribute selection, and will reduce the size of attributes in order to facilitate application of explainability.

3.1 Association Rules Feature Selection More Large (ARFSL)

We propose the model shown in Fig. 2, which uses association rules to provide an order to the features, and then uses a learning search model to derive a new ordering of attributes, such that by extracting the subset of attributes based on their sizes using the k-best strategy, we will only have better subsets of attributes. The learning search model considers the order of attributes as a pattern.

The ARFSL proposed in this paper and presented in Algorithm 2 must first calculate the confidence of the set of frequent item sets of size 2 denoted L_2 between the attribute modalities and the category denoted $\{A = v, C = c\}$ from the L_2 mining algorithm of Qu [5] to lines 2 and 3 in Algorithm 2. Then, on line 4, we group together all the sets of items whose attribute is A, then we associate the confidence of this rule with each association rule. We then select the maximum confidence of this group of items such that the rule is $\{A = v\} \Rightarrow \{C = c\}$, this score will represent the score of the attribute A. We will have a score attribute vector called selected attribute vector A_{select} by defining minimum support and minimum confidence. The confidence of a rule is used here to measure the correlation between attributes and categories.

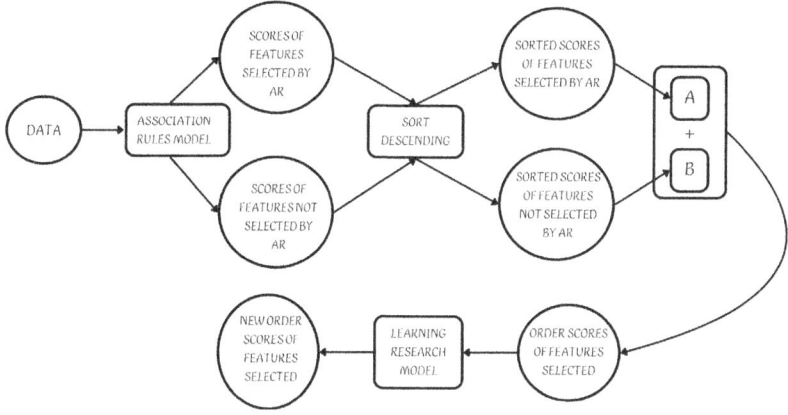

Fig. 2. Specific model representation

Due to minimal support and minimal trust, some rules will be removed, which will result in some attributes being removed. The attributes thus deleted will be used to form the forgotten attribute vector A_{forget} to the lines 5 and 6. The forgotten attribute vector A_{forget} will be constructed by extracting attributes that belong to the starting attribute set, but do not belong to the attribute set of the selected attribute vector. Next, calculate the prediction performance[2] of each forgotten attribute using the learning model Ft. Then, the selected A_{select} and forgotten A_{forget} attribute vectors are arranged in descending order up to lines 7 and 8, and will be concatenated on line 9 to obtain the attribute score vector, which will be passed to the GLRFSL Algorithm 3.

Algorithm 2: Association Rules Feature Selection more Large (ARFSL)

Input: sup_min : minimum support threshold, conf_min : minimum confidence threshold
Output: set_opt : Best features subset
Data: D : Dataset

1 *Init Ft // Decision Tree*
2 $T_2 \leftarrow Apriori(sup\_min, D)$
3 $R_2 \leftarrow Association\_Rules(T_2, conf\_min)$
4 $A_{select} \leftarrow MAX(R_2)$
5 $A_{forget} \leftarrow Get\_feature\_forget(D, A_{select})$
6 $A_{forget} \leftarrow Get\_Feature\_Prediction(Ft, D, A_{forget})$
7 $A_{select} \leftarrow Sort\_decreasing(A_{select})$
8 $A_{forget} \leftarrow Sort\_decreasing(A_{forget})$
9 $A_{Att} \leftarrow A_{select} + A_{forget}$
10 $d \leftarrow divide\_lenght$
11 $set\_opt \leftarrow GLRFSL(A_{Att}, Ft, d)$
12 **return** set_opt

---

[2] According to the chosen metric.

Algorithm 3: Global and Local Research of Feature Subset by Learning (GLRFSL)

Input: A_{Att} : Scores vector of feature, Ft-CS : Learning model, d : step
Output: opt : best features subset
Data: D : Dataset

1 $\beta \leftarrow |A_{Att}|$
2 $i \leftarrow 1$
3 **while** $divide == False$ **do**
4       $l.add(A^i_{Att_d})$
5       $g.add(A^i_{Att_d})$
6       $opt[|l|] \leftarrow Max(\eta_{pred}(opt[|l|], D, Ft), \eta_{pred}(l, D, Ft))$
7       $opt[|g|] \leftarrow Max(\eta_{pred}(opt[|g|], D, Ft), \eta_{pred}(g, D, Ft))$
8       $f \leftarrow Max(\eta_{pred}(l, D, Ft), \eta_{pred}(g, D, Ft))$
9   **if** $\eta_{pred}(f, D, Ft) > \eta_{pred}(f_{best}, D, Ft)$ **then**
10          $opt[|l|], f_{best}, g \leftarrow f, f, f$
11   update f_{best} in A_{Att_d} with descending order
12   **else**
13          $g.pop()$
14   SBS step on $opt[m]$ and update A_{Att} if needed
15   Test $[opt[m], A^i_{Att_d}]$ and update A_{Att} if needed
16   **if** $i > \beta$ **then**
17          $divide \leftarrow True$
18      $i \leftarrow i + d$
19 **return** opt

We can then search for the best subsets of attributes based on the size of the subset using the GLRFSL (Global and local Research Feature Subset by Learning scored vector) search algorithm proposed in this paper in Algorithm 3. The idea of this algorithm is to leave the current attribute order to provide a new attribute order in such a way that it allows us to extract subsets of attributes with better prediction performance.

$\eta_{pred}(f, D, Ft)$[3] returns the prediction performance for a training set D, on features f using a prediction model Ft. First, we add the feature A^i_{Att} to the vectors l and g in lines 4 and 5, then we adjust $opt[|l|]$ and $opt[|g|]$ locally on lines 6 and 7 if the prediction performances on the attribute subsets l and g are respectively higher than the prediction performances on the attribute subsets $opt[|l|]$ and $opt[|g|]$. Then put in f the attribute subset with the highest prediction performance (line 8) and compare f to the current best attribute subset f_{best}, adjust A_{Att} from f if f has a prediction performance strictly superior to that of f_{best}. Then, on line 14, a step of the SBS (Sequential Backward Selection) strategy is used to have the best subset of reduced size among that selected by the SFS strategy.

This idea is taken from the SFFS (Sequential Floating Forward Selection) algorithm by [17]. During this process, an adjustment of the attribute score vector is performed whenever a new subset of attributes with better prediction performance is discovered. Test the new attribute subset on line 15 to select better attribute subsets by concatenating $opt[m]$ to A^i_{Att}, during this process, adjustments to the score vector A_{Att} can be done in case of improvement in

---
[3] f : Set of attributes, D: Dataset, Ft: Model prediction.

Table 2. Example of Data set

A	B	C	Target
0	0	1	1
1	0	0	1
0	0	0	0
1	0	1	0
1	1	0	1

Table 3. Rules obtained with a confidence of 0.4

Ant	Cons	Conf
A=0	Target=1	0.5
A=1	Target=1	0.66
A=0	Target=0	0.5
B=0	Target=1	0.5
B=0	Target=0	0.5
B=1	Target=1	1.0
C=1	Target=1	0.5
C=0	Target=0	0.66
C=1	Target=0	0.5

Table 4. Rules obtained with a confidence of 0.6

Ant	Cons	Conf
A=1	Target=1	0.66
B=1	Target=1	1.0
C=0	Target=0	0.66

Table 5. Rules obtained with a confidence of 0.7

Ant	Cons	Conf
B=1	Target=1	1.0

prediction performance. The time complexity of the ARFSL algorithm is the same as that of the SFFS algorithm presented in [17]. ARFSL[4] can be used with all learning algorithms.

3.2 Application Example

The Table 2 presents an example of a dataset. The objective of this example is to show how association rules are used in the proposed ARFSL algorithm.

In the first case we assume that we have a confidence of 0.4 and therefore we obtain the Table 2 which represents the antecedent, the consequent and the confidence of the rule at the end of the use of the Algorithm 1. We already notice that the antecedent (Ant) of each rule is an attribute value and the consequent ($Cons$), a value of the target attribute. Then, the rules whose antecedent have the same attribute are grouped together. In the case of the Table 2, we group together all the rules whose associated attribute is the attribute A, then the attribute B and finally the attribute C. From there, we assign as a score for each attribute the highest confidence among those with which it is associated. In the case of attribute A, the score assigned to it will be $Max(0.5, 0.66, 0.5) = 0.66$. The same process will be carried out on attribute B and C and they will have score values of 1.0 and 0.66. For the Table 4 where we have imposed a confidence of 0.6 we carry out the same process.

The observation made is that at the end of this process on Tables 3 and 4 all attributes of the data table have a score where the second phase of the ARFSL algorithm is not necessary. On the other hand, in Table 5 the only attribute

---
[4] The metric can be adjusted depending on the context in which we find ourselves.

selected by the association rules will be B with a score of 1.0 and therefore those which have not been selected by the association rules are A and C, hence the second phase of the ARFSL algorithm will be necessary.

4 Experiments Results and Discussion

In this part, we experiment with the ARFSL algorithm in order to evaluate these capabilities in terms of classification performance. The data used in the experiment are: Glass Identification Dataset [23], German Credit Data numeric [24], Australian Credit Approval [25], Breast Cancer Wisconsin Dataset [26], Contraceptive Method Choice Dataset [28], Speaker Accent Recognition Dataset [29], and Sensor Reading Dataset [30].

This experiment was carried out on a 16GB RAM using the Scikit-learn[5] Python tool for learning models.

4.1 Datasets

We start by applying the ARFSL algorithm on 5 different datasets. Among which Table 6:

- Glass Identification Dataset [23]: This dataset of 214 instances gathers information from various glasses from the USA Forensic Science Service, where each glass has 9 attributes and a target attribute whose target represents whether a glass is of type "float" or not.
- German Credit Data numeric [24]: This data set classifies people described by a set of attributes as good or bad credit risk. It has 24 attributes and one target attribute.
- Australian Credit Approval [25]: The Australian Credit Approval Dataset has 14 attributes that represent information about individuals applying for a credit card and one target attribute whose classes represent an acceptance or refusal of a credit card assignment.

Table 6. Datasets

Dataset	Instances	Attributs	Classe
Glass	214	9	6
German	1000	24	2
Australian	690	14	2
Cmc	1473	9	3
Accent-mfcc-1	329	12	6
Wdbc	569	30	2
Ionosphere	351	34	2
Sensor_Reading	5456	24	4

---

[5] https://scikit-learn.org/.

- Breast Cancer Wisconsin Dataset (Diagnostic) [26]: This dataset of 569 instances, whose 30 attributes were calculated from a digitized image of a fine needle aspiration of a breast mass and a target attribute whose targets gather information on the diagnosis of cancer or not.
- Contraceptive Method Choice Dataset [27]: This dataset of 1473 instances, 9 attributes, and 1 target attribute is a subset of the Indonesian National Contraceptive Prevalence Survey 1987. This dataset presents demographic and socioeconomic information from married women on their contraceptive methods (non-use, long-term, or short-term methods).
- Speaker Accent Recognition Dataset [28]: This data set contains 329 instances collecting accent information from six different countries for detection and recognition. It contains 12 attributes obtained using MFCC on the original time-domain audio of lectures of up to 1 word and one target attribute.
- Ionosphere Dataset [29]: For the 351 instances and 34 attributes in this dataset, the target attribute is "good" for those whose characteristics show the presence of some type of structure in the ionosphere and the target attribute is "bad" for instances whose characteristics show no type of ionosphere structure: their signals pass through the ionosphere.
- Sensor Reading [30]: This dataset contains 24 attributes representing information from various ultrasonic sensors of a robot moving around a room following the wall clockwise in 4 turns and a target attribute whose targets are the next actions to be performed next based on the actions that have already been performed.

4.2 Evaluation Metrics

We evaluate our results in terms of accuracy, F-measure and precision. In order to obtain statistically significant experimental results, a 10-fold cross-validation experiment was used to take into account the average of bad and good separations of data in train and test.

4.3 Description of Results and Observations

We will describe on the one hand the results of the best subsets of selected attributes and on the other hand the results of the best subsets of attributes selected according to the size of the attributes, on all the datasets presented above and using the algorithms presented in this paper.

A - Observations of the results for the best subset of attributes selected

The Table 7 present the best results in terms of prediction performance, accuracy, F-measure and precision respectively, on the 8 datasets presented above from the CART model. The Table 8 present the number of attributes selected following the performance results in terms of accuracy, F-measure and precision obtained in Table 7.

Table 7. Results in terms of Accuracy, F-measure and Precision

Metrics	Base		Filter		Wrapper		Embedded		Proposed
	CART	ARFS	MI	ReliefF	SFS	RFE-SVM	LASSO	RIDGE	ARFSL
Accuracy									
Glass	0.6822	0.5129	0.7054	0.6822	0.7242	0.6822	0.7054	0.6865	**0.7575**
Wdbc	0.9367	0.8946	0.9384	0.9314	0.9508	0.9368	0.9437	0.9507	**0.9631**
German	0.6632	0.7174	0.7476	0.7194	0.7507	0.7341	0.7143	0.7195	**0.7549**
Accent-mfcc-1	0.6898	-	0.6898	0.6898	0.7111	0.6898	0.6898	0.6898	**0.7232**
Australian	0.8275	0.8579	0.8550	0.8623	0.8681	0.8608	0.8681	0.8666	**0.8710**
Cmc	0.4623	0.4602	**0.5166**	0.4854	**0.5166**	0.4900	**0.5166**	**0.5166**	**0.5166**
Ionosphere	0.9001	0.9061	0.9060	0.9059	0.9373	0.8945	0.8888	0.8888	**0.9488**
Sensor Reading	0.9954	0.9946	0.9956	0.9957	**0.9970**	0.9957	0.9957	0.9957	0.9967
Average	0.7696	-	0.7943	0.7840	0.8069	0.7854	0.7903	0.7892	**0.8164**
StDev	0.1654	-	0.1481	0.1581	0.1504	0.1558	0.1497	0.1517	0.1501
F-measure									
Glass	0.5915	0.4496	0.60	0.5915	0.6271	0.6480	0.60	0.6198	**0.6888**
Wdbc	0.9172	0.8868	0.9344	0.9268	0.9495	0.9323	0.9392	0.9471	**0.9561**
German	0.6241	0.4472	0.6660	0.6558	0.6784	0.6487	0.6560	0.6620	**0.6789**
Accent-mfcc-1	0.5871	-	0.5871	0.5871	0.6151	0.6013	0.5871	0.5871	**0.6423**
Australian	0.8248	0.8576	0.8546	0.8609	0.8669	0.8601	0.8662	0.8658	**0.8689**
Cmc	0.4370	0.4215	0.4651	0.4577	**0.4943**	0.4675	**0.4943**	**0.4943**	**0.4943**
Ionosphere	0.8694	0.8991	0.8971	0.8983	0.9383	0.8857	0.8787	0.8787	**0.9439**
Sensor Reading	0.9951	0.9945	0.9951	0.9951	**0.9966**	0.9951	0.9951	0.9951	0.9959
Average	0.7307	-	0.7499	0.7466	0.7707	0.7548	0.7520	0.7562	**0.7836**
StDev	0.1838	-	0.1816	0.1842	0.1768	0.1754	0.1764	0.1750	0.17
Precision									
Glass	0.60	0.4447	0.6064	0.60	0.6458	0.6607	0.6077	0.6254	**0.7046**
Wdbc	0.9168	0.8907	0.9346	0.9272	0.9486	0.9319	0.9424	0.9484	**0.9562**
German	0.6302	0.5926	0.6880	0.6572	**0.8082**	0.6688	0.6583	0.6641	**0.8082**
Accent-mfcc-1	0.6044	-	0.6050	0.6054	**0.6958**	0.6526	0.6044	0.6044	0.6809
Australian	0.8279	0.8634	0.8611	0.8632	0.8680	0.8636	0.8684	0.8683	**0.8727**
Cmc	0.4389	0.4461	0.4894	0.4619	0.4684	0.4733	**0.5022**	**0.5022**	**0.5022**
Ionosphere	0.8789	0.8602	0.9013	0.9032	0.9344	0.8901	0.8893	0.8903	**0.9451**
Sensor Reading	0.9944	0.9950	0.9944	0.9947	0.9958	0.9946	0.9947	0.9947	**0.9962**
Average	0.7471	-	0.76	0.7516	0.7956	0.7669	0.7584	0.7622	**0.8082**
StDev	0.1815	-	0.1737	0.1811	0.1686	0.1672	0.1735	0.1722	0.1583

Of the 8 data sets, the proposed ARFSL algorithm performed best on 8 data sets regardless of the metric used. These 8 datasets are: Glass, Ionosphere, German, Australian, Wdbc, Accent-mfcc-data and Cmc, Sensor Reading. The experiments in terms of performance presented on the Table 7 and in terms of the number of selected characteristics presented on the Table 8, show that ARFSL obtains the best results in the majority.

The results show that on the Wdbc and Cmc datasets, the algorithm *ARFSL* in addition to having selected the subsets with the best accuracy, F-measure and precision performances in the Table 7, it also selects the fewest attributes

Table 8. Results in terms of number of attributes selected from Accuracy, F-measure and Precision

Metrics	Base		Filter		Wrapper		Embedded		Proposed
	CART	ARFS	MI	ReliefF	SFS	RFE-SVM	LASSO	RIDGE	ARFSL
Accuracy									
Glass	9	3	8	9	7	9	8	8	**6**
Wdbc	30	2	18	18	12	25	21	24	**7**
German	24	2	**3**	9	8	8	22	21	11
Accent-mfcc-1	12	-	12	12	**8**	11	12	12	**8**
Australian	14	2	**1**	4	4	3	6	3	5
Cmc	9	2	2	4	**2**	5	**2**	**2**	**2**
Ionosphere	34	8	**3**	15	16	28	31	31	8
Sensor Reading	23	16	19	21	11	20	21	21	**8**
Average	19.375	-	8.25	11.5	8.5	13.625	15.375	15.25	**6.875**
StDev	9.0820	-	6.8145	5.8094	4.1833	8.8308	9.2457	9.8710	2.4717
F-measure									
Glass	9	3	8	9	**6**	7	8	8	8
Wdbc	30	2	18	18	9	25	21	24	**4**
German	24	2	**3**	23	18	23	22	21	19
Accent-mfcc-1	12	-	12	12	9	11	12	12	**8**
Australian	14	2	**1**	4	4	3	6	3	5
Cmc	9	3	6	4	**2**	5	**2**	**2**	**2**
Ionosphere	34	8	**3**	15	11	28	31	31	11
Sensor Reading	23	15	23	23	11	23	23	23	**8**
Average	19.375	-	9.25	13.5	8.75	15.62	15.62	15.5	**8.12**
StDev	9.0820	-	7.3442	7.1239	4.63	9.4728	9.4198	10.0374	4.8846
Precision									
Glass	9	3	**6**	9	8	7	8	8	8
Wdbc	30	2	17	5	**4**	24	21	24	6
German	24	2	**4**	23	**4**	8	22	21	**4**
Accent-mfcc-1	12	-	7	10	**8**	11	12	12	**8**
Australian	14	2	**1**	4	4	3	6	5	5
Cmc	9	3	3	4	3	5	**2**	**2**	**2**
Ionosphere	34	1	**3**	15	15	**3**	31	17	11
Sensor Reading	23	16	23	21	**11**	21	21	21	**11**
Average	19.375	-	8	11.375	7.125	10.25	15.375	13.75	**6.875**
StDev	9.0820	-	7.2972	7.0522	3.9508	7.5291	9.2457	7.6770	3.0181

compared to other selection algorithms presented in Table 8. Also, in the accuracy and F1-measure metrics, the ARFSL algorithm selects the fewest features and gives better performance on the Wdbc, Accent-mfcc-data and Cmc datasets in Tables 7 and 8.

On the German, Australian, and Ionosphere datasets, the MI algorithm selected the fewest attributes, but, it did not achieve the best performance, which is not very interesting. One could justify that $ARFSL$ selected more attributes compared to MI because, in these specific cases, as performance increases, the selected attributes increase.

In the Cmc data set $ARFSL$, LASSO, Ridge achieved the best results in terms of accuracy, F-measure and precision prediction performance how presented in Table 7 and they select the least attributes in this data set as shown in Table 8. In these same figures, the Sensor Reading dataset, SFS algorithm achieved the best prediction performance in terms of accuracy and F-measure, which are 0.9970 and 0.9966, respectively, followed by $ARFSL$, RFE-SVM, LASSO and Ridge. On the accuracy metric, $ARFSL$ on this dataset achieved a performance of 0.9967 which is very close to the result of SFS which is 0.9970 and selected 8 attributes compared to SFS which selected 11 attributes which gives to think about when we position ourselves in a context of explainability of learning models.

In terms of precision metric and with the Sensor Reading data set, $ARFSL$ gives the best performance and further reduces the attributes. $ARFSL$ selects the fewest attributes from the accuracy and F-measure metrics, in 4 data sets[6] and on all datasets from metric *Precision*.

In average, $ARFSL$ obtained the best performance in terms of accuracy, F1-measure and precision which are 0.8164, 0.7836 and 0.8082 respectively, with standard deviation (StDev) values of 0.1501, 0.17 and 0.1583, respectively, showing that the average prediction performance is very close to the prediction performance obtained by $ARFSL$ on each data set.

On the other hand, $ARFSL$ also obtains the lowest number of features selected on average in terms of accuracy, F-measure and precision which are 6.875, 8.12, and 6.875 respectively, and the results in terms of standard screen show that the average number of features selected is close to the number of features selected for each dataset[7].

These observations show that ARFSL not only selects the attribute subsets with the best prediction performance, but also the smallest number of attributes compared to state-of-the-art algorithms such as MI, Relief, SFS, SVM-RFE, LASSO, RIDGE.

We observe that $ARFSL$ performs better compared to ARFS on all subsets of the data. A major disadvantage of ARFS is the fact that it has a high probability that after filtering, association rules extracted from Apriori algorithm do not contain the rules sensitive to the constraint "having as an antecedent an attribute modality and as a consequence a modality of the class attribute", which is the case of the Accent-mfcc dataset. $ARFSL$ solved this problem by doing the second phase.

---

[6] On datasets: Wdbc, Accent-mfcc-1, Cmc, Sensor Reading.

[7] SFS comes second for F-measure and precision, and MI for accuracy.

Overall, the average gains of $ARFSL$ over MI, Relief, SFS, RFE-SVM, LASSO and Ridge algorithms are 3.02%, 3.64% and 5.24% in terms of accuracy, F-measure, precision respectively[8].

B - Observations of the results for the best subset of attributes selected based on size

Figures 3 and 4 show the curves for each data set. These curves represent the performance prediction curves of the CART model in terms of accuracy in Fig. 3 and the F-measure in Fig. 4 respectively, depending on the size of the selected attributes. On the abscissa of each curve, we have the number of selected attributes, and on the ordinate, we have the prediction performance in terms of accuracy and F-measure respectively.

And so, we have the prediction performance curves as a function of the size of the selected attribute subset for the algorithms MI (blue), ReliefF (green), SFS (red), RFE-SVM (cyan), LASSO (purple), Ridge (yellow) and ARFSL (black). To select attribute subsets of specific sizes, the MI, ReliefF, RFE-SVM, LASSO and Ridge algorithms use the best k attributes.

Concerning the results, we observe a great dominance of the ARFSL and SFS algorithms over the other algorithms, which are Wapper type algorithms. For most of the datasets cited in this paper, we observe that the black curve which represents the $ARFSL$ algorithm is practically above the other curves, which shows that the $ARFSL$ algorithm allows to select the subsets of attributes having the best prediction performance in terms of accuracy and F-measure depending on the sizes of the subsets compared to other attribute selection algorithms. It is followed by the SFS algorithm which also provides very appreciable prediction performance. These results can be explained by the fact that the search algorithm used in $ARFSL$ and proposed in this paper has a learning nature, which is not the case of SFS and RFE-SVM.

C - Conclusion of the experiments

The results of these experiments allowed us to highlight certain hidden disadvantages of ARFS as listed during the observations, which allowed us to propose an algorithm which will make it possible to overcome these. These results also allow us to realize that association rules are an interesting model for modeling the relationships that exist between variables. As part of this work, the first aspect of selecting the subset of attributes with the best prediction performance is generally taken into account when we need to have a model with the best possible performance. However, the second aspect of this work is that of attribute selection based on the size of the subset of attributes to be selected, which is generally used when priority is given to the explainability of the models.

---

[8] The calculation of this average gain is done by calculating the average deviation between the mean of the prediction performances of $ARFSL$ and those of the other algorithms.

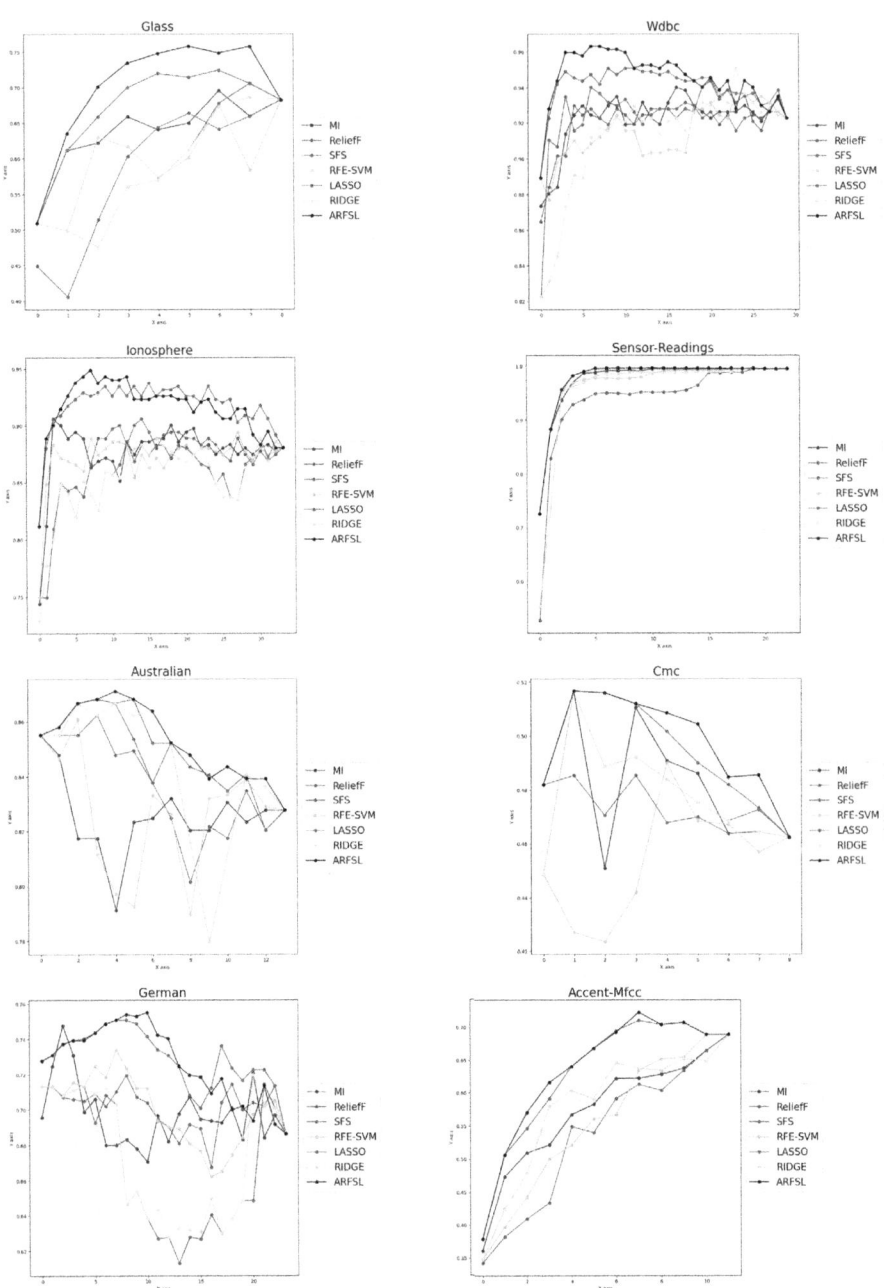

Fig. 3. For each dataset, the performance in terms of accuracy of the selected attributes based on the sizes of the selected attribute subsets (Color figure online)

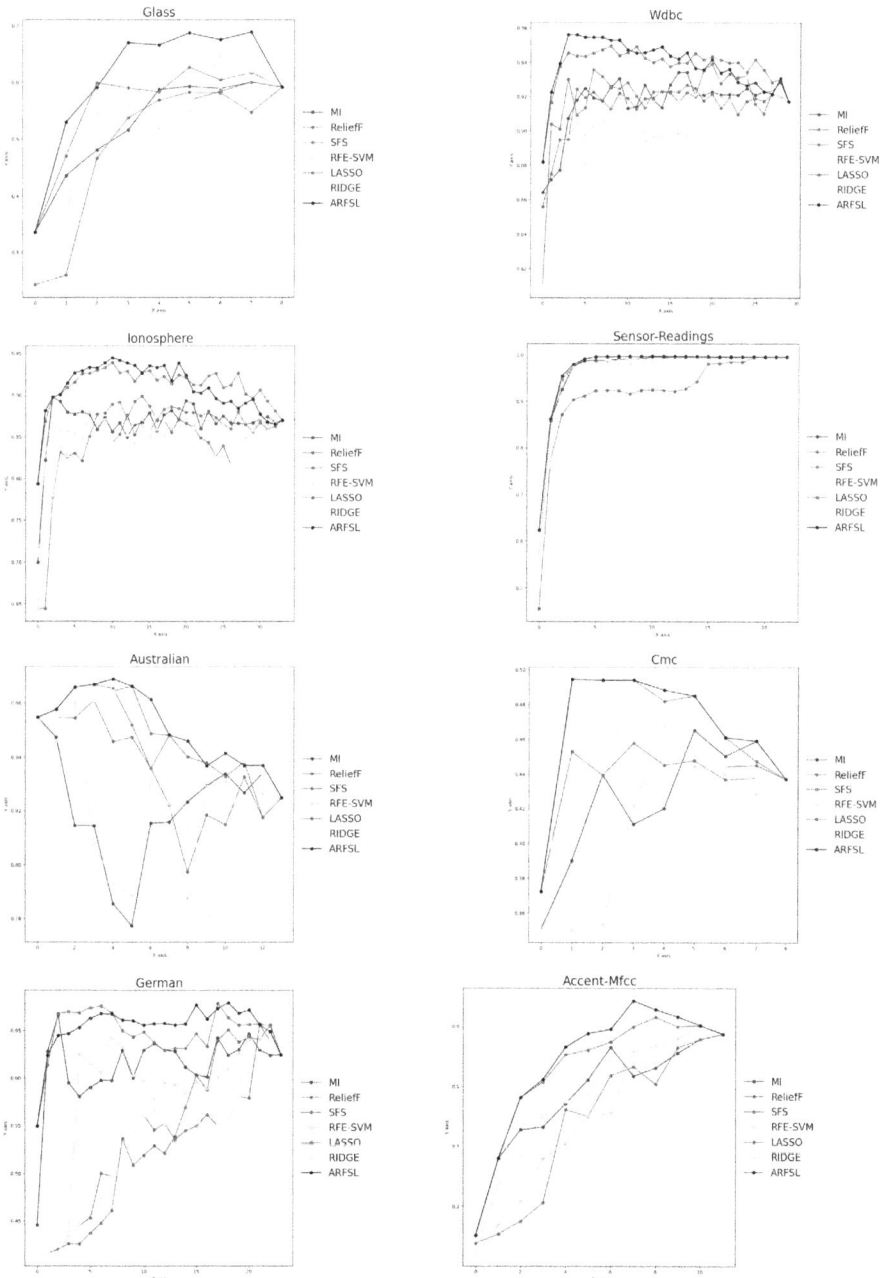

Fig. 4. For each dataset, the performance in terms of F-measure of the selected attributes based on the sizes of the selected attribute subsets (Color figure online)

5 Conclusion

The objective of this work was to select a subset of attributes from the association rules, using as a comparison criterion the performance of the classification model in terms of accuracy, F-measure and precision on the selected datasets. This work proposes to carry out a second phase when mining the best subsets of attributes by considering the attributes that have not been selected by the association rules and by considering the ordered vector of attributes as a model. The experimental results show that ARFSL is better in terms of prediction performance and number of selected attributes on the datasets presented above on accuracy, F-measure and precision metrics. It also allows you to select subsets of attributes with the best performance based on the number of attributes selected. ARFSL in the majority of cases produces better results compared to SFS and when it does not, it reduces the number of selected attributes. In further work, we will study the impact of taking cost sensitivity into account on association rules in the context of attribute selection.

References

1. Akhiat, Y., Chahhou, M., Zinedine, A.: Feature selection based on graph representation. In: 2018 IEEE 5th International Congress on Information Science and Technology (CiSt), pp. 232–237. IEEE (2018)
2. Liu, H., Setiono, R., et al.: A probabilistic approach to feature selection-a filter solution. In: ICML, vol. 96, pp. 319–327. Citeseer (1996)
3. John, G.H., Kohavi, R., Pfleger, K.: Irrelevant features and the subset selection problem. In: Machine Learning Proceedings 1994, pp. 121–129. Elsevier (1994)
4. Zhou, Z.: Machine Learning Beijing (2016)
5. Qu, Y., Fang, Y., Yan, F.: Feature selection algorithm based on association rules. J. Phys. Conf. Ser. **1168**, 052012 (2019)
6. Tibshirani, R.: Regression shrinkage and selection via the Lasso. J. Roy. Stat. Soc. Ser. B Methodol. **58**(1), 267–288 (1996)
7. Hoerl, A.E., Kennard, R.W.: Ridge regression: biased estimation for nonorthogonal problems. Technometrics **12**(1), 55–67 (1970)
8. Raman, B., Ioerger, T.R.: Instance-based filter for feature selection. J. Mach. Learn. Res. **1**(3), 1–23 (2002)
9. Kononenko, I.: Estimating attributes: analysis and extensions of RELIEF. In: European Conference on Machine Learning, pp. 171–182. Springer, Berlin, Heidelberg (1994)
10. Kohavi, R., John, G.H.: Wrappers for feature subset selection. Artif. Intell. **97**(1–2), 273–324 (1997)
11. Battiti, R.: Using mutual information for selecting features in supervised neural net learning. IEEE Trans. Neural Netw. **5**(4), 537–550 (1994)
12. Chandrashekar, G., Sahin, F.: A survey on feature selection methods. Comput. Electr. Eng. **40**(1), 16–28 (2014)
13. Guyon, I., Weston, J., Barnhill, S., Vapnik, V.: Gene selection for cancer classification using support vector machines. Mach. Learn. **46**(1), 389–422 (2002)
14. Salma, M.U., et al.: Reducing the feature space using constraint-governed association rule mining. J. Intell. Syst. **26**(1), 139–152 (2017)

15. Chawla, S.: Feature selection, association rules network and theory building. In: Feature Selection in Data Mining, pp. 14–21. PMLR (2010)
16. Pandey, G., Chawla, S., Poon, S., Arunasalam, B., Davis, J.G.: Association rules network: definition and applications. Stat. Anal. Data Min. ASA Data Sci. J. **1**(4), 260–279 (2009)
17. Pudil, P., Novovičová, J., Kittler, J.: Floating search methods in feature selection. Pattern Recogn. Lett. **15**(11), 1119–1125 (1994)
18. Yu, L., Liu, H.: Efficient feature selection via analysis of relevance and redundancy. J. Mach. Learn. Res. **5**, 1205–1224 (2004)
19. Robnik-Sikonja, M., Kononenko, I.: Theoretical and empirical analysis of relieff and rrelieff. Mach. Learn. **53**, 23–69 (2003)
20. Tang, J., Alelyani, S., Liu, H.: Feature selection for classification: a review. In: Algorithms and Applications, Data Classification, p. 37 (2014)
21. Fonti, V., Belitser, E.: Feature selection using lasso. VU Amsterdam Rese. Pap. Bus. Anal. **30**, 1–25 (2017)
22. Bouchlaghem, Y., Akhiat, Y., Amjad, S.: Feature selection: a review and comparative study. In: E3S Web of Conferences, vol. 351, pp. 01046. EDP Sciences (2022)
23. German, B.: Glass identification. In: UCI Machine Learning Repository (1987). https://doi.org/10.24432/C5WW2P
24. Hofmann, H.: Statlog (German Credit Data). In: UCI Machine Learning Repository (1994). https://doi.org/10.24432/C5NC77
25. Quinlan, R.: Statlog (Australian Credit Approval). In: UCI Machine Learning Repository. https://doi.org/10.24432/C59012
26. Wolberg, W.M.: Breast cancer Wisconsin (diagnostic). In: UCI Machine Learning Repository (1995). https://doi.org/10.24432/C5DW2B
27. Lim, T.-S.: Contraceptive method choice. In: UCI Machine Learning Repository (1997). https://doi.org/10.24432/C59W2D
28. Speaker Accent Recognition. In: UCI Machine Learning Repository (2020). https://doi.org/10.24432/C52329
29. Sigillito, V., Wing, S., Hutton, L., Baker, K.: Ionosphere. In: UCI Machine Learning Repository (1989). https://doi.org/10.24432/C5W01B
30. Vergara, A.: Gas sensor array drift dataset. In: UCI Machine Learning Repository (2012). https://doi.org/10.24432/C5RP6W

Stationary Wavelet Transform Based Watermarking for Telemedicine Image Security

Aminata Ngom[1,2(✉)], Samba Sidibé[2], Ndeye Fatou Ngom[2], and Oumar Niang[2]

[1] LACGAA Laboratory, Cheikh Anta Diop University, Dakar, Senegal
myangoma@gmail.com
[2] LTISI Laboratory, Thies Polytechnic School, Thies BP A10, Senegal
https://ept.edu.sn/, https://www.ucad.sn/

Abstract. In the rapidly developing field of telemedicine, the security of sensitive medical data remains a critical concern. This paper presents an integrated digital watermarking and encryption method designed to enhance the security of both medical images and associated textual data. Using the Stationary Wavelet Transform (SWT), this method embeds a digital watermark into medical images to ensure their integrity and traceability. At the same time, both the image and the associated textual data are secured using a combination of RSA digital signatures and AES encryption, reinforcing the confidentiality and integrity of the data. This dual approach not only protects against unauthorized data manipulation and access, but also ensures that the watermark is resistant to a wide range of digital threats. Extensive evaluations confirm the robustness of our proposed solution against common and sophisticated attacks, setting new standards for secure telemedicine data transmission. The proposed solution is essential for safeguarding patient privacy and trust in digital health systems and provides a comprehensive framework for the protection of medical data.

Keywords: Telemedicine · Stationary Wavelet Transform · Watermarking · Digital signature · Cyber Security

1 Introduction

The digital transformation of healthcare, particularly through telemedicine, has fundamentally changed access to medical services. It enables rapid and remote consultation, diagnosis and treatment planning. However, this transformation posess significant challenges in ensuring the security and integrity of sensitive medical data. The protection of this data is critical not only for the maintenance of patient confidentiality, but also for preserving the authenticity and integrity of the information shared across networks. Telemedicine relies heavily on transmitting high-resolution medical images and detailed textual medical records between providers and patients. These transmissions pose significant risks to patient safety and privacy because they are vulnerable to interception, unauthorised access and manipulation. Increasingly sophisticated cyber threats require the development of robust security solutions that protect data from tampering and ensure confidentiality during transmission. In this paper, we present a robust digital watermarking technique combined with encryption and digital signatures to enhance the security of medical images and related textual data in telemedicine environments. The proposed architecture uses Stationary Wavelet Transform (SWT) to embed digital watermarks in medical images and combines RSA signatures and AES encryption to secure both the image and textual data. This approach ensures that all forms of medical data are protected from unauthorised access and manipulation, while maintaining their usability and integrity. Our dual-layer security mechanism strengthens the protection of medical data and facilitates the traceability of its origin and modification, which is critical for legal and medical audit purposes. The solution ensures that even if data is intercepted, its integrity and authenticity can be verified, supporting non-repudiation. The paper presents a detailed discussion of the methodology, implementation and testing of the proposed security solution, highlighting its effectiveness through experimental results and comparisons with existing security measures. The main contributions of this paper are as follows:

- Thecombination of digital watermarking and encryption methods to enhance the security of both medical images and associated textual data.
- The use of Stationary Wavelet Transform (SWT) in the embedding step of the digital watermark in medical images to ensure their integrity and traceability.
- The combination of RSA digital signatures and AES encryption to secure both the image and the associated textual data, strengthening the confidentiality and integrity of the data.

The rest of the paper is structured as follows. Section 2 discusses previous work on security solutions in telemedicine. Section 3 presents concepts such as stationary wavelet transform (SWT), AES encryption, RSA digital signature embedding and LSB embedding. Section 4 describes the design of the proposed solution and its compliance with medical security standards. Section 6 analyses the performance and discusses the results of the experiment. Section 6 concludes our work and gives some perspectives.

2 Related Work

Digital watermarking has emerged as a key technique for ensuring the integrity and authenticity of medical images. Watermarking techniques can be broadly classified into spatial domain and frequency domain techniques. Spatial domain techniques, such as the Least Significant Bit (LSB) method [14], involve directly modifying the pixel values of the host image. Although easy to implement, these methods often lack robustness against common imaging attacks, including compression, noise addition, and cropping.

Frequency domain techniques embed watermarks in the transformed coefficients of the image. One of the earliest and most popular among them is the discrete cosine transform (DCT) [5]. DCT transforms the image into the frequency domain, allowing watermarks to be embedded in significant frequency coefficients, making them less perceptible. However, DCT-based watermarking is susceptible to geometric attacks, which limits its robustness in dynamic telemedicine environments. The Discrete Wavelet Transform (DWT) [1,6], offers improved robustness compared to DCT by providing multi-resolution analysis of the image. DWT divides the image into different frequency bands, allowing watermarks to be embedded in less perceptible regions. However, DWT can suffer from information loss due to downsampling during the transformation process. To address these limitations, the Stationary Wavelet Transform (SWT) [7] has been proposed as a superior alternative. Unlike the DWT, the SWT is shift-invariant and does not involve down-sampling, making it more robust to geometric attacks and noise. The redundancy of SWT increases its robustness, although this also increases computational complexity and storage requirements [2–4]. In the study of Shokrollahi and Yazdi [11], a robust blind watermarking scheme based on SWT is proposed that uses all subband decompositions of the image to embed the watermark. Their results show significant improvements in robustness against various attacks, as evaluated by NCC and PSNR metrics. Another study [18] highlights the advantages of applying SWT in the frequency domain for medical image watermarking. The authors emphasize that embedding the watermark in the SWT coefficients, especially within the first subband, significantly increases resistance to attacks compared to spatial domain methods. The results confirm the effectivenes of this approach in maintaining image quality and robustness, as evidenced by high PSNR and low Bit Error Ratio (BER) values. Moreover, the integration of SWT in a two-level watermarking scheme, coupled with chaos-based encryption, demonstrates superior performance in securing medical images within telemedicine [19]. By using SWT and SVD, this method achieves high PSNR and Normalized Cross Correlation (NCC) values, underscoring the efficacy of SWT in preserving both the quality and integrity of medical images under various attacks. Collectively, these studies illustrate the critical role of SWT in advancing the security and robustness of medical image processing.

In addition to SWT based watermarking, encryption techniques play a critical role in securing medical data. Advanced Encryption Standard (AES) [9] and RSA encryption [10] encryption are widely used to protect textual medical records and provide non-repudiation mechanisms. While these techniques are highly effective, integrating them with robust watermarking strategies such as SWT provides a comprehensive solution to the challenges of securing medical data in telemedicine. Despite advances in watermarking and encryption techniques, traditional methods often fall short when it comes to providing the comprehensive traceability and verification mechanisms that are essential in a medical setting.

In this paper, we combine SWT-based watermarking with RSA and AES to create a more robust and secure framework for the protection of medical data in a telemedicine environment. In this paper, we combine SWT-based watermarking with RSA and AES to create a more robust and secure framework for the protection of medical data in a telemedicine environment.

3 Preliminaries

The basic concepts and techniques underlying the proposed methodology are presented in this section.

3.1 Stationary Wavelet Transform (SWT)

The Stationary Wavelet Transform (SWT) [7] is a wavelet transform algorithm designed to overcome the lack of translation invariance in the Discrete Wavelet Transform (DWT) [6]. Unlike DWT, SWT avoids downsampling during decomposition and maintains consistent resolution by inserting zeros after filtering, preserving signal integrity and enabling more accurate analysis. This makes SWT robust and cost-effective, ideal for securing medical images in telemedicine [8]. SWT provides multi-scale and multi-directional analysis, enhancing redundancy and shift invariance [15]. SWT is applied at a single level to decompose the medical images into different subbands in the proposed solution of this paper. This allows the watermark to be embedded in an efficient manner, while ensuring that the image quality is preserved and the system remains robust to various attacks. Consider an image $f(x,y)$ with dimensions $H \times W$. The decomposition at the level i using SWT can be described mathematically by the Eq. 1.

$$\begin{cases} S_{i+1}(a,b) = \sum_j \sum_l g_j^i g_l^i S_i(a+j, b+l) \\ S_{i+1}^h(a,b) = \sum_j \sum_l h_j^i g_l^i S_i(a+j, b+l) \\ S_{i+1}^v(a,b) = \sum_j \sum_l g_j^i h_l^i S_i(a+j, b+l) \\ S_{i+1}^d(a,b) = \sum_j \sum_l h_j^i h_l^i S_i(a+j, b+l) \end{cases} \quad (1)$$

In the Eq. 1, $a = 1, 2, ..., H$ and $b = 1, 2, ..., W$, g_j^i and g_l^i are the LP filters, while h_j^i and h_l^i are the HP filters. S_i and S_{i+1} denote the low-frequency subband at levels i and $i+1$, respectively, with S_{i+1}^h, S_{i+1}^v, and S_{i+1}^d representing the horizontal, vertical, and diagonal detail coefficients at level $i+1$.

The inverse SWT, which is used to reconstruct the original signal from the decomposed subbands, is calculated by the Eq. 2.

$$\begin{aligned} \tilde{S}_i(a,b) = &\sum_j \sum_l \tilde{g}_j^i \tilde{g}_l^i \tilde{S}_{i+1}(a+j, b+l) \\ &+ \sum_j \sum_l \tilde{h}_j^i \tilde{g}_l^i \tilde{S}_{i+1}^h(a+j, b+l) \\ &+ \sum_j \sum_l \tilde{g}_j^i \tilde{h}_l^i \tilde{S}_{i+1}^v(a+j, b+l) \\ &+ \sum_j \sum_l \tilde{h}_j^i \tilde{h}_l^i \tilde{S}_{i+1}^d(a+j, b+l) \end{aligned} \quad (2)$$

In this inverse process, $\tilde{g}_j^i$ and $\tilde{g}_l^i$ are the reconstruction of the LP filters, while $\tilde{h}_j^i$ and $\tilde{h}_l^i$ are the reconstruction of the HP filters. $\tilde{S}_i$ and $\tilde{S}_{i+1}$ represent the reconstruction of the low-frequency subband at levels i and $i+1$, respectively. Similarly, $\tilde{S}_{i+1}^h$, $\tilde{S}_{i+1}^v$, and $\tilde{S}_{i+1}^d$ correspond to the reconstructed horizontal, vertical, and diagonal detail coefficients, respectively.

3.2 AES Encryption

The Advanced Encryption Standard (AES) [9] is a widely used symmetric encryption algorithm known for its efficiency and strong security. AES encrypts data in blocks of fixed size, typically 128 bits. It uses key sizes of 128, 192 or 256 bits. Because of its high efficiency, AES is suitable for encrypting large amounts of data, including sensitive medical records. The strength of AES lies in its resistance to brute-force attacks, achieved through the use of larger key sizes. For example, breaking a 128-bit AES key would require 2^{128} attempts, making it a computational infeasible task. AES encryption involves several rounds of transformations, the number of which depends on the size of the key: 10 rounds for a 128-bit key, 12 rounds for a 192-bit key, and 14 rounds for a 256-bit key. Each round consists of four main operations:

1. Non-linear substitution (SubBytes): each byte is replaced with another according to a predefined substitution box (S-box), enhancing confusion in the encryption process.
2. Transposition (ShiftRows): each row in the state is shifted cyclically by a certain number of bytes, contributing to the diffusion of the plaintext.
3. MixColumns operation: mixes the bytes within each column of the state, further enhancing diffusion by combining the four bytes in each column.
4. AddRoundKey: each byte of the state is combined with a round key derived from the cipher key using a key schedule. This ensures that the ciphertext is heavily dependent on the key, providing strong security.

Mathematically, the AES encryption process can be described Eq. 3.:

$$C = E_K(P) \qquad (3)$$

where P is the plaintext, C is the resulting ciphertext, and K is the encryption key. The decryption process, which reverses the encryption to recover the original plaintext, is given by Eq. 4:

$$P = D_K(C) \qquad (4)$$

where D_K represents the AES decryption function. In the proposed architecture, AES is used to encrypt both the medical text data and the image data, along with their respective digital signatures. This approach guanrantees that the data remains confidential and secure throughout transmission. The process begins by combining the medical records with their respective signatures into a single data structure. A random AES key is then generated for encryption. The combined data is encrypted using this AES key, converting the plaintext data into ciphertext, which is then securely transmitted over the network. This ensures that even if the data is intercepted, it cannot be interpreted without the corresponding decryption key, thus maintaining the confidentiality and integrity of the transmitted medical information.

3.3 RSA Digital Signatures

RSA is an asymmetric cryptographic algorithm widely used to secure digital signatures [10], ensuring data integrity, authenticity and non-repudiation. In our methodology, RSA is used to sign both the medical text and image data. This provides a robust mechanism for verifying the origin and integrity of the data. The process of creating a digital signature using RSA involves two key steps: hashing and encryption.

First, the plaintext message M is hashed using a secure hash algorithm, such as SHA-256, to produce a fixed-size hash value $H(M)$. This hash value uniquely represents the content of the message.

$$H(M) = \text{Hash}(M) \tag{5}$$

Next, the hash value $H(M)$ is encrypted using the sender's private key d to generate the digital signature S. This step ensures that only the sender, who possesses the private key, can create this signature.

$$S = H(M)^d \mod n \tag{6}$$

Here, n is the modulus, which is a component of both the public and private keys in RSA. The verification process involves decrypting the digital signature using the sender's public key e to retrieve the hash value $H(M)$:

$$H(M) = S^e \mod n \tag{7}$$

The plaintext message M is hashed again to produce a new hash value $H'(M)$. The hash value $H(M)$, obtained from the signature, is then compared with the newly computed hash value $H'(M)$. If they match, the signature is valid, confirming that the data has not been altered and verifying the sender's identity.

RSA offers several advantages, including robust security and ensuring data integrity and authenticity. However, it also has some limitations, such as computational complexity and the need for secure key management. In our architecture, RSA digital signatures are used to sign both the medical text data and the image data. This involves hashing the data and encrypting the hash with the sender's private key to create a signature. The signed data, along with the signature, are then encrypted using AES to ensure confidentiality during transmission. On receipt, the recipient decrypts the data using AES, verifies the signatures using RSA and confirms the integrity and authenticity of the data.

3.4 Least Significant Bit (LSB) Embedding

Least Significant Bit (LSB) embedding is a spatial domain technique used to embed secret data in an image. It involves modifying the least significant bits of the pixel values in the host image to hide the secret data. This technique is widely used because of its simplicity and ease of implementation. Consider a cover image with pixel values represented in binary form. To embed a secret message, the least significant bit of each pixel value is replaced with a bit from the secret message. For example, if the binary representation of a pixel value is 11001010 and the bit from the secret message is 1, the modified pixel value becomes 11001011.

The embedding process can be mathematically represented as:

$$\text{Pixel}_{new} = \left\lfloor \frac{\text{Pixel}_{old}}{2} \right\rfloor \times 2 + \text{bit}_{secret} \qquad (8)$$

where Pixel_{old} is the original pixel value, $\lfloor \cdot \rfloor$ denotes the floor function, and bit_{secret} is the bit from the secret message. By dividing the original pixel value by 2 and applying the floor function, the least significant bit is effectively removed, equivalent to a bitwise right shift. Multiplying the result by 2 shifts the bits to the left, making room for a new LSB, equivalent to a bitwise left shift. Finally, adding the secret bit embeds it in the least significant position of the pixel value. The LSB is easy to implement, computationally efficient, and offers a high capacity for data insertion, especially for large images. However, it is vulnerable to image processing attacks such as compression, noise addition, cropping, and the hidden data can be easily detected and extracted if the embedding method is known.

To address these vulnerabilities, we first apply the Stationary Wavelet Transform (SWT) to the secret image, decomposing it into different subbands without downsampling. This preserves the resolution of the image and ensures shift invariance. This increases the robustness of the embedded data against common image processing attacks such as compression, noise addition and cropping. The benefits of using SWT before LSB embedding include enhanced robustness, preservation of image quality and shift invariance. By decomposing the image into subbands, SWT allows LSB embedding to be applied to a transformed version of the image, making the embedded data less vulnerable to attack. SWT preserves the resolution of the image, ensuring that the visual quality of the cover image is maintained after embedding. SWT's redundancy and shiftinvariance properties improve the stability and reliability of the embedded data. In this paper, the secret medical image is first compressed using SWT, which generates subbands containing different frequency components of the image. The approximate subband containing the most significant information is then used for LSB embedding. This method ensures that the embedded data is less detectable and more resistant to tampering. After embedding the SWT-compressed image into the cover image using LSB, the resulting embedded image is transmitted along with the encrypted textual medical data and their respective signatures. On reception, the embedded image is extracted, decompressed using inverse

SWT and verified for integrity and authenticity using the associated RSA signatures. This multi-layered approach enhances the security and robustness of medical data transmission in telemedicine environments.

4 Proposed Scheme

In this section, we describe the overall architecture of our proposed scheme for securing medical images and textual data using a combination of digital watermarking, encryption, and digital signatures. The scheme is designed to protect sensitive medical data during transmission in telemedicine applications. The process involves several steps that ensure data confidentiality, integrity, authenticity of the transmitted medical information and robustness against attacks.

Figure 1 describes the general diagram of the proposed scheme. The diagram illustrates the detailed process of securing medical data in a telemedicine environment, including both textual and image data. The workflow starts with the user acting as the sender, creating and signing the medical record using RSA, then encrypting it together with the image data using AES. The image is first compressed using Stationary Wavelet Transform (SWT) and then embedded into a cover image using Least Significant Bit (LSB). The combined encrypted data and embedded image are then transmitted to the receiver, typically a doctor. Upon receiving the data, the receiver decrypts the data, verifies the signatures, extracts the compressed image from the cover image and finally decompresses the image. Figure 2 complements the general diagram by introducing key security measures. Before any data processing or transmission takes place, the patient device and the telemedicine server authenticate each other to ensure that both parties are legitimate. This mutual authentication process leads to the establishment of a session key, which is then used to encrypt the medical data during transmission. The session key ensures secure communication throughout the session, protecting both text and image data from unauthorized access. This additional layer of security enhances the overall integrity and confidentiality of the telemedicine process.

4.1 Embedding Stage

The embedding stage is a critical part of the proposed scheme, where sensitive medical data and images are securely processed and embedded into a cover image. This process involves several key steps: creating and signing the medical record, compressing the secret image using the Stationary Wavelet Transform (SWT), and embedding the compressed image into a cover image using Least Significant Bit (LSB) embedding. Each step is described in detail below, including the relevant mathematical equations.

Medical Record Creation and Signing: The medical record containing sensitive patient information is first created and converted into JSON format. To

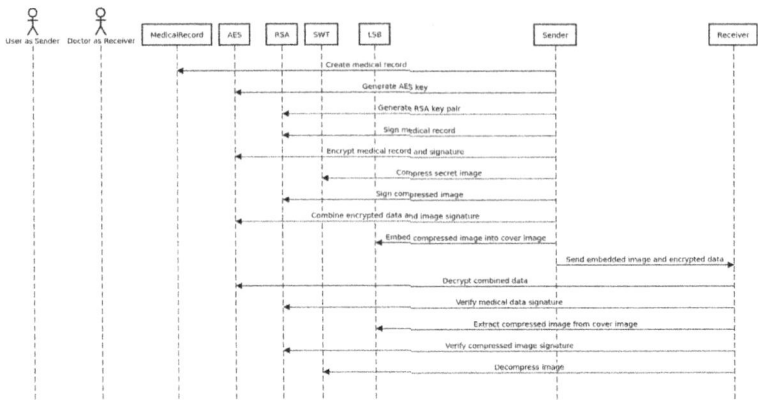

Fig. 1. General Diagram of the Proposed Scheme.

ensure its authenticity and integrity, the record is digitally signed using RSA. The SHA-256 hash of the JSON-encoded medical record is computed as follows:

$$H_{\text{record}} = \text{SHA256}(\text{medical\_record\_JSON}) \tag{9}$$

This hash is then encrypted with the sender's private RSA key to generate the digital signature:

$$\text{Signature}_{\text{record}} = \text{RSA\_Sign}(H_{\text{record}}, \text{private\_key}) \tag{10}$$

Secret Image Compression Using Stationary Wavelet Transform (SWT): The secret image is decomposed into its color channels (e.g., Red, Green, Blue channels). Each channel undergoes a single-level decomposition using the Stationary Wavelet Transform (SWT). SWT decomposes the image into four subbands: approximation (cA), horizontal detail (cH), vertical detail (cV), and diagonal detail (cD). The decomposition at level 1 for an image I is given by:

$$I_{\text{SWT}} = \text{SWT}(I) = (cA, cH, cV, cD) \tag{11}$$

The approximation subband cA is retained and used to represent the compressed version of the image, which contains the most significant information. The compressed image is then reconstructed as:

$$I_{\text{compressed}} = cA_R \oplus cA_G \oplus cA_B \tag{12}$$

where cA_R, cA_G, and cA_B are the approximation subbands of the Red, Green, and Blue channels, respectively. An SHA-256 hash of the compressed image is generated:

$$H_{\text{image}} = \text{SHA256}(I_{\text{compressed}}) \tag{13}$$

This hash is then signed using RSA to produce the digital signature for the compressed image:

$$\text{Signature}_{\text{image}} = \text{RSA Sign}(H_{\text{image}}, \text{private\_key}) \tag{14}$$

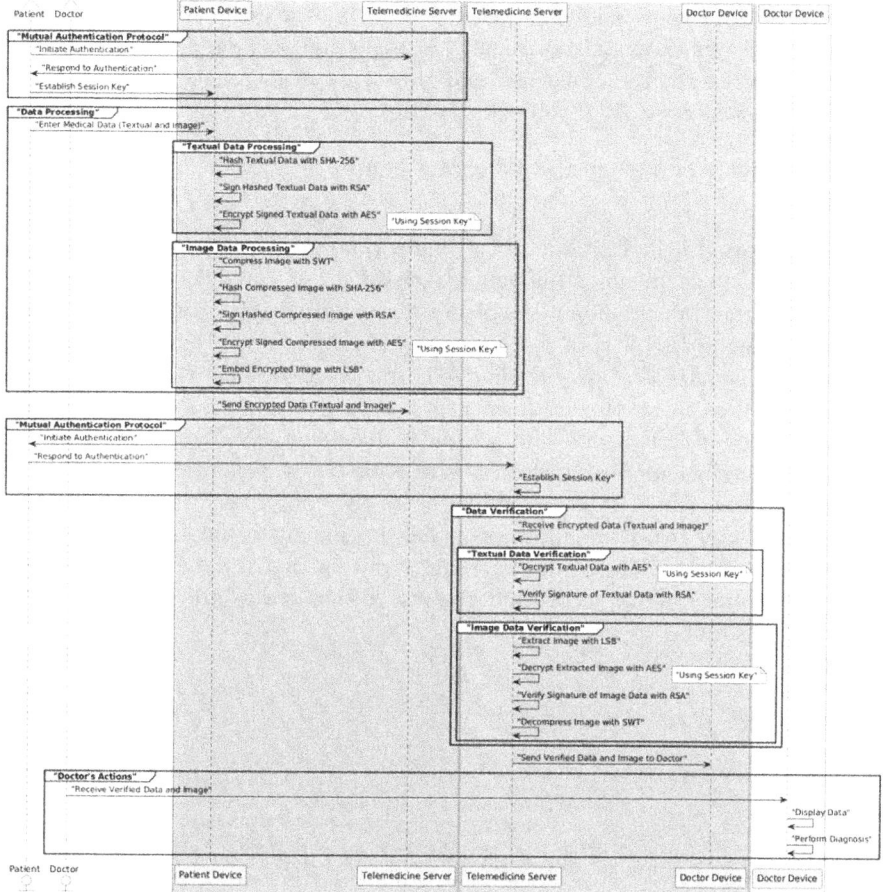

Fig. 2. Logic Architecture of the Proposed Scheme.

Combining and Encrypting Data. Before encryption, we assume that a secure authentication protocol has been established between the communicating parties. This protocol is responsible for verifying the identity of the sender and receiver and securely negotiating a session key. This session key is then used for encrypting the data. Once authentication is complete and the session key is securely established, the combined data is encrypted using the Advanced Encryption Standard (AES) in Cipher Block Chaining (CBC) mode with the session key. The encryption process is mathematically defined as:

$$C = \text{AES}_{\text{encrypt}}(\text{combined data JSON}, \text{AES key}) \qquad (15)$$

where *AES key* is the session key generated during the authentication protocol. The resulting ciphertext C represents the securely encrypted combined data. The medical record, its signature, and the compressed image's signature are combined into a single JSON object:

$$\text{combined data} = \{\text{medical record}, \text{Signature}_{record}, \text{Signature}_{image}\}$$

Transmission. In the last step of the embedding process, the encrypted image is transmitted to the recipient along with the AES-encrypted combined data. We assume that the transmission takes place over a secure network where an authentication protocol [12,13] is in place to verify the identity of the communicating parties. This ensures that only authorized users can access the data. In addition, the use of a session key for AES encryption further enhances security by protecting the confidentiality of data within each session. SWT compression prior to LSB embedding increases the robustness of the watermark against various types of attacks, while LSB embedding hides the compressed image within the cover image. This two-layer approach makes it difficult for unauthorized parties to detect or tamper with the hidden data, ensuring that the medical record and compressed image, along with their respective signatures, are securely embedded and transmitted.

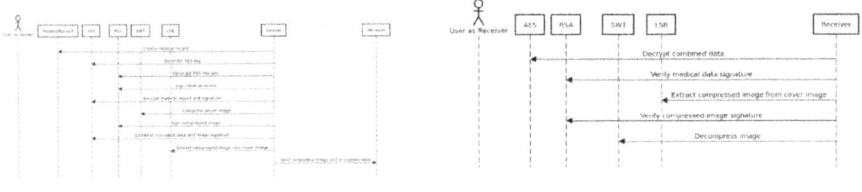

(a) Embedding Process Diagram of the Proposed Scheme

(b) Extraction process diagram of the proposed scheme.

Fig. 3. Extraction Diagram Process of the Proposed Scheme.

The Fig. 3a outlines the secure transmission of medical data in a telemedicine system. It starts with the sender creating a medical record, which is then signed using RSA and encrypted using AES. At the same time, a secret image is compressed using Stationary Wavelet Transform (SWT), signed and embedded into a cover image using Least Significant Bit (LSB). The encrypted data and embedded image are securely transmitted to the recipient, ensuring the integrity, authenticity and confidentiality of the medical information. Once the data has been transmitted, Fig. 4 shows the steps taken by the recipient to securely retrieve and verify the medical data. Upon receiving the data, the receiver first decrypts the combined data using AES. It then verifies the authenticity of the medical data by checking the RSA signature. The receiver then extracts the compressed image from the cover image using the LSB technique, verifies the image signature using RSA, and finally decompresses the image using Stationary Wavelet Transform (SWT). This process ensures that the medical data received is both authentic and intact.

4.2 Extraction Stage

The extraction stage is the inverse of the embedding process, where the hidden and encrypted medical data, along with the secret image, are securely retrieved and verified. This stage includes the decryption of the combined data, verification of the digital signatures, and decompression of the hidden image. Below is the detailed explanation of this process.

Retrieving and Decrypting the Combined Data. Once the encoded image and encrypted data are received, the first step is to extract the hidden compressed image from the cover image using LSB decoding. The decoding process is the reverse of the LSB embedding process. Each pixel of the encoded image is examined to retrieve the least significant bit, which corresponds to the secret image data. The secret image is reconstructed using:

$$\text{bit}_{\text{secret}} = \text{Pixel}_{\text{new}} \& 1 \tag{16}$$

The entire secret image is then reconstructed by combining the retrieved bits. Once the secret image is retrieved, the combined data (which includes the medical record and the signatures) is decrypted using the AES key that was used during the encryption stage. The AES decryption in CBC mode can be represented as:

$$\text{combined\_data\_json} = \text{AES}_{\text{decrypt}}(C, \text{AES\_key}) \tag{17}$$

where C is the ciphertext and AES_key is the symmetric key used during encryption.

Verification of Digital Signatures. After decryption, the JSON object containing the medical record and the digital signatures is parsed. The first verification step is to check the integrity and authenticity of the medical record using its digital signature. The SHA-256 hash of the decrypted medical record is computed:

$$H_{\text{record\_retrieved}} = \text{SHA256}(\text{medical\_record\_retrieved}) \tag{18}$$

This hash is then verified against the decrypted signature using the sender's public RSA key:

$$\text{RSA\_Verify}(H_{\text{record\_retrieved}}, \text{Signature}_{\text{record\_retrieved}}, \text{public\_key}) \tag{19}$$

Similarly, the signature of the compressed image is verified by computing the hash of the retrieved compressed image:

$$H_{\text{image\_retrieved}} = \text{SHA256}(I_{\text{compressed\_retrieved}}) \tag{20}$$

and then verifying it using the public RSA key:

$$\text{RSA\_Verify}(H_{\text{image\_retrieved}}, \text{Signature}_{\text{image\_retrieved}}, \text{public\_key}) \quad (21)$$

Successful verification of these signatures confirms that the data has not been tampered with during transmission.

Decompressing the Image with SWT. Once the signatures are verified, the next step is to decompress the retrieved compressed image. The secret image, which was compressed using the Stationary Wavelet Transform (SWT) during the embedding stage, is now decompressed to recover the original image. The inverse Stationary Wavelet Transform (iSWT) is applied to the approximation subband coefficients obtained during the embedding stage:

$$I_{\text{decompressed}} = \text{iSWT}(cA_R, cA_G, cA_B) \quad (22)$$

where cA_R, cA_G, and cA_B are the approximation subbands of the Red, Green, and Blue channels, respectively. The decompressed image is reconstructed by combining these subbands to obtain the final image.

Reconstructing the Original Medical Data and Image. The original medical data and the secret image are reconstructed in the final step. The verified and decrypted medical record, together with the decompressed image, represents the original data before embedding. This reconstructed data is then presented to the recipient, ensuring that the integrity, confidentiality and authenticity of the medical data and image are maintained. The extraction stage effectively reverses the embedding process, ensuring that the hidden data is accurately retrieved, verified and reconstructed. The use of SWT for image compression and LSB for embedding, combined with AES encryption and RSA digital signatures, provides a robust and secure method for transmitting sensitive medical data in telemedicine environments.

4.3 Compliance with Medical Security Standards

When it comes to securing medical data, it's essential to comply with established standards such as the Health Insurance Portability and Accountability Act (HIPAA) in the United States and the General Data Protection Regulation (GDPR) in Europe. These standards set strict requirements for the protection, confidentiality and integrity of patient data. For example, HIPAA requires that medical data be encrypted both in transit and at rest, and that access to this data be controlled by strong authentication mechanisms. In addition, HIPAA emphasises the importance of data integrity, ensuring that medical records cannot be altered without detection. Similarly, GDPR imposes strict controls on the processing of personal data, requiring data controllers to implement appropriate technical and organisational measures to protect data from unauthorised access, accidental loss or damage. Our proposed scheme addresses the following security objectives recommended by these standards:

- Confidentiality: The use of AES encryption ensures that both medical images and textual data are protected from unauthorised access during transmission and storage.
- Integrity: RSA digital signatures offer a robust mechanism for verifying that medical data has not been tampered with, ensuring data integrity.
- Authentication: The process of signing data with RSA not only verifies integrity, but also authenticates the identity of the sender.
- Non-repudiation: Digital signatures prevent the sender from denying the origin of the data, fulfilling the requirement for non-repudiation.
- Access control: The secure distribution and management of keys and the implementation of session keys help to control access to sensitive medical data.

Table 1. Compliance with Security Objectives According to HIPAA and GDPR

Security Objective	HIPAA Compliance [16]	GDPR Compliance [17]
Data Confidentiality	✓	✓
Data Integrity	✓	✓
Data Availability	✓	✓
Encryption of Sensitive Data	✓	✓
Authentication and Access Control	✓	✓
Audit Controls and Monitoring	✓	✓
Data Minimization	N/A	✓
Data Subject Rights (e.g., access, correction)	N/A	✓
Data Breach Notification	✓	✓

As shown in Table 1, our proposed scheme meets the critical security objectives set forth by HIPAA and GDPR, thereby providing a comprehensive framework for the secure transmission of medical data in telemedicine environments.

5 Results and Discussion

5.1 Performance Analysis

In this section, we evaluate the performance of the proposed watermarking scheme by calculating the Peak Signal-to-Noise Ratio (PSNR) and Normalized Cross-Correlation (NCC) under various attacks. These metrics are crucial in assessing the robustness and fidelity of the watermarking scheme. Initially, the PSNR between the cover image and the encoded image was calculated to be **65.91 dB**, indicating high visual quality of the watermarked image. The NCC between the compressed image and the recovered compressed image was found to be **1.0000**, indicating that the watermark was perfectly preserved in the absence of attacks. The attacks were designed to simulate common manipulations that a watermarked image might undergo, either intentionally or unintentionally, in real-world scenarios. These include rotation, scaling, noise addition, compression, and cropping. The purpose of calculating PSNR and NCC after these attacks is to measure the resilience of the watermark to such distortions.

PSNR is a widely used metric for assessing the quality of reconstructed images. It is defined as:

$$\text{PSNR} = 10 \cdot \log_{10}\left(\frac{\text{MAX}^2}{\text{MSE}}\right) \qquad (23)$$

where MAX is the maximum possible pixel value of the image and MSE is the Mean Squared Error between the original and the distorted image. Higher PSNR values indicate better image quality, with less noticeable distortions.

NCC is a measure of similarity between the original watermark and the extracted watermark. It is defined as:

$$\text{NCC} = \frac{\sum(I_{\text{original}} \cdot I_{\text{extracted}})}{\sqrt{\sum(I^2_{\text{original}}) \cdot \sum(I^2_{\text{extracted}})}} \qquad (24)$$

where I_{original} and $I_{\text{extracted}}$ are the original and extracted watermark images, respectively. NCC values close to 1 indicate a high correlation between the two images, meaning that the watermark has been successfully extracted. For rotation attacks of 10^{circ}, 20^{circ} and 30^{circ}, the PSNR values decreased significantly to 9.18 dB, 8.92 dB and 8.68 dB respectively. These low PSNR values indicate a significant degradation in image quality due to rotation. The NCC values also decreased to 0.33, 0.29 and 0.23 respectively, showing that the integrity of the watermark was increasingly compromised as the degree of rotation increased. The scaling attack, applied with a scaling ratio of 2, resulted in a PSNR of 39.52 dB and an NCC of 1.00. This PSNR indicates that the image quality was well preserved, and the NCC of 1.00 indicates that the watermark was perfectly resilient to the scaling operation. For the Gaussian noise attacks with increasing variance (0.01 to 0.05), the PSNR values gradually decreased from 20.52 dB to 14.26 dB, indicating a moderate to significant degradation in image quality. However, the NCC values ranged from 0.95 to 0.81, demonstrating that the watermark was still largely intact despite the addition of noise. The JPEG2000 compression attack resulted in a PSNR of 31.64 dB and an NCC of 1.00, demonstrating the robustness of the watermark against compression. Finally, the cropping attack resulted in both low PSNR (9.42 dB) and NCC (0.33) values, indicating that cropping is highly effective in degrading both image quality and watermark integrity. The speckle noise attack resulted in a PSNR of 5.17 dB and an NCC of 0.31, showing that this attack severely degrades both image quality and watermark integrity. Figures 4, 5 and 6 illustrate the various stages of our testing process.

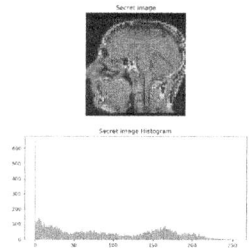
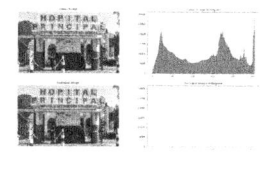
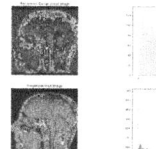
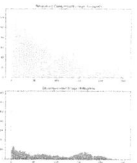

Fig. 4. Secret Image and its histogram.

Fig. 5. The cover image, the encoded image and their histograms.

Fig. 6. The recovered compressed image, the decompressed image and their histograms.

5.2 Discussion

In our study, by integrating Stationary Wavelet Transform (SWT) with cryptographic techniques such as RSA digital signatures and AES encryption, we aimed to improve the robustness and security of watermarking. Our results show that our method provides significant security advantages, which are particularly important for medical data protection, although the peak signal-to-noise ratio (PSNR) and normalised cross-correlation (NCC) values are sometimes lower than those reported by Shokrollahi and Yazdi (2017) [11]. For example, Shokrollahi and Yazdi reported strong robustness against rotation and noise attacks, with PSNR values slightly higher than those observed in our study. However, our method addresses the broader security needs in telemedicine environments by integrating digital signatures and encryption, which ensure the authenticity, integrity and confidentiality of the data Fig. 2. Under rotation attacks, our PSNR values dropped significantly, indicating a weakness in maintaining visual quality Table 3. However, the NCC values remained relatively stable, showing that the watermark can still be recovered, albeit with some loss of quality. This is an important consideration in scenarios where watermark integrity is more important than image quality, such as legal or medical verification (Table 2).

In the case of scaling and JPEG2000 compression attacks, our method performed exceptionally well, with NCC values of 1.00, indicating perfect watermark recovery. This highlights the robustness of the SWT-based watermarking process, especially when combined with the redundancy provided by not downsampling during the transformation process. This is a notable improvement over Shokrollahi and Yazdi's method, which, although robust, did not provide the same level of cryptographic security. In addition, our approach's integration of cryptographic techniques provides a layered defense, which is critical for protecting sensitive medical data. By using RSA digital signatures, we ensure that any change to the data can be detected, preventing unauthorised changes. The use of AES encryption further secures the data against unauthorised access, ensur-

Table 2. Comparison of PSNR and NCC Values with Shokrollahi and Yazdi (2017)

Attack	PSNR (dB)/NCC (Our Method)	PSNR (dB)/NCC (Shokrollahi et al.) [11]
Rotation 10^{circ}	9.18/0.33	10.48/0.95
Rotation 20^{circ}	8.92/0.29	9.40/0.94
Rotation 30^{circ}	8.68/0.23	9.60/0.94
Scaling (Ratio 2)	39.52/1.00	33.11/0.99
Gaussian Noise 0.01	20.52/0.95	14.60/0.98
Gaussian Noise 0.02	17.74/0.91	12.30/0.97
Gaussian Noise 0.03	16.17/0.87	10.31/0.96
Gaussian Noise 0.04	15.08/0.84	9.42/0.95
Gaussian Noise 0.05	14.26/0.81	8.12/0.94
JPEG2000 Compression	31.64/1.00	36.12/0.99
Salt & Pepper Noise	14.03/0.82	12.64/0.97
Cropping	9.42/0.33	13.69/0.97
Speckle Noise	5.17/0.31	14.05/0.98

ing that even if the watermark is tampered with, the underlying data remains protected.

Table 3. Comparison of Security Objectives Achieved

Security Objective	Our Method	Shokrollahi & Yazdi (2017)
Confidentiality (Images & Text)	Yes (Both)	No (Images Only)
Integrity (Images & Text)	Yes (Both)	No (Images Only)
Authenticity (Images & Text)	Yes (Both)	No (Images Only)
Non-Repudiation	Yes	No
Comprehensive Data Protection	Yes (Images & Text)	No (Images Only)

The Table 3 compares the security objectives achieved by our method with those of Shokrollahi and Yazdi (2017). It highlights that our approach provides a more comprehensive strategy for securing medical data. Unlike Shokrollahi and Yazdi's method, which focuses solely on protecting images, our approach extends security measures to both images and textual data, an essential aspect in telemedicine. By incorporating AES encryption and RSA digital signatures, we ensure the confidentiality, integrity, and authenticity of all medical data. Furthermore, our method supports non-repudiation, which is critical for legal and medical audits, and offers a more holistic data protection strategy, better suited to the complex security needs of telemedicine, where both visual and textual data require stringent protection.

6 Conclusion

In this paper, we have proposed an innovative method to secure medical images and associated textual data in the context of telemedicine. The proposed approach combines the stationary wavelet transform (SWT) to embed digital watermarks with RSA digital signatures and AES encryption to protect data integrity and confidentiality. Although our results show that metrics such as PSNR and NCC are sometimes lower compared to existing methods such Asokrollahi and Yazdi (2017), our method offers significant advantages. In particular, the proposed solution not only preserves the integrity of the watermark under various attacks but also improve the overall security by integrating robust cryptographic techniques. The inclusion of RSA digital signatures ensures the authenticity and non-repudiation of medical data before encryption, while AES encryption protects the data from unauthorized access. These additional layers of security are critical in the medical field, where data confidentiality and trust are paramount. In addition, using SWT before the embedding of the watermark provides better robustness against geometric transformations, which is essential in telemedicine environments where images may be subject to various manipulations. Our method strikes an optimal balance between image visual quality, watermark robustness, and data security, making it a robust and secure solution for the transmission of medical data in telemedicine. As the proposed scheme relies on the use of multiple keys (AES, RSA), we recommend the adoption of rigorous key management practices. The use of key management protocols, such as Public Key Infrastructure (PKI), would be beneficial to ensure the secure distribution and storage of keys, thereby reducing the risk of key compromise.

For future work, we plan to explore additional techniques to improve robustness against attacks such as cropping and speckle noise, while maintaining the security benefits inherent in our approach. Beyond enhancing robustness against specific attacks, we will also explore the integration of artificial intelligence (AI) techniques such as machine learning and deep learning in our future work. These technologies could enable the adaptive selection of watermarking strategies based on content or anticipated attack vectors, thereby optimizing security and robustness of the data in various scenarios.

References

1. Ngom, A., Djimnaibeye, S., Ngom, N.F., Sidibé, S., Niang, O.: A new wavelet based steganography method for securing medical data. In: Mambo, A.D., Gueye, A., Bassioni, G. (eds.) Innovations and Interdisciplinary Solutions for Underserved Areas, pp. 132–143. Springer, Cham (2022). ISBN: 978-3-031-23116-2. https://doi.org/10.1007/978-3-031-23116-2_10
2. Nagarjuna, P.V., Ranjeet, K.: Robust blind digital image watermarking scheme based on stationary wavelet transform. In: 2013 Sixth International Conference on Contemporary Computing (IC3), pp. 451–454. IEEE, New York (2013). Keywords: Watermarking, Discrete wavelet transforms, PSNR, Digital images, Stationary wavelet transforms (SWT), Watermarking, Peak signal to noise ratio (PSNR), Normalized cross correlation (NCC). https://doi.org/10.1109/IC3.2013.6612238

3. Novamizanti, L., Suksmono, A., Danudirdjo, D., Budiman, G.: Robust reversible watermarking using stationary wavelet transform and multibit spread spectrum in medical images. Int. J. Intell. Eng. Syst. **15**, 343–354 (2022). https://doi.org/10.22266/ijies2022.0630.29
4. Assini, I., Badri, A., Safi, K., Sahel, A. Abdennaceur, B.: Méthode de Tatouage Robuste pour la Sécurité des Images Mammographiques basée sur SWT-FWHT (2018)
5. Alhatami, E., Bhatti, U., Huang, M., Feng, S.: Review and enhancement of discrete cosine transform (DCT) for medical image fusion, pp. 89–97 (2023). ISBN: 978-981-19-9330-5. https://doi.org/10.1007/978-981-19-9331-2_8
6. Prasad, Pournami, S., Surekha, B., V., Krishnappa, H.K: Medical image fusion techniques using discrete wavelet transform. In: 2019 3rd International Conference on Computing Methodologies and Communication (ICCMC), pp. 614–618 (2019). https://doi.org/10.1109/ICCMC.2019.8819672
7. Chao, Z., Duan, X., Jia, S., Guo, X., Liu, H., Jia, F.: Medical image fusion via discrete stationary wavelet transform and an enhanced radial basis function neural network. Appl. Soft Comput. **118** (2022). Article 108542. https://doi.org/10.1016/j.asoc.2022.108542
8. Novamizanti, L., Suksmono, A., Danudirdjo, D., Budiman, G.: Robust reversible watermarking using stationary wavelet transform and multibit spread spectrum in medical images. Int. J. Intell. Eng. Syst. **15**, 343–354 (2022). https://doi.org/10.22266/ijies2022.0630.29
9. Shete, P., Kohle, S.: Image encryption using AES algorithm: study and evaluation. Int. J. Res. Appl. Sci. Eng. Technol. **10**, 1134–1137 (2022). https://doi.org/10.22214/ijraset.2022.46619
10. Aufa, F.J., Endroyono, Affandi, A.: Security system analysis in combination method: RSA encryption and digital signature algorithm. In: 2018 4th International Conference on Science and Technology (ICST), pp. 1–5 (2018). https://doi.org/10.1109/ICSTC.2018.8528584
11. Shokrollahi, Z., Yazdi, M.: A robust blind watermarking scheme based on stationary wavelet transform. J. Inf. Hiding Multimedia Signal Process. **8**, 676–687 (2017)
12. Djimnaibeye, A., Ngom, A., Sow, A.: Post-quantum cryptography for healthcare: a number theory based two-factor mutual authentication and key exchange protocol over lattices for TMIS. AADM, **41** (2023). https://pphmjopenaccess.com/index.php/aadm/article/view/1212, https://doi.org/10.17654/0974165824001
13. Djimnaibeye, S., Ngom, A., Tchappi, I., Mahamat Hassan, B., Najjar, A.: Improvement of cloud-assisted identity-based anonymous authentication and key agreement protocol for secure WBAN. In: Safe, Secure, Ethical, Responsible Technologies and Emerging Applications - First EAI International Conference, SAFER-TEA 2023, Yaoundé, Cameroon, October 25-27, 2023, Proceedings, Lecture Notes of the Institute for Computer Sciences, Social Informatics and Telecommunications Engineering, vol. 566, pp. 58–70 (2023). https://doi.org/10.1007/978-3-031-56396-6_4
14. Abikoye, O., Ogundokun, R.: Efficiency of LSB steganography on medical information. Int. J. Electri. Comput. Eng. (IJECE) **11**, 4157–4164 (2021). https://doi.org/10.11591/ijece.v11i5.pp4157-4164
15. Nason, G.P., Silverman, B.W.: The stationary wavelet transform and some statistical applications. In: Antoniadis, A., Oppenheim, G. (eds.) LNS, vol. 103, pp. 281–299. Springer, Cham (1995). https://doi.org/10.1007/978-1-4612-2544-7_17

16. U.S. Department of Health and Human Services: Health Insurance Portability and Accountability Act of 1996 (HIPAA). https://www.hhs.gov/hipaa/for-professionals/index.html. Accessed 06 Aug 2024
17. European Parliament and Council of the European Union: Regulation (EU) 2016/679 of the European Parliament and of the Council of 27 April 2016 on the Protection of Natural Persons with Regard to the Processing of Personal Data and on the Free Movement of Such Data (General Data Protection Regulation, GDPR). https://eur-lex.europa.eu/eli/reg/2016/679/oj. Accessed 06 Aug 2024
18. A-Ajlan, A.S.: Stationary wavelet transform-based semi-blind medical image watermarking. In: Proceedings of the 2024 Conference on Computing and Communication, New York, NY, USA. Association for Computing Machinery (2024). https://doi.org/10.1145/3644713.3644734
19. Abirami, R., Malathy, C.: Medical image security by crypto watermarking using enhanced chaos and fruit fly optimization algorithm with SWT and SVD. Multimedia Tools Appl. **83**(27), 70451–70476 (2024). https://doi.org/10.1007/s11042-024-19019-9

Exploring Human Personality Traits in Phishing Success: Contextual Cybersecurity Study

Robert Makila Beni[1(✉)], Landry Mbale[1], and Antoine Bagula[1,2]

[1] Universté Nouveaux Horizons (UNH), Lubumbashi, Democratic Republic of Congo
robert.makila@unhorizons.org
[2] ISAT Laboratory, Univerity of the Western Cape (UWC), Cape Town, South Africa
abagula@uwc.ac.za
http://www.unhorizons.org, https://www.uwc.ac.za

Abstract. In the dynamic landscape of cybersecurity, safeguarding computer systems remains pivotal. With privacy gaining prominence, notably under the GDPR in Europe and POPI act in South Africa, private data emerges as a powerful entity. Despite technological advancements, the human factor remains a vulnerable and enticing target for malicious actors. This paper delves into the multifaceted realm of successful phishing attacks, recognizing the psychological dimension as a pivotal battleground. Focused on the vulnerabilities inherent in the human psyche, we undertake a nuanced exploration of social engineering techniques directed at the weakest link in security humans. Leveraging real-world scenarios and deploying Natural Language Processing (NLP) and machine learning, our study illuminates the heightened sensitivity of successful attacks, particularly among the demographic of young individuals. The key contribution of this paper is to go beyond traditional technical paradigms to scrutinize the impact of contextual parameters, specifically delving into the influence of emotional states on the success of phishing attacks and proposing the reinforced defensive awareness framework (RDAF). By immersing ourselves in authentic situations, we unravel the intricate relationship between the mood in which an attack unfolds and its efficacy. This analysis sheds light on the evolving dynamics of cyber threats, especially within the context of the younger generation.

Keywords: Vishing · Smishing · Quishing · Natural Language Processing · Sentiment Analysis · Social engineering · Cybersecurity

1 Introduction

The rapidly advancing landscape of technology has ushered in an era where the security of computer systems stands as one of the most sensitive and crucial domains. With the pervasive digitization of personal information and the advent

---

Universté Nouveaux Horizons.

of stringent data protection regulations worldwide, the intricate dance between cybersecurity and the vulnerabilities inherent in human behavior takes center stage. As organizations strive to fortify their defenses against cyber threats, social engineering attacks, particularly phishing, have emerged as potent adversaries [1].

In the wake of digital transformations, the respect for privacy and the safeguarding of sensitive data have become paramount concerns. Stringent regulations, both in Europe and globally, underscore the gravity of these concerns. The General Data Protection Regulation (GDPR), a landmark regulation in Europe, has set a precedent for safeguarding individuals' privacy rights and imposing stringent obligations on organizations handling personal data [2].

Beyond the confines of Europe, other regions have enacted regulations aimed at fortifying data protection. Notably, the Protection of Personal Information (POPI) Act in South Africa stands as a testament to the global recognition of the need for robust data protection measures. The POPI Act, akin to the GDPR, establishes principles for the lawful processing of personal information, emphasizing transparency, accountability, and the rights of data subjects [3].

Amidst this regulatory landscape, the attack vector in the cybersecurity realm continues to pivot towards the human factor. Phishing attacks have increasingly targeted critical infrastructure sectors such as oil refineries, electricity grids, and other industrial control systems [4–6]. These attacks can have severe consequences, including operational disruptions, financial losses, and safety hazards. A crucial aspect of these attacks is the human dimension, as they often exploit human vulnerabilities to gain access to secure systems. This article directs its focus towards the psychological dimensions of successful phishing attacks, examining how social engineering exploits the susceptibilities of individuals. Real-world scenarios, analyzed through the lenses of Natural Language Processing (NLP) and machine learning, offer insights into the nuanced interplay between contextual factors and the efficacy of attacks, especially among demographic segments like the youth.

To comprehensively address successful phishing attacks, it is imperative to delve into the rich tapestry of academic research. This involves synthesizing findings from studies exploring the intricate dynamics of social engineering attacks. The objective is to uncover the nuanced vulnerabilities inherent in human psychology, spanning cognitive processes, personality traits, and emotional responses.

The study in this paper aims not only to contribute to the academic discourse but also to offer practical insights for cybersecurity practitioners, researchers, and policymakers. As technology evolves and attackers adapt, fortifying the human element in cybersecurity becomes not just a tactical maneuver but a strategic imperative. This research presents substantial contributions by examining the interplay between human psychology, particularly personality characteristics and emotional conditions, and the susceptibility to phishing attacks. The importance of this research is also rooted in its comprehensive approach to cybersecurity, which amalgamates human elements with the RDAF. It enhances training protocols adherence by highlighting the necessity to mitigate psychological vulnerabilities within cybersecurity methodologies, ultimately leading to more efficacious prevention of social engineering assaults.

2 Literature Review

Phishing emails manipulate the psychological vulnerabilities of their targets; however, there exists a notable deficiency in the scholarly literature that correlates the characteristics of phishing content with the personality traits of victims. This study posits a decision support system that employs the Five-Factor Model of personality traits to forecast the specific types of phishing emails to which individuals may exhibit heightened susceptibility. The system, which was conceived through an experimental framework simulating a virtual stock market, has the potential to assist organizations in delivering tailored phishing awareness training and fortifying their defenses against phishing incursions [7].

The research investigated the influence of three social engineering methodologies: authority, scarcity, and social proof on users' evaluations regarding the safety of email links. The authority principle emerged as the most compelling strategy for persuading users to perceive an email link as secure, whereas users demonstrated optimal performance in identifying phishing attempts when social proof was employed. Users exhibited considerable difficulty in differentiating authentic emails from spear-phishing attempts, particularly in scenarios where the authority principle was leveraged. Moreover, individuals exhibiting lower levels of impulsivity tended to be less inclined to regard fraudulent links as trustworthy. The study posits educational and training ramifications informed by these results [8].

As cybersecurity measures become increasingly sophisticated, cybercriminals are progressively employing social engineering tactics to exploit the human element within an organization's security framework. Social engineering assaults manipulate human psychological tendencies to circumvent technical safeguards, rendering them exceptionally effective and challenging to combat due to their absence of distinct patterns. This manuscript endeavors to deliver a comprehensive examination of the mechanisms through which social engineering-driven cyberattacks are executed, the psychological vulnerabilities exploited in recent security breaches, as well as the pre-existing countermeasures, including those employing machine learning algorithms, to mitigate the impact of these attacks [9].

The central thesis of this discourse posits that although investigations into marketing and deception have delineated various principles of persuasion that impact human decision-making, the existing literature exhibits a degree of fragmentation, with disparate taxonomies concentrating on particular contexts. Three taxonomies frequently cited in the realm of fraud and scam research : Cialdini's principles of influence, Gragg's psychological triggers, and Stajano et al.'s principles of scams demonstrate both overlapping and complementary dimensions. The authors advocate for an integrated and enhanced compilation of these principles and conduct an analysis of phishing emails to illustrate the utilization of specific combinations of these principles. While the analysis is grounded in peer-reviewed research, the proposed methodology could be implemented in a more holistic and systematic manner than the original taxonomies, necessitating further investigation to facilitate the automation of the process [10].

The researchers conducted a critical review of existing literature to examine how personality traits such as those in the Big Five Personality model, along with cognitive factors, affect individual susceptibility to online phishing attacks. The study identified gaps in current research, particularly in how factors like urgency cues, online habits, and the Covid-19 pandemic influence risk levels. By investigating the interplay between these psychological variables, this study broadens the scope of understanding regarding online phishing susceptibility [11].

The pilot study furthers the exploration of personality traits and their relationship to susceptibility. Using the Big Five Personality model, the research found that individuals scoring high in agreeableness and extroversion were more prone to social engineering attacks. This result highlights the importance of psychological diversity in understanding vulnerability, providing a starting point for further research into how personality interacts with different social engineering techniques in [12]. The study discusses the growing sophistication of social engineering attacks as cybercriminals adapt to more robust cybersecurity defenses. This research emphasizes how attackers exploit specific human vulnerabilities, such as trust and emotion, to bypass technical security measures. The paper stresses the complexity of social engineering attacks, which are difficult to detect due to their dynamic and evasive nature. The analysis concludes with recommendations for further understanding the human element in cybersecurity and employing machine learning methods to counter these attacks [13].

The authors examined how three specific social engineering strategies:authority, scarcity, and social proof affect users' judgments of email safety. The findings reveal that authority is the most effective tactic for convincing users to click on malicious links, while social proof was associated with the best user performance in detecting phishing attempts. The study suggests that users who are less impulsive are more likely to identify fraudulent emails, highlighting the need for tailored education and training in [14].

The research deepens the exploration of personality traits in phishing susceptibility by conducting a spear-phishing simulation within a software development company. Employees' susceptibility to phishing attacks was measured before and after cybersecurity training, and the results indicated that certain personality traits made individuals more vulnerable under specific conditions. This study underscores the need for targeted cybersecurity measures based on personality profiles, as well as the value of training interventions to reduce susceptibility [15].

Lastly authors provides a broader organizational perspective by examining common social engineering attack methods, such as phishing and spear-phishing, and the importance of employee awareness training. This semi-comprehensive literature review, conducted using the PRISMA method, highlights major security breaches at Yahoo and Sony to exemplify the severe consequences of such attacks. The study recommends a multi-layered defense strategy that combines technical solutions with ongoing employee training. This approach aims to mitigate the human vulnerabilities exploited in social engineering attacks, stressing the importance of continual adaptation to evolving threats [16] (Table 1).

Table 1. Summary of Literature

Reference	Key Findings	Implications
[7]	Fake invoice scam is a highly successful and urgent social engineering attack	Urgent response and incapacitated decision-making characterize victims
[8]	Authority in phishing messages significantly impacts vulnerability	Perceived authority plays a crucial role in phishing susceptibility
[13]	Cybercriminals adapt social engineering tactics as cybersecurity strategies evolve	Constant evolution in tactics demands adaptive cybersecurity measures
[14]	Authority is the most successful tactic in persuading users	Users struggle to differentiate between phishing and legitimate emails
[10]	Merged principles provide a comprehensive framework for understanding phishing emails	Offers a systematic approach to analyzing and categorizing phishing tactics
[11]	Psychological determinants, including personality traits, impact susceptibility	Insights into factors influencing vulnerability can inform targeted cybersecurity measures
[12]	Users scoring high in agreeableness and extraversion are more vulnerable	Personality traits influence susceptibility to social engineering attacks
[15]	Personality traits affect susceptibility to spear-phishing attacks under specific conditions	Understanding individual traits can inform personalized cybersecurity training
[16]	Multi-layered defense, including employee awareness training, is crucial	PRISMA methodology emphasizes a comprehensive approach to mitigate vulnerabilities
[17]	Social engineering attacks have detrimental effects on information security linked to human behavior	Highlights the need for understanding the human factor in cybersecurity strategies
[18]	Personality traits and experiences impact susceptibility to phishing attacks	Insights into individual characteristics can inform targeted awareness training
[19]	LLMs can simulate human responses to social engineering attacks	Potential for using simulations to understand and mitigate human vulnerability
[20]	Conceptual model explains social engineering attack mechanisms, emphasizing human vulnerabilities	Framework for understanding and categorizing mechanisms, vulnerabilities, and attack techniques
[21]	Human vulnerabilities influence susceptibility; ongoing vulnerability assessments are crucial	Calls for continuous vulnerability assessments and consideration of insider threat-actors

3 The Social Engineering Attack Approach

Our social engineering attack approach as methodology, encompasses various techniques, including Smishing, Quishing, and Vishing.

3.1 Smishing

An SMS sent to students that contains a link that leads to a WIX-created website. Just like in the last web programming class, students were given an assignment to make a website or blog for use as an online communication tool. Thus, it was the ideal opportunity to employ social engineering strategies to gauge the student's susceptibility. The text message says, "Bonjour, voici comment faire votre site/blog avec l'intelligence artificielle en cinq minutes." Which is unambiguously in English: Hi, this is how to use AI to develop a website or blog in five minutes. Therefore, when they clicked on the SMS's embedded link, the landing page simply said "Travailles sans AI" which implies that work without AI in English. Here in Fig. 2 we notice that the correlation between words is still an essential element of our analysis (Figs. 1 and 3).

Fig. 1. Smishing

3.2 Quishing

In order to assess human's vulnerability to quishing attacks, the following message was encoded into a QR code:
"*Merci, vous vous êtes fait piraté. Toutes vos données m'appartiennent désormais. Déchiffrer le Code suivant pour libérer vos données :*" (Table 2)

Table 2. I'm the CyberProphet ! —-ROMAK—-

1C1 2E1 3S	1U2	1F3 2A3 3U	1P4 2I4 3R4 4A4 5T4 6A4	1S5 2O5 2I	1C6 1A6 3L6
4T1	2N2	4X3	7G4 8E4	4S5	4M6 !

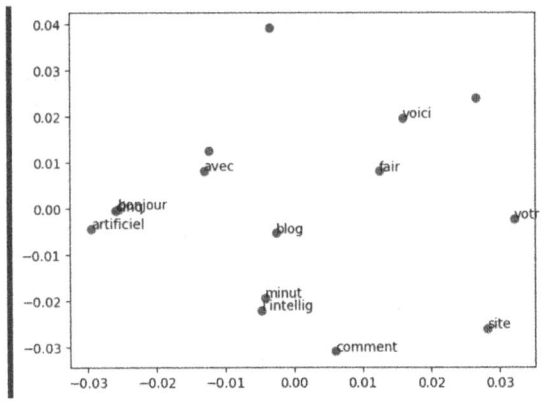

Fig. 2. Smishing ML analysis

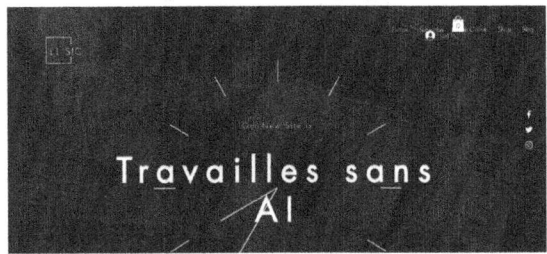

Fig. 3. Answer AI

It is very evident from the content that you have been hacked. Thank you. Now, all of your info is mine. To release your data, decode the following code. By taking into account the element in the middle of every block, the code contains a secret message that says, C'EST UN FAUX PIRATAGE. CALME SOIS! indicating that it is a phony hack. Remain composed! In the hypothetical case, the lecturer simply projected the QR code on the topic slide for one minute during the presentation, on top, written "scan me." They scanned and became alarmed that they had been hacked all of a sudden. As the result, out of 164, 98 scans

$$\text{MESSAGE} = \begin{cases} 1C1\ 2E1\ 3S1\ 4T1\ 000\ 000\ 000\ 000 \\ 1U2\ 2N2\ 000\ 000\ 000\ 000\ 000\ 000 \\ 1F3\ 2A3\ 3U3\ 4X3\ 000\ 000\ 000\ 000 \\ 1P4\ 2I4\ 3R4\ 4A4\ 5T4\ 6A4\ 7G4\ 8E4. \\ 1S5\ 2O5\ 2I4\ 4S5\ 000\ 000\ 000\ 000 \\ 1C6\ 1A6\ 3L6\ 4M6!\ 000\ 000\ 000\ 0000 \end{cases}$$

Fig. 4. Quishing

were from unique devices, 66 scans were repeated from some devices and having a total 84 scans. Consequently, only 3 were able to decipher the code instantly (Fig. 4).

3.3 Vishing

An employee of a university was involved in an accident involving a conference where students were competing and the best French writers were being awarded. We were asked to perform an audit or survey to confirm that all winners had received their awards because the event report was not entirely clear. We used social engineering strategies, specifically the vishing attack, to obtain information from students during that audit. And it really did work; after eight calls, we had favorable outcomes.

Using NLP, we want to use machine learning to carry out an in-depth analysis of the speech and determine the correlation between the prevailing sentiment and the probability of success of an attack based on deception or manipulation of the emotional state of the person interlocutor. With Vishing we direct our interviewee towards a favorable emotional state, according to the feeling and we thus manage to extract information from them. The question remains, to what extent does the success of such an attack depend on the general mood of the conversation? Could it be true that this constitutes a key element? For conducting a best analysis for Vishing, in the First step, we collected conversation recordings in audio format of around 24 min in which there was a conversation as mentioned in the previous paragraph. Secondly we used machine learning to transform audio into text; for this we used whisper as a framework with the medium parameter. Given the size and for in-depth analysis, we divided the entire audio into 8 parts of 3 min each, in which we did an analysis and a transformation in part. We noticed that the probability correlation was no more relevant.

4 Experimental Results

In this section, we delve into the experimental results obtained through the utilization of the skip-gram technique to discern distributed representations of words within a continuous vector space. The skip-gram model operates by taking a target word as input and endeavors to predict the words within its contextual vicinity. During training, the model is optimized to maximize the probability of predicting context words given the target word.

Our objective was to establish a correlation between the probability of word occurrences, considering the context, and to explore the connection with the emotional state requisite for the success of the attack. This exploration was conducted across eight diverse dialogues, focusing particularly on Vishing scenarios.

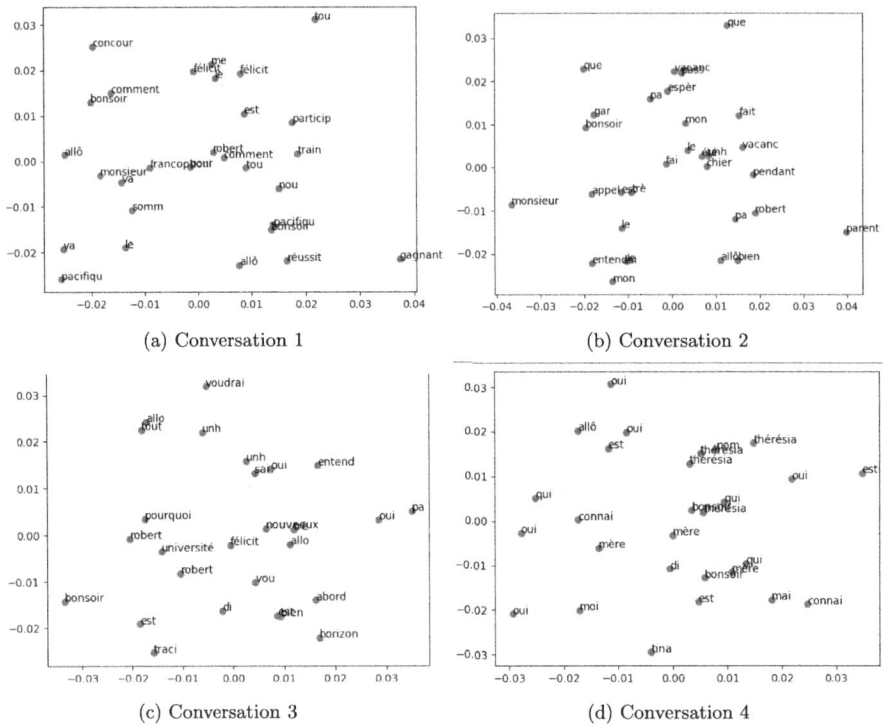

Fig. 5. Vectorized word correlation

4.1 NLP Process

In the realm of our NLP study, preprocessing was carried out on the gathered words. An examination of embedding allowed us to pinpoint contextual similarities that indicate susceptibility to vishing within the examined subjects. This task was accomplished through vector analysis employing a dimensionality of 100 and a context window of 10. The initial phase involved data collection via vishing, subsequent speech-to-text transcription with a 97% accuracy rate utilizing Whisper. Following this, preprocessing was executed to filter out non-essential words utilizing the preprocess string function. The conversion of the refined text into vectors facilitated the identification of key words contributing to the vulnerability of individuals to vishing attacks within our specific scenario. These identified words are illustrated in Figs. 5a to 5d, emphasizing that certain manipulative words can either facilitate successful vishing attacks or aid in their detection (Fig. 7).

These visual representations showcase the correlation of probabilities through vectors, underscoring the closeness of word occurrences in four out of eight audio samples. Lastly, our machine learning algorithm was deployed to scrutinize the entire text, ensuring a thorough assessment that yields pertinent and significant findings. Through our analysis, we determined that the success of a vishing

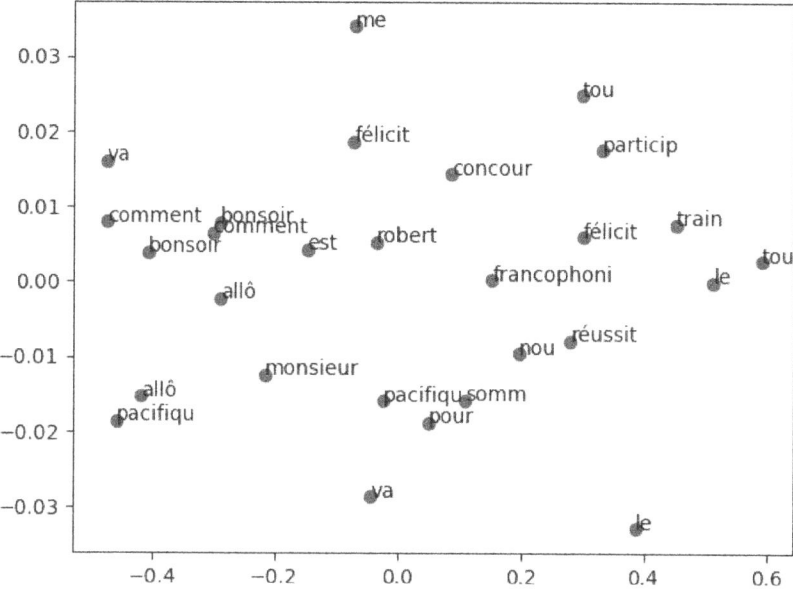

Fig. 6. General emotional state analysis

attack hinges not solely on the quality of terms or words utilized, but predominantly on the emotional response elicited by such language. In our observations, we discerned that the success of the attack is contingent not only on the quality of the terms or words employed but more critically on the emotional state engendered by these words. Figure 6 encapsulates this nuanced comprehension, shedding light on specific words with a high likelihood of influencing the emotional state of the recipient. Moreover, Fig. 8 delineates the outcomes of a quishing attack in a scenario involving a sample of 23 individuals, where 17 individuals

Fig. 7. Quishing result

succumbed to the quishing trap. It is imperative to acknowledge the substantial impact of the environment on the success of the quishing attack in this particular context.

5 Discussion

In our analysis, we established a robust correlation between the probability of word appearances in a conversation and the success of a vishing attack. This correlation, depicted in the vector representation presented in the figure, underscores the pivotal role of context in influencing attack outcomes across various conversational settings.

From the distributed representations of words, we gleaned insights into the personality traits that significantly influence the effectiveness of different types of social engineering attacks.

In the context of a vishing attack, the victim's openness, consciousness, extraversion, agreeableness, and neuroticism emerged as crucial factors that could be exploited.

For a smishing attack, we found that openness, consciousness, agreeableness, and neuroticism play pivotal roles. The victim's attention is captivated by compelling content, compelling them to swiftly click on the provided link.

Conversely, a quishing attack is more successful when the victim exhibits traits of openness and agreeableness. The scenario for a quishing attack needs to be straightforward to appeal to these traits.

5.1 Sensibility from the Attack

The sensitivity matrix (Table 3) summarizes the impact of personality traits on different attack vectors. It provides a quick reference guide, highlighting the traits that are most relevant for each type of attack.

Table 3. Sensibility from the attack

	Quishing	Smishing	Vishing
Openness	X		X
Conscientiousness		X	X
Extraversion			X
Agreeableness		X	X
Neuroticism	X	X	X

5.2 Final Results

The final results (Table 4) distill the key parameters for success in each attack vector. It emphasizes the critical role of trust, curiosity, and content in vishing, smishing, and quishing attacks, respectively.

Table 4. Final results

Quishing	Curiosity	Content
Smishing	Content	Curiosity
Vishing	Trust	Content

5.3 Sample Analysis

The sample analysis (Table 5) provides a practical application of the findings to real-world scenarios. It showcases specific words and phrases that align with the identified personality traits and illustrates their potential impact on the emotional state of the victim.

Table 5. Sample Analysis

	Vishing	Smishing	Quishing
Openess	Allo, Bonsoir, Comment tu vas		Scan me
Conscientiousness	Participation, francophonie, reussite, concour	Comment	
Extraversion	Somme, train		
Agreableness	Bonsoir, Monsieur, Robert	AI	
Neurotism	Felicitation, Reussite, somme	5 min	Scan me

These findings not only enrich academic discussions on cybersecurity but also provide practical insights for policymakers and practitioners. As the human factor remains a persistent target, understanding the intricate interplay of content and context in phishing attacks becomes a strategic imperative. Adopting a holistic approach that combines technological defenses with a deep comprehension of human susceptibility is vital to fortify the weakest link and advance collective resilience against phishing attacks.

6 Recommendations

To mitigate the probability of experiencing an attack, we advocate for the implementation of a Defense Awareness Framework predicated upon enhanced training methodologies (Fig. 8 and Table 6).

Table 6. Recommendations

Untrusted channel verification	Engagement in the process of validating whether the source constitutes a legitimate request and conducting preliminary scans of the QR-Code prior to advancing
Trusted channel verification	It is imperative to remain vigilant regarding potential insider threat actors. The unforeseen attacks pose significant risks
Emotional intelligence	Emphasizing the importance of identifying and regulating emotional reactions to unforeseen or time-sensitive communications in high-stress contexts. Exhibiting resilience through judicious reflection prior to responding
Cognitive behavioral reinforcement	Executing consistent real-world simulations of smishing, quishing, and vishing scenarios, with the objective of rewarding those who exhibit positive learning outcomes
Individual vulnerability assessment	Conducting profiling of the trainee based upon their browsing histories, communication patterns, and prior failures
Technology empowerment	Implementing mobile security applications capable of detecting and identifying malicious calls and links
Threat Reporting	Any communication deemed suspicious must be duly reported

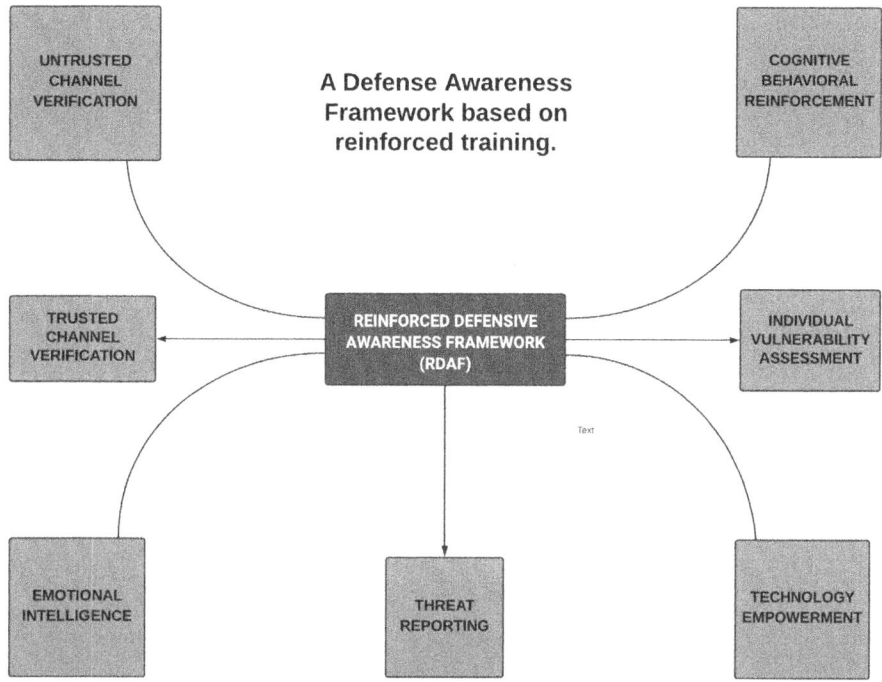

Fig. 8. Proposed Framework

7 Conclusion and Future Work

7.1 Limitations and Considerations for Future Work

Despite the valuable insights gained, our study has certain limitations that warrant consideration for future research. Firstly, our analysis focuses on a specific set of personality traits, and expanding the scope to encompass a broader spectrum could provide a more comprehensive understanding of susceptibility.

Additionally, the study predominantly relies on textual content analysis, overlooking potential non-verbal cues and multi-modal elements that could influence the success of phishing attacks. Incorporating diverse data sources, such as voice and video, would contribute to a more holistic examination of the nuanced interplay between attackers and victims.

Moreover, it is essential to note that our study employed a reduced sample size, which may limit the generalizability of the findings. Future research should aim to overcome this limitation by involving a larger and more diverse participant pool, enhancing the external validity of our conclusions and ensuring a more representative reflection of real-world scenarios.

7.2 Practical Implications and Future Directions

Notwithstanding these limitations, our study extends beyond academic discourse to offer tangible value for both policymakers and practitioners. The insights gained provide a foundation for refining defense strategies, emphasizing the importance of considering psychological factors in cybersecurity measures.

Looking forward, future research endeavors should aim to address the identified limitations, delving into a broader array of personality traits, incorporating multi-modal data, and diversifying the participant pool. This iterative process ensures a more robust and adaptable framework for understanding and mitigating the evolving landscape of social engineering attacks.

As we navigate the intricate challenges of an ever-evolving cybersecurity landscape, the call for a holistic defense approach resonates. By amalgamating advanced technological defenses with a nuanced comprehension of human susceptibility, we not only fortify the weakest link but also advance collective resilience against phishing attacks, thereby securing the digital frontier in our increasingly interconnected world.

References

1. Zubaedah, P.A., Harliyanto, R., Situmeang, S.M.T., Siagian, D.S., Septaria, E.: The legal implications of data privacy laws, cybersecurity regulations, and AI ethics in a digital society (2024)
2. Amin, M.: The importance of cybersecurity and protecting of digital assets and understanding the role of cybersecurity laws in safeguarding digital assets. Indian J. Public Adm. (2024)
3. Ehimuan, B., Ogugua Chimezie, O., Akagha, O.V., Reis, O., Oguejiofor, B.B.: Global data privacy laws: a critical review of technology's impact on user rights. World J. Adv. Res. Rev. (2024)
4. Kostarev, A., Kotenko, I., Skormin, V.: Advanced persistent threats in critical infrastructures: phishing, smishing and other cyberattack vectors. In: Communications in Computer and Information Science, vol. 1214, pp. 55–69. Springer, Cham (2020)
5. Smith, R., Simpson, J.: Cybersecurity in industrial control systems: the threat landscape and defensive measures. Int. J. Crit. Infrastruct. Prot. **34**, 100412 (2021)
6. Antova, V., Kurnikov, A.: Phishing and its implications for critical infrastructure protection. J. Inf. Secur. Appl. **64**, 103039 (2022)
7. Cummings, A.B., Eftekhary, D., House, F.G.: A decision support system for personality based phishing susceptibility analysis. J. Sketchy Phys. **13**(2), 46–129 (2003)
8. Butavicius, M., Parsons, K., Pattinson, M.: Breaching the human firewall: social engineering in phishing and spear-phishing emails. In: Australasian Conference on Information Systems (2015)
9. Siddiqi, M.A., Pak, W., Siddiqi, M.A.: A study on the psychology of social engineering-based cyberattacks and existing countermeasures. Appl. Sci. **12**(12) (2022). https://www.mdpi.com/2076-3417/12/12/6042
10. Ferreira, A., Coventry, L., Lenzini, G.: Principles of persuasion in social engineering and their use in phishing (2015)

11. Bright, C., Wziatka, M., Ngaruko, W.: An examination of the role of big five personality traits, cognitive processes and heuristics on individuals' phishing attack susceptibility levels (2022). https://doi.org/10.31234/osf.io/c5uvj
12. Cusack, B., Adedokun, K.: The impact of personality traits on user's susceptibility to social engineering attacks. In: Proceedings of the 16th Australian Information Security Management Conference (2022). https://doi.org/10.31234/osf.io/c5uvj
13. Siddiqi, M.A., Parsons, K., Pattinson, M.: A study on the psychology of social engineering-based cyberattacks and existing countermeasures. In: Australasian Conference on Information Systems (2022)
14. Butavicius, M.A., Parsons, K., Pattinson, M.R., McCormac, A.: Breaching the human firewall: social engineering in phishing and spear-phishing emails. CoRR, abs/1606.00887 (2016). http://arxiv.org/abs/1606.00887
15. Eftimie, S., Moinescu, R., Rcuciu, C.: Spear-phishing susceptibility stemming from personality traits. IEEE Access **10** (2022)
16. Broberg, R., Sinnott, P.: The human element of cybersecurity: a literature review of social engineering attacks and countermeasures (2023)
17. Li, M.: Environmental factors affect social engineering attacks. Ph.D. dissertation (2021)
18. Anawar, S., Kunasegaran, D.L., Mas'ud, M.Z., Zakaria, N.A.: Analysis of phishing susceptibility in a workplace: a big-five personality perspectives. J. Eng. Sci. Technol. **14**(5), 2865–2882 (2019)
19. Asfour, M., Murillo, J.C.: Harnessing large language models to simulate realistic human responses to social engineering attacks: a case study. Int. J. Cybersecur. Intell. Cybercrime (2023)
20. Wang, Z., Zhu, H., Sun, L.: Social engineering in cybersecurity: effect mechanisms, human vulnerabilities and attack methods. IEEE Access **9**, 11 895–11 910 (2021)
21. Papatsaroucha, D., Nikoloudakis, Y., Kefaloukos, I., Pallis, E., Markakis, E.K.: A survey on human and personality vulnerability assessment in cyber-security: challenges, approaches, and open issues. arXiv preprint arXiv:2106.09986 (2021)

Optimizing Real-Time Video Analytics for Resource-Constrained Environments

Rodrique Kafando[1(✉)], Aminata Sabané[2], and Tégawendé F. Bissyandé[1,2]

[1] Centre d'Excellence CITADEL, Université Virtuelle du Burkina Faso, Ouagadougou, Burkina Faso
rodrique.kafando@citadel.bf
[2] Département d'Informatique, UFR/SEA, UJKZ, Ouagadougou, Burkina Faso
https://citadel.bf/

Abstract. Developing countries face a growing demand for video analytics, yet often lack sufficient computational resources. This paper addresses this challenge by proposing and evaluating optimization techniques for efficient video stream processing on resource-constrained devices, including edge systems. We introduce and evaluate several techniques, including image resizing, frame skipping, parallel processing, threading, queue management, memory optimization, and buffering. Experimental results demonstrate substantial improvements in frames per second (FPS) and memory usage, enabling real-time video analytics without compromising accuracy namely in object detection. By effectively balancing performance and resource consumption, our methods facilitate the deployment of advanced AI-driven video analysis in resource-limited environments, paving the way for practical real-time monitoring and alert systems.

Keywords: RTSP stream · Real-time Video Analytics · Computational Optimization · Post-Training Optimization

1 Introduction

Real-time object detection and tracking demand exceptionally low processing and transmission latencies to be effective. These systems are critical in various applications requiring immediate alerts, such as surveillance, access control, and anomaly detection. For instance, in sensitive areas, unauthorized intrusions must be detected and reported instantly. Retail environments rely on rapid theft detection to prevent losses, while traffic monitoring systems necessitate real-time accident alerts for efficient emergency response.

Developing regions often face significant limitations in computational resources, hindering the deployment of advanced video analytics systems. These systems typically demand substantial processing power, making them impractical in environments with constrained infrastructure and budgets. To bridge this gap, our research focuses on developing optimization strategies that enable efficient video analytics on resource-limited platforms.

We introduce in this study a suite of optimization techniques to accelerate the processing and delivery of Real Time Streaming Protocol (RTSP) video streams while maintaining low latency. By employing image resizing, frame skipping, MSE-based frame skipping, parallel processing, threading, queue management, memory optimization, and buffering, we aim to optimize real-time video analytics for resource-constrained environments. Our findings demonstrate substantial improvements in processing efficiency, enabling the reliable operation of real-time monitoring and alert systems in such settings. These results highlight the feasibility of deploying advanced video analytics solutions that can function reliably in developing regions.

2 Related Work

Object detection techniques are a key area of artificial intelligence, with popular algorithms such as You Only Look Once (YOLO) and its improved versions (YOLOv2 to YOLOv10). These algorithms are noted for their speed and accuracy, processing images in a single pass to provide the positions and categories of detected objects [6]. Successive versions of YOLO have brought improvements in batch normalization, the use of high-resolution images, and multi-scale training [2]. Other detection methods include Convolutional Neural Networks (CNNs) used in models like SSD (Single Shot MultiBox Detector) and Faster R-CNN, which balance processing speed and accuracy. For instance, SSD achieves an average precision of 74.3% mAP on the VOC2007 test at a speed of 59 FPS, surpassing Faster R-CNN and YOLO in terms of both speed and accuracy [5].

Recent research has explored distributed real-time video analytics using optimized YOLOv8 models on CPU nodes. This approach utilizes cloud platforms like Microsoft Azure and data streaming tools such as Apache Kafka to efficiently manage and process video streams [3]. OpenVINO [4] is used for both pre-training and post-training optimization, enhancing model efficiency by converting the YOLOv8 model into an IR format with FP32 precision, followed by post-training quantization to create an INT8 version of the model. This technique enhances processing speed while maintaining accuracy.

In [7] authors show that the magnitude pruning reduces computational complexity by removing low-magnitude weights from the network, followed by fine-tuning to recover performance. Results indicate that the optimal pruning rate for balancing performance and accuracy is around 0.5. This approach also allows a reduction in parameters and computations while maintaining good detection accuracy.

Optimized models allow for more efficient use of memory and processing resources, which is essential for resource-constrained devices like CPU edge nodes. Faster and more efficient models enable real-time detection and instant alerting, which is critical for surveillance and security applications [1]. The increasing demand for video storage and the complexities associated with processing large volumes of video data require robust and scalable solutions. Tools like Apache Kafka and Microsoft Azure Cloud play a crucial role in managing and processing real-time video in a distributed manner [4].

In addition to algorithm-specific detection techniques, it is essential to consider post-processing strategies that can be applied independently of the specific detection algorithm used. These strategies include image resizing, frame skipping, and the use of parallel processing and threading to manage real-time video streams. Efficient queue management for processed frames and memory optimization with tools like tracemalloc are also crucial for maintaining high performance and low latency. This article proposes and evaluates these post-processing strategies, demonstrating their effectiveness in optimizing object detection systems, regardless of the specific detection algorithm [8].

3 Proposed Approaches

3.1 Image Resizing

Image resizing is a fundamental optimization technique used to enhance the performance of real-time video analytics systems, especially in resource-constrained environments. By reducing the resolution of video frames, the computational load on the processing system is significantly decreased, enabling faster processing speeds and lower memory usage. This section details the image resizing technique, its implementation, and its impact on the computational efficiency of object detection and tracking systems.

Interpolation methods reduce the number of pixels while preserving as much visual information as possible. The common interpolation methods include:

- Nearest Neighbor Interpolation: Selects the nearest pixel value to the target pixel. It is the simplest and fastest method but may result in blocky images.
- Bilinear Interpolation: This method takes the average of the four nearest pixel values to compute the target pixel value. It produces smoother images than nearest neighbor interpolation.
- Bicubic Interpolation: This method considers the nearest sixteen pixels and produces even smoother images. It is more computationally intensive than the previous methods but provides better visual quality.

3.2 Frame Skipping

Frame skipping is an optimization technique designed to reduce the computational load of real-time video analytics systems by processing only a subset of the frames in a video stream. This method can significantly enhance processing speed and reduce memory usage, making it an effective strategy for resource-constrained environments.

Frame skipping selectively processes frames at regular intervals, skipping a predefined number of frames between each processed frame. The interval at which frames are processed is referred to as the skip rate (sk). For example, a skip rate of 2 means that every second frame is processed, while a skip rate of 5 means that every fifth frame is processed. The primary parameters involved in frame skipping are:

- Skip Rate: The number of frames to skip between each processed frame. Higher skip rates result in fewer processed frames, leading to faster processing times but potentially missing some critical information.
- Resolution: The resolution of the frames being processed, which can further influence the computational load.

3.3 MSE-Based Frame Skipping

MSE-based frame skipping calculates the Mean Squared Error between consecutive frames. If the MSE value exceeds a predefined threshold, the frame is processed; otherwise, it is skipped. This method analyzes only frames with substantial differences, optimizing computational resource usage.

The primary parameters involved in MSE-based frame skipping are:

- Skip Rate (sk): The interval at which frames are checked for processing based on the MSE value. MSE Threshold (th): The threshold value above which frames are processed. Lower thresholds result in more frames being processed, while higher thresholds lead to more frames being skipped.

Other techniques besides MSE can be used for frame skipping, each with its advantages and limitations. Some notable methods include:

- Structural Similarity Index (SSIM): This technique compares the structural similarity between frames. SSIM is more sensitive to changes in structure, luminance, and contrast, making it suitable for applications where visual quality is paramount.
- Histogram Difference: This method calculates the difference in color histograms between frames. It is computationally less intensive than MSE and can quickly detect changes in the overall color distribution of frames.
- Optical Flow: This technique estimates the motion between frames by calculating the flow of pixels. Optical flow is effective for detecting motion and can be used to skip frames with minimal motion, thereby focusing processing on dynamic scenes.

$$\text{MSE} = \frac{1}{n}\sum_{i=1}^{n}(I_1(i) - I_2(i))^2 \qquad (1)$$

where I_1 and I_2 are two consecutive frames, and n is the number of pixels.

3.4 Parallel Processing with ThreadPoolExecutor

Parallel processing with ThreadPoolExecutor creates a pool of threads to execute tasks concurrently. Each frame of the video stream is treated as a separate task, which can be processed in parallel by the threads in the pool. By distributing the computational load across multiple threads, parallel processing reduces processing time and increases efficiency. For instance, the ThreadPoolExecutor from the concurrent futures library in Python provides a flexible and efficient way to implement parallel processing. The following steps outline the implementation strategy:

- Initialize the ThreadPoolExecutor: Create a ThreadPoolExecutor with a specified number of worker threads.
- Submit Tasks to the Executor: Submit the frame processing tasks to the executor.
- Process Frames Concurrently: Each worker thread processes a frame concurrently.
- Retrieve and Display Results: Collect the processed frames and display them.

$$T_p = \frac{T_s}{N} \tag{2}$$

Where T_p is the parallel processing time, Ts is the sequential processing time, and N is the number of threads.

3.5 Threading for Concurrent Video Stream Processing

Threading involves creating multiple threads within a single process, allowing different tasks to be executed concurrently. In the context of real-time video stream processing, threading can be used to handle multiple video streams simultaneously or to parallelize the processing of frames within a single stream. The primary techniques used in threading include:

- Thread Creation: Initializing and managing threads for concurrent execution.
- Synchronization: Coordinating the execution of threads to prevent race conditions and ensure data integrity.
- Queue Management: Using queues to buffer frames and manage the flow of data between threads.
- Thread Pooling: Utilizing a pool of reusable threads to handle tasks efficiently.

$$T_t = \frac{T_s}{N} + \text{Overhead} \tag{3}$$

Where T_t is the threading processing time, T_s is the sequential processing time, N is the number of threads, and $Overhead$ is the additional time due to context switching and synchronization.

3.6 Queue Management for Processed Frames

Queue management involves using data structures called queues to temporarily store frames as they move through the different stages of processing. Queues help to manage the flow of frames between the frame capture stage, the processing stage, and the display stage. The key components of the queue management approach include:

- Frame Queue: Buffers frames captured from the video stream before they are processed.
- Processed Queue: Buffers frames after they have been processed and before they are displayed.
- Max Queue Size: Defines the maximum number of frames that can be stored in the queue at any given time, preventing memory overflow and ensuring smooth processing.

By using queues to buffer frames and manage the flow of data between various stages of processing, queue management ensures efficient handling of video streams and reduces latency.

$$\text{Queue Size} = \min(\text{Max Size}, \text{Input Rate} \times \text{Processing Time}) \quad (4)$$

Where $InputRate$ is the rate at which frames are added to the queue and $ProcessingTime$ is the time taken to process each frame.

3.7 Memory Management with Tracemalloc

Memory management is the process of efficiently allocating, utilizing, and freeing memory resources within a computer system. It ensures that applications have sufficient memory to execute while optimizing the overall performance and stability of the system. Effective memory management involves tracking memory usage, preventing memory leaks, and ensuring that memory is allocated and deallocated in a way that maximizes system efficiency and prevents resource exhaustion. This is critical in environments with limited computational resources, as it helps maintain optimal performance and avoid system crashes or slowdowns. The Python library *tracemalloc* designed to trace memory allocations. It provides detailed information about memory usage, including the size and location of allocated memory blocks. An effective memory management ensures that the system can handle large volumes of video data without running out of memory or experiencing significant performance degradation. The implementation of memory management with tracemalloc involves the following steps:

- Initialize tracemalloc: Start tracing memory allocations at the beginning of the program.
- Track Memory Usage: Monitor memory usage during the execution of the program.
- Analyze Memory Usage: Retrieve and analyze memory statistics to identify memory usage patterns and potential issues.

– Stop tracemalloc: Stop tracing memory allocations and clean up resources.

$$\text{Memory Usage} = \sum_{i=1}^{n} \text{Memory Block Size}_i \tag{5}$$

Where n is the number of memory blocks allocated.

3.8 Optimization Through Buffering

Buffering is the process of temporarily storing data in a memory buffer while it is being transferred between two locations, typically to accommodate differences in data processing rates between the source and destination. In the context of real-time video analytics, buffering helps to manage the flow of video frames, ensuring smooth and efficient processing by mitigating the impact of fluctuations in data processing speeds. Buffering plays a crucial role in maintaining a consistent data stream, reducing latency, and preventing bottlenecks in the processing pipeline.

The implementation of buffering in real-time video analytics involves creating queues that act as buffers for incoming and outgoing frames. The queue.Queue class in Python provides a thread-safe FIFO (First In, First Out) queue, which is ideal for this purpose. The key techniques in buffering include:

– Input Buffering: Temporarily storing incoming video frames before they are processed. This helps to accommodate variations in frame capture rates and ensures a steady supply of frames to the processing pipeline.
– Output Buffering: Storing processed frames before they are displayed or transmitted. This helps to handle variations in processing time and ensures smooth playback or transmission.
– Buffer Size Management: Adjusting the size of the buffers to balance memory usage and processing efficiency. Larger buffers can handle more variation in processing times but require more memory.

$$\text{Buffer Size} = \text{Input Rate} \times \text{Buffer Time} \tag{6}$$

4 Experimental Setup and Discussion

In this section, we detail the experimental setup used to evaluate the performance of various optimization strategies for real-time video analytics systems. The primary goal is to assess the impact of each strategy on processing speed (FPS), memory usage, and overall system efficiency. The strategies evaluated include image resizing, frame skipping, MSE-based frame skipping, parallel processing, threading, queue management, memory management with tracemalloc, and buffering. We provide the source code for replication, accessible from our GitHub repository.

4.1 Hardware and System Configuration

The experiments were conducted using a Dahua IR DOME NETWORK CAMERA with a wired connection (RJ-45) for video input. To facilitate easy replication, the reported results were obtained using a free online video from Pexels[1]. Additionally, the yolov8n.pt[2] model from Ultralytics was employed for object detection, using the default classes and parameters (such as confidence, etc.) provided by the model.

The PC used for the experiment has the following system configuration is as follows:

- Operating System: Linux #35 22.04.1-Ubuntu SMP PREEMPT_DYNAMIC Tue May 7 09:00:52 UTC 2 (Release: 6.5.0-35-generic)
- operating system: x86_64
- Processor: i7
- Number of Cores: 8
- Max CPU Frequency: 4700.0 MHz
- Total Memory: 15.34 GB
- GPU Info: GPUtil not installed

4.2 Results and Discussion

Table 1 below summarizes the performance metrics for each optimization strategy applied in our real-time video analytics system. The strategies include image resizing, frame skipping, MSE-based frame skipping, parallel processing, threading, queue management, memory management with tracemalloc, and buffering. For each strategy, we present the skip rate, resolution, maximum queue size, number of frames processed, total processing time, frames per second (FPS), current memory usage, and peak memory usage. These results highlight the effectiveness of each optimization technique in enhancing processing speed and efficiency, particularly in a resource-constrained environment. Figure 1 and Fig. 2 respectively represent the evolution of FPS and the memory usage across the different strategies.

Image resizing significantly increased FPS and reduced memory usage. Reducing the resolution from 1920×1080 to 640×480 improved FPS from 4.32 to 6.90, and further reducing to 320×240 increased FPS to 9.37, proving highly effective for improving processing speed in resource-constrained environments. In practice, the optimal resolution may vary depending on the specific application and the complexity of the scenes being analyzed.

Frame skipping showed notable improvements in FPS and memory usage. With a skip rate of 5, the FPS increased to 10.24 for 640×480 resolution. MSE-based (same for other technics) frame skipping provided a balance between processing efficiency and accuracy of object detection and tracking. Using a threshold of 500 with a skip rate of 5 yielded an FPS of 9.70, while higher thresholds

---

[1] https://www.pexels.com/video/dancers-performing-a-choreography-on-a-promenade-14691550/.

[2] https://github.com/ultralytics/assets/releases/download/v8.2.0/yolov8n.pt.

Table 1. Performance metrics across optimization strategies

Strategy	SkRate	Resol	MxQSize	NbFrames	Time(s)	FPS	C.Mem(MB)	PeakMem(MB)
Default	–	1920 × 1080	–	705	163.27	4.32	201.67	220.08
IR	–	640 × 480	–	705	102.11	6.90	175.22	187.41
IR	–	320 × 240	–	705	75.25	**9.37**	66.65	79.01
FSkip	2	640 × 480	–	353	64.96	5.43	88.46	100.90
FSkip	5	640 × 480	–	141	13.76	**10.24**	36.84	49.28
MSESkip	5	640 × 480	–	141	14.54	9.70	37.46	53.12
ParlProcess	2	640 × 480	–	352	33.74	**10.43**	89.44	104.86
ParlProcess	5	640 × 480	–	141	14.85	9.49	47.39	62.81
Threading	2	640 × 480	–	352	46.72	7.53	89.05	104.72
Q.M.	5	640 × 480	10	141	14.23	9.91	48.07	62.81
Q.M.	5	640 × 480	20	141	13.86	**10.17**	48.07	64.07
M.M	5	640 × 480	10	141	16.18	8.71	91.80	108.64
M.M	5	640 × 480	20	141	14.95	9.43	81.45	108.33
Buff.	5	640 × 480	10	141	15.54	9.07	81.74	108.32
Buff	5	640 × 480	20	141	15.08	**9.35**	81.45	108.31

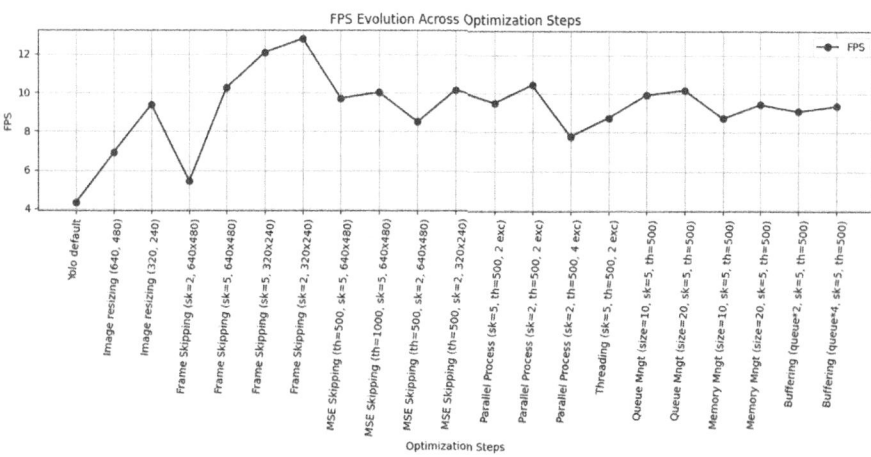

Fig. 1. FPS evolution across optimization steps.

resulted in slightly better FPS. This method is especially useful for detecting significant changes in video frames, maintaining a balance between performance and accuracy where not every frame needs to be processed.

Parallel processing improved FPS by distributing the computational load across multiple threads. With 2 executors, the FPS increased to 10.43 for 640 × 480 resolution. However, increasing the number of executors to 4 resulted in a slight decrease in FPS due to the overhead of managing more threads, indicating a balance must be struck in thread management.

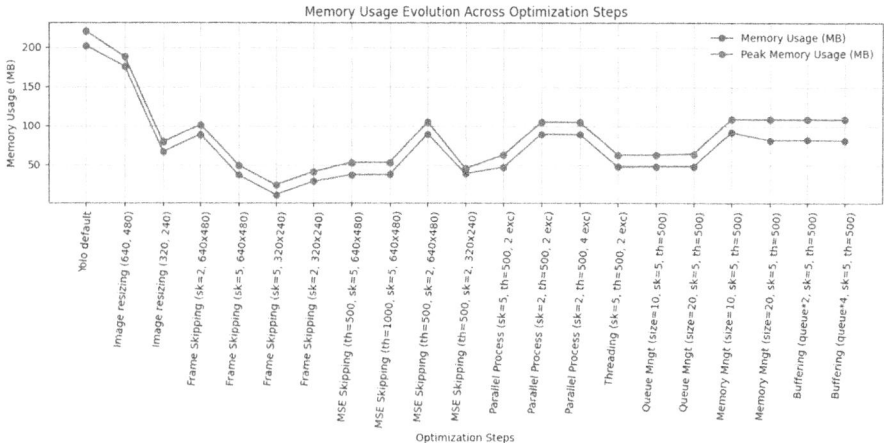

Fig. 2. Memory usage evolution across optimization steps.

Threading allowed for concurrent processing of multiple video streams, enhancing FPS. With 2 threads, the FPS was 7.53 for 640 × 480 resolution. This strategy is effective for systems that need to handle multiple video streams simultaneously, ensuring improved throughput and responsiveness. Balancing the number of threads is important, to avoid overhead associated with managing too many threads.

Queue management using buffers helped smooth out fluctuations in processing time, leading to more consistent performance. Increasing the max queue size to 20 improved FPS to 10.17 for 640 × 480 resolution. This approach is beneficial for managing data flow and reducing latency, ensuring a steady stream of frames for processing. It is important to balance the maximum queue size to avoid excessive memory usage while maintaining low latency.

Memory management with tracemalloc provided valuable insights into memory usage and helped optimize system performance. The results showed that increasing the max queue size reduced memory usage variability and improved FPS. This strategy is essential for detecting memory leaks and ensuring efficient memory usage, contributing to overall system stability. However, it is essential to balance memory usage and processing efficiency to ensure optimal performance.

Buffering smoothed out variations in processing time, leading to consistent FPS and reduced memory usage variability. With a max buffer size of 20, the FPS improved to 9.35 for 640 × 480 resolution. This technique is effective for maintaining a steady data flow and preventing bottlenecks, ensuring continuous and efficient processing of video streams. The optimal buffer size depends on the specific hardware configuration and the nature of the video stream being analyzed.

5 Conclusion

This paper has addressed the critical need for optimization strategies in real-time video analytics, particularly in resource-constrained environments such as developing countries and edge systems. Through the introduction and evaluation of several techniques—including image resizing, frame skipping, MSE-based frame skipping, parallel processing, threading, queue management, memory management with tracemalloc, and buffering—we have demonstrated significant improvements in processing efficiency and memory usage. Our experimental results show that these strategies collectively enhance frames per second (FPS) and reduce memory consumption, ensuring that real-time video analytics systems can operate effectively even with limited computational resources.

By balancing processing efficiency and accuracy, the proposed strategies make advanced AI-driven video analysis feasible in environments with restricted resources. This not only facilitates real-time monitoring and alert systems but also broadens the accessibility of sophisticated video analytics technologies to regions and applications where computational capabilities are limited. Additionally, this paper provides a practical guide for implementing these optimization techniques, offering valuable insights and actionable steps for practitioners and researchers aiming to optimize their video analytics systems.

References

1. Girshick, R.: Fast R-CNN. In: Proceedings of the IEEE International Conference on Computer Vision, pp. 1440–1448 (2015)
2. Jiang, P., Ergu, D., Liu, F., Cai, Y., Ma, B.: A review of Yolo algorithm developments. Procedia Comput. Sci. **199**, 1066–1073 (2022)
3. Kastrinakis, D., Petrakis, E.G.: Video2flink: real-time video partitioning in apache flink and the cloud. Mach. Vis. Appl. **34**(3), 42 (2023)
4. Khadka, S., Ghimire, S.K.: Scalable solutions for efficient real-time distributed video analytics with vehicle detection on CPU edge nodes. In: Proceedings of the 2024 7th International Conference on Computers in Management and Business, pp. 73–79 (2024)
5. Liu, W., et al.: SSD: single shot MultiBox detector. In: Leibe, B., Matas, J., Sebe, N., Welling, M. (eds.) ECCV 2016, Part I. LNCS, vol. 9905, pp. 21–37. Springer, Cham (2016). https://doi.org/10.1007/978-3-319-46448-0_2
6. Redmon, J., Divvala, S., Girshick, R., Farhadi, A.: You only look once: unified, real-time object detection. In: Proceedings of the IEEE Conference on Computer Vision and Pattern Recognition, pp. 779–788 (2016)
7. Sultana, F., Sufian, A., Dutta, P.: A review of object detection models based on convolutional neural network. In: Mandal, J.K., Banerjee, S. (eds.) Intelligent Computing: Image Processing Based Applications. AISC, vol. 1157, pp. 1–16. Springer, Singapore (2020). https://doi.org/10.1007/978-981-15-4288-6_1
8. Zhao, Z.Q., Zheng, P., Xu, S.t., Wu, X.: Object detection with deep learning: a review. IEEE Trans. Neural Netw. Learn. Syst. **30**(11), 3212–3232 (2019)

A New Convolutional Neural Network Approach for Image Classification: The Case of Tomatoes

Kopoin N. D. Charlemagne[1](✉), Koffi Dagou[1], and Zouneme Boris[2]

[1] Ecole Supérieure Africaine des TIC, Abidjan-Treichville, Côte d'Ivoire
charlemagne.kopoin@esatic.edu.ci
[2] Université Nangui Abrogoua, Abidjan, Côte d'Ivoire

Abstract. Pattern recognition, in particular image classification, is a computationally intensive process. The best performing algorithmic models in this field are convolutional neural networks with a multi-layer convolution architecture, such as ResNet, GoogleNet or DenseNet. Most of these algorithms are computationally intensive and have high algorithmic complexity. In this paper, we propose KDZnet, a simple CNN architecture that is shallower and more robust and gives results as satisfactory as the CNN architectures in the literature. Two main technologies are used in our model, making it performant. First, we use the acyclic learning technique, which achieves fast convergence rates and high learning performance. We then apply the Batch normalization technique to optimize the network. Our model was tested on Fruits-360 dataset, mainly on tomato plants. The results obtained show that KDZnet achieves satisfactory results comparable to DenseNet or GoogleNet, and takes 10 times less time to run, and the algorithmic complexity is lower.

Keywords: CNN · image classification · Batch normalization

1 Introduction

Pattern recognition is a vast field that includes technologies for image classification and detection [1, 2], video classification [3], prediction of protein-protein interactions [4], disease prediction [5, 6], etc. Image classification is one of the most widely used technologies, given the new prospects offered by the development of AI and IoT technologies, mainly in precision agriculture [7]. This success has been made possible by the development of high-performance algorithms such as convolutional neural network (CNN) algorithms [8].

CNNs are a type of neural network inspired by mammalian vision. In the literature, several CNN architectures have been proposed for image classification [9–13]. Alexnet [14], for example, is a very successful model.. This model was used to classify handwritten images of numbers from 0 to 9. Overall, the performance results obtained were satisfactory. Given its success, several other architectures based on Alexnet [13, 15, 16] have been developed to improve its performance. Imagenet is a CNN model that has been used to classify several images. Its architecture consists of 3 convolutional layers and 3 fully connected layers. It used batch and adam techniques to optimize the network. Googlenet, a CNN model that was used to classify images of the architecture consists of 20 convolutional layers and 3 fully connected layers. Learning rate technologies were used. ResNet is a 50 convolutional layers architecture. DenseNet has been proposed. Several versions have been proposed, including densent 100 and DenseNet 201. Densent is a block architecture, each block being a condesnsed of a convolutional layer but also pooling layer. Its performance has been observed on 360 fruit images and many other images. More recently, models using image segmentation [17, 18] have been introduced. We can cite the models of rich, which is a 3-layer convolution architecture using segmentation coupled with performance. This architecture has been trained on testla images and obtained interesting performances.

We also note that one of the fields that has recently made extensive use of CNN algorithms is precision agriculture, specifically plant image recognition. Here, CNNs can be used to identify plants that are diseased, ripe, rotting, etc., with the aim of increasing production.

Although several architectures have been proposed with satisfactory results, it should be noted that each architecture corresponds to the classification of a particular image. There is no general architecture that can be adapted to all kinds of images. In addition, most of the architectures developed that deliver good performance are architectures with many convolution layers, making them very computationally intensive, with higher algorithmic complexity and longer execution times. This considerably reduces the testing of large-scale data. There are two main ways to improve the performance of your CNN architecture. Either you propose a multi-layer architecture such as ResNet or DenseNet, or you optimize the hyperparameters. In the context of precision agriculture for example, where these CNN algorithms will often have to be implemented, high energy consumption by certain data analysis tools such as sensors could compromise their operation. It's in this context that we place our study. We have developed KDZnet, which proposes an architecture with fewer convolution layers (4 layers to be exact) but introduces cyclic learning rate and batch normalization technologies to make the model less greedy and more efficient. In the following, we first present a general overview of a CNN architecture, followed by the Fruits-360 dataset, then present our KDZnet architecture model.

2 Architecture of CNN

2.1 General Information

Convolutional Neural Networks (CNNs) are particularly effective for tasks related to image analysis, such as classification, object detection, and segmentation. Indeed, these models are capable of learning multi-level representations of visual data, where higher-level features depend on lower-level ones. This process allows the model to recognize complex patterns and make highly accurate predictions. CNNs follow a series of steps, starting with the input image to be analyzed and ending with the predicted image output (Fig. 1).

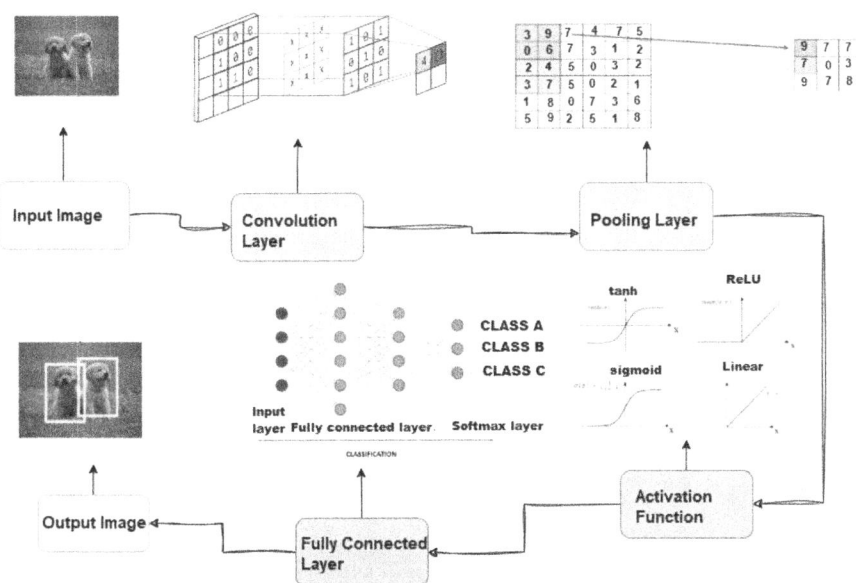

Fig. 1. Different phases of the CNN [28]

2.2 The Differents CNN Layers

A Convolutional Neural Network (CNN) typically consists of several layers (see Fig. 1, Table 1), each serving a specific role within the model. According to various researchers [19–21], the main types of layers in CNNs include the convolutional layer, the pooling layer, and the fully connected layer. Table 1 outlines these layers and their respective functions within the network.

Table 1. The different layers of the CNN and their function (adapted from [21])

Layer	Function
Convolutional layer	Applies a convolution operation to the input image using a set of trainable filters to generate a set of feature maps
Pooling layer	Decreases the spatial dimensions of the feature maps generated by the convolutional layer by selecting the maximum or average value from non-overlapping regions
Fully connected layer	Connects each neuron in the previous layer to each neuron in the current layer, usually used at the end of the network to produce the final output

Convolutional Layer. Considered the heart of the CNN [21, 22], convolution is a mathematical process that merges two signals or functions to generate a third signal.

This resulting signal reflects the impact of one signal on the other, weighted by the shape of the second signal. The mathematical expression of convolution can be represented by Eq. 1:

$$(g \times h)[n] = \sum_{m=-\infty}^{\infty} g[m] h[n-m] \qquad (1)$$

where g and h represent two functions that can be discrete or continuous, and n is the position or time index of the output signal. The convolution operation is designated by the symbol $\times$.

If we consider the case where the input signals are discrete, the above equation becomes as Eq. 2:

$$(g \times h)[n] = \sum_{m=-\infty}^{\infty} g[m] h[n-m] \Delta m \qquad (2)$$

where Δm is the sampling interval. For continuous input signals, the equation can be written as follows:

$$(g \times h)[t] = \int_{-\infty}^{\infty} g(\rho) h(t-\rho) d\rho \qquad (3)$$

with t, the time index of the output signal.

Convolution is used to extract various features from the input. The first convolution layer identifies basic features such as contours, lines and corners. Higher layers extract more advanced features.

Pooling Layer. The pooling layer is employed to decrease the spatial dimensions of the feature maps produced by the convolutional layer [19]. Its purpose is to minimize the size of these maps, thereby improving the robustness of feature extraction and preventing overfitting. Typically positioned between two convolutional layers, the size of the feature maps in the pooling layer is defined by the movement of the kernels. Common pooling operations include average pooling, which mathematically corresponds to $f(x) = \frac{1}{n} \sum_{i=1}^{n} x_i$ and the max pooling which corresponds mathematically to $_i^{max} x_i$ (Fig. 2).

Max pooling, a commonly used technique, splits the image into rectangular sub-regions and returns only the maximum value within each sub-region. A typical max pooling size is 2×2. A key aspect of pooling, designed to decrease the complexity of the subsequent layers, is down sampling, which can be compared to reducing the resolution in image processing. Pooling does not change the number of filters.

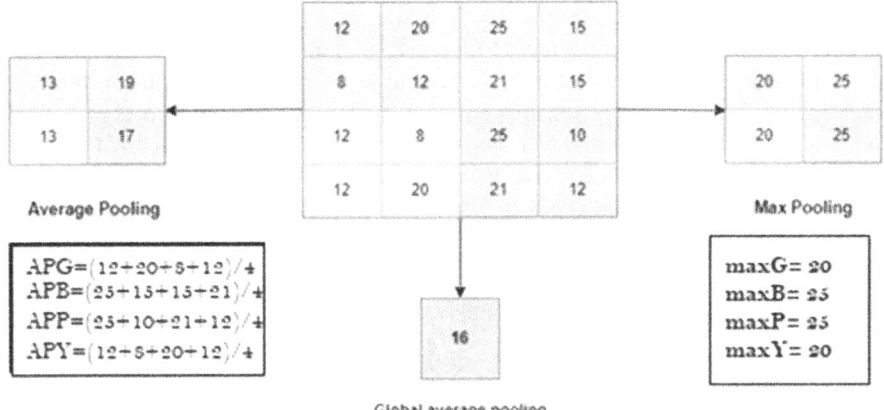

Fig. 2. Pooling layers. Here, APG refers to the average value of the window marked in green, while maxG represents the maximum value within the same green window (adapted from [22, 28])

Fully Connected Layer. Typically used at the end of the network to produce the final output. The fully connected layer is a standard neural network layer that establishes connections between every neuron in the previous layer and every neuron in the current layer.

3 Our Approach

The KDZnet model we propose for image classification has a shallow architecture but is rigorous and efficient in terms of prediction performance.

3.1 KDZnet Architecture

The architecture of our KDZnet model consists of 4 convolutional layers, 4 pooling layers and 3 fully connected layers (Fig. 3).

Convolutive Section. To increase the efficiency of our model, features as described below have been applied. It should be noted that these characteristics are obtained from certain experiments on which we have based ourselves and those we have carried out as shown in Table 2, and from data in the literature. We applied a pooling layer after each convolution layer (four to be exact) with filters of size 2×2 and a stride of 2 to reduce the input to a quarter of its original size. This scales the image by a factor of ½. This means that a window of size 2×2 is used, so the height of the output is equal to half the height at the input and the width and height are therefore reduced to 50 pixels each. For convolutional layers, the former applies 16 filters of size 3×3. Consequently, each filter here consists of a matrix of 3 pixels by 3 pixels. This was followed by max pooling with a 2×2 filter and a 2 stride, ensuring that the pooled regions did not overlap. The second convolutional layer applies 32 filters of size 3×3, producing 32 activation maps.

The same type of pooling as for the first layer, i.e. a 2 × 2 filter and stride 2, has been applied. The third convolutional layer applies 64 3 × 3 filters, followed by another layer of maximum pooling in the form of 2 × 2 and stride 2. Finally, the fourth convolutional layer applies 128 3 × 3 filters, followed by an average pooling layer of 2 × 2 shape and stride 2. This last pooling layer feeds a fully connected layer with 1024 inputs. 3 × 3 filters are effective for capturing local patterns and fine details in an image. Basic features such as textures and edges are efficiently extracted. Here, the choice of 3 × 3 size filters for convolutional layers therefore enables the model to capture local patterns and details in the input image. Also, with a stride of 1, the filter moves one pixel at a time across the layer, allowing more features to be extracted.

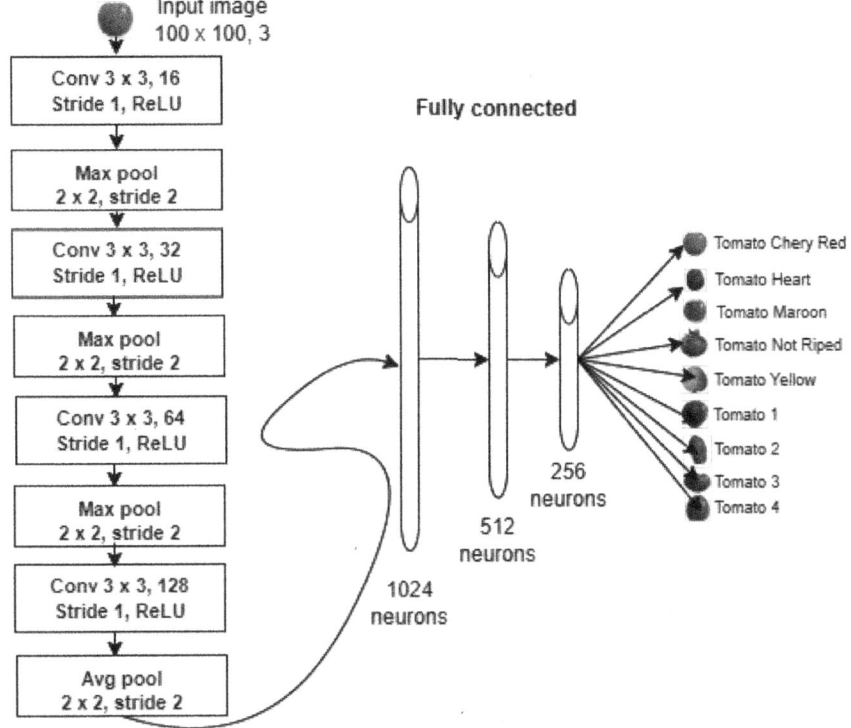

Fig. 3. KDZnet model architecture

Table 2. Convolutional parameters

Name	Proposed	Recommended
Convolution layers	3, 4, 5, 6, 7, 8	4
kernel	(3 × 3), (5 × 5), (7 × 7)	(3 × 3)
Stride	1 × 1, 2 × 2	1 × 1

(*continued*)

Table 2. (*continued*)

Name	Proposed	Recommended
Activation function	relu, sigmoid, softmax, tanh	relu

Fully Connected Section. This section describes a classical neural network, and for our model we have three fully connected layers of 1024, 512 and 256 neurons respectively. The output layer corresponds to the 9 reconstructed tomato classes.

3.2 KDZnet Optimization

The optimization of convolutional networks is a crucial task for the implementation of such systems. Loss layers, generally located at the end of the network, penalize it when it produces outputs different from those expected. Various loss functions exist, such as the softmax function, used to predict one class from a set of disjoint classes. Batch normalization [23], normalizes the inputs of the previous layer for each batch, keeping the values in a comparable range with a mean of 0 and a standard deviation of 1. This prevents model activations from being biased towards a particular point, increases execution speed, improves training stability, accelerates convergence, and acts as a form of regularization.

Using the gradient descent algorithm, we can optimize the weights of the convolutional neural network. During this iterative process, it is essential to carefully set key parameters such as the basic learning rate. The cyclic learning rate method [24] has been used to achieve better validation accuracy in a reduced number of epochs. This involves varying the learning rate within a range of values over a specific number of iterations. Here, the Adadelta optimizer was applied with a learning rate whose values lie between $[1e^{-6}; 1e^{-1}]$. The factor $\rho = 0.5$ has been applied to reduce the apprenticeship rate. We also used the Batch Normalization technique, which normalizes the inputs from the previous layer to each batch, keeping the values within a comparable range, with a mean equal to 0 and a standard deviation equal to 1. This ensures that our model activations are not skewed at any point, and increases execution speed, improves training stability, speeds up convergence and acts as a form of regularization.

As for the other hyperparameters, we optimized the most important ones, such as learning rate and batch size, by exploiting different values while keeping the other hyperparameters constant. Table 3 shows the other hyperparameter values used in the network.

Table 3. Optimisation parameters

Name	Proposed	Recommended
Epoch	16, 25, 32, 64, 50	25
Batch-size	25, 50, 75, 100	50

(*continued*)

Table 3. (*continued*)

Name	Proposed	Recommended
Per-parameter adaptive learning rate methods	SGD, RMSprop, Adagrad, Adadelta, Adam, Adamax, Nadam	Adadelta
Dropout rate	0.1, 0.2, 0.3, 0.4	0.1

4 The "Fruits-360" Dataset

"Fruits-360" is a large dataset of reference fruit images from the work of [25] which has been used by several studies to evaluate the models they propose [11, 26, 27] (available on https://www.kaggle.com/moltean/fruits, Version: 2020.05.18.0).

Images were obtained by filming the fruit in slow rotation at 3 rpm, then extracting individual frames. A diffusion filling algorithm was used to extract the background from the images. Marked pixels are considered the background, the rest being the object of interest. The dataset contains 90,483 images divided into 131 classes.

In this study, we were more interested in tomato images, divided into 9 types: Tomato 1, Tomato 2, Tomato 3, Tomato 4, Red Cherry Tomato, To-mate Heart, Brown Tomato, Unripe Tomato and Yellow Tomato (Fig. 4). Tomatoes for which no scientific or popular name has been found are labelled with numbers: Tomato 1, Tomato 2, Tomato 3, Tomato 4.

Data Augmentation. To overcome the problem of small sample sizes, authors often resort to data augmentation. In this study, the method used is augmentor [28, 29]. This method is based on a pipeline for stochastic image enhancement. The user can chain operations such as shearing, rotating and cropping, passing images through this pipeline to generate new data. All operations in the pipeline are applied randomly, both in terms of the probability of each operation being applied to an image, and the parameters of each operation, which are randomly selected from user-specified ranges. This enables sampling from a distribution of possible images, generated by the pipeline at runtime.

To create Training Set 2, comprising 10,000 images, we used the augmentor tool to apply geometric rotations combined with elastic distortions to the Training Set 1. Elastic distortions enable modifications to be made to an image while preserving its proportions. The number of trainings set 1 and training set 2 images, as well as test images, for each tomato type, is shown in Table 4.

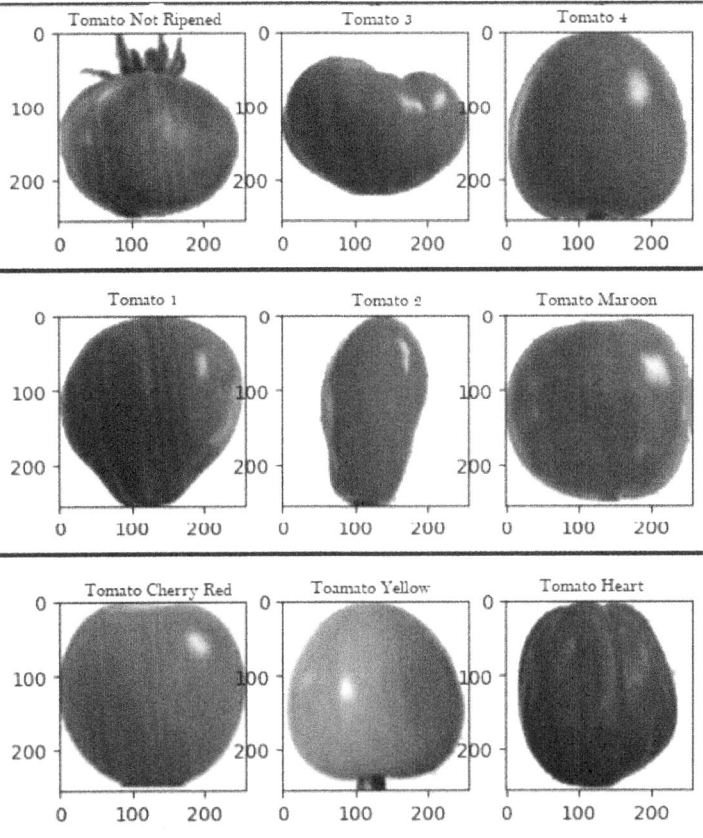

Fig. 4. Image of each tomato by category

Table 4. The number of images of each tomato type in trainings sets 1 and 2 and in the test set (Adapted from [22]).

Tomato type	Training set1	Training set 2	Testing set
Tomato 1	738	1440	246
Tomato 2	672	1316	225
Tomato 3	738	1419	246
Tomato 4	479	938	160
Tomato Cherry Red	492	989	164
Tomato Maroon	367	788	127
Tomato Heart	684	1325	228
Tomato Not Ripened	474	895	158
Tomato Yellow	459	890	153

(*continued*)

Table 4. (*continued*)

Tomato type	Training set1	Training set 2	Testing set
Total	5103	10000	1707

5 Results

In this section, we present the results obtained from training the KDZnet network using the Fruits-360 dataset. Figure 5 displays the training and validation loss curves for our KDZnet model. We trained the model with 9.1 million parameters for 25 epochs, using a batch size of 50 images. As shown in Fig. 5, the model rapidly achieves higher validation accuracy (before the 5th epoch) and significantly reduces validation loss. This performance is attributed to the use of the cyclic learning rate technique and Batch Normalization. Prior to the 15th epoch, the validation loss curve was below the training loss curve, indicating underlearning. Afterward, a higher cyclic learning rate was applied, narrowing the gap between the two curves, which then tended to decrease together towards zero. At the conclusion of the 25 epochs, we achieved a validation accuracy of 100%, with the training accuracy also reaching 100%, demonstrating effective learning and generalization by the model.

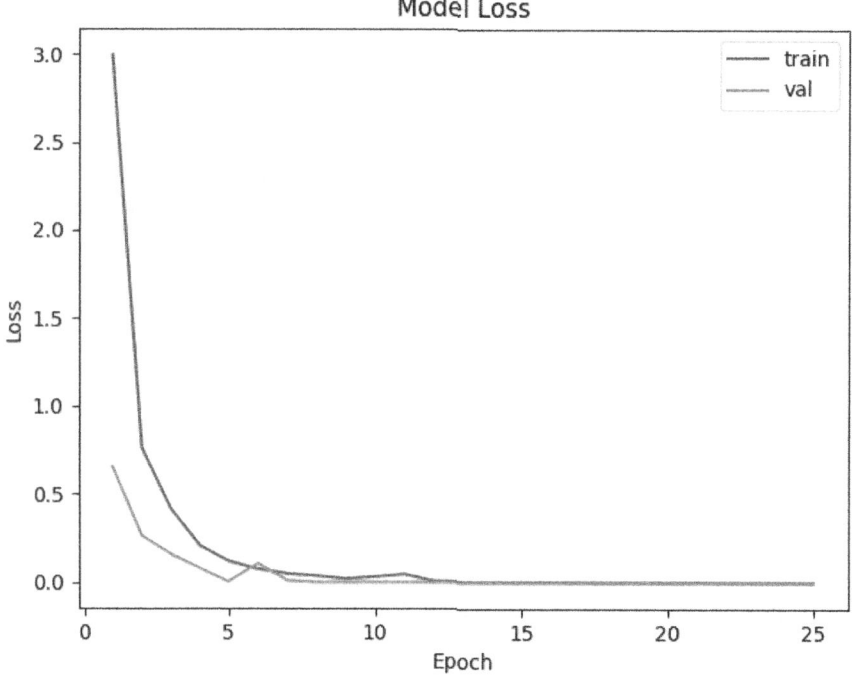

Fig. 5. KDZnet train loss and validation loss curves

Below, we compare the performance of our KDZnet model with some models in the literature, such as GoogleNet [13], ResNet [30], and DenseNet-121 [11], which we have implemented. We emphasize that all these networks have been trained with the hyperparameter values that give the best performance. GoogleNet, consisting of 22 convolution layers, is a convolutional neural network model based on the Inception architecture [31].

Table 5 shows the execution time and performance results obtained on training set 1, made up of original images of Fruits-360. The results obtained by the different models on training set 2, obtained after applying a data augmentation technique to training set 1, are shown in Table 6.

Table 5. Performance comparison on training set 1

Models	Execution time (s)	Validation accuracy (%)	Test accuracy (%)
GoogleNet	1,663	98.61	99.75
ResNet	5,721	100	100
DenseNet	3,698	100	100
KDZnet	**643**	**100**	**100**

Table 6. Performance comparison on training set 2

Modèles	Execution time (s)	Validation Accuracy (%)	Test accuracy (%)
GoogleNet	2,510	99.69	100
ResNet	11,398	99.79	100
DenseNet	7,148	100	100
KDZnet	**1,175**	**100**	**100**

The results presented in Table 5 demonstrate that, across all models, the validation performance values for accuracy are very close to the test values, with performance exceeding 94%. This indicates that all models are capable of effectively extracting and learning features. The ResNet, DenseNet, and our KDZnet models all achieve 100% accuracy on both the validation and test datasets. This level of performance suggests that these three models have learned the features well and are able to generalize to new data with high accuracy. The GoogLeNet model shows a validation performance of 98.91% and a test performance of 99.75%. In terms of execution time, our KDZnet model had the shortest runtime at 643 s. The longest execution time belongs to ResNet with 5,721 s, then DenseNet with 3,698 s and finally GoogleNet with 1,663 s. In terms of network performance, we can say that our model, in addition to displaying an accuracy rate of 100% in both validation and test, on a par with the ResNet and DenseNet models, has an execution time well below that of ResNet and DenseNet.

According to Table 6, we can see that GoogleNet's validation performance increased by over 1%. We can therefore say that this model captures features better when the training data is larger. Both our KDZnet and DenseNet models maintained their 100% performance in validation and testing with the new training data. This shows that the DenseNet model and our model have not overlearned and are able to generalize correctly on new data. In terms of execution times, our KDZnet model maintains the shortest time with 1,175 s. As for the other models, times have almost all doubled, with 2,510, 11,398 and 7,148 s respectively for GoogleNet, ResNet and DenseNet. This clearly shows how cumbersome these networks can be when the dataset becomes large.

6 Discussion

In this work, we present a CNN model that reduces memory cost while maintaining good performance. The architecture of our proposed CNN, named KDZnet, consists of 4 convolutional layers with a kernel size of 3×3, a stride of 1×1, and employs the ReLU activation function (Table 2). In our model, we utilize a cyclic learning rate during the training phase, which results in identical performance in terms of learning and testing accuracy, as shown in Tables 5 and 6. We believe that periodically increasing the learning rate through the cyclic learning rate technique allows for a broader exploration of the parameter space, helping to avoid local minima and facilitating the discovery of better global solutions. This technique helps stabilize and accelerate the training of deep neural networks by reducing the internal covariate shift (i.e., the changes in input distribution for each layer during training), making the learning process more efficient. Regarding execution time, based on the number of operations in Floating Point Operations (FLOPS), we observe that the execution time of KDZnet needs to be multiplied by a factor ranging from 26 to 50 to match the time required for the other architecture discussed in this work. We believe that this efficiency is primarily due to the architecture of KDZnet, which consists of 4 layers and a 3×3 kernel size, requiring less computation time while delivering strong performance.

However, we acknowledge that our KDZnet model has not been tested on large datasets like ImageNet or MNIST. Additionally, we have not evaluated it on datasets with a wide range of classes. Errors may arise from the diversity of classes, particularly when some classes are underrepresented. In such cases, regularization techniques like L1/L2 could help address this issue by improving the model's ability to generalize more effectively.

7 Conclusion and Prospects

This study proposes a CNN network model that offers good performance without being computationally intensive or having many layers. Experimental results have shown that our KDZnet model performs as well as recent models in literature, and with a relatively small execution time. The use of a cyclic learning rate and the Batch normalization technique not only accelerated learning but also improved the model's performance. This work highlights several factors that contribute to KDZnet's performance. For instance, we can highlight its ability to extract relevant features and its quick execution time, which makes it less computationally demanding compared to state-of-the-art CNN networks. Looking ahead, we aim to further strengthen our model by testing it on other image datasets such as MNIST or ImageNet. Additionally, we plan to implement regularization techniques like L1/L2 regularization to improve the model's generalizability. We also intend to integrate the model into a software application for practical use, such as in agriculture.

References

1. Nouar, F., Bouchenine, R., (Encadreur) Bouatmane, S.: Classification d'images des cellules sanguines leucémiques à l'aide des techniques d'apprentissage profond. Thesis, Université de Jijel (2023). http://dspace.univ-jijel.dz:8080/xmlui/handle/123456789/14376. Accessed 23 Mar 2024
2. Chen, W., Su, L., Chen, X., Huang, Z.: Rock image classification using deep residual neural network with transfer learning. Front. Earth Sci. **10** (2023). https://www.frontiersin.org/articles/https://doi.org/10.3389/feart.2022.1079447. Accessed 3 Jan 2024
3. Li, Y., et al.: MViTv2: improved multiscale vision transformers for classification and detection. In: Proceedings of the IEEE/CVF Conference on Computer Vision and Pattern Recognition, pp. 4804–4814 (2022). http://openaccess.thecvf.com/content/CVPR2022/html/Li_MViTv2_Improved_Multiscale_Vision_Transformers_for_Classification_and_Detection_CVPR_2022_paper.html. Accessed 4 Apr 2024
4. Hu, L., Wang, X., Huang, Y.-A., Hu, P., You, Z.-H.: A survey on computational models for predicting protein–protein interactions. Brief. Bioinform. **22**(5), bbab036 (2021). https://doi.org/10.1093/bib/bbab036
5. Krishnamoorthi, R., et al.: A novel diabetes healthcare disease prediction framework using machine learning techniques. J. Healthc. Eng. **2022** (2022). https://www.hindawi.com/journals/jhe/2022/1684017/1000/. Accessed 4 Apr 2024
6. Ahmed, U., et al.: Prediction of diabetes empowered with fused machine learning. IEEE Access **10**, 8529–8538 (2022)
7. Botta, A., Cavallone, P., Baglieri, L., Colucci, G., Tagliavini, L., Quaglia, G.: A review of robots, perception, and tasks in precision agriculture. Appl. Mech. **3**(3), Article no 3 (2022). https://doi.org/10.3390/applmech3030049
8. Jiang, Y., Xie, J., Zhang, D.: An adaptive offset activation function for CNN image classification tasks. Electronics **11**(22), Article no 22 (2022). https://doi.org/10.3390/electronics11223799
9. Abai, Z., Rajmalwar, N.: DenseNet models for tiny ImageNet classification (2020)
10. Hu, K., Zou, A., Wang, Z., Leino, K., Fredrikson, M.: Unlocking deterministic robustness certification on ImageNet. Adv. Neural Inf. Process. Syst. **36**, December 2023. https://proceedings.neurips.cc/paper_files/paper/2023/hash/863da9d40547f1d1b18859519ce2dee4-Abstract-Conference.html. Accessed 24 Feb 2024
11. Lu, T., Han, B., Chen, L., Yu, F., Xue, C.: A generic intelligent tomato classification system for practical applications using DenseNet-201 with transfer learning. Sci. Rep. **11**(1), Article no 1 (2021). https://doi.org/10.1038/s41598-021-95218-w
12. He, F., Liu, T., Tao, D.: Why resnet works? Residuals generalize. IEEE Trans. Neural Netw. Learn. Syst. **31**(12), 5349–5362 (2020)
13. Yang, L., et al.: GoogLeNet based on residual network and attention mechanism identification of rice leaf diseases. Comput. Electron. Agric. **204**, 107543 (2023)
14. Chen, H.-C., et al.: AlexNet convolutional neural network for disease detection and classification of tomato leaf. Electronics **11**(6), 951 (2022)

15. Kaddoun, S.S., Aberni, Y., Boubchir, L., Raddadi, M., Daachi, B.: Convolutional Neural Algorithm for palm vein recognition using ZFNet architecture. In: Proceedings of the 2021 4th International Conference on Bio-Engineering for Smart Technologies (BioSMART), pp. 1–4. IEEE (2021). https://ieeexplore.ieee.org/abstract/document/9677799/. Accessed 4 Apr 2024
16. Prasetyo, E., Suciati, N., Fatichah, C.: Multi-level residual network VGGNet for fish species classification. J. King Saud Univ.-Comput. Inf. Sci. **34**(8), 5286–5295 (2022)
17. Gené-Mola, J., et al.: AmodalAppleSize_RGB-D dataset: RGB-D images of apple trees annotated with modal and amodal segmentation masks for fruit detection, visibility and size estimation. Data Brief **52**, 110000 (2024)
18. Zhang, Y., Gong, Y., Cui, D., Li, X., Shen, X.: DeepGI: an automated approach for gastrointestinal tract segmentation in MRI scans. arXiv: arXiv:2401.15354, 27 January 2024. http://arxiv.org/abs/2401.15354. Accessed 4 Apr 2024
19. Taye, M.M.: Theoretical understanding of convolutional neural network: concepts, architectures, applications, future directions. Computation **11**(3), Article no 3 (2023). https://doi.org/10.3390/computation11030052
20. Li, Z., Liu, F., Yang, W., Peng, S., Zhou, J.: A survey of convolutional neural networks: analysis, applications, and prospects. IEEE Trans. Neural Netw. Learn. Syst. **33**(12), 6999–7019 (2022). https://doi.org/10.1109/TNNLS.2021.3084827
21. Krichen, M.: Convolutional neural networks: a survey. Computers **12**(8), Article no 8 (2023). https://doi.org/10.3390/computers12080151
22. Kamagate, B.H., Kopoin, N., Koffi, D.D.A., Asseu, O.P.: A robust convolutional neural network model for fruit image classification. Ingénierie Systèmes Inf. **29**(5) (2024). https://doi.org/10.18280/isi.290504. Accessed 15 Dec 2024
23. Bjorck, N., Gomes, C.P., Selman, B., Weinberger, K.Q.: Understanding batch normalization. Adv. Neural Inf. Process. Syst. **31**, 7694–7705 (2018)
24. Yu, T., Zhu, H.: Hyper-parameter optimization: a review of algorithms and applications. arXiv: arXiv:2003.05689, 12 March 2020. http://arxiv.org/abs/2003.05689. Accessed 16 Mar 2024
25. Mureşan, H., Oltean, M.: Fruit recognition from images using deep learning. Acta Univ. Sapientiae Inform. **10**(1), 26–42 (2018). https://doi.org/10.2478/ausi-2018-0002
26. Siddiqi, R.: Effectiveness of transfer learning and fine tuning in automated fruit image classification. In: Proceedings of the 2019 3rd International Conference on Deep Learning Technologies, in ICDLT 2019, pp. 91–100. Association for Computing Machinery, New York, July 2019. https://doi.org/10.1145/3342999.3343002
27. Kodors, S., Lacis, G., Zhukov, V., Bartulsons, T.: Pear and apple recognition using deep learning and mobile. Eng. Rural Dev. **20**, 1795–1800 (2020)
28. Xu, M., Yoon, S., Fuentes, A., Park, D.S.: A comprehensive survey of image augmentation techniques for deep learning. Pattern Recognit. **137**, 109347 (2023). https://doi.org/10.1016/j.patcog.2023.109347
29. Bloice, M.D., Stocker, C., Holzinger, A.: Augmentor: an image augmentation library for machine learning. arXiv: arXiv:1708.04680, 11 August 2017. https://doi.org/10.48550/arXiv.1708.04680
30. Koonce, B.: ResNet 50. In: Convolutional Neural Networks with Swift for Tensorflow, pp. 63–72. Apress, Berkeley (2021). https://doi.org/10.1007/978-1-4842-6168-2_6
31. Lee, H., Kwon, H.: Going deeper with contextual CNN for hyperspectral image classification. IEEE Trans. Image Process. **26**(10), 4843–4855 (2017). https://doi.org/10.1109/TIP.2017.2725580

Text-to-OWL: Automated Ontology Construction for Tuberculosis Treatment Recommendation Using Generative AI

Zonabo Ouédraogo[1,2](✉), Lydie Simone Tapsoba[2], Aminata Sabane[1,2], Rodrique Kafando[1,3], Abdoul Kader Kabore[4], and Tegawendé F. Bissyande[1,4]

[1] Interdisciplinary Center of Excellence in AI for Development (CITADEL), Ouagadougou, Burkina Faso
aminata.sabane@ujkz.bf,
{rodrique.kafando,tegawende.bissyande}@citadel.bf
[2] University Joseph KI-ZERBO, Ouagadougou, Burkina Faso
ozenabo3@gmail.com
[3] Virtual University of Burkina Faso, Ouagadougou, Burkina Faso
[4] University of Luxembourg, Luxembourg City, Luxembourg
abdoulkader.kabore@citadel.bf

Abstract. This paper presents an automated approach for building ontologies to improve treatment recommendations for tuberculosis (TB), in particular multidrug-resistant tuberculosis (MDR-TB) cases in Burkina Faso, using generative language models such as GPT-3. The aim is to facilitate the personalization of treatments according to the patient profile and drug resistance. Two approaches were explored: an automated approach based on the DaVinci GPT-3 model to generate OWL axioms from natural language sentences and a semi-automated approach using text extraction and natural language processing (NLP) techniques. The automated approach was fine-tuned with a dataset consisting of technical guidelines on TB management. The automated approach created an ontology composed of 158 classes, 55 object properties and 57 data properties, outperforming the semi-automated approach in terms of efficiency and accuracy. The axioms generated were validated using Protégé and integrated into a formal knowledge base. The study demonstrates that the use of language models such as GPT-3 can efficiently automate ontology generation, reducing human intervention. This approach is particularly well-suited to the management of complex MDR-TB cases and paves the way for standardization of treatment recommendations, while remaining adaptable to local specificities.

Keywords: Tuberculosis · Generative AI · Ontologies · Medical Decision Support Systems · Text-to-Ontology

1 Introduction

Tuberculosis (TB) remains a significant public health issue in many developing countries, particularly in Burkina Faso, where health systems face increased challenges in managing cases of multidrug-resistant tuberculosis (MDR-TB)[1]. MDR-TB significantly complicates standard treatment regimens as it evades conventional treatments, thereby increasing mortality and prolonging treatment periods[2]. In this context, the integration of advanced technologies like artificial intelligence (AI) and ontology-based systems becomes crucial to improve treatment recommendations and tailor medical interventions to the specific needs of patients[3].

Current therapeutic recommendation systems for tuberculosis principally rely on clinical guidelines and standardized protocols, often based on recommendations from the World Health Organization (WHO). While these systems are effective for common cases of tuberculosis, they reveal their limitations when faced with complex cases, like those of multidrug-resistant tuberculosis (MDR-TB), where resistance to standard drugs complicates therapeutic decisions [1].

To address this gap, this study proposes an innovative model for the automatic generation of ontologies aimed at improving treatment recommendations for TB, particularly for MDR-TB cases [2]. The hypothesis is that the use of generative models based on Large Language Models (LLMs), like GPT-3, can transform technical guides and local data into a formal ontology [3]. This ontology facilitates the personalization of treatment recommendations based on the patient's profile and drug resistances.

In the following sections of this article, we present a review of the literature on ontology construction approaches and recommendation systems for tuberculosis treatment. Next, we detail the methodology utilized to generate ontologies from management guidelines. Definitively, we present the results obtained and discuss the implications for case management of multidrug-resistant tuberculosis (MDR-TB) in Burkina Faso.

2 Related Work

There are several relevant works related to the use of ontologies for the treatment of tuberculosis (TB). We have grouped the articles into two distinct groups. The first group consists of articles using ontologies in the treatment or monitoring of tuberculosis. The second includes articles that utilize tools to generate ontologies or offer predictions to understand the construction approaches that can be considered for our work.

2.1 Ontologies in Tuberculosis Treatment and Monitoring

Several studies explore the use of ontologies in tuberculosis (TB) treatment and monitoring.

Surveillance Systems: Gadicherla *and al.* [4] propose a TB surveillance system using a manual ontology for real-time data collection and analysis. While effective for identifying high-risk areas, limitations include narrow scope (excluding financial aspects) and a lack of focus on resource management.

---

[1] Rapport mondial sur la tuberculose (OMS).
[2] http://cns.bf/IMG/pdf/mshp_profil_du_burkina_sur_la_tuberculose.pdf.
[3] https://www.scidev.net/afrique-sub-saharienne/news/l-intelligence-artificielle-une-solution-aux-problemes-de-sante-de-l-afrique/.

TB Adherence Ontology: Olukunle Ayodeji Ogundele et al. [5] develop an ontology to capture factors influencing TB treatment adherence behavior in sub-Saharan Africa. This ontology offers a modern perspective on adherence factors and their interrelationships.

Epidemiological Surveillance in Gabon: Raymond Ondzigue Mbenga [6] developed a decision support system for the epidemiological surveillance of tuberculosis in Gabon. The system combines a spatiotemporal decision-making tool (SOLAP-TB) and a multi-agent simulation model (SMA-TB). This approach is distinguished by the use of complex modeling to monitor the evolution of TB in real-time, although the complexity of the model may limit its transferability to other contexts.

Tuberculosis Management: Kumar Abhishek [1] presents an ontology-based formalization for the Revised National Tuberculosis Control Program (RNTCP) in India. He utilizes a decision support system (DSS) and semantic web technologies to improve tuberculosis management and control. The proposed system integrates ontologies and SWRL rules for diagnosis and treatment, following WHO recommendations. The ontologies facilitate knowledge representation and decision-making based on logical rules. The article concludes with the potential extension of the system to track patients with multi-drug resistant tuberculosis and those co-infected with HIV.

Ontology Enrichment: Desi Ramayanti [7] leverages the existing Epidemiology Ontology (EPO) to create a TB-specific ontology through a semi-automatic approach. This approach emphasizes reducing time and costs associated with manual enrichment. These studies showcase the potential of ontologies for TB management but also highlight limitations in scope and automation.

2.2 Ontology Generation and Prediction Tools

Research efforts explore tools for ontology generation and prediction:

Automatic Ontology Construction: Fatima N. Al-Aswadi [8] discusses challenges and approaches in automatic ontology construction from text. The focus is on reducing human intervention and improving relation/axiom discovery. Deep learning approaches are seen as promising avenues for subsequent exploration.

Ontology Generation Frameworks: Samaa Elnagar and al. [9] propose a framework for automating ontology generation from unstructured knowledge sources. This framework promotes efficiency and reduces costs compared to manual methods, but limitations exist in addressing complex OWL structures.

Term Extraction and Taxonomy Generation: Gerhard W. et al. [10] (2016) evaluate the effectiveness of word2vec for ontology creation by extracting terms and generating taxonomies from text. While efficiently, word2vec's results can be influenced by input terms, impacting relevance.

Large Language Models for Ontology Enrichment: Patricia M. and Adrian G. [11] present a Protégé plugin that leverages large language models (like GPT-3) to automatically convert natural language sentences into OWL axioms. This approach aims to accelerate ontology development but necessitates evaluation of its impact on general quality and reliability. These studies explore diverse tools for ontology generation and enrichment, highlighting a trend towards automation and the use of advanced language models.

2.3 Comparison of Approaches

Table 1. Table summarizing the advantages and disadvantages of different ontology-building approaches.

Approaches	Advantages	Disadvantages
Using word2vec for ontology learning	Simple implementation, impressive ability to extract relevant terms	Results sometimes too closely related to seed terms, difficulty in generating accurate taxonomic relations (about 50% accuracy)
Methods for automatic extraction and generation of ontologies from unstructured corpus	Cost and time reduction through automation, ability to use Knowledge Graphs (KGs) for dynamic representation	Often domain-specific approaches, still require manual interventions, KG quality issues (uncertain reliability and completeness)
Semi-automatic ontologies (Desi Ramayanti)	Cost and time reduction in ontology development	Still partially manual, not completely automated
Large language models (Patricia M.)	Automation of OWL axioms from natural language sentences	Requires evaluation of the quality and reliability of the axioms

Among the various articles, the works of Kumar Abhishek have addressed the complexity of managing cases of multidrug-resistant tuberculosis (MDR-TB) and comorbidities, highlighting the persistent challenges in this field. The main objective of this thesis is to create an ontology that proposes suitable treatments for these specific cases of tuberculosis. For the implementation of the knowledge base, the approach adopted relied on the works of Patricia M. and Adrian G., who utilize large-scale language models, such as GPT-3, to translate sentences written in natural language into OWL axioms. These works show progress towards the automation of ontologies in TB management, but they also reveal gaps in adapting to local specificities, such as managing MDR-TB in Burkina Faso. Our research proposes to explore these approaches while leveraging the use of large language models to generate ontologies adapted to local contexts (Table 1).

3 Material and Methodology

3.1 Material

This section describes the tools and methods used to construct an ontology from technical guidelines for tuberculosis management, particularly for managing multidrug-resistant tuberculosis (MDR-TB). Two approaches are presented: an automatic approach and a semi-automatic approach.

Protégé: protégé is a widely used open-source ontology editor for creating and validating ontologies using the OWL language[4]. It allows for the syntactic validity of generated axioms to be checked and integrated into a formal knowledge base.

Apache Jena Fuseki: apache Jena Fuseki is a SPARQL server used to query, manipulate, and store RDF triples [12]. This server allowed us to execute queries on semantic data and integrate the results into the ontology.

GPT-3: designed by OpenAI in 2018, GPT-3 represent a deep learning model belonging to the GPT (generative pre-trained transformer) family developed by the similar company. It is a pre-trained generative model for automatic natural language processing (ANLP) or natural language processing (NLP)[5]. With its 175 billion parameters, GPT-3 is one of the large language models (LLMs) and is used for tasks like question-answering, translation, text writing, problem solving and application code generation.

DaVinci: the DaVinci model was utilized for the automatic translation of natural language sentences into OWL axioms[6]. This natural language processing model, developed by OpenAI, was fine-tuned for this specific task of axiom generation. Its ability to comprehend and generate complex texts makes it an ideal tool for developing ontologies in specialized fields like tuberculosis.

PyPDF2: PyPDF2 is a Python library operated to extract raw text from PDF files[7]. We used PyPDF2 to read the PDF files of the technical guidelines for tuberculosis management, thus enabling automated extraction of textual information.

SpaCy: SpaCy is an open-source natural language processing (NLP) library[8]. It was utilized to segment the extracted text into sentences, recognize named entities (NER), and perform syntactic and morphological analyses.

3.2 Proposed Approaches

We explored two approaches to construct the ontology from textual documents: an automatic approach and a semi-automatic approach.

---

[4] https://www.imgt.org/textes/IMGTeducation/Enseignements/_FR/Giudicelli-MEDBioinformatique_ontologies_23_Mai_2013.pdf.
[5] https://www.ibm.com/topics/machine-learning, https://www.journaldunet.fr/intelligence-artificielle/guide-de-l-intelligence-artificielle/1516205-gpt-3-le-modele-de-langue-geant-d-openai/.
[6] https://www.actuia.com/actualite/openai-officialise-une-nouvelle-version-pour-\discretionary-son-modele-de-langage-gtp-3/.
[7] https://nanonets.com/blog/pypdf2-library-working-with-pdf-files-in-python/.
[8] https://spacy.io/.

Automatic Approach: In this approach, we utilize the fine-tuning technique on the Davinci model [11]. Fine-tuning is a method that allows adapting a pre-trained Machine Learning model to a specific task.

Figure 1 illustrates this approach in detail, highlighting the various steps of the process.

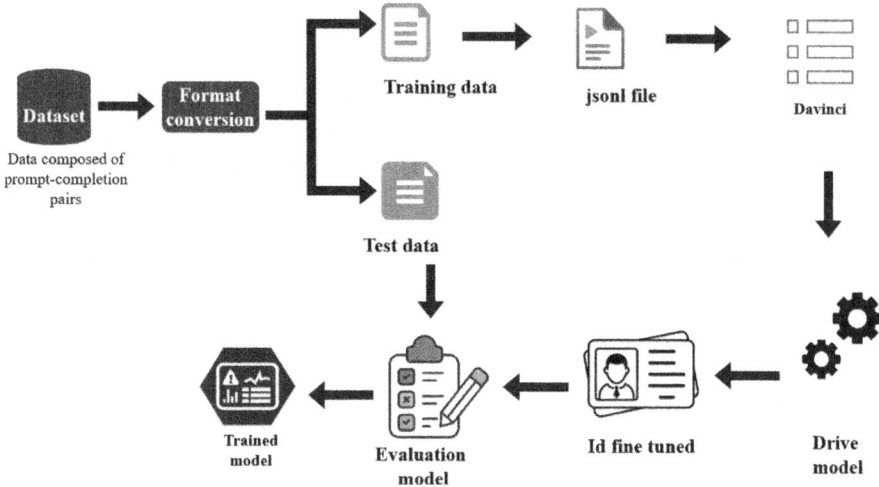

Fig. 1. Diagram of the automatic approach.

According to Fig. 1, the following steps are involved:

- data collection and preparation: we built a dataset consisting of 182 auto-completion pairs from two technical guidelines for tuberculosis management in Burkina Faso;
- conversion to JSONL Format: the sentences were converted to JSONL (JavaScript Object Notation Lines) format, a format suitable for training natural language processing models. Each line of the file represents a pair consisting of a sentence written in natural language and its translation into an OWL axiom;
- training and Fine-Tuning the GPT-3 Model: the DaVinci model of GPT-3 was fine-tuned using these data pairs. This fine-tuning process adjusts the model's parameters to generate precise and coherent OWL axioms from sentences written in natural language. A test dataset was used to evaluate the model's performance after training;
- generation and validation of OWL Axioms: Once the model was trained, it was utilized to automatically generate OWL axioms. The generated axioms were then validated using Protégé to verify their syntactic accuracy before integration into the ontology.

Semi-automatic Approach: The semi-automatic approach uses a combination of text extraction from PDF files and NLP (Natural Language Processing) analysis to extract triplets. Here are the main steps of this approach:

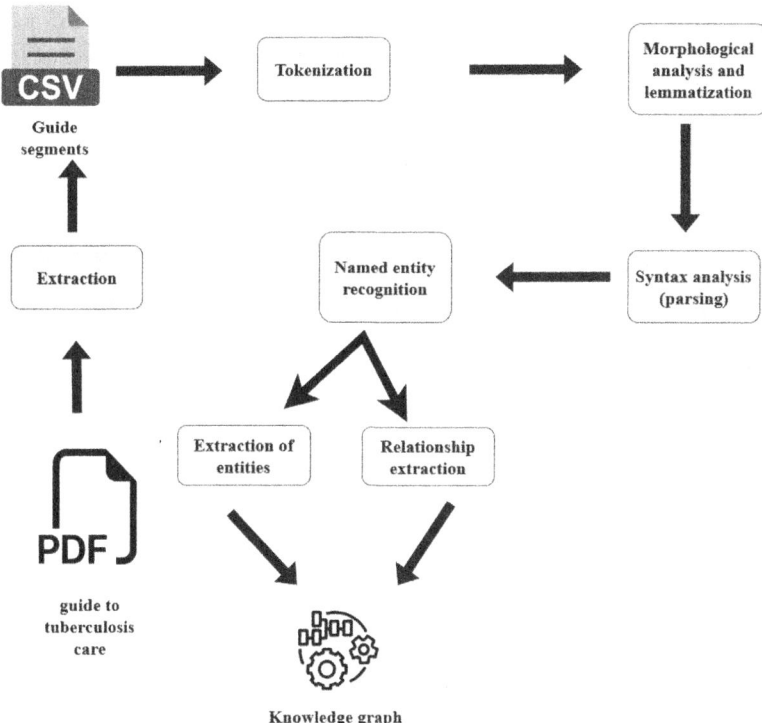

Fig. 2. Diagram of PDF text extraction.

Figure 2 the steps involved in extracting triplets from PDF files.
According to Fig. 2, the following steps are involved:

- text extraction from PDF Files: the text from the technical guides was extracted using a PyPDF2 library. This script automated the extraction of relevant information from large PDF files while preserving their structure. The raw text was then cleaned to remove unwanted characters and extra spaces;
- sentence segmentation and NLP Analysis: after extraction, the text was segmented into sentences using SpaCy. SpaCy identified named entities and performed syntactic and morphological analysis of the sentences, facilitating the extraction of RDF triples;
- data organization in CSV: the triples were organized into a CSV file for more structured data management;
- knowledge graph generation: we built a knowledge graph to visualize the relationships between the triples.

Using the DaVinci model allows for fully automated generation of OWL axioms with increased accuracy, especially for complex sentences. Additionally, the fine-tuning process enables the model to adapt specifically to the domain of tuberculosis, thereby reducing the need for human intervention. In contrast, the semi-automatic approach, while functional, requires more manual intervention, particularly for text extraction and segmentation, as well as RDF triple generation. This approach is also less efficient in handling complex concepts, as it relies on additional steps of data cleaning and structuring. In summary, the automatic approach proved to be faster and more accurate for generating OWL axioms, requiring minimal human intervention. It is therefore more suitable for constructing a formal ontology in complex domains like the management of multidrug-resistant tuberculosis.

4 Experiments

4.1 Results of the Semi-automatic Approach

The two approaches we have mentioned are two distinct methods for extracting information from texts and converting it into a structured form. Table 2 is an excerpt of the obtained triplets.

Table 2. Results of the Semi-Automatic Approach

Subjects	Predicate	Object
Patient	is	person
Patient	assumes	PresumedCase
PresumedCase	follows	PreventiveTreatment
Patient	isInfectedBy	TuberculosisCase
Patient	isUnder	Surveillance
Patient	takesA	XpertTest
Patient	interrupts	Treatment
TuberculosisCase	hasA	TherapeuticRegimen
Antitubercular	_hasFor_	MajorEffect
Antitubercular	hasFor__	MinorEffect
MajorEffect	__hasFor	RecommendedAction
MinorEffect	__hasFor_	RecommendedAction

The Semi-Automatic Approach focuses on extracting subject-predicate-object triplets from texts. These triplets can help identify different classes in PDF files. For example, in the context of tuberculosis treatment, a triplet could be "Patient assumes PresumedCase," where "Patient" is the subject, "assumes" is the predicate, and "PresumedCase" is the object.

4.2 Results of the Automatic Approach

We used an automatic approach to generate ontologies from natural language sentences. The model, based on GPT-3 (DaVinci), was fine-tuned with 182 pairs of natural language sentences and their translations into OWL axioms.

- **Model performance:** After several training steps, the model showed high accuracy in generating axioms. For example, the sentence *'A patient is a person'* was correctly translated into an OWL axiom by declaring the `Patient` class and establishing a subclass relationship with `Person`.
- **Obtained metrics:** During training, the training loss (a measure of the model's error) gradually decreased, reaching a value as low as 0.0002, indicating that the model learned well from the training data and is capable of generating accurate results.

Table 3 The table below shows the different metrics.

Table 3. Training and Validation Results

Step	Train Loss	Train Accuracy	Valid Loss	Valid Mean Token Accuracy
1	4.0779	0.31818	-	-
2	2.69302	0.59259	-	-
3	3.85006	0.40816	-	-
4	3.23567	0.50980	-	-
5	2.58106	0.55556	-	-

Table 4 illustrates the results obtained using the automatic approach.

Table 4. Results of the Automatic Approach

Prompt	Results
A patient is a person.	Declaration(Class(:Patient))
	Declaration(Class(:Person))
	SubClassOf(Patient :Person)
A patient is a class, but disjoint from Doctor.	Declaration(Class(:Patient))
	DisjointClasses(Patient :Doctor)
A person is a class. A patient is a subclass of person. A patient is a person.	Declaration(Class(:Patient))
	SubClassOf(Patient :Person),
	Declaration(Individual(:Florence))
	ClassAssertion(Patient :Person),
	Declaration(Individual(:Paul))
	ClassAssertion(Patient :Person)
A tuberculosis case is any patient for whom tuberculosis has been confirmed bacteriologically or diagnosed clinically.	Declaration(Class(:Tuberculosis_Case)),
	Declaration(Class(:Patient)),
	Declaration(ObjectProperty(:confirmed_by_Bacteria)),
	Declaration(ObjectProperty(:diagnosed_Clinically))

Here are some examples of axioms generated by the automatic approach:

- **Natural language sentence:** "A patient is a person"
  - **OWL Axiom:** `Declaration(Class(:Patient))`, `SubClassOf(:Patient :Person)`

These results show the model is capable of efficiently converting sentences into formal axioms, thereby facilitating the creation of a comprehensive ontology for tuberculosis care.

For the continuation of our work, we have opted for the automatic approach. Several reasons justify this choice. On the one hand, this approach does not require constant expert intervention, saving time. On the other hand, the axioms generated by this method greatly facilitate the creation of the ontology in the Protégé software. After generating these axioms, we obtained 158 classes, 55 object properties, and 57 data properties. Figure 3 illustrates the graph of the proposed ontology.

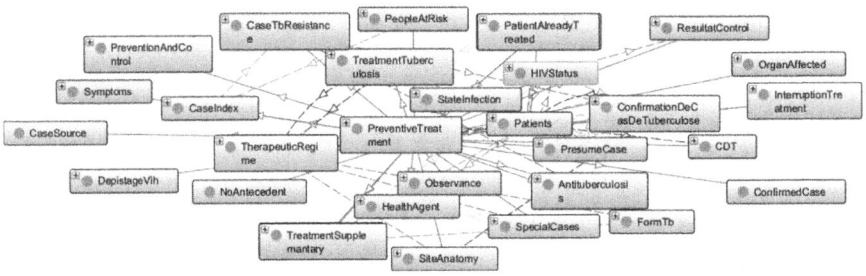

Fig. 3. A sample of the proposed Ontology Graph

Figure 3 shows a sample of the generated ontology. It presents the relationships between medical concepts related to tuberculosis, like Patient, Tuberculosis Case, and Treatment. This graph highlights how these concepts are connected, thus allowing a better understanding of the relationships between the different entities.

We used an Apache Jena Fuseki to execute SPARQL queries. These queries allowed us to explore and query the data represented in the knowledge base. In Fig. 4, a query was performed to select information on the phases of tuberculosis (TB) treatment and the details associated with these phases, like treatment duration, antibiotics used, TB cases, and medication dosages (Fig. 5).

The results allow us to extract information on the different phases of tuberculosis treatment from an RDF database. These details, like treatment durations, antibiotics used, and resistant drug dosages, are essential for proposing a treatment plan for a tuberculosis case.

Figure 6 is a query that interrogates an RDF database to retrieve information on antibiotics, their major side effects, and the associated management guidelines (Fig. 7).

The query results are presented in the form of URIs, which is essential for uniquely identifying each entity and establishing relationships between them in the RDF database. This query helps provide information on the expected reactions to antibiotics and the actions to take in case of adverse effects.

```
PREFIX a: <http://www.semanticweb.org/asus/ontologies/2023/8/untitled-ontology-3#>

SELECT ?CaseTb ?Phase (GROUP_CONCAT(?value; separator=', ') AS ?Antibiotic) ?Dure ?Posologie
WHERE {
  {
    a:phase1 a:composeFrom ?uri .
    BIND("phase1:Intensive or first phase" AS ?Phase)
    a:phase1 a:duration_Phase ?Dure.
    BIND(STRAFTER(STR(?uri), "#") AS ?value)
    BIND("Pharmacosensitive" AS ?CaseTb)
    OPTIONAL { a:phase1 a:has_for_dosage ?Posologie. }
  }
  UNION
  {
```

Fig. 4. *Query on the phases of tuberculosis (TB) treatment.*

CaseTb	Phase	Antibiotic	Dure	Posologie
Pharmacosensible	phase1:Intensive or f	Ethambutol, Isoniazi	Two months	
TB-MR/RR	1st phase	Bedaquiline, Ethaml	14 days	Bdq 4 cp/day (2 cp
TB-MR/RR	1st phase	Bedaquiline, Ethaml	13 weeks	Bdq 2 tablets 3 time: (Monday, Wednesda
Pharmacosensible	phase2: Continuatio	Isoniazide, Rifampic	four months	
TB-MR/RR	2nd phase	Ethambutol, Pyrazin	2 months	Bdq 2 cp/day (2 cp 2 cp evening)
TB-MR/RR	2nd phase	Bedaquiline, Ethaml	7 weeks	Bdq 2 tablets 3 time: (Monday, Wednesda

Fig. 5. Result of the query on the phases of tuberculosis (TB) treatment.

```
PREFIX a: <http://www.semanticweb.org/asus/ontologies/2023/8/untitled-ontology-3#>

SELECT ?Antibiotic ?majorEffect ?conductToBeObserved
WHERE {
  ?a a:antibioticName ??Antibiotic.
  ?Antibiotic a:has_forMajorEffect ?MajorEffect.
  ?MajorEffect a:has_for ?conduct.

  BIND(STR(?MajorEffect) AS ?majorEffect)
  BIND(STR(?conduct) AS ?conductToBeObserved)
}
```

Fig. 6. Query: Antibiotics, Side Effects, and Management Guidelines.

Table   Response   7 results in 0.181 seconds   Simple view   Ellipse   Filter query results   Page size: 50

	Antibiotic	majorEffect	conductToBeObserved
1	<http://www.semanticweb.org/asus/ontologies/2023/8/untitled-ontology-3#Etham...	http://www.semanticweb.org/asus/ontologies/2023/8/untitled-ontology-3#Ef...	http://www.semanticweb.org/asus/ontologies/2023/8/untitled-ontology-3#cond...
2	<http://www.semanticweb.org/asus/ontologies/2023/8/untitled-ontology-3#Isonia...	http://www.semanticweb.org/asus/ontologies/2023/8/untitled-ontology-3#Ef...	http://www.semanticweb.org/asus/ontologies/2023/8/untitled-ontology-3#cond...
3	<http://www.semanticweb.org/asus/ontologies/2023/8/untitled-ontology-3#Isonia...	http://www.semanticweb.org/asus/ontologies/2023/8/untitled-ontology-3#Ef...	http://www.semanticweb.org/asus/ontologies/2023/8/untitled-ontology-3#cond...
4	<http://www.semanticweb.org/asus/ontologies/2023/8/untitled-ontology-3#Rifam...	http://www.semanticweb.org/asus/ontologies/2023/8/untitled-ontology-3#Ef...	http://www.semanticweb.org/asus/ontologies/2023/8/untitled-ontology-3#cond...
5	<http://www.semanticweb.org/asus/ontologies/2023/8/untitled-ontology-3#[illegible]...	http://www.semanticweb.org/asus/ontologies/2023/8/untitled-ontology-3#Ef...	http://www.semanticweb.org/asus/ontologies/2023/8/untitled-ontology-3#cond...
6	<http://www.semanticweb.org/asus/ontologies/2023/8/untitled-ontology-3#Pyraz...	http://www.semanticweb.org/asus/ontologies/2023/8/untitled-ontology-3#Ef...	http://www.semanticweb.org/asus/ontologies/2023/8/untitled-ontology-3#cond...
7	<http://www.semanticweb.org/asus/ontologies/2023/8/untitled-ontology-3#Pyrazi...	http://www.semanticweb.org/asus/ontologies/2023/8/untitled-ontology-3#Ef...	http://www.semanticweb.org/asus/ontologies/2023/8/untitled-ontology-3#cond...

Showing 1 to 7 of 7 entries

Fig. 7. Result of the query to display antibiotics, their side effects, and management guidelines.

5 Discussion

This study aimed to develop a model using large language models (GPT-3 DaVinci) to automatically generate ontologies dedicated to the management of multidrug-resistant tuberculosis (MDR-TB). The objective was to optimize clinical decision-making by minimizing human intervention while providing reliable and tailored treatment recommendations.

The results show the automatic approach enabled the creation of a rich ontology, comprising 158 classes, 55 object properties, and 57 data properties. These results surpass those obtained by the semi-automatic method, which requires more human intervention and produces less accurate results. The use of GPT-3 has thus proven its effectiveness in automating the generation of OWL axioms.

Our results align with research on tuberculosis management while providing significant advancements.

Raymond Ondzigue's Work: Raymond Ondzigue's thesis focuses on the epidemiological surveillance of tuberculosis in Gabon, using a multi-agent simulation model (SMA-TB) and spatio-temporal analysis to model the evolution of the disease. Our approach stands out through the complete automation of ontology generation for clinical decision-making. While Ondzigue's approach focuses on monitoring and modeling epidemiological data, our work aims to optimize the clinical recommendation process for MDR-TB based on textual data, reducing reliance on human expertise.

Kumar Abhishek's Work: Kumar Abhishek's article proposes an ontology-based decision support system for the Revised National Tuberculosis Control Program (RNTCP) in India, using SWRL rules. Although this work offers a formalized approach to managing drug-sensitive tuberculosis, it requires significant human intervention to manually define relationships between concepts. Our method goes further by fully automating the creation of OWL axioms from natural language sentences, enabling the handling of more complex cases, like MDR-TB, which were sufficiently uncovered in Abhishek's work.

The strengths of our approach are multiple:

- **Complete automation**: The use of GPT-3 DaVinci allows the generation of OWL axioms without significant human intervention, improving the efficiency and speed of the process.
- **Improved efficiency in terms of time and resources**, which is particularly relevant in the context of Burkina Faso.

However, this study presents certain limitations:

- **dependence on data quality**: the GPT-3 model relies on the quality of the training data. Ambiguous or poorly structured sentences can affect the quality of the generated axioms;
- **human supervision**: although the approach is automated, supervision is still necessary to validate the clinical relevance of the axioms, especially for complex cases;
- **lack of clinical validation**: the treatment recommendations generated still need to be validated in a clinical setting to assess their real impact on decision-making.

Our study makes a unique contribution to the field of automatic ontology generation applied to tuberculosis management, particularly for MDR-TB cases. Unlike previous work, like that of Kumar Abhishek or Raymond Ondzigue, our approach offers an automated solution for generating OWL axioms from natural language sentences, significantly simplifying the ontology creation process. This approach allows for the standardization of treatment recommendations in local contexts, while adapting to regional specificities.

6 Conclusion

This study set out to develop a model leveraging large language models, specifically GPT-3 DaVinci, for the automatic generation of ontologies aimed at supporting the clinical management of multidrug-resistant tuberculosis (MDR-TB). Through an automated approach, we successfully created a rich ontology comprising 158 classes, 55 object properties, and 57 data properties. This approach surpassed the semi-automatic method in terms of efficiency, accuracy, and the need for minimal human intervention.

The findings demonstrate that GPT-3, when fine-tuned for domain-specific tasks, can effectively automate the generation of OWL axioms from natural language sentences, which is essential for building robust medical decision support systems. By automating the process, our work not only enhances the speed of ontology generation but also improves the personalization and relevance of treatment recommendations for MDR-TB cases.

Comparisons with previous work, like the epidemiological surveillance system for TB in Gabon developed by Raymond Ondzigue, and the ontology-based decision support system for tuberculosis in India by Kumar Abhishek, highlight the novelty of our approach. While their systems focus on specific aspects of TB management, such as epidemiological surveillance and decision-making based on predefined rules, our model automates the entire ontology creation process. This automation allows for greater flexibility and scalability in clinical decision-making, particularly in the context of MDR-TB treatment, which remains a critical challenge in regions like Burkina Faso.

Looking forward, future work will focus on extending the ontology to cover additional aspects of tuberculosis management, including diagnostics and predictive models for patient outcomes. Moreover, clinical validation of the treatment recommendations generated by our system will be a key area of exploration, ensuring that the theoretical advancements achieved translate into tangible benefits in real-world healthcare settings.

Acknowledgments. This work was conducted as part of the Artificial Intelligence for Development in Africa (AI4D Africa) program, with the financial support of Canada's International Development Research Centre (IDRC) and the Swedish International Development Cooperation Agency (Sida).

References

1. Abhishek, K., Singh, M.: An ontology based decision support for tuberculosis management and control in India. Int. J. Eng. Technol. **8**(6), 2860–77 (2016)
2. Du, Y., Ranwez, S., Sutton-Charani, N., Ranwez, V.: Apports des ontologies aux systèmes de recommandation : état de l'art et perspectives. In: 30es Journées Francophones d'Ingénierie des Connaissances, IC 2019. AFIA. Toulouse, France: AFIA, pp. 64–77. Ffhal-02329644 (2019)
3. Menad, S., Abdeddaïm, S., Soualmia, L.F.: Fusion d'ontologies biomédicales par des modèles siamois et validation par modèles de langue. In: 35es Journées francophones d'Ingénierie des Connaissances (IC 2024) @ Plate-Forme Intelligence Artificielle (PFIA 2024). La Rochelle, France (2024). Ffhal-04636888f
4. Gadicherla, S., et al.: Envisioning a learning surveillance system for tuberculosis. PLoS ONE **15**(12), e0243610 (2020)
5. Olukunle Ayodeji Ogundele, A.W.P., Deshendran, M., Seebregts, C.J.: An ontology for factors affecting tuberculosis treatment adherence behavior in sub-Saharan Africa. Patient Preference and Adherence (2016);10:669–81. https://www.tandfonline.com/doi/abs/10.2147/PPA.S96241
6. Ondzigue Mbenga, R., Devogele, T., Maghendji, S., Peralta, V., Ngoungou, E.B.: Un système d'information géographique décisionnel pour la surveillance épidémiologique de la tuberculose en Afrique subsaharienne : Cas du Gabon; 2019. Poster. Francophone International Conference on Spatial Analisys and Geomatics (Sageo 2019). https://hal.science/hal-02375898
7. Pellison, F.C., et al.: Data integration in the Brazilian Public Health System for Tuberculosis: use of the semantic web to establish interoperability. JMIR Med. Inform. **8**(7), e17176 (2020)
8. Al-Aswadi, F.N., Chan, H.Y., Gan, K.H.: Automatic ontology construction from text: a review from shallow to deep learning trend. Artif. Intell. Rev. **53**, 3901–28 (2020)
9. Elnagar, S., Yoon, V., Thomas, M.A.: An automatic ontology generation framework with an organizational perspective. arXiv preprint arXiv:2201.05910 (2022)
10. Wohlgenannt, G., Minic, F.: Using word2vec to build a simple ontology learning system. In: ISWC (Posters and Demos), pp. 1–7 (2016)
11. Mateiu, P., Groza, A.: Ontology engineering with large language models. arXiv preprint arXiv:2307.16699 (2023)
12. Chokshi, H.J., Panchal, R.: Using Apache Jena Fuseki server for execution of SPARQL queries in job search ontology using semantic technology. Int. J. Innov. Res. Comput. Sci. Technol. **10**(2), 497–504 (2022)

Using a Bidirectional Decoder Model with Attention Mechanisms for Biomedical Named Entity Recognition

Konan Marcellin Brou[1,2](✉), Adama Samassi[1,2], Appoh Kouamé[1,2], and Kidjégbo Augustin Touré[1]

[1] Ecole Doctorale Polytechnique, Institut National Polytechnique (INP-HB), Yamoussoukro, Ivory Coast
{marcellin.brou,appoh.kouame,kidjegbo.toure}@inphb.ci

[2] Laboratoire de Recherche en Informatique et Télécommunication (LARIT), Yamoussoukro, Ivory Coast

Abstract. Named Entity Recognition is an important task in the biomedical domain. State-of-the-art models for this task use neural network encoders for capturing contextual information of words in the input sentence and linear conditional random fields decoders to predict the most probable label sequence. However, the linear conditional random fields can only model dependencies among adjacent output labels. In this paper, we propose a bidirectional decoder model that uses two recurrent decoders to handle all the dependencies between labels. We introduced attention mechanisms in each decoder layer to help them to focus on the important words in the input sequence. We experimented with three types of attention mechanism. We observed that these attention mechanisms improve the performance of our model in the MedMentions and i2b2 2010 datasets.

Keywords: Named Entity Recognition · Sequence Labeling · Deep Learning · Attention Mechanism

1 Introduction

Named entity recognition (NER) is an important task of Natural Language Processing in the biomedical research. It aims to identify entities from text and classify them into entity types. Several methods have been proposed for this task. However, the deep learning methods are more efficient than the traditional methods [1–4]. Deep learning methods rely on sequence labeling models [5, 6] or seq2seq models [7, 8]. These models are trained on sentences annotated (Fig. 1) by labeling scheme [9].

Kidney/B-DISEASE failure/I-DISEASE destroys/O the/O kidneys/B-ORGAN ./O

Fig. 1. Example of an annotated sentence.

T. Koné et al. (Eds.): AFRICOMM 2024, LNICST 653, pp. 295–303, 2025.
https://doi.org/10.1007/978-3-032-01910-3_19

The sequence labeling models such as the BiLSTM-CRF [10] model uses a conditional random fields (CRF) [11] decoder, However, according to Cui et al. [12], CRF can only manage the dependencies between adjacent labels (Fig. 2).

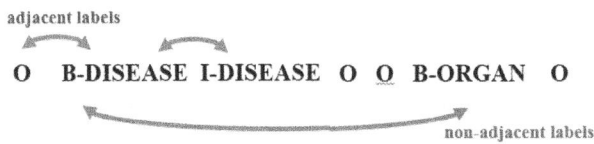

Fig. 2. Example of dependencies between labels in a sequence.

The seq2seq model proposed in [8] uses a Long Short-term Memory (LSTM) [13] decoder. This decoder can handle short and long-range dependencies between labels in a single direction. Therefore, we propose to use two decoders based on recurrent neural networks to handle label dependencies in two directions. In addition, we introduced attention mechanisms [14] in each decoder layer. Theses attention mechanisms help the decoder to focus on only the informative words in the input sentence. Here, we investigated the global attention and the local attention mechanisms proposed in [14]. We investigated their impact on the performance of our model in the recognition of biomedical named entities on MedMentions [15] and the i2b2 2010 [16] datasets. We use these datasets because they are publicly available.

In this study, we proposed a model that uses two recurrent decoders to capture label dependencies in both forward and backward directions. In addition, we introduced attention mechanisms [14] in each decoder layer. Theses attention mechanisms allow our decoders to focus on only the informative words in the input sentence. We evaluated our model on the MedMentions and the i2b2 2010 datasets. In addition, we experimented with three types of attention mechanisms: the *concat*, *dot* and *local* attentions [14].

This study is organized as follows. In addition to the previous section, five others organize our study. Section 2 focuses on related works. In Sect. 3, we detail our method for biomedical named entity recognition. Section 4 presents the experiments we carried out. The results of the experiments are discussed in Sect. 5. Finally, we conclude the study in Sect. 6.

2 Related Work

The neural models for biomedical named entity recognition typically contain an encoder layer and a decoder layer. In the studies [5, 6, 17, 18], the researchers used a CRF decoder. This allowed them to obtain good results. Nevertheless, CRF can only manage adjacent label dependencies [12]. To address this issue, authors [8, 19] proposed models based on recurrent neural networks. Regarding [8], the authors proposed a model where the encoder and the decoder are based on LSTM. But, this model uses a single decoder. Recently, Samassi et al. [19] proposed a bidirectional encoder-decoder model. This model is based on Gated Recurrent Unit (GRU) [20] and attention mechanisms. This decoder allows the model to manage a bidirectional context at the level of labels. However, they only experimented with the global attention mechanism [13] in the decoder layer. In this paper, we also experimented with the local attention mechanism [13].

3 Methods

We describe our model contains four modules: The Embedder module, the Encoder module, the LR-Decoder module and the RL-Decoder module. We describe all these modules in the following sub sections.

3.1 Embedder Module

The Embedder Module (EM) to convert the input sentence $X = (x_1, x_2, \ldots, x_n)$ into a sequence of word embeddings $V = (v_1, v_2, \ldots, v_n)$.

$$V = EM(x_1, x_2, \ldots, x_n) \tag{1}$$

3.2 Encoder Module

The Encoder Module contains the *forward LSTM encoder* ($\overrightarrow{FLE}$) and the *Backward LSTM Encoder* ($\overleftarrow{BLE}$). The encoder $\overrightarrow{FLE}$ reads the sequence V in the forward direction to build a sequence of vectors $\{\overrightarrow{h}_i\}_{i=1}^n$. While the encoder $\overleftarrow{BLE}$ reads the sequence V in the backward direction to build a sequence of vectors $\{\overleftarrow{h}_i\}_{i=1}^n$.

We computed $\overrightarrow{h}_i$ and $\overleftarrow{h}_i$ as:

$$\overrightarrow{h}_i = \overrightarrow{FE}(\overrightarrow{h}_{i-1}, v_i) \tag{2}$$

$$\overleftarrow{h}_i = \overleftarrow{BE}(\overleftarrow{h}_{i+1}, v_i) \tag{3}$$

$\overrightarrow{FE}$ and $\overleftarrow{BE}$ are LSTMs. $\overrightarrow{h}_i$ and $\overleftarrow{h}_i$ represent respectively the left context and the right context of the word x_i. We concatenated $\overrightarrow{h}_i$ and $\overleftarrow{h}_i$ to build h_i, which is the bidirectional contextual representation of the word x_i [19]. Finally, we represented the vectors generated by the Encoder Module as $H = \{h_i\}_{i=1}^n$. In what follows, we describe the decoder modules, which employ LSTM networks.

3.3 LR-Decoder Module

The LR-Decoder takes the sequence $H = \{h_i\}_{i=1}^n$ as input. Then it sequentially generates the vectors $\{\overrightarrow{d}_i\}_{i=1}^n$ in the forward direction. We defined each vector $\overrightarrow{d}_i$ as [19]:

$$\overrightarrow{d}_i = \overrightarrow{FD}(\overrightarrow{d}_{i-1}, [e(\overrightarrow{y}_{i-1}); h_i; \overrightarrow{c}_i]) \tag{4}$$

According the equation above (Eq. 4.), $\vec{d}_i$ represents the left context of the label $\vec{y}_i$. $\vec{FD}$ is an LSTM cell, and $e(\vec{y}_{i-1})$ is the embedding of the label $\vec{y}_{i-1}$ predicted at the previous time step $i - 1$. $\vec{c}_i$ is a context vector, calculated according to an attention mechanism [13]. This vector allows the decoder to select the vectors of the sequence $\{h_i\}_{i=1}^n$ that it must use to predict the label $\vec{y}_i$. We considered the *Global attention* and *Local attention* mechanisms proposed by Luong et al. [13].

Global Attention. The *Global attention* focuses on all the vectors $\{h_i\}_{i=1}^n$ generated by the encoder [13]:

$$\vec{c}_i = \sum_{j=1}^n \vec{\alpha}_{ij} h_j \qquad (5)$$

$\vec{\alpha}_{ij}$ is the weight assigned to the vector h_j by the attention mechanism [13]:

$$\vec{\alpha}_{ij} = \frac{exp(score(\vec{s}_i, h_j))}{\sum_{k=1}^n exp(score(\vec{s}_i, h_k))} \qquad (6)$$

$score(\vec{s}_i, h_j)$ is the alignment score [13]:

$$score(\vec{s}_i, h_j) = \begin{cases} \vec{v}_b^T tanh(\vec{W}_a[\vec{s}_i; h_j]) & concat \\ \vec{s}_i . h_j & dot \end{cases} \qquad (7)$$

Local Attention. The *Local attention* focuses only on a few vectors of the sequence $H = \{h_i\}_{i=1}^n$ within the window $[p_i - D_w, p_i + D_w]$. p_i is The alignment position, computed at time step i as [13]:

$$p_i = S.sigmoid(v^T tanh(Wh_i)) \qquad (8)$$

where S is the length of the sentence; v^T and W are parameters [13].

Finally, the context vector $\vec{c}_i$ is computed as [13]:

$$\vec{c}_i = \sum_{j=p_i-D_w}^{p_i+D_w} \vec{\alpha'}_{ij} h_j \qquad (9)$$

where $\vec{\alpha'}_{ij}$ is the attention weight [13]:

$$\vec{\alpha'}_{ij} = \alpha_{ij}.exp(-\frac{(j-p_i)}{2\sigma^2}) \qquad (10)$$

σ is the standard deviation, set to $\frac{D_w}{2}$. D_w is the window size, set to 3.

Label Prediction

We used a log-softmax to assign a prediction score to each label $\vec{y}_i$ at time step i as:

$$p(\vec{y}_i | \vec{y}_{i-1}; V) = \log(softmax(\vec{W}_o [\vec{d}_i; h_i] + \vec{U}_c \vec{c}_i + \vec{b}_o)) \qquad (11)$$

3.4 RL-Decoder Module

The RL-Decoder takes the sequence $H = \{h_i\}_{i=1}^{n}$ as input. Then it sequentially generates the vectors $\{\overleftarrow{d}_i\}_{i=1}^{n}$ in the backward direction. We defined a vector $\overleftarrow{d}_i$ as [19]:

$$\overleftarrow{d}_i = \overleftarrow{BD}(\overleftarrow{d}_{i+1}, [e(\overleftarrow{y}_{i+1}); h_i; \overleftarrow{c}_i]) \quad (12)$$

$\overrightarrow{d}_i$ represents the right context of the label $\overrightarrow{y}_i$. $\overrightarrow{FD}$ is an LSTM cell, and $e(\overleftarrow{y}_{i+1})$ is the embedding of the label $\overleftarrow{y}_{i+1}$ predicted at the previous time step $i+1$.

Global Attention. The *Global attention* mechanism [13] computes the context vector $\overleftarrow{c}_i$ as:

$$\overleftarrow{c}_i = \sum_{j=1}^{n} \overleftarrow{\alpha}_{ij} h_j \quad (13)$$

where

$$\overleftarrow{\alpha}_{ij} = \frac{exp(score(\overleftarrow{s}_i, h_j))}{\sum_{k=1}^{n} exp(score(\overleftarrow{s}_i, h_k))} \quad (14)$$

and

$$score(\overleftarrow{s}_i, h_j) = \begin{cases} \overleftarrow{v}_b^T tanh\left(\overleftarrow{W}_s[\overleftarrow{s}_i; h_j]\right) Concat \\ \overleftarrow{s}_i . h_j \, Dot \end{cases} \quad (15)$$

Local Attention. The *Local attention* [13] computes the context vector $\overleftarrow{c}_i$ as:

$$\overleftarrow{c}_i = \sum_{j=p_i-D_w}^{p_i+D_w} \overleftarrow{\alpha}'_{ij} h_j \quad (16)$$

$$\overleftarrow{\alpha}'_{ij} = \overleftarrow{\alpha}_{ij} . exp\left(-\frac{(j-p_i)^2}{2\sigma^2}\right) \quad (17)$$

Label Prediction

We used a log-softmax to assign a prediction score to each label $\overleftarrow{y}_i$ at time step i as:

$$P(\overleftarrow{y}_i | \overleftarrow{y}_{i+1}; V) = log(softmax(\overleftarrow{W}_o\left[\overleftarrow{d}_i; h_i\right] + \overleftarrow{U}_c \overleftarrow{c}_i + \overleftarrow{b}_o)) \quad (18)$$

3.5 Training

We trained the LR-Decoder and the RL-Decoder by maximizing the negative log-likelihood (*LL*) with respect to the training data $\{(X^d, Y^d)\}_{m=1}^{D}$.

$$-LL(\theta|D) = -\sum_{m=1}^{|D|} \sum_{i=1}^{n} \frac{1}{2}(logP(\overrightarrow{y}_i^m | \overrightarrow{y}_{i-1}^m, X^m; \theta) + logP(\overleftarrow{y}_i^m | \overleftarrow{y}_{i+1}^m, X^m; \theta)) \quad (19)$$

4 Experiments

4.1 Datasets

We use three datasets. The Table 1 shows the number of entity types in each datasets.

The i2b2 2010 dataset contains three named entity types, which are *tests*, *problems* and *treatments* [16]. The MedMentions-SemType10 and the MedMentions-SemType15 [21] are two subsets of the MedMentions [15]. The entity types in the MedMentions are Semantic types of the UMLS [22].

Table 1. Number of Entity Types for the MedMentions SemType10 and SemType15 datasets.

Dataset	Entity Types
I2b2 2010	3
SemType10	10
SemType15	15

4.2 Evaluation

We used three metrics to evaluate the performance of our model: F1-score (F1), precision (P) and recall (R).

$$precision = \frac{TP}{TP + FP} \quad (20)$$

$$recall = \frac{TP}{TP + FN} \quad (21)$$

$$F1 - score = \frac{2 \times precision \times recall}{precision + recall} \quad (22)$$

TP is the number of named entities correctly predicted by the model. FN is the number of named entities that the model fails to predict. FP is the number of named entities misidentified by the model.

4.3 Training and Testing

The hyper-parameters used to train our model are reported in Table 2. They are selected according to the performance of our model on the development dataset. Once the optimal values for the parameters are set, then we evaluate its performance in the test dataset.

Table 2. The parameters used for model evaluation.

Parameters	Value
Batch size	100
Learning rate	0.001
Epochs	30
Dropout	0.3
LSTM Hidden Layer dimension	256

5 Results

We compare the effect of the three types of attention mechanism on the results of our model for the three corpora.

5.1 Effectiveness of Attention Mechanisms

We observe (Table 3) that the *Dot* alignment in the global attention mechanism significantly improves the performance of our model in terms of F1 measurement compared to the *Concat*. The *Dot* alignment in the local attention mechanism is the least efficient.

Table 3. Results for i2b2 2010, MedMentions SemType10pv and SemType15pv datasets.

Attention	SemType15pv			SemType10pv			I2b2 2010		
	P	R	F1	P	R	F1	P	R	F1
None	52.53	30.04	38.23	59.53	34.95	44.05	64.03	56.82	60.21
Global (Concat)	50.51	31.31	38.66	58.55	45.69	51.32	76.54	70.47	73.38
Global (Dot)	**87.89**	**87.78**	**87.84**	**87.54**	**87.30**	**87.42**	77.24	78.42	**77.83**
Local (Dot)	61.67	40.27	48.72	65.37	45.66	53.77	74.57	73.25	73.90

5.2 Training Time

We observe (Table 4) that the training time of our model is shorter with the *Dot* alignment in the global attention compared to the *Concat* alignment. With the *Dot* alignment in the local attention, the training time of our model is the longest.

Table 4. Training Time (s).

Attention	st15pv	st15pv	i2b2 2010
None	[226,232]	[223,232]	[118–123]
Concat	[217,230]	[215,221]	[117,127]
Dot	[206,214]	[203,207]	[114,124]
Local	[258,265]	[255,259]	[153,172]

5.3 Discussion

Despite the improved performance results provided by our proposal, it suffers from the exposure-bias problem. This is because our decoders take into account the labels that have been previously predicted to predict the label at time step i (see Eq. 4 and 12). However, this prediction could be wrong if one of the previously predicted labels is wrong. We intend to address this issue in our future work, by going and drawing in-depth inspiration from the solution orientation in Yang et al. [23] and Najafi et al. [24].

6 Conclusion

We proposed a seq2sq model for biomedical named entity recognition. The model uses an encoder based on LSTM networks and a bidirectional decoder based LSTM and attention mechanisms. We experimented with three types of attention mechanism at the decoder level: *Concat*, *Dot* and *Local*. The results obtained showed that these attention mechanisms improve the performance of a seq2seq model in the MedMentions-SemType10 (SemType10) and MedMentions-SemType15 (SemType15) datasets. However, our model suffers from the exposure-bias problem because it uses recurrent neural networks in the decoder layer. We intend to address this issue in our future work. In addition, we will evaluate our model in the MedMentions-full dataset.

References

1. Makino, T., Ohta, Y., Tsujii, J.I.: Tuning support vector machines for biomedical named entity recognition. In: Proceedings of the ACL-02 Workshop on Natural Language Processing in the Biomedical Domain, pp. 1–8, July 2002
2. Zhang, J., Shen, D., Zhou, G., Su, J., Tan, C.L.: Enhancing HMM-based biomedical named entity recognition by studying special phenomena. J. Biomed. Inform. **37**(6), 411–422 (2004)
3. Kang, N., Singh, B., Afzal, Z., van Mulligen, E.M., Kors, J.A.: Using rule-based natural language processing to improve disease normalization in biomedical text. J. Am. Med. Inform. Assoc. **20**(5), 876–881 (2013)
4. Rahman, H.U., Chowk, N.G.T.K., Hahn, T., Segall, R.: Disease named entity recognition using conditional random fields. In Proceedings of the 7th International Symposium on Semantic Mining in Biomedicine (2016)

5. Chalapathy, R., Borzeshi, E.Z., Piccardi, M.: Bidirectional LSTM-CRF for clinical concept extraction. arXiv preprint arXiv:1611.08373 (2016)
6. Cho, H., Lee, H.: Biomedical named entity recognition using deep neural networks with contextual information. BMC Bioinform. **20**, 1–11 (2019)
7. Wang, Y., Li, Y., Zhu, Z., Xia, B., Liu, Z.: SC-NER: a sequence-to-sequence model with sentence classification for named entity recognition. In: Yang, Q., Zhou, Z.H., Gong, Z., Zhang, M.L., Huang, S.J. (eds.) Advances in Knowledge Discovery and Data Mining. PAKDD 2019. Lecture Notes in Computer Science, vol. 11439, pp. 198–209. Springer, Cham (2019). https://doi.org/10.1007/978-3-030-16148-4_16
8. Straková, J., Straka, M., Hajič, J.: Neural architectures for nested NER through linearization. arXiv preprint arXiv:1908.06926 (2019)
9. Ramshaw, L.A., Marcus, M.P.: Text chunking using transformation-based learning. In: Armstrong, S., Church, K., Isabelle, P., Manzi, S., Tzoukermann, E., Yarowsky, D. (eds.) Natural Language Processing Using Very Large Corpora. Text, Speech and Language Technology, vol. 11, pp. 157–176. Springer, Dordrecht (1999). https://doi.org/10.1007/978-94-017-2390-9_10
10. Huang, Z., Xu, W., Yu, K.: Bidirectional LSTM-CRF models for sequence tagging. arXiv preprint arXiv:1508.01991 (2015)
11. Lafferty, J., McCallum, A., Pereira, F.C.: Conditional random fields: probabilistic models for segmenting and labeling sequence data (2001)
12. Cui, L., Zhang, Y.: Hierarchically-refined label attention network for sequence labeling. arXiv preprint arXiv:1908.08676 (2019)
13. Hochreiter, S., Schmidhuber, J.: Long short-term memory. Neural Comput. **9**(8), 1735–1780 (1997)
14. Luong, M.T., Pham, H., Manning, C.D.: Effective approaches to attention-based neural machine translation. arXiv preprint arXiv:1508.04025 (2015)
15. Mohan, S., Li, D.: Medmentions: a large biomedical corpus annotated with UMLS concepts. arXiv preprint arXiv:1902.09476 (2019)
16. Uzuner, Ö., South, B.R., Shen, S., DuVall, S.L.: 2010 /VA challenge on concepts, assertions, and relations in clinical text. J. Am. Med. Inform. Assoc. **18**(5), 552–556 (2011)
17. Unanue, I.J., Borzeshi, E.Z., Piccardi, M.: Recurrent neural networks with specialized word embeddings for health-domain named-entity recognition. J. Biomed. Inform. **76**, 102–109 (2017)
18. Zhu, Q., Li, X., Conesa, A., Pereira, C.: GRAM-CNN: a deep learning approach with local context for named entity recognition in biomedical text. Bioinformatics **34**(9), 1547–1554 (2018)
19. A bidirectional encoder-decoder model with attention mechanism for nested named entity recognition. Int. J. Adv. Res. (Mar), 382–394. https://doi.org/10.21474/IJAR01/18405. ISSN 2320-5407
20. Chung, J., Gulcehre, C., Cho, K., Bengio, Y.: Empirical evaluation of gated recurrent neural networks on sequence modeling. arXiv preprint arXiv:1412.3555 (2014)
21. https://github.com/javiagu13/MedicalNER. Accessed 01 Jun 2024
22. Bodenreider, O.: The unified medical language system (UMLS): integrating biomedical terminology. Nucleic Acids Res. **32**(suppl_1), D267–D270 (2004)
23. Yang, P., Sun, X., Li, W., Ma, S., Wu, W., Wang, H.: SGM: sequence generation model for multi-label classification. arXiv preprint arXiv:1806.04822 (2018)
24. Najafi, S.: Sequence labeling and transduction with output-adjusted actor-critic training of RNNs (2018)

Detection of COVID-19 Using Machine Learning Techniques

Diako Doffou Jérome[1,2,3(✉)], Johnson Grâce Yénin Edwige[1,2,3], Sandjé Marcelin[2,3], and Patrice E. Mensah[2]

[1] Ecole Supérieur Africaine des Tics, Abidjan, Ivory Coast
kingdjako@gmail.com
[2] Inphb, Yamoussoukro, Ivory Coast
[3] LARIT, LASTIC, Abidjan, Ivory Coast

Abstract. In December 2019, a new coronavirus emerged in Wuhan, Hubei province, China, giving rise to the disease named COVID-19, caused by SARS-CoV-2, a highly contagious severe acute respiratory virus. Rapidly spreading outside China, the WHO declared a pandemic in March 2020. Symptoms of infection include fever, weakness, dry cough, headache, dyspnoea, myalgia, as well as blood abnormalities and other biochemical indicators. In view of the rapid spread of COVID-19, it is becoming imperative to explore the use of machine learning techniques for a variety of applications, such as accurate and rapid diagnosis, as well as the detection of individuals most likely to contract the disease. The aim of this article is to present a method for the early identification of patients at increased risk of developing severe symptoms of COVID-19, using a database available in Côte d'Ivoire. Through the application of machine learning techniques, we solve a classification problem to predict the state (negative, positive) of individuals in relation to COVID-19.

Models were trained on 80% of the dataset, while the remaining 20% was used for testing. The results of the model performance evaluation indicate that the decision tree model shows the highest accuracy, reaching 97%.

Keywords: COVID-19 · SARS-CoV-2 · Machine Learning

1 Introduction

A new coronavirus appeared in the city of Wuhan (Hubei province, China) in December 2019. The disease, named COVID-19, is caused by the severe acute respiratory syndrome coronavirus 2 (SARS-CoV-2) and is highly contagious. The virus spread rapidly outside China and the World Health Organisation (WHO) recognised the epidemic as a pandemic in March 2020. SARS-CoV-2 infection is characterised by fever, generalised weakness, dry cough, headache, dyspnoea, myalgia, as well as leukopenia, lymphopenia, neutrophilia, elevated levels of C-reactive protein, D-dimer and cytokines, muscle stiffness and loss of sense of smell and taste in the early stages of infection. However, the condition can rapidly progress to acute respiratory distress syndrome (ARDS), cytokine storm, coagulation dysfunction, acute cardiac injury, acute renal failure and multi-organ dysfunction if the disease is not resolved, leading to the patient's death. Given the rapid spread of COVID-19, there is a need to focus on the use of machine learning techniques on various fronts, such as rapid and accurate diagnosis and identification of those most susceptible to the disease.

The aim of this article is to make a prognosis or early identification of patients at increased risk of developing severe symptoms of COVID-19 using a database available from the Ivorian government. Using machine learning techniques, a classification problem can be solved with the aim of predicting the status (negative, positive) of people in relation to COVID-19, on the basis of individual information, in addition to various co-morbidities and clinical symptoms. This process can be of great importance in helping hospitals to make decisions, as resources become more limited every day. Patients classified as having a more serious illness may be given priority in this case. Machine learning is capable of detecting viral diseases and infections more accurately, so that patients' illnesses can be diagnosed at an early stage, dangerous stages of disease can be avoided, and fewer patients die. In this article, we look at how Machine Learning can be used to develop intelligent solutions for diagnosing COVID-19 in people.

In order to address the subject and answer the questions raised, a re-research plan was drawn up. Firstly, we conducted interviews with professionals. The empirical research was supplemented by extensive reading on the subject.

In this work, we relied on a labelled epidemiological dataset for positive and negative cases of COVID-19 in Côte d'Ivoire and on supervised learning algorithms such as the decision tree, the random drill and gradient boosting.

2 State of the Art on the Prediction of COVID19 Disease Using Machine Learning Algorithms

Swapnarekha et al., (2020) presented a literature review on the use of intelligent algorithms in the prediction of COVID19 disease. These include machine learning algorithms, deep learning algorithms and algorithms based on mathematical and statistical models. According to the study, an analysis of the literature reveals that 39% of research is focused on the use of deep learning algorithms, 37% on the use of machine learning algorithms and the remaining 24% is attributed to the application of mathematical and statistical models. These intelligent computing approaches have been used to good effect in the prediction and detection of COVID19 pandemic [1].

Kwekha-Rashid et al., (2021) showed that among the works using machine learning algorithms, supervised algorithms are used a lot compared to unsupervised algorithms. In this study, their use is estimated at 92.9% and the use of unsupervised algorithms at 7.1%. In addition, 86% of the models built are based on classification, 7% on regression models and 7% on clustering-based models. This study focuses on logistic regression, artificial neural networks, convolutional neural networks, linear regression, K-means, K-NN and Naïve Bayes. Although this study presents the advantages of using supervised algorithms, we note that this list is not exhaustive. Indeed, in the context of the use of machine learning algorithms for the prediction of the COVID19 disease, several other algorithms have been used in recent years for predictions [2].

Prakash et al., (2020) presented a framework for analysing COVID19, with a view to understanding how it affects people. The study reveals that people aged between 20 and 50 are most affected by the disease. Machine learning algorithms such as SVM, KNN + NCA, Decision Tree, Gaussian Naïve Bayes, Multilinear Regression, Logistic Regression and XGBoost were used to build prediction models. The data used were characterised by age, number of deaths, number cured, number of confirmed foreigners and number of confirmed nationals. RF performed best with an accuracy of 96%[3].

Rustam et al., (2020) demonstrated the ability of machine learning models to predict the number of patients affected by COVID19. Four prediction models were used, namely linear regression (LR), least absolute selection and shrinkage operator (LASSO), support vector machine (SVM) and exponential smoothing (ES). The aim of this study was to perform three types of prediction, such as the number of new cases of infection, the number of deaths and the number of recoveries in the next 10 days. The results showed that the ES was best suited to the study of the 3 cases mentioned above, followed by the LR and the LASSO. However, SVM performed poorly in all prediction scenarios [4].

Another study by N. N. Sun et al. (2020) aimed to extract risk factors from the clinical data of patients infected with COVID19 using four algorithms: LR, SVM, DT, RF and DNN. The results indicate that the LR predictive model performed better in terms of precision, sensitivity and accuracy [5].

This article describes the ability of machine learning methods to improve the precision and speed of early diagnosis of this disease.

A great deal of work has been done on the use of machine learning algorithms to predict COVID19, mainly over the last two years. These are summarised in Table 1 below. This table gives an overview of the machine learning algorithms used in the 2020 and 2022.

3 Proposed Approach

3.1 Dataset

This study is based on an epidemiological dataset of COVID-19 positive and negative cases in Côte d'Ivoire. These data were collected by the National Institute of Public Health (INHP). The dataset comes from the Epidemiological Surveillance System. The dataset includes 10,000 records, with 13 features, including symptoms (Tables 2 and 3).

Table 2. Description of features

Features	Descriptions
N°	Unique identifier for each COVID-19 case
Fever	Increase in body temperature above normal
Fever sensation	Feeling of warmth or boiling in the body
Fatigue	Feeling of tiredness or exhaustion

(continued)

Table 2. (*continued*)

Features	Descriptions
Cough	Expulsion of air from the lungs
Body aches	Musclepain
Loss of taste and/or smell	Loss of the ability to taste or smell
Headache	Pain in the head
Diarrhea	Production of an excessive amount of liquid or loose stools
Contact with signs	A person who has been in close contact with a person infected with COVID-19
Contactcasconfirms	A person who has been in close contact with a person who has tested positive for COVID-19
comorbidities	Pre-existing medical conditions that can increase the risk of complications from COVID-19
daily treatment	Treatment that the person receives for COVID-19

Table 3. Profile information of the dataset

N°	Fever	Fever sensation	Fatigue	Cough	Body aches	Loss of taste and/or smell	Headache	Diarrhea	Contact with signs	Contactcasconfirms	comorbidities	daily treatment	Decision
001	1	1	1	1	1	1	1	1	1	1	0	0	1
002	1	1	1	1	1	1	1	0	0	1	0	0	1
003	1	0	1	1	1	1	1	1	0	1	0	0	1
004	1	0	1	1	1	1	1	1	1	1	0	0	1
...	...	...	...	...	...	...	...	...	...	...	...	...	...

3.2 Algorithm IDPATIANT

This algorithm, named IDPATIANT, identifies patients from preprocessed data through several simple steps: loading data, splitting into training and test sets, scaling features, developing models, training and evaluation, displaying scores and graphs, generating decision tree rules, and visualizing the decision tree. The aim of this algorithm is to provide an effective method for patient identification and visual data analysis.

Table 1.

Year	Authors	Algorithms used	Best Algorithms
2020	Prakash et al. [3]	RF, SVM, DT, GNB, MLR, LR, XGBoost, KNN	RF
	Rustam et al. [4]	LR, LASSO, SVM, ES	ES
	Batista et al. [6]	RN, RF, GBT, LR, SVM	SVM
	Swapna Rekha et al. [1]	SVM, RF, FFT-Gabor Sheme	SVM
	Schwab et al. [7]	LR, RN, SVM, RF, GB	SVM, RF et XGB
	Sun et al. [5]	LR, RN, SVM, RF, DT, DNN	LR
2021	Zoabi et al. [8], Kukar et al. [9]	XGBoost	XGBoost
	Rahman et al. [10]	CSDC-SVM, LR, LR/CNN	CSDC-SVM
	Muhammad et al. [11]	DT, SVM, Naïve Bayes, LR, ANN	DT
	Charlyn et al. [12]	J48 DT, RF, SVM, KNN, Naïve Bayes	SVM et RF
	Dutta et al. [13]	KNN, RF, Bagging	RF
2022	Sharma et al. [14]	SVM, FS-SVM, HPO-FS-SVM	HPO-FS-SVM

Algorithm IDPATIANT
Var
Data, train_set, test_set
Results :Dictonary
Graphs: Graph
decision_tree_rules: rules
Begin

   # Step 1: Load preprocessed data
   data = load_preprocessed_data()

   # Step 2: Split data into training and test sets
   train_set, test_set = split_data(data)

   # Step 3: Scale features
   train_set, test_set = scale_features(train_set, test_set)

   # Step 4: Develop models and hyperparameter search grids
   models, hyperparameters = develop_models_and_search_grids()

   # Step 5: Dictionaries to store results
   results = {}

   # Step 6: Train and evaluate models
   for model, params in zip(models, hyperparameters):
      trained_model = train_model(train_set, params)
      scores = evaluate_model(trained_model, test_set)
      results[model_name] = scores

   # Step 7: Display scores
   display_scores(results)

   # Step 8: Plot graphs
   graphs = plot_graphs(results)

   # Step 9: Bar plot of accuracy, precision, recall, and fscore scores
   bar_plot(graphs)

   # Step 10: Display graphs
   display_graphs(graphs)

   # Step 11: Generate decision tree rules
   decision_tree_rules = generate_decision_tree_rules(decision_tree_model)

   # Step 12: Display decision tree image
   display_decision_tree_image(decision_tree_rules)
End

3.3 Experimentation

The following supervised machine learning algorithms, decision tree, random forest and gradient boosting, were run using the Python programming language in a Windows operating system environment deployed on a Thinkpad (laptop), Corei7 computer system with 16 GB RAM and a processor speed of 2.9 GHz. All the necessary libraries were installed on a Python notebook and used for data analysis, including correlation analysis and model development. The models were evaluated using a performance measure of accuracy, sensitivity and specificity to determine their effectiveness and quality.

3.4 Results and Discussion

Early patient prediction of COVID-19 is very useful as it reduces the burden on healthcare systems by helping to diagnose patients with COVID-19. In this work, decision tree, random forest and gradient boosting models for the prediction of COVID-19 infection using an epidemiological dataset for COVID-19 positive and negative cases in Côte d'Ivoire were developed. The performance of all models was evaluated on the basis of the following performance indicators: accuracy, recall and precision. The model performance results are presented in Table 4.

Table 4. Evaluation de performance

Model	Accuracy	Precision	Recall
Random Forest	0.87	0.85	0.875
Gradient Boosting	0.8	0.85	0.875
Decision Tree	0.97	0.98	0.925

Our results show that the performance of the models used is particularly high. Indeed, the decision tree model achieved an accuracy of 97% and a sensitivity of 92.5%, outperforming the other models. The random forest model achieved an accuracy of 87% and a sensitivity of 87.5%, while gradient boosting achieved an accuracy of 80% and a sensitivity of 87.5%. These results are comparable or even superior to those of previous studies. The work of Muhammad et al. (2021) reported an accuracy of 85% with a decision tree model, while that of Rahman et al. (2021) obtained a sensitivity of 82% with a CSDC-SVM model.

Our decision tree model therefore outperforms these approaches in terms of accuracy and sensitivity, two crucial measures for early diagnosis and health resource management.

We also observed an increased robustness of our approach to data variations. The F1 score obtained with our decision tree model is 0.95, showing a good balance between precision and recall. The random forest and gradient boosting models both achieved an F1 score of 0.86, illustrating considerable robustness. In comparison, Dutta et al. (2021) reported an F1 score of 0.78 for their random forest model, demonstrating the significant improvement of our models in reducing classification errors, for both false positives and false negatives.

To illustrate these results, the following graph shows a detailed comparison of performance indicators (accuracy, sensitivity, F1-score) for each model studied, as well as previous work. These graphs provide a clear visualization of the differences in performance between the models (Figs. 1 and 2).

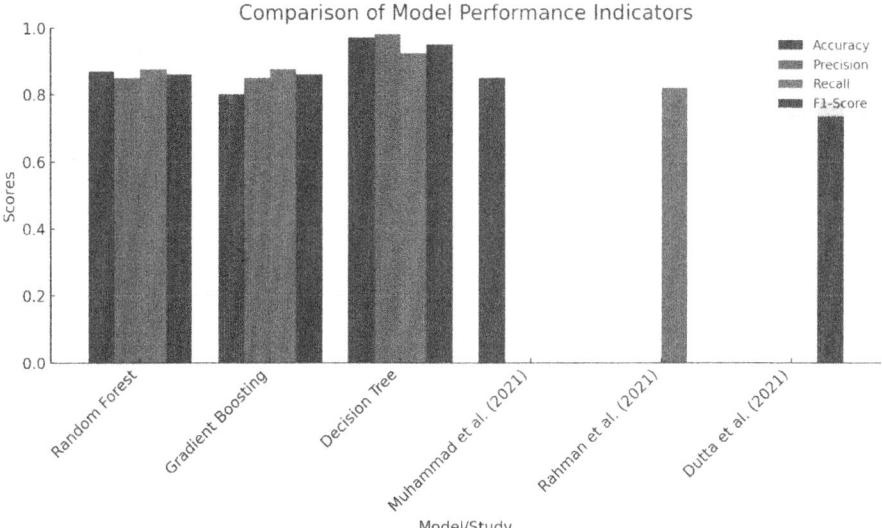

Fig. 1. Comparison of model performance indicators

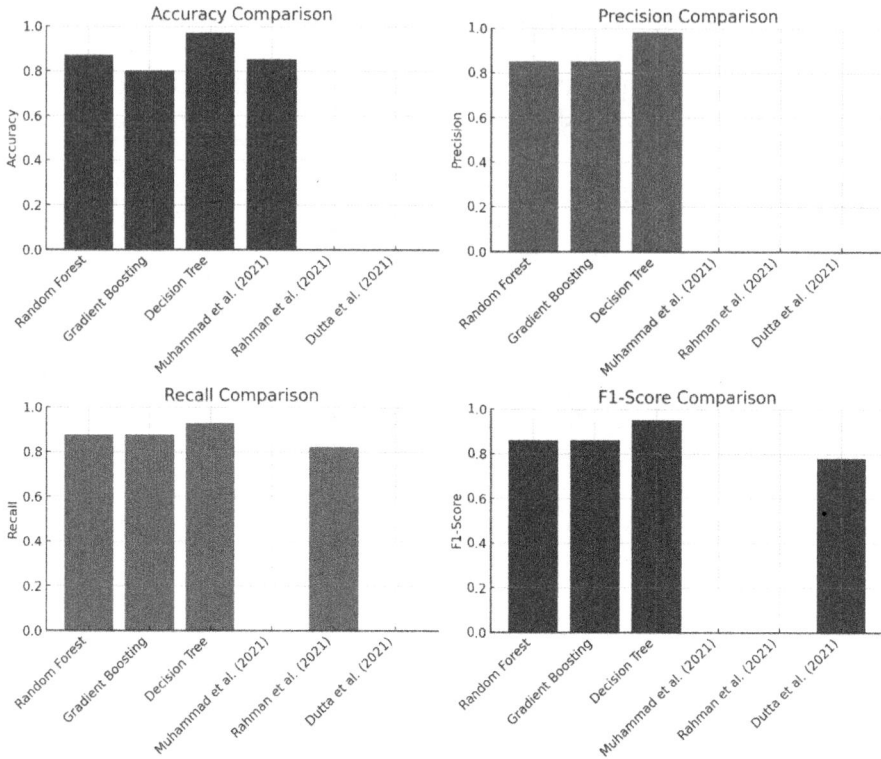

Fig. 2. Comparison of Scores

Computation time is a crucial aspect for real-time applications, especially in hospital environments. We have optimized our models to run with an average time of 2 s per prediction, enabling practical use in emergency situations. In comparison, Sharma et al. (2022) reported an average execution time of 5 s for their HPO-FS-SVM model, which may be less efficient in situations where every second counts.

In addition to the good performance of our models, we have also focused on interpretability. Our decision tree model uses techniques such as partial dependency graphs to provide detailed information on the risk factors associated with disease severity. This not only boosts users' confidence in the model's predictions, but also provides valuable information for patient management. This level of interpretability is often lacking in previous work, such as the study by Kukar et al. (2021), which focuses solely on prediction accuracy without offering an analysis of influential variables.

3.5 Generating Rules for Our Best Model

The best model for high precision and high recall is the Decision Tree.

The rules generated.

```
|--- Contactcasconfirme <= 0.50
| |--- comorbidites <= 0.50
| | |--- class: 0
| |--- comorbidites > 0.50
| | |--- class: 0
|--- Contactcasconfirme > 0.50
| |--- Pertedegoutetouodorat <= 0.50
| | |--- Fatigue <= 0.50
| | | |--- Fievre <= 0.50
| | | | |--- class: 0
| | | |--- Fievre > 0.50
| | | | |--- class: 0
| | |--- Fatigue > 0.50
| | | |--- Courbatures <= 0.50
| | | | |--- class: 0
| | | |--- Courbatures > 0.50
| | | | |--- Mauxdetete <= 0.50
| | | | | |--- class: 0
| | | | |--- Mauxdetete > 0.50
| | | | | |--- class: 1
| |--- Pertedegoutetouodorat > 0.50
| | |--- Mauxdetete <= 0.50
| | | |--- class: 0
| | |--- Mauxdetete > 0.50
| | | |--- Fatigue <= 0.50
| | | | |--- Toux <= 0.50
| | | | | |--- class: 0
| | | | |--- Toux > 0.50
| | | | | |--- class: 1
| | | |--- Fatigue > 0.50
| | | | |--- Courbatures <= 0.50
| | | | | |--- class: 1
| | | | |--- Courbatures > 0.50
| | | | | |--- class: 1
```

These rules are used to predict whether a person has COVID-19.

- If contact with a confirmed case is less than 0.5, then the class is 0 (no COVID-19).
- If contact with a confirmed case is greater than 0.5, then the class is 1 (COVID-19).
- If contact with a confirmed case is greater than 0.5 and the loss of taste or smell is less than 0.5, then the class is 0 (no COVID-19).
- If contact with a confirmed case is greater than 0.5 and the loss of taste or smell is greater than 0.5, then the class is 1 (COVID-19).

In other words, these rules indicate that:

- If a person has not been in contact with a confirmed case of COVID-19, then they are probably negative for the virus.
- If a person has been in contact with a confirmed case of COVID-19, then they are more likely to be positive for the virus.
- If a person has been in contact with a confirmed case of COVID-19 and has symptoms such as loss of taste or smell, then they are more likely to be positive for the virus.

These rules can be used to help doctors identify people who may have COVID-19 (Fig. 3).

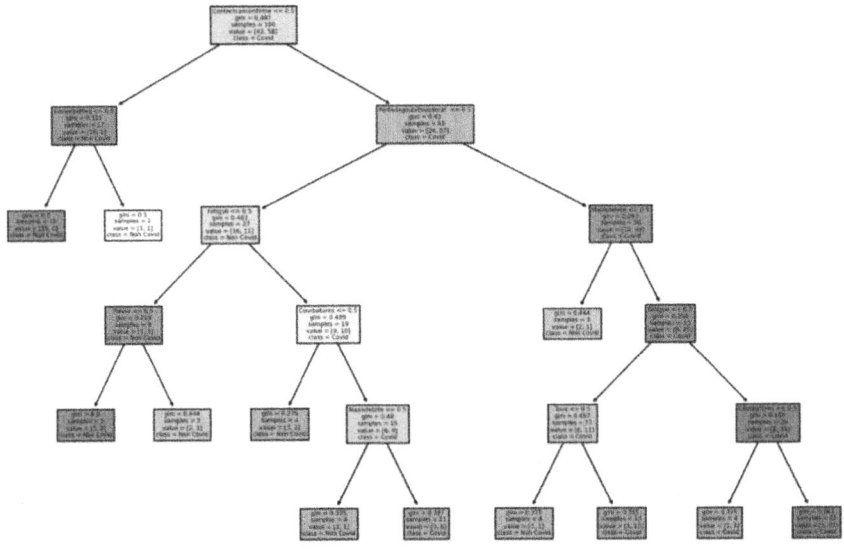

Fig. 3. Decision tree model for predicting COVID-19 infection.

- A doctor can use these rules to assess a person's risk of contracting COVID-19.
- A laboratory can use these rules to automate the process of diagnosing COVID-19.
- A mobile application can use these rules to help people track their sym toms and determine whether they need to be tested for COVID-19.

3.6 Application

To deploy our application that predicts the presence of COVID-19 using the decision tree model, we used the Streamlit framework. Streamlit is a powerful tool for creating interactive web applications for machine learning and data science projects. The algorithmic code of our application is as follows (Fig. 4).

Algorithm Identify_COVID19

```
Var
   contact, comorbidities, loss_of_smell, fatigue, fever, aches, headache, cough: Real
   patient_id, patient_name, patient_first_name: Text
   data, input_data: Table
   prediction, max_depth, min_samples_split: Integer
   model: Model
Functions
   Load_Data(): DataFrame
   Train_Model(data: DataFrame, max_depth: Integer, min_samples_split: Integer): Model
   Predict(model: Model, input_data: DataFrame): Integer

Begin
   Display_Title("Identifying Individuals Likely to Have COVID-19")
   uploaded_file = Upload_File("Upload your CSV file")
   If uploaded_file is not null Then
      data = Read_CSV(uploaded_file)
      Display("Preview of uploaded data:", data.head())

      X = Drop_Columns(data, ["N", "Decision"])
      y = Extract_Column(data, "Decision")

      max_depth = Select_Value("Maximum depth of the tree", 1, 10, 3)
      min_samples_split = Select_Value("Minimum number of samples required to split a node", 2, 2,10)

      model = Train_Model(X, y, max_depth, min_samples_split)

      Display_SubTitle("Patient Information:")
      patient_id = Enter_Text("Patient ID")
      patient_name = Enter_Text("Patient Name")
      patient_first_name = Enter_Text("Patient First Name")
      Contact_with_signs = Select_Value("Contact with signs", [-1.0, 0.0, 1.0])
      comorbidities = Select_Value("Comorbidities", [-1.0, 0.0, 1.0])
      Diarrhea = Select_Value("Diarrhea", [-1.0, 0.0, 1.0])
      Confirmed_contact = Select_Value("Confirmed contact", [-1.0, 0.0, 1.0])
      aches = Select_Value("Aches", [-1.0, 0.0, 1.0])
      fatigue = Select_Value("Fatigue", [-1.0, 0.0, 1.0])
      loss_of_smell = Select_Value("Loss of smell", [-1.0, 0.0, 1.0])
      cough = Select_Value("Cough", [-1.0, 0.0, 1.0])
      fever = Select_Value("Fever", [-1.0, 0.0, 1.0])
      Fever_sensation = Select_Value("Fever sensation", [-1.0, 0.0, 1.0])
      daily_treatment = Select_Value("Daily treatment", [-1.0, 0.0, 1.0])

      If Button("Predict") Then
```

The application predicts whether a person is likely to have COVID-19 using a decision tree model. Users upload a CSV file containing the data, input symptoms and contact information through a user interface, and the algorithm uses this information to make a prediction. The result, indicating whether the person is likely to be positive or negative for COVID-19, is displayed along with the decision rules used by the model. This is a demonstration of our model.

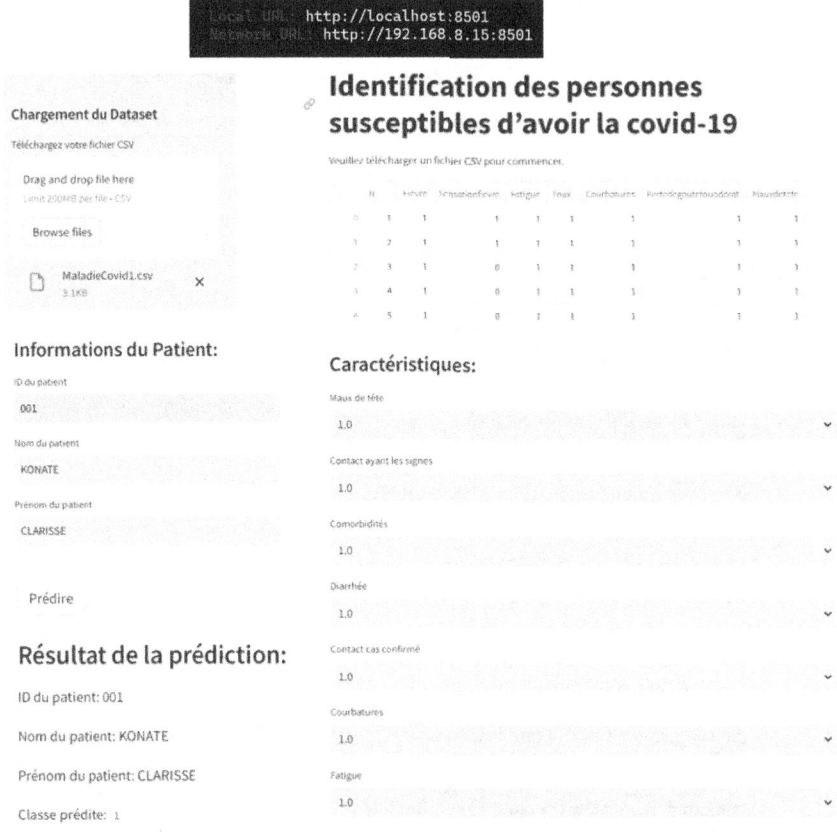

Fig. 4. Application

4 Conclusion

In conclusion, early prediction of COVID-19 patients is extremely useful as it reduces the burden on healthcare systems by facilitating the diagnosis of those affected by the disease. In this work, decision tree, random forest, and gradient boosting models were developed to predict COVID-19 infection using an epidemiological dataset of positive and negative cases in Côte d'Ivoire. The performance of these models, evaluated based on accuracy, precision, and recall, shows that the decision tree is the most effective model, with high precision and recall.

The rules generated by the decision tree allow for effective prediction of whether a person has COVID-19, primarily based on contact with a confirmed case and the presence of specific symptoms such as loss of taste or smell. These rules indicate that a person who has not been in contact with a confirmed COVID-19 case is probably negative for the virus, while a person who has been in contact with a confirmed case and presents symptoms is more likely to be positive.

These rules can be used to help doctors identify people who may have COVID-19, automate the diagnostic process in laboratories, and assist users of mobile applications in tracking their symptoms and determining whether they need to be tested. In summary, the application of these models and rules can significantly contribute to more effective management of the COVID-19 pandemic.

Looking ahead, the models developed in this study could be improved. The integration of real-time data and the use of more advanced machine learning techniques, such as deep neural networks, could also improve the accuracy and responsiveness of predictions.

References

1. Swapnarekha, H., Behera, H.S., Nayak, J., Naik, B.: Role of intelligent computing in COVID-19 prognosis: a state-of-the-art review. Chaos Solitons Fractals **138**, 109947 (2020). https://doi.org/10.1016/j.chaos.2020.109947
2. Kwekha-Rashid, A.S., Abduljabbar, H.N., Alhayani, B.: Coronavirus disease (COVID-19) cases analysis using machine-learning applications. Appl. Nanosci., 0123456789, May 2021. https://doi.org/10.1007/s13204-021-01868-7
3. Prakash, K.B.: Analysis, prediction and evaluation of COVID-19 datasets using machine learning algorithms. Int. J. Emerg. Trends Eng. Res. **8**(5), 2199–2204 (2020). https://doi.org/10.30534/ijeter/2020/117852020
4. Rustam, F., et al.: COVID-19 future forecasting using supervised machine learning models. IEEE Access **8**, 101489–101499 (2020). https://doi.org/10.1109/ACCESS.2020.2997311
5. Sun, N.N., et al.: A prediction model based on machine learning for diagnosing the early COVID-19 patients. medRxiv, pp. 1–12 (2020). https://doi.org/10.1101/2020.06.03.20120881
6. Afm, B., et al.: COVID-19 diagnosis prediction in emergency care patients: a machine learning approach. medRxiv **102** (2020). https://doi.org/10.1101/2020.04.04.20052092
7. Schwab, P., DuMont Schütte, A., Dietz, B., Bauer, S.: Clinical predictive models for COVID-19: systematic study. J. Med. Internet Res. **22**(10), e21439 (2020). https://doi.org/10.2196/21439
8. Zoabi, Y., Deri-Rozov, S., Shomron, N.: Machine learning-based prediction of COVID-19 diagnosis based on symptoms. NPJ Digit. Med. **4**(1), 3 (2021). https://doi.org/10.1038/s41746-020-00372-6
9. Kukar, M., et al.: COVID-19 diagnosis by routine blood tests using machine learning. Sci. Rep. **11**(1), 10738 (2021). https://doi.org/10.1038/s41598-021-90265-9
10. Atta-ur-Rahman, et al.: Supervised machine learning-based prediction of COVID-19. Comput. Mater. Continua **69**(1), 21–34 (2021). https://doi.org/10.32604/cmc.2021.013453
11. Muhammad, L.J., Algehyne, E.A., Usman, S.S., Ahmad, A., Chakraborty, C., Mohammed, I.A.: Supervised machine learning models for prediction of COVID-19 infection using epidemiology dataset. SN Comput. Sci. **2**(1), 11 (2021). https://doi.org/10.1007/s42979-020-00394-7
12. Villavicencio, C.N., Macrohon, J.J.E., Inbaraj, X.A., Jeng, J.H., Hsieh, J.G.: Covid-19 prediction applying supervised machine learning algorithms with comparative analysis using weka. Algorithms **14**(7) (2021). https://doi.org/10.3390/a14070201

13. Sharma, D.K., Subramanian, M., Malyadri, P., Reddy, B.S., Sharma, M., Tahreem, M.: Classification of COVID-19 by using supervised optimized machine learning technique. Mater. Today Proc. **56**, 2058–2062 (2022). https://doi.org/10.1016/j.matpr.2021.11.388
14. Dutta, P., Paul, S., Kumar, A.: Comparative analysis of various supervised machine learning techniques for diagnosis of COVID-19. In: Electronic Devices, Circuits, and Systems for Biomedical Applications, pp. 521–540. Elsevier (2021). https://doi.org/10.1016/B978-0-323-85172-5.00020-4

Text Mining for Thematic Keyword Extraction: Enriching a French Lexicon on Food Security

Rabiatou Zampaligre[1,2,3,4]✉, Aminata Sabane[1,2,3,4], Rodrique Kafando[1,2,3,4], Abdoul Kader Kabore[1,2,3,4], and Tégawendé F. Bissyande[1,2,3,4]

[1] Interdisciplinary Center of Excellence in AI for Development (CITADEL), Ouagadougou, Burkina Faso
rabiatouzampaligre@gmail.com, tegawende.bissyande@citadel.bf
[2] University Joseph Ki-Zerbo, Ouagadougou, Burkina Faso
[3] Virtual University of Burkina Faso, Ouagadougou, Burkina Faso
[4] University of Luxembourg, Luxembourg, Luxembourg

Abstract. Food security is a major concern in many countries in West Africa, particularly Burkina Faso. Early warning systems for food security and famines rely primarily on numerical data for analysis, while textual data, which is more complex to process, is seldom used. In this paper, we propose a textual analysis approach using text mining techniques on French language corpus (press papers and YouTube video transcripts) to enrich the lexicon related to food security. This study involves the extraction of food security domain terminology to enhance surveillance systems. The process is conducted in three steps: initially, relevant documents are selected based on an expert lexicon; then, terms are extracted from these pertinent documents; finally, the initial lexicon is enriched using the newly extracted terms. This methodology ensures a comprehensive and up-to-date lexicon for improved food security monitoring and analysis.

Keywords: food security · text mining · textual data · corpus · lexicon

1 Introduction

According to the definition provided at the World Food Summit (1996) [1], "food security exists when all people, at all times, have physical and economic access to sufficient, safe, and nutritious food that meets their dietary needs and food preferences for an active and healthy life. As the global population continues to grow and food systems become increasingly complex, ensuring safe and nutritious food for all has become a critical concern. In the face of this pressing challenge, research and innovation in the field of food security play an essential role in ensuring sustainable and high-quality food systems.

One of the cornerstones of food security lies in a deep understanding of its various components. This involves not only monitoring food risks but also implementing effective prevention and intervention mechanisms. Despite their usefulness, early warning systems (EWS) used to anticipate food crises rely mainly on numerical data and little on textual data available online, such as news articles or social media posts. With the rise of digital technologies, these textual data sources are becoming increasingly abundant and easily accessible, offering a valuable opportunity to complement traditional analyses and detect early warning signals of food crises [2].

To meet these challenges, access to a rich and up-to-date database is essential. However, food security is a field that extends far beyond conventional data, encompassing diverse information such as weather data, market data, public health data, supply chain data, and much more. The complexity of these heterogeneous data sources makes their analysis and effective use a major challenge.

The aim of this study is to propose a set of terms and concepts specific to the field of food security that can be used to analyze data from different sources and at different scales. This study builds on previous work [8,9,12]. Among the contributions of this study is the enrichment of the lexicon related to food security, specifically through the proposition of approaches that allow the automatic extraction of relevant terms related to this theme from a corpus, and the spatial distribution of these terms. To achieve this, we will propose a text-mining-based approach to extract thematic keywords from a corpus of French-language documents in order to enrich a lexicon related to food security monitoring.

This study is composed of four parts. First, a literature review will present the study of existing work on automatic terminology extraction techniques and lexicon enrichment. Second, the overall process will be detailed. Next, the various data used will be described, and finally, the results will be presented.

2 Related Work

In this section, we review and compare the existing research on terminology extraction and lexicon enrichment related to food security.

A notable initial contribution in this field is by Chloé Choquet [12], who worked on enriching a lexicon dedicated to food security. Her approach is based on an advanced natural language processing system capable of self-improvement. This system identifies the main themes of documents using unsupervised learning models such as LDA (Latent Dirichlet Allocation) and Word2Vec. Choquet's method is distinguished by its ability to handle large sets of unstructured data while capturing underlying thematic relationships.

In addition, Mathieu Roche et al. [8] developed a text-mining approach focused more on the structural aspect of terminology extraction. Their method begins with grammatical tagging using the TreeTagger tool [11], which assigns a grammatical function to each word by using binary decision trees. Once the texts are tagged, specific terms are extracted using the Biotex and Gentex tools. This approach ensures precise term extraction, though it is less flexible in unstructured contexts or for real-time analyses.

In contrast, Rose et al. [9] adopted a different method with RAKE, an unsupervised, domain- and language-independent keyword extraction algorithm. Unlike the previous methods that rely on complex models or grammatical tagging, RAKE allows for quick and direct keyword extraction from a corpus, such as news articles. To evaluate the keywords, metrics for exclusivity, essentiality, and generality were defined, allowing the system to identify key terms without manual annotations. This simplicity and speed make RAKE an interesting tool, though it is less precise in specialized domains.

Finally, going beyond term extraction, Xiao et al. [13] proposed an innovative framework for the automatic detection of food crises. Their method begins with the extraction of characteristic keywords using the TF-IDF technique [10], followed by named entity recognition using a Bi-LSTM-CNN-CRF model [14]. In addition, each article is classified based on the weighted keywords and named entities using the single-pass clustering technique [7]. This integrated approach allows real-time monitoring of critical events in food security by combining terminology extraction and automatic article classification.

Comparative Analysis

Although these methods share the common goal of extracting and structuring relevant information from textual corpora, they differ in their approaches and application:

Choquet's approach is particularly useful for handling large unstructured text corpora and detecting underlying themes through unsupervised learning models. However, this approach requires significant computational resources for training models such as LDA and Word2Vec.

Roche et al.'s method stands out for its rigor in terminology extraction through grammatical tagging. This method is ideal for well-structured texts but may lack flexibility for real-time data analysis or more informal contexts.

RAKE (Rose et al.), on the other hand, offers a quick and computationally inexpensive solution for extracting keywords without concern for the grammatical structure of texts. However, its raw statistical approach may lack precision in highly specialized fields like food security.

Xiao et al.'s method intelligently combines several techniques for detecting food crises, including both keyword extraction and named entity recognition. While this approach is highly effective for real-time detection, it requires a sophisticated technical infrastructure and models like Bi-LSTM-CNN-CRF, which can be costly to implement.

3 Proposed Approach

In order to enrich the food security lexicon, we have developed a comprehensive methodology that combines advanced machine learning techniques with traditional keyword extraction methods. This approach is specifically designed to address the unique requirements of the food security domain, where it is essential to capture a diverse range of thematic concepts, from agricultural practices to socio-economic and environmental factors. By combining multiple extraction algorithms, we aim to create a lexicon that reflects the complexity of food security and improves the performance of early warning systems.

Figure 1 presents an overview of the main steps in our methodology, which includes document selection, data preprocessing, keyword extraction, and lexicon enrichment.

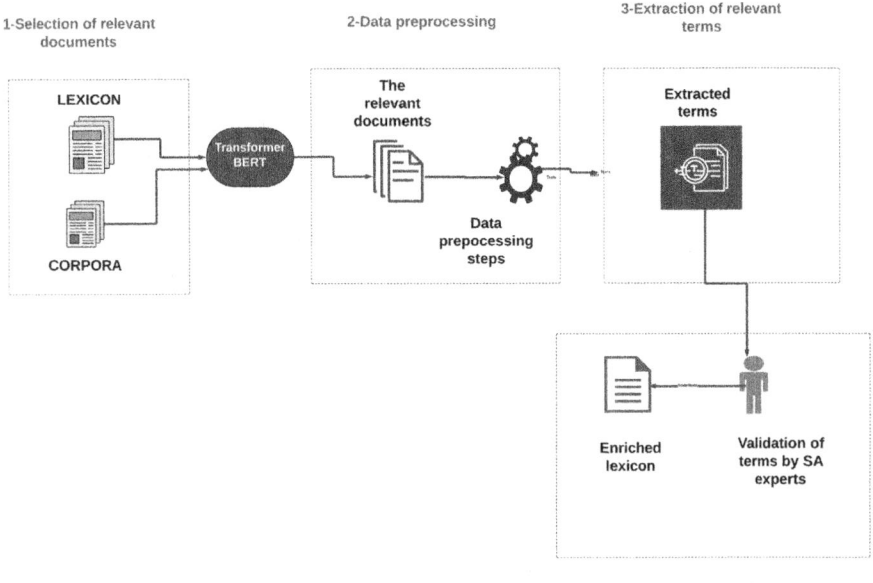

Fig. 1. Diagram of the methodological approach.

Below, we detail the key steps of our methodology.

3.1 Selection of Relevant Documents

The first step of our methodology is to identify relevant documents for the enrichment of the food security lexicon. Food security encompasses a broad set of concepts, often requiring specific regional knowledge. To capture this contextual relevance, we use the BERT model (Bidirectional Encoder Representations from Transformers) to calculate semantic similarity scores between the corpus documents and an existing lexicon.

– **BERT** is particularly useful for capturing contextual relationships between words and phrases, allowing us to identify the most relevant documents

with enhanced precision. This is especially important for food security, as it involves context-dependent terminology that varies by region and socioeconomic factors.
- **Expected outcome**: A selection of documents containing potentially useful terms for lexicon enrichment.

3.2 Data Preprocessing

Once the relevant documents are selected, we move on to the text preprocessing phase to normalize the data and facilitate term extraction. Preprocessing helps ensure the consistency and quality of terms extracted, especially given the variety of sources within food security data. We use the NLTK (Natural Language Toolkit) library to perform the following operations:

- **Tokenization**: Splitting texts into units (tokens).
- **Stopword removal**: Eliminating common words (like "the", "of", "in", etc.) that do not provide specific information.

3.3 Extraction of Relevant Terms

To extract important terms from the preprocessed corpus, we employ a combination of term extraction methods. Using multiple algorithms allows us to capture both general and domain-specific terms, enhancing the lexicon's thematic diversity and relevance for food security.

- **TF-IDF (Term Frequency-Inverse Document Frequency)**: This method weighs terms based on their frequency in a document relative to their frequency across the entire corpus, helping detect document-specific terms.
- **RAKE (Rapid Automatic Keyword Extraction)**: An unsupervised algorithm that extracts keywords based on word co-occurrence patterns, ideal for identifying multi-word phrases that are common in food security documents.
- **YAKE (Yet Another Keyword Extractor)**: Another unsupervised algorithm that identifies keywords based on several factors like word distribution in the text, effective for single-document analysis.
- **Biotex**: This tool is used for extracting complex and multi-word terms by combining statistical and linguistic approaches, making it suitable for identifying scientific and technical terminology within food security.

Each algorithm is applied independently to the corpus, providing a unique set of terms. The combination of these methods allows us to capture a comprehensive range of terms, including both single words and multi-word expressions that are essential for an accurate food security lexicon. The most relevant terms are selected based on a comparison of results from each algorithm, followed by a filtering process to retain contextually appropriate keywords.

3.4 Lexicon Enrichment

The extracted terms are then used to enrich the existing lexicon. Given the importance of precision in the food security domain, the selected terms are validated by food security experts to ensure they align with domain-specific concepts.

The final steps of our methodology ensure that the enriched lexicon is both accurate and contextually relevant to the field of food security.

Final steps:

- Manual validation by food security experts.
- Updating the lexicon with validated terms.

4 Experiments and Analysis

4.1 Datasets and Lexicons Used

In this study, we worked with two main corpora containing information documents about West Africa, as well as three lexicons provided by food security experts. The data and lexicons, which are essential for the terminological analysis, were provided by the UTM Paris laboratory.

- **The corpora:** Two corpora were used in this research: the BF Corpus and the FRESA Corpus. Both corpora are in French and focus on events and issues in West Africa.

    BF Corpus: The BF corpus consists of 22,856 articles from Burkinabé newspapers, published by Le Faso.net and Burkina 24 between 2009 and 2018. This corpus covers a wide period of current events on various topics, with food security being one of the analyzed subjects. It is particularly relevant for studying the situation in Burkina Faso during that time.

    FRESA Corpus: This corpus is composed of automatic transcriptions of news videos from YouTube, as well as news articles. The documents cover West African countries, particularly Benin, Burkina Faso, and Senegal. While this corpus has broader geographical and thematic coverage, it is still being processed for future analyses.

    Table 1 summarizes the characteristics of each corpus, detailing the type of documents, the period covered, the geographical focus, and the total number of documents included. This information is crucial for understanding the data foundation upon which our methodology is applied.

- **The lexicon**

    Three lexicons, developed in different contexts, were used to evaluate the relevance of documents related to food security. Each lexicon brings a unique perspective on food security-related terms.

Table 1. Characteristics of the corpora used in the food security study

Corpus name	Document type	Temporal Coverage	Geographical Scope	Number of documents
BF Corpus	News articles	2009 to 2018	Burkina Faso	22,856 papers
FRESA Corpus	Automatic transcriptions of YouTube news videos and news articles	2004-present	West Africa - Burkina Faso - Benin - Sénégal	26,178 papers

The Experts Lexicon: The Experts Lexicon contains terms specific to food security and was created by experts in the field. This lexicon, tailored to the context of Burkina Faso for the period between 2009 and 2018, was also utilized in the study by [4]. It consists of three sub-lexicons:
- **LEXG**: General lexicon on food security, containing 21 expressions.
- **LEXA**: Detailed lexicon on food security, containing 84 expressions.
- **LEXC**: Detailed lexicon on crises, containing 83 expressions.

This lexicon was used to identify relevant documents in the BF corpus during our experiments.

The KEOPS Lexicon: This lexicon was developed as part of the LEAP4FNSSA project (Long-term EU-AU Research and Innovation Partnership for Food and Nutrition Security and Sustainable Agriculture) to feed the Knowledge Extractor Pipeline System (KEOPS). It consists of 331 keywords associated with 12 concepts, including 22 keywords specifically related to food security.

The Fraiberger Lexicon: This lexicon was built from a large corpus of online newspapers in English. Keywords related to risk factors for food security were extracted using word embedding models, then statistically filtered to obtain a final list of 164 keywords. These were manually grouped into 12 semantic clusters[1].

Table 2 summarizes the characteristics of each lexicon, including its source, the number of terms, and the main concepts covered.

Data Structure Used: The data is organized to facilitate processing and analysis. Each corpus contains articles or transcriptions that are accompanied by metadata such as publication date, source, and geographical information when available.

- **Corpus Metadata:** The articles in each corpus are associated with information such as the date, source, and, where possible, geographical indications (country, region, etc.). This metadata is crucial for the thematic and spatio-temporal analyses carried out in the study.

---
[1] https://bit.ly/3LctN5D.

Table 2. Characteristics of the lexicons used in the food security study

Lexicon Name	Details	Number of Terms	Concepts Covered
Expert Lexicon	Lexicon provided by food security experts (adapted to the Burkinabé context 2009–2018)	188 terms (LEXG, LEXA, LEXC)	Food security and crises
KEOPS Lexicon	Lexicon developed within the LEAP4FNSSA project	331 keywords	Food security and related concepts
Fraiberger Lexicon	Keywords extracted from online newspapers, statistically filtered, and manually grouped	164 keywords	Food security risk factors

- **Lexicon Terms:** The terms extracted from the lexicons (particularly the expert lexicon) are used as selection criteria to determine the relevance of documents. The identified terms are associated with relevant documents from the BF corpus to examine the frequency and distribution of food security-related terms.

4.2 Selection of Relevant Documents

In this experiment, the BERT transformer model was used to generate vector representations of both the corpus documents and the lexicon terms. BERT, which is particularly suited for natural language processing tasks, captures the semantics of words in their context.

The first step involved tokenizing both the lexicon and the corpus. Each term from the lexicon and each document from the corpus were converted into tokens, after which their respective embeddings were computed. These vector embeddings represent the semantic relationships between terms, helping to capture the nuances of concepts related to food security.

Once the embeddings were computed, the cosine similarity measure was employed to assess the proximity between each document and the lexicon terms. This measure quantifies the semantic similarity between a document and a lexicon term, thereby determining the relevance of each document to food security topics.

Finally, a relevance threshold was defined to identify relevant documents. This threshold represents the value above which a document is considered relevant to the study. Documents with a similarity score higher than the threshold were selected for further analysis[2].

Figure 2 illustrates the process for calculating these similarity scores, which helps in selecting documents most relevant to the thematic focus of food security.

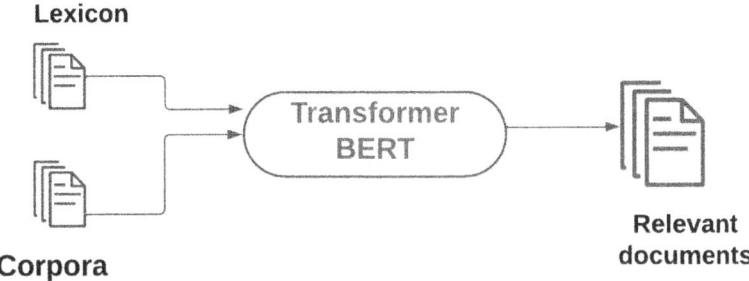

Fig. 2. Calculations of similarity score.

Determining the Relevance Threshold

The relevance threshold was determined based on the results obtained from the BF corpus. After calculating the similarities between the documents and the lexicon, we observed that the similarity scores ranged between 0.35 (lower bound) and 0.52 (upper bound).

To validate the threshold to be used, we manually annotated the relevance of the articles. The corpus was sorted in descending order of similarity, allowing us to verify that the relevance of documents related to food security was well correlated with their similarity scores. This manual annotation step aimed to assess the quality of the correlation between the score and the subject of the articles.

We also evaluated the top 50 documents before definitively setting the threshold. Based on these evaluations, we chose an experimental relevance threshold of 0.50. Thus, any document with a similarity score equal to or greater than 0.50 was considered relevant and related to food security.

4.3 Data Preprocessing

After selecting the relevant documents, a preprocessing phase was applied to the corpus to enhance data quality for further analysis. The preprocessing was carried out using the NLTK (Natural Language Toolkit) library, which provides a set of specialized tools for natural language processing. This process involves several key steps:

- **Tokenization**: The documents were converted to lowercase and then split into lexical units (tokens) to facilitate processing.

---

[2] https://bit.ly/3WntJqw.

- **Stopword Removal**: Common and non-informative words, such as articles, conjunctions, or prepositions, were removed from the corpus. We used the French stopword list provided by NLTK for this step.
- **Punctuation Cleaning**: All punctuation marks were stripped from the documents, allowing us to focus solely on the essential keywords.

Figure 3 outlines the data preprocessing steps, which include tokenization, stopword removal, and punctuation cleaning to ensure consistency across the corpus.

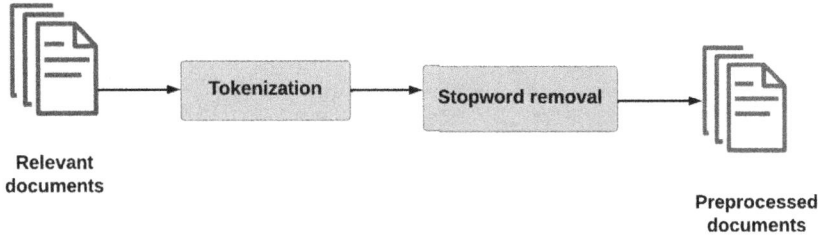

Fig. 3. data preprocessing.

After these operations, we obtained a cleaned and preprocessed corpus, ready for more advanced stages of analysis. The combination of NLTK tools for stopword removal and tokenization, along with Python's standard library for punctuation handling, allowed for optimized data preparation.

4.4 Extraction of Relevant Terms

Various methods exist for extracting terms from different sources, often utilizing a range of tools to achieve optimal results. In this study, we applied four specific keyword extraction algorithms TF-IDF [10], RAKE [9], YAKE [3], and Biotex [6] to explore their effectiveness in identifying relevant terms related to food security within our corpus. Each algorithm has its own approach to determining keyword importance, and the combination of their results provides insight into the most effective strategies for enriching the lexicon with diverse thematic terms[3].

Description of Algorithms

TF-IDF (Term Frequency-Inverse Document Frequency): TF-IDF is a statistical measure used to evaluate the importance of a term in a document relative to a corpus. The term frequency (TF) reflects how often a word appears in a document, while the inverse document frequency (IDF) penalizes words that are common across many documents, thus highlighting unique terms.

---

[3] https://bit.ly/3ycYHYc.

Process

- Tokenization of the text.
- Calculation of term frequency and inverse document frequency.
- Extraction of terms with the highest TF-IDF scores.

RAKE (Rapid Automatic Keyword Extraction): RAKE is a domain-independent keyword extraction algorithm that identifies key phrases in a document by analyzing word co-occurrences and evaluating word frequency and degree.

Process:

- Split the text into phrases by removing stopwords and punctuation.
- Calculate scores for each phrase based on word co-occurrence and frequency.
- Rank phrases according to their scores.

YAKE (Yet Another Keyword Extractor): YAKE is a lightweight unsupervised method that extracts keywords by using text features such as word frequency, word position, and casing. Unlike TF-IDF, it does not rely on a reference corpus and instead focuses solely on the input document.

Process

- Tokenization of text and filtering of stopwords.
- Evaluation of keyword candidates based on statistical features like position, casing, and frequency.
- Ranking of terms by score to identify the most relevant keywords.

Biotex: Biotex is a terminology extraction tool specifically designed for scientific and technical texts. It combines various statistical measures and linguistic patterns to extract terms related to the specific domain.

Process:

- Tokenization of text and extraction of candidate terms.
- Evaluation of candidates using statistical measures.
- Final selection of domain-specific keywords.

Results of Keyword Extraction

The table below (Table 3) summarizes the top keywords extracted by each algorithm:

Each algorithm contributed unique keywords that, when combined, provided a more comprehensive and contextually rich lexicon for food security. TF-IDF and Biotex were particularly effective at identifying precise, domain-specific terms that align closely with food security, forming a foundation of essential vocabulary. Meanwhile, RAKE and YAKE introduced complementary multi-word expressions and document-specific terms that added thematic diversity to the lexicon. This combined approach allowed us to leverage the strengths of each algorithm to enrich the lexicon with terms that are both contextually relevant and thematically comprehensive.

Table 3. Results of Keyword Extraction

Algorithm	Top Keywords
TF-IDF	eau (0.489), spiruline (0.375), station (0.293)
RAKE	a (60), site (35), project (23)
YAKE	pays (0.383), programme (0.375), instauré (0.375)
BIOTEX	pays (36.2), développement (32.2), directeur (30.3)

4.5 Lexicon Enrichment

The expert lexicon was initially used to calculate the similarity scores of papers to determine their relevance for food security analysis. To improve the identification of relevant documents, we aimed to enrich this lexicon with additional terms.

The terms extracted in the previous keyword extraction step were insufficient for enriching the lexicon due to the nature of the documents in the corpus, which often contained overly generic language. This limitation prevented the identification of terms with the specificity required for food security in West Africa. To address this, we turned to the Agrovoc Thesaurus resource [5], a specialized thesaurus in the agricultural field coordinated by the Food and Agriculture Organization (FAO) of the United Nations. This resource offers a structured collection of agricultural concepts, terms, definitions, and relationships, providing access to "linked open data on agriculture".

We began by searching for "Food Security" in the French version of Agrovoc's thesaurus, from which we explored related concepts. Based on the knowledge gained during this project, 15 new relevant terms were manually selected and presented to food security experts for validation.

However, relying on a single external source like Agrovoc to enrich the lexicon presents some limitations. While Agrovoc is a comprehensive resource in agriculture, it may not sufficiently cover specific aspects of food security unique to certain regions or contexts. Furthermore, using only one external source may limit terminological diversity, which could be improved by combining multiple databases or thesauri specializing in related fields, such as economics, climate, or nutrition.

4.6 Term Validation

Fifteen terms were selected for validation by food security experts. Each term was evaluated to determine its relevance for inclusion in the lexicon. This validation step is crucial in the field of food security, where terminology can be highly context-specific and nuanced. The inclusion of human expertise ensures that the lexicon reflects accurate, contextually relevant terms that automated algorithms alone may not fully capture. While computational methods can identify a broad set of terms, expert validation helps refine these results to align closely with field-specific language and ensure high accuracy for applications in food security monitoring.

The experts were presented with a table listing each term, where they indicated whether the term should be added to the lexicon. This process adds a layer of quality control, as the inclusion of a term ultimately depends on its validation by domain experts, which helps maintain consistency with the specific requirements and complexity of the food security domain.

Below are the terms extracted from the AGROVOC resource, as presented in Table 4. These additional terms aim to provide a more comprehensive coverage of food security concepts.

Table 4. Proposed terms for addition to the "Food Security" lexicon.

Agrovoc (English)	Agrovoc (French)
Inanition	Inanition
Food rationing	Rationnement des denrées
Food sovereignty	Souveraineté alimentaire
Seed insecurity	Insécurité semencière
Agrarian reform	Réforme agraire
Food availability	Disponibilité alimentaire
Nutritional security	Sécurité nutritionnelle
Food stock	Stock alimentaire
Food shortage	Pénurie alimentaire
Nutritional requirement	Besoin nutritionnel
Food intake	Prise alimentaire
Food resource	Ressource alimentaire
Undernutrition	Sous-alimentation
Satiety	Satiété
Meal frequency	Fréquence des repas

Out of the 15 proposed terms, eight were selected for inclusion in the general lexicon, four were chosen for a specialized lexicon, and three were designated for a lexicon focusing on crises. This categorization was done based on expert feedback, ensuring that the lexicon meets the specific needs of different aspects of food security, from general monitoring to crisis response.

4.7 Impact of Lexicon Enrichment

The lexicon enrichment had a significant impact in terms of both the quantity and quality of the included terms. Before the study, the initial lexicon contained *188* terms, distributed as follows: *21* terms for **LEXG**, *84* terms for **LEXA**, and *83* terms for **LEXC**.

After adding the new terms extracted from the Agrovoc thesaurus, the lexicon now contains *203* terms, representing an increase of *15* terms. This corresponds to an increase rate of **7.98%**, calculated using the following formula:

$$\text{Increase rate} = \frac{\text{New terms}}{\text{Initial number of terms}} \times 100 = \frac{15}{188} \times 100 = 7.98\%$$

This increase better reflects key concepts related to food security, thereby improving the relevance of the analyzed documents. Thanks to this study, the lexicon was not only enriched in terms of quantity but also in terms of quality. The addition of new terms expanded the scope of analysis, facilitating more accurate identification of relevant documents and enhancing the relevance of the results.

This approach contributes to a better understanding of food security issues at various scales.

5 Conclusion

In this study, we developed a methodology to enrich the food security lexicon by leveraging a dataset to identify relevant documents, preprocess data, extract terms, and integrate resources like the Agrovoc thesaurus. The BERT model was employed for vector representation, with cosine similarity for relevance evaluation, complemented by traditional algorithms like TF-IDF and RAKE.

Challenges arose with BERT's tokenization, which fragmented terms, limiting extraction quality. Future work could focus on refining tokenization, fine-tuning domain-specific models, and incorporating diverse resources to enhance thematic coverage. Despite these challenges, the study successfully enriched the lexicon and highlighted areas for improvement in food security terminology extraction.

Acknowledgments. This work was conducted as part of the Artificial Intelligence for Development in Africa (AI4D Africa) program, with the financial support of Canada's International Development Research Center (IDRC) and the Swedish International Development Cooperation Agency (Sida). Thanks to the UMR TETIS Laboratory, Montpellier, which provided the necessary data for the experiments, enabling the scientific advances achieved in this study.

References

1. Banque mondiale: Qu'est-ce que la sécurité alimentaire?. https://www.banquemondiale.org/fr/topic/agriculture/brief/food-security-update/what-is-food-security
2. Becker-Reshef, I., Justice, C., Barker, B., et al.: Strengthening agricultural decisions in countries at risk of food insecurity: the geoglam crop monitor for early warning. Remote Sens. Environ. **237**, 111553 (2020). https://doi.org/10.1016/j.rse.2019.111553
3. Campos, R., Mangaravite, V., Pasquali, A., Jorge, A., Nunes, C., Jatowt, A.: Yake! Keyword extraction from single documents using multiple local features. Inf. Sci. **509**, 257–289 (2020)

4. Deléglise, H.: Mise en relation de données hétérogènes pour le renforcement des systèmes de sécurité alimentaire – cas de la production agricole en afrique de l'ouest
5. Food, Organization, A.: Page Agrovoc c_10967 (Année de publication). https://agrovoc.fao.org/browse/agrovoc/fr/page/c_10967
6. Lossio-Ventura, J.A., Jonquet, C., Roche, M., Teisseire, M.: Biotex: a system for biomedical terminology extraction, ranking, and validation. In: ISWC: International Semantic Web Conference, pp. 157–160. No. 1272 (2014)
7. Papka, R., Allan, J., et al.: On-line new event detection using single pass clustering. University of Massachusetts, Amherst **10**(290941.290954) (1998)
8. Roche, M., et al.: Extraction automatique des mots-clés á partir de publications scientifiques pour l'indexation et l'ouverture des données en agronomie. Cahiers Agric. **24**(5), 313–320 (2015)
9. Rose, S., Engel, D., Cramer, N., Cowley, W.: Automatic keyword extraction from individual documents. In: Text Mining: Applications and Theory, pp. 1–20 (2010)
10. Salton, G., Buckley, C.: Term-weighting approaches in automatic text retrieval. Inf. Process. Manag. **24**(5), 513–523 (1988)
11. Schmid, H.: Probabilistic part-of-speech tagging using decision trees. In: New Methods in Language Processing, p. 154 (2013)
12. Souchon, A., Choquet, C.: Analyse de données textuelles sur la sécurité alimentaire en afrique de l'ouest - chloé choquet. Afrique de l'Ouest
13. Xiao, K., Wang, C., Zhang, Q., Qian, Z.: Food safety event detection based on multi-feature fusion. Symmetry **11**(10), 1222 (2019)
14. Yu, H.: Named Entity Recognition with Deep Learning. Ph.D. thesis, Auckland University of Technology (2019)

Improving Web User Tracking Systems Through Browser Fingerprinting

Goya Alama Désiré Dao[1,2(✉)], Abdoul Kader Kabore[1], Aminata Sabane[1,2], Rodrique Kafando[1], and Tégawendé F. Bissyande[1,2]

[1] Centre d'Excellence CITADEL Université Virtuelle du Burkina Faso Ouagadougou Burkina Faso, Ouagadougou, Burkina Faso
{abdoulkader.kabore,rodrique.kafando,tegawende.bissyande}@citadel.bf,
aminata.sabane@ujkz.bf

[2] Laboratoire de Mathématiques et d'Informatique Université Joseph KI-ZERBO Ouagadougou Burkina Faso, Ouagadougou, Burkina Faso
daogoyaalamadesire@gmail.com

Abstract. Browser fingerprinting is a technique that involves collecting unique information from a user's web browser to create a distinct profile. This method can be used for identification, targeted advertising, or enhancing web security. This article proposes an approach to improve browser fingerprinting for web tracking systems. We developed a JavaScript-based browser fingerprinting system that generates stable and diverse fingerprints, addressing existing systems' stability and diversity issues. Through a series of tests, we evaluated our system and obtained conclusive results regarding the stability, diversity, and compatibility of the fingerprints generated by our system.

Keywords: Browser fingerprinting · stable fingerprints · diverse fingerprints · compatibility

1 Introduction

Today, the development of information and communication technologies has opened up many benefits and opportunities for Internet users [3,9,11,16]. The Internet allows access to information, global communication, remote work, and more. The web has become an essential tool for carrying out these various tasks. However, as with any technology, the web has developed with its own set of drawbacks, namely threats such as computer hacking, identity theft and cyber harassment, all of which fall under the umbrella of cybercrime [2]. According to the Central Brigade for the Control of Cybercrime (BCLCC), in 2022 some 3,028 complaints were received and processed in Burkina Faso, with 33 people referred to legal institutions for financial losses of around 1,108,382,906 CFA francs [1]. With this in mind, it is important for institutions fighting cybercrime to find effective solutions to combat these scourges. Browser Fingerprinting technology can provide a solution for tracking and tracing suspects and cybercriminals across the web [8,10,19]. Indeed, it was Ekersley et al. [7] who discovered this technique, known as browser fingerprinting, which makes it possible to collect browsing information from internet users through their browsers and create a digital fingerprint. This solution can be used for profiling and also to detect cybercriminal behaviour in cyberspace. However, challenges such as stability and diversity issues remain in browser fingerprinting technology [14]. The main objective of this thesis is to improve the stability and diversity of fingerprints generated by browser fingerprinting systems by proposing an approach to improve the stability and diversity factors of browser fingerprints. Stability is a factor that states that machine fingerprints remain unchanged over time [14]. Diversity is a factor of browser fingerprints that states that no two machines have similar fingerprints to each other [14].

The structure of this article is as follows: Sect. 2 presents the state of the art of our study. Section 3 describes our methodology. Section 4 is dedicated to the results and their discussion, and we conclude this work in Sect. 5.

2 Related Works

In the field of browser fingerprinting, a number of studies have been conducted in different research areas since the first scientific journal mentioned this technology. For example, authors such as Desheng Zhang et al. [20], Pierre Laperdrix et al. [12] and others [5,18] have conducted extensive studies on this technology. Their aim was to understand and review the latest findings in this field. This includes technical analysis of the methods used to identify a user from browser settings such as installed extensions, screen size, fonts, system language. They have also studied the different types of browser fingerprints that exist, the technologies and methods used to obtain them at the browser level, and the methods used to obtain authentic and high quality fingerprints from a browser. The results of their studies have shown that despite the many benefits that this technology can offer, it faces significant challenges. In addition, it can be used to identify and track users on the Web, providing a solution to scourges such as cybercrime.

In the same vein, authors such as Salomatin et al. [17], Gabryel et al. [8] and Y. Cao et al. [6,15] have conducted studies using random browser features and combining them to create browser fingerprints. At the end of these studies, we found that the methods used were not reliable for creating an effective browser fingerprinting approach.

Muhammad Mudassar et al. [14] proposed a system to create unique cross-platform (Windows, Linux and Android) fingerprints to identify and capture user interest. To do this, they combined the characteristics of the device (computer, smartphone) with those of the browser (user agent, language, screen resolution) to create a more stable and unique fingerprint for users of web platforms. Our observation regarding this study is that the selection of browser and device characteristics for the design of the browser fingerprint has not been done in a sufficiently objective manner, resulting in near-random feature selection.

The majority of previous studies have had shortcomings in their process of constructing browser fingerprints. In fact, they have failed to reconcile two important aspects of browser fingerprints, namely stability and diversity.

For example, authors such as Vicki Wei Qi Lee et al. [13] began a process of establishing a list of reliable browser attributes that would help create stable and diverse browser fingerprints. To do this, the authors collected information from browsers and processed it using machine learning algorithms, including clustering algorithms such as *EM, FarthestFirst, FilteredClusterer, HierarchicalClusterer, MakeDensityBasedClusterer and SimpleK-Means*. When processing the browser data, the goal was to determine which browser features had a high degree of uniqueness.

At the end of their study, the authors identified five browser features with high entropy, i.e. high uniqueness within a particular browser.

Our work will consist of improving the study by Vicki Wei Qi Lee et al. [13] in order to design a browser fingerprinting system based on their results, implementing the results of their research in a concrete way to confirm or not their veracity.

3 Methodology

In the process of proposing an approach for improving web user tracking systems through browser fingerprinting, our methodology is structured in several steps. In fact, we will first identify the different characteristics that we will collect and used to create browser fingerprints [13]. After this step, we will implement the JavaScript code that will allow us to collect these different characteristics; code that we will then integrate into a web page. Then, when users connect to the web page, the different characteristics are automatically collected from the browser and stored in a database. Note that a hash of the collected information is generated and stored at the same time as the information in the database; this hash is considered the browser's fingerprint. We then move on to the system testing phase, which consists of making changes to the browser to check that these changes do not result in a change to the user's browser fingerprint. If the results are satisfactory, we will now compare them with the results of similar work carried out previously, then interpret the results obtained and draw a conclusion at the end. The diagram below shows our methodological approach (Fig. 1).

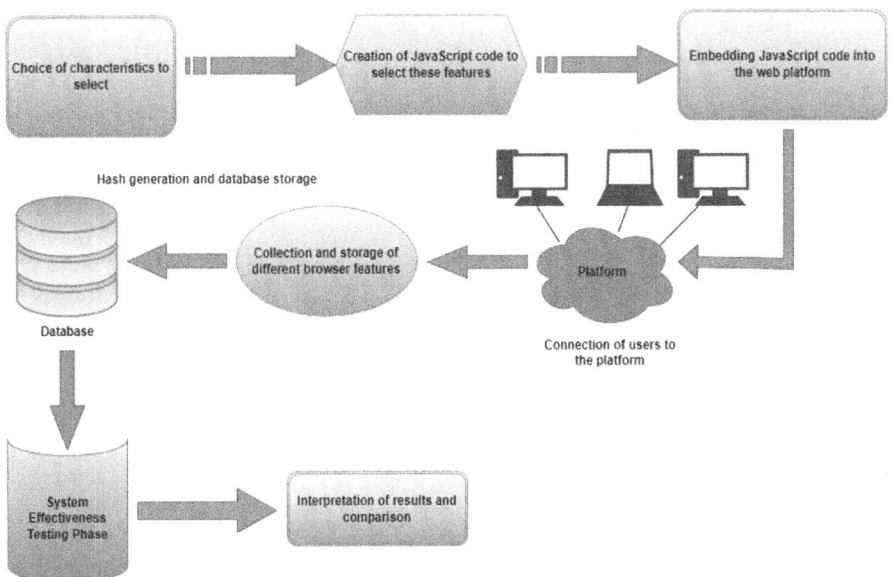

Fig. 1. Methodology

3.1 Selecting Browser Features

This step is crucial in our approach. Indeed, it constitutes the very basis of our work, in the sense that we must choose the right features that allow us to identify the browser with the greatest possible precision and stability. Selected features include: *The speech recognition engine, the inner window screen, the keys of the HTML elements, the image data, the header connection* [13].

- **The speech recognition engine**: This is a speech recognition system that recognizes and translates spoken language into text using computational linguistics. It is also called speech recognition or computer speech recognition.
- **Screen window inner or screen inner window**: This is the number of pixels displayed in width and height on a computer screen or television. It is the ratio between the definition of the screen panel and the size of the screen itself.
- **HTML element keys or HTML element keys**: HTML element keys designate the identifiers of HTML tags.
- **Image Data or image data**: This term designates the image data in the browser.
- **Header connection or header connection**: This designates the connection information between the client and the server.

Two additional features were added to enhance robustness, namely the *platform* and the *time zone*, to increase the robustness and efficiency of the generated fingerprint.

3.2 Implementation of Javascript Code

The implementation of JavaScript code is a step that takes place after the selection of browser features. It consists in creating a JavaScript code that allows to collect the information specified in the previous step. The browser information is collected when the user logs into the web page. Not only is this collection done without user awareness and stored in a remote database (Fig. 2).

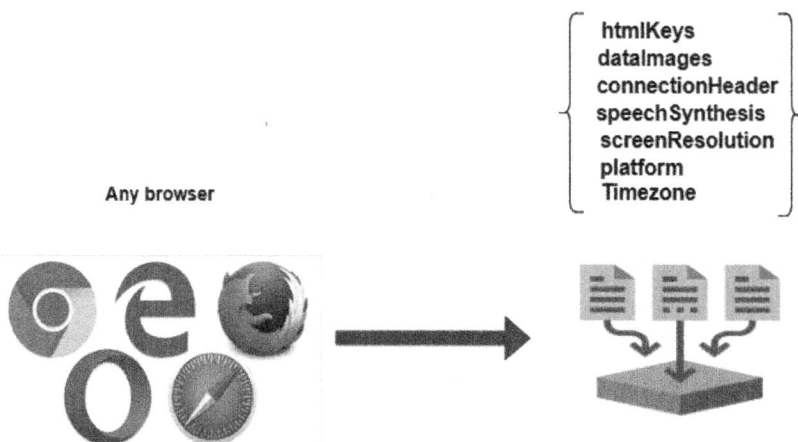

Fig. 2. Collection of characteristics

The figure below shows us the algorithm executed by the JavaScript code for feature selection (Fig. 3).

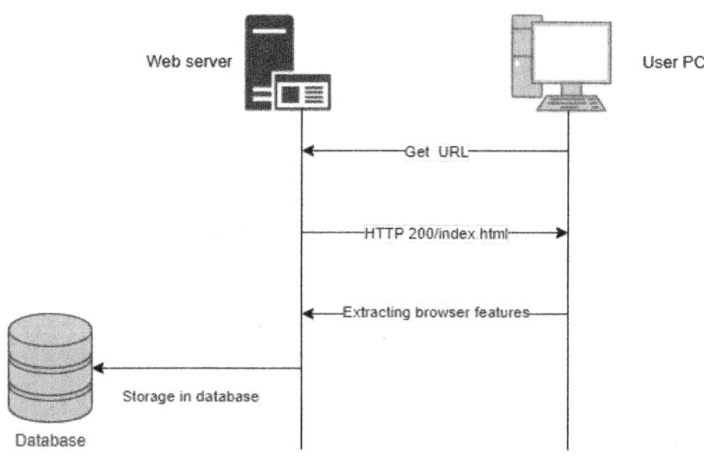

Fig. 3. Browser Feature Extraction Flow

3.3 Hash Generation

The generation of a hash with the collected data is done at the same time as the collection of information in such a way that the browsing data of a specific user is stored in the database at the same time as the hash generated from this data (Fig. 4).

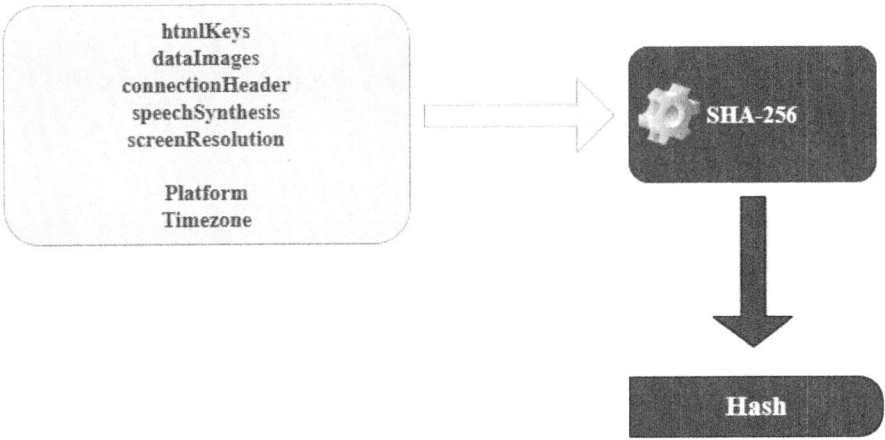

Fig. 4. Hash generation

4 Results, Discussions and Challenges

After implementing our system following the defined methodology, we carried out tests to verify the effectiveness of our system. After the testing phase, we obtained results which will be presented below.

4.1 Testing Phase

The testing phase is mainly composed of three types of tests.

- The stability test
- The diversity test
- The inter-compatibility test

The Stability Test. consists of testing the stability of the fingerprint generated with the information collected at the browser level by making modifications to it. The figure below shows us that the stability test is successful because the browser fingerprint remains stable despite changes made at the browser level (Fig. 5).

- **Stability test**

	hash
Before the test	d29c1d6d4302058909daa56569fdeb97b6eec0e16bb4dff327...
After the test	d29c1d6d4302058909daa56569fdeb97b6eec0e16bb4dff327...

Fig. 5. The stability test result

The Diversity Test. involved testing the fingerprinting system on another device and seeing if the fingerprint generated is different from the one generated on the other machine based on each user. Following this test, we noted that the generated fingerprint is very different from that generated on the other machine. This result then reinforces our position to say that our system manages to identify users through their browsers precisely. The following figure illustrates our result (Fig. 6).

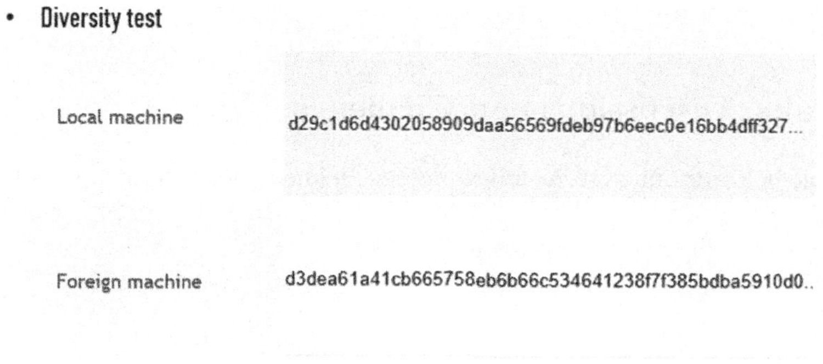

- **Diversity test**

Local machine	d29c1d6d4302058909daa56569fdeb97b6eec0e16bb4dff327...
Foreign machine	d3dea61a41cb665758eb6b66c534641238f7f385bdba5910d0..

Fig. 6. The diversity test result

The Inter-compatibility Test. consisted of using different browsers to access the web page, and seeing if the different browsers were able to correctly identify the user through their browser, that is to say if the different browsers had the same hash for a given user. The observation we made was that the browsers had the same hash. This shows that our browser fingerprinting system generates identifiers that help identify a user across different browsers. The following figure illustrates our result (Fig. 7).

- **Inter-compatibility test**

  Edge — d29c1d6d4302058909daa56569fdeb97b6eec0e16bb4dff327...

  Opera — d29c1d6d4302058909daa56569fdeb97b6eec0e16bb4dff327...

  Chrome — d29c1d6d4302058909daa56569fdeb97b6eec0e16bb4dff327...

Fig. 7. The inter-compatibility test result

4.2 Comparison of Results with Previous Work

Through the results that we obtained, we notice that we have very good results compared to previous work that had been carried out, in the sense that our system passed the various tests to which it was subjected. The table below illustrates our assertion (Table 1).

Table 1. Comparative table of results

Systems	Stability	Diversity	Intercompatibility
Our system	Yes	Yes	Yes
Károly Boda et al. [4]	No	Yes	Yes
Yinzhi Cao et al. [6]	Yes	No	Yes

Our system gives satisfactory results in the tests it has had to undergo. This reinforces our idea that our approach to improving user tracking systems on the web using browser fingerprinting is good. However, although our system has passed all the tests, it would be dishonest to assert that our system is 100 effective like any system.

5 Conclusion

During our work, we proposed an approach for improving web user tracking systems through browser fingerprinting. Our approach passed with flying colors the various tests to which it was subjected, thus confirming our opinion, which is that our approach is a promising solution for the development of fingerprint systems for browsers.

The solution can be implemented as a plugin for integration into IT systems in order to perform tasks such as advertising tracking, fraud prevention and security analyses. The prospects consist of improving our system by subjecting it to other types of tests and seeing the possibilities of combining artificial intelligence technologies for better efficiency.

Acknowledgments. We would like to warmly thank the Interdisciplinary Center of Excellence in Artificial Intelligence for Development (CITADEL) in Burkina Faso, for its unwavering support throughout this project.

References

1. Brigade centrale de lutte contre la cybercriminalité - BCLCC — ouagadougou. https://fr-fr.facebook.com/bclcc.bf
2. CBR technologies. https://sites.google.com/view/cbr-technologies/accueil
3. World internet users statistics and 2023 world population stats. https://www.internetworldstats.com/stats.htm
4. Boda, K., Földes, Á.M., Gulyás, G.G., Imre, S.: User tracking on the web via cross-browser fingerprinting. In: Laud, P. (ed.) NordSec 2011. LNCS, vol. 7161, pp. 31–46. Springer, Heidelberg (2012). https://doi.org/10.1007/978-3-642-29615-4_4
5. Bujlow, T., Carela-Español, V., Sole-Pareta, J., Barlet-Ros, P.: A survey on web tracking: mechanisms, implications, and defenses. Proc. IEEE **105**(8), 1476–1510 (2017)
6. Cao, Y., Li, S., Wijmans, E.: (cross-) browser fingerprinting via OS and hardware level features. In: Proceedings 2017 Network and Distributed System Security Symposium. Internet Society (2017)
7. Eckersley, P.: How unique is your web browser? In: Atallah, M.J., Hopper, N.J. (eds.) PETS 2010. LNCS, vol. 6205, pp. 1–18. Springer, Heidelberg (2010). https://doi.org/10.1007/978-3-642-14527-8_1
8. Gabryel, M., Grzanek, K., Hayashi, Y.: Browser fingerprint coding methods increasing the effectiveness of user identification in the web traffic. J. Artif. Intell. Soft Comput. Res. **10**(4), 243–253 (2020)
9. Gniniguè, M., Wonyra, K.O., Tchagnao, A.F., Bayale, N.: Participation of developing countries in global value chains: what role for information and communication technologies? Telecommun. Policy **47**(3), 102508 (2023)
10. Kaur, N., Azam, S., Kannoorpatti, K., Yeo, K.C., Shanmugam, B.: Browser fingerprinting as user tracking technology. In: 2017 11th International Conference on Intelligent Systems and Control (ISCO), pp. 103–111. IEEE (2017)
11. Kurniawati, M.A.: Analysis of the impact of information communication technology on economic growth: empirical evidence from Asian countries. J. Asian Bus. Econ. Stud. **29**(1), 2–18 (2022)
12. Laperdrix, P., Bielova, N., Baudry, B., Avoine, G.: Browser fingerprinting: a survey. ACM Trans. Web (TWEB) **14**(2), 1–33 (2020)
13. Lee, V.W.Q., Ooi, S.Y., Pang, Y.H.: Assessing the importance of browser fingerprint attributes towards user profiling through clustering algorithms. In: 2023 IEEE 13th Symposium on Computer Applications and Industrial Electronics (ISCAIE), pp. 326–331. IEEE (2023)
14. Mudassar, M., et al.: An analysis of browser and machine fingerprinting techniques. In: 2023 International Conference on Business Analytics for Technology and Security (ICBATS), pp. 1–8. IEEE (2023)

15. Nair, K.V., RoseLalson, E.: The unique id's you can't delete: browser fingerprints. In: 2018 International Conference on Emerging Trends and Innovations In Engineering And Technological Research (ICETIETR), pp. 1–5. IEEE (2018)
16. Quaglio, G., et al.: Information and communications technologies in low and middle-income countries: survey results on economic development and health. Health Policy Technol. **5**(4), 318–329 (2016)
17. Salomatin, A.A., Iskhakov, A.Y., Iskhakova, A.O.: Web user identification based on browser fingerprints using machine learning methods. IFAC-PapersOnLine **54**(13), 582–587 (2021)
18. Segers, W.: A survey and evaluation of browser fingerprinting techniques (2021)
19. Vastel, A., Laperdrix, P., Rudametkin, W., Rouvoy, R.: Fp-stalker: tracking browser fingerprint evolutions. In: 2018 IEEE Symposium on Security and Privacy (SP), pp. 728–741. IEEE (2018)
20. Zhang, D., et al.: A survey of browser fingerprint research and application. Wirel. Commun. Mob. Comput. **2022** (2022)

Monitoring the Compliance and Response to the COVID-19 Lockdown in South Africa, and Analysing the Impact Thereof

Avuya Shibambu, Nelisiwe Dlamini, Sthembile Mthethwa(✉), Nenekazi Mkuzangwe, Motlatsi Mantsi, and Thato Boateng

Defence and Security, Council for Scientific and Industrial Research, 627 Meiring Naude Road, Pretoria 0001, Republic of South Africa (RSA)
{ashibambu,ndlamini2,smthethwa,nmkuzangwe,amantsi, tboateng}@csir.co.za

Abstract. In 2020, the world was confronted with a global pandemic. The Coronavirus disease (COVID-19) originated in Wuhan City, China, in December 2019. On 5 March 2020, the first case of the virus was confirmed in South Africa (SA). In response, the President of SA announced a national lockdown, prompting efforts to track and monitor public compliance with the newly introduced regulations. This paper examines the impact of COVID-19 in SA, with a focus on the monitoring of non-compliance incidents through online platforms. Data was collected from social media sources and analysed using descriptive and inferential statistics to assess trends in regulatory adherence. Social media users actively participated in online surveillance activities to closely monitor non-adherence to the lockdown regulations and reporting violations of lockdown measures. The findings show that, initially, most of the people disregarded the regulations observed through numerous incidents of non-compliance reported, where the surveilled people were mostly moving around unauthorized and breaking the regulations related to social distancing. Looting and fraud became popular categories during the period of April and May; protests also emerged as many people, especially public healthcare workers, became frustrated over the lack of personal protective equipment (PPE) provided for their safety while working. It was concluded that the government needed to do more to monitor and enforce regulations, as it was evident that there is a correlation between non-adherence to the regulations and the spread of COVID-19.

Keywords: Covid-19 · Lockdown · South Africa

1 Introduction

When a pneumonia broke out in Wuhan City, China, in December 2019, no one knew it was a start of a worldwide pandemic that would drastically change the way we live. On 31 December 2019, the World Health Organization (WHO) was made aware of a series of cases of a Novel Coronavirus infected pneumonia reported in China local hospitals [1]. The outbreak was traced to a local seafood market in Wuhan which sold wild animals; it was consequently closed on 1 January 2020 [2]. The WHO coined a term for this virus, 2019 novel coronavirus (2019-nCoV) – which was later officially named the coronavirus disease 2019 (COVID-19) on 11 February 2020 [3]. The outbreak was recognized as a pandemic by WHO on 11 March 2020 [4]. It is the fifth documented pandemic but first documented COVID-19 pandemic [5]. On 5 March 2020, the first positive case was confirmed in South Africa (SA) by the National Institute for Communicable Diseases (NICD) [6]. The President of SA, Cyril Ramaphosa, stated in his first speech that, "never before in the history of our democracy have, we been confronted by such a severe situation" [7]. For SA, this was the beginning of a unique period for the Government and citizens alike, after a long time.

The index case was a man from Hilton, KwaZulu Natal (KZN), who had travelled to Italy with his wife and 8 others. He had returned on 1 March, and on 3 March reported some symptoms and went to see a private doctor and started self-isolating: the doctor self-isolated as well. On 5 March he was confirmed to have the virus. Not long after that, on the 7th, a woman who was in the same travel group returning to Gauteng Province (GP) had also tested positive for the virus [8]. The people from the group continued to test positive and SA had its first report of confirmed local transmission cases on 17 March [9]. Prior to this, South Africans were watching, from a distance, the mysterious COVID-19 pandemic and how it was quickly killing people in different parts of the world. On 11 February, the death global toll had climbed over the 1000 mark – less than two months after the virus came into the spotlight [10]. It was almost like a tale when cases were reported in SA as many people did not take it seriously. Some went to the lengths of saying it is for a certain race and social class. Because the first case was of a person coming from an international trip, there are people in the lower social class who believed it is for the rich, not knowing that COVID-19 has no respect for race, age, gender and social class.

The SA Government was now in the spotlight. Countries all over the world were announcing lockdowns in efforts to minimize the spread of the virus. On 15 March, President Cyril Ramaphosa, for the first time, declared a National State of Disaster whereby a lot of restrictions had to be put in place to curb the spread of the virus [11]. This caused a lot of commotion as there were a lot of social events that had to be cancelled or postponed. The National Coronavirus Command Council (NCCC) was formed on 17 March with the mandate to "lead the nation's plan to contain the spread and mitigate the negative impact of the coronavirus" [12]. A government gazette was signed on 18 March by the Minister of Cooperative Governance and Traditional Affairs (COGTA), Nkosazana Dlamini Zuma, which outlined several restrictions including limiting the number of patrons at restaurants, pubs and night clubs to 50 [13]. Several parliamentary activities were also suspended; schools and most universities were closed on 18 March. The first Presidential address around COVID-19 in SA was delivered on the 23rd of March where the President, announced a 21-day national lockdown period effective from March 26 to 16 April 2020 [7]. The deployment of the South African National Defense Force (SANDF) to assist the Government in enforcing the lockdown rules was also announced, which introduced the beginning of a unique phase for the Country.

People's movements were to be restricted, for their own good, but it sounded extreme to some that they had to be policed. On 9 April, the lockdown period was extended by the President until the end of April. Only essential workers – were allowed to move around during the prescribed times. The lockdown was further divided into Alert levels with the aim of stimulating the economy in a controlled manner, each phase stating which activities were allowed and prohibited. The Alert levels range from one to five, five being the one with more stringent regulations. With each step down a level; more services, economic sectors, social activities etc., will be allowed to operate. Two main factors contributed to the decision to change alert levels, namely, current infection rate, and how overwhelmed the available health resources were [14]. The lockdown alert levels are as follows:

- Alert level 5 – drastic measures to contain the spread of the virus and save lives.
- Alert level 4 – extreme precautions to limit community transmission and outbreaks, while allowing some activity to resume.
- Alert level 3 – restrictions on many activities, including at workplaces and socially, to address a high risk of transmission.
- Alert level 2 – physical distancing and restrictions on leisure and social activities to prevent a resurgence of the virus.
- Alert level 1 – most normal activity can resume, with precautions and health guidelines. Population prepared for an increase in alert levels if necessary.

It was, therefore, important to monitor the movements and behaviour of people during the first alert level to the third to keep track of the patterns of how people respond to the regulations and to track the correlation between the spread of the virus and people's behaviours. The aim of this paper is to present the findings established from examining the public discourses and emotions shared on various online media platforms about the pandemic and ways people responded to the regulations stipulated to combat the spread of the virus in SA. The trends and patterns that had a direct impact on the safety, security, and stability of the Nation are also highlighted. It is important for the Government to know the effectiveness of the lockdown and how the regulations were responded to by the general public so as to gain insight into the future. This paper may assist a country to have better understanding of certain behaviour that erupts during a time such as a lockdown. Such insight may assist with better planning, monitoring and better distribution of resources to enforce certain regulations that were observed to be broken easily or frequently. It is vital to be cognisant of how people responded during the previous lockdowns and plan accordingly for the future.

The remainder of the paper is structured as follows. Section 2 gives insight on the methods followed to track and monitor nonadherence incidents in SA; Sect. 3 contains the analysis of the different lockdown regulations that were disregarded during the observation period; Sect. 4 gives a discussion on the work that was carried out and the impact of the lockdown on the Country; Sect. 5 provides recommendations based on the findings; Sect. 6 gives limitations to the study; Sect. 7 is the conclusion.

2 Methodology

To track and monitor nonadherence incidents during lockdown, a few methods had to be adopted to have a defined strategy. The process followed was data collection, data verification and data analysis by means of descriptive and inferential statistics. The following subsections provide details of the methods that were adopted.

2.1 Data Collection

For the dataset, the engagement on online media platforms was used as a window into some of the concerns that the public in SA had or concerns about COVID-19 in general and the regulations imposed to fight against the spread of the Coronavirus. The use of social media platforms has made things easier enabling creating and sharing which are two ways that social media can be used as a communication tool in the digital era [15]. Four online media platforms were used for collecting data, namely; news websites, WhatsApp, Twitter and Facebook. In total 347 incidents were reported through these platforms. These sources were chosen because they are reliable (particularly the news websites), and the events were updated as and when they occurred. Arianto and Pui [15] state that currently, Twitter (currently known as X) is one of the familiar social media platforms, and the dataset used clearly shows that people use twitter more as a lot of concerns were posted on this platform (as depicted in Fig. 1), thus it became the main source of data collection. It is worth noting that collecting data via WhatsApp proved to be a challenge as it is a private platform and one can only collect from their inner circle. This is evident through the number of data collected through this platform which is depicted in Fig. 1.

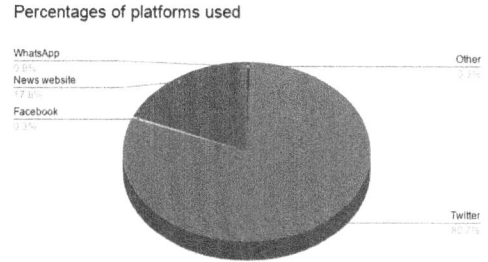

Fig. 1. Percentages of platforms used for data collection.

To collect data on Twitter, a Tweet Sentiment Visualisation tool [16] was used, whereby a list of COVID-19 related hashtags were used as search terms. Various hashtags depicted in Fig. 2 were trending on Twitter and these were constantly changing depending on what was happening at that time. However, some remained constant throughout the process of collecting data. A set of categories had to be established as patterns and were picked up during the process of collecting data. These categories were used to group the nonadherence incidents into meaningful subsets which later aided in analysing the data. These were in line with the stipulated regulations. However, it can be noted that some of the categories did not come directly from the regulations, but certain events led to people not following the stipulated regulations. Thus, from the frequency of these events new categories were classified. The following categories (Table 1) were associated with the regulations:

Fig. 2. Word Cloud about COVID-19 in SA.

Table 1. Categories associated with lockdown regulations.

Category	Regulation [17]
Breaking social distancing	"keep a distance of at least one square meter from each other."
Moving around unauthorized	"every person is confined to his or her place of residence, unless strictly for the purpose of performing an essential service."
Public gathering	"gatherings are prohibited, except for funerals."
Buying of nonessential goods Rendering nonessential services	"selling or buying of non-essential goods is prohibited."
Ignoring safety and health measures	"Hygienic conditions are adhered to."
Place or premises not closed to public	"Places and premises closed to the public, e.g. night clubs."

The following categories were not directly linked to regulations, however, they are included as part of the categories because whilst performing these acts, certain regulations were ignored.

- Crime incidents.
- Fraud – for example; stealing food parcels intended for struggling citizens.
- Looting – people robbing shops or distributing trucks for food, money etc.
- Price hiking – whereby prices went up unexpectedly.

It can be noted that, at a later stage fraud and looting were merged into the category of crime incidents. These were the main categories that came up throughout the process of data collection. However, other categories were identified based on the content of the stories and were included at the end for analysis purposes and these included panic buying, protests, informal trade permits refusal, protective equipment concern, no protective equipment, people exercising in groups, surfing, denial of funeral permits, and permits for doing groceries. The next step of the process was to verify the collected data.

2.2 Data Verification

As the data was sourced mostly from online public domains, in most cases when data is gathered from these sources, one cannot guarantee its quality, correctness and accuracy. Especially since the concerns about the reliability of digital information shared on these platforms are increasing [18]. It was, therefore, mandatory that the collected data undergoes a process of data verification, whereby the various forms of data; such as text, videos and photos collected online, are confirmed to be authentic, uploaded at the time when it was said to be uploaded and not recycled, etc. Without this process, the work done could easily be discredited. The data verification process assisted to ascertain that this data was evidence based. To do this, upon collection, the data was consolidated into a repository and prepared for analysis. The data verifier had to back track to the data sources to check the existence of the data on a per record basis, in some instances this data would not exist. This occurred mostly when the post or news article was deleted. To verify the data, the method depicted in Fig. 3 was followed.

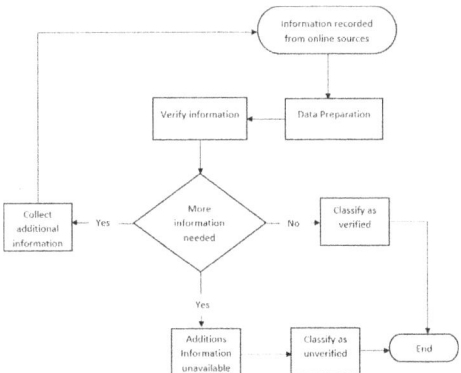

Fig. 3. Data Verification Process.

1. Data Preparation was first applied to identify if there was any missing information pertaining to the gathered data.
2. Provided there was no additional information required for data before verification, a suitable tool was selected depending on the data that had to be verified. For example, on a platform such as Twitter, users shared photos and added captions stating various incidents. To examine the user's activity, Twitter account analysis, as suggested by Africa Check (a fact checking organisation), was used [19]. This tool provides profound details about the Twitter account such as the user's profile date of creation, latest Twitter post, and their historic activity which would be evidence of how long

they have been a user and their activity or identify whether a bot is tweeting. This would help the data verifier to determine the user's intentions before even analysing if the photos and videos were authentic and taken during the lockdown period. Reverse Image search Application Programming Interface (API), such as Google Reverse Image Search was then used to verify digital content such as shared photos, to ascertain that these were not recycled or edited to support the incidents that occurred during this time. These are a few examples of tools that were used in this method to ensure reliable results.
3. Additional information was gathered, if the consolidated data in the repository was insufficient during verification, e.g. when there was no category included for a particular story. However, there were instances where additional information was unavailable and there were no means of verifying that data. This concluded the verification process for that story, and it would be classified as 'could not be verified'.
4. When the data stored in the repository was sufficient and complete, it was classified as 'verified', successfully concluding the verification process for that story.

Following this method ensured that, the data that was classified as verified was accurate. The following sections provides details of the steps that were taken to perform statistical analysis on the stories.

2.3 Statistical Analysis

After data verification, data cleaning was conducted where incidents that could not be verified were removed, etc. After data cleaning, 300 incidents were left, and data analysis was conducted on these incidents. Descriptive statistics were drawn showing the counts of the nonadherence categories of the stories at national, provincial and city/town levels. These counts were used to determine:

- the most occurring nonadherence incidents nationally, provincially and in cities/towns within each province
- the province with the highest nonadherence incidents and
- the cities/towns with the highest nonadherence incidents

It was observed that some stories were included in more than one nonadherence category. Initially, this was handled by counting such a story in the first category it fell into, which resulted in loss of information. At a later stage, it was decided that such a story must be counted in all the categories it fell into to prevent information loss. This resulted in the overall count being higher, but this was better than losing information. The obtained counts were displayed on different graphs. Furthermore, counts of the nonadherence categories of the stories over time at national and provincial levels were determined and displayed using a line graph. The daily counts were observed on a weekly basis and used to depict the behaviour associated with nonadherence during that particular week. Section 3 provides an overview of some of the stories and how they were captured in the graphs.

A chi square test for independence [20] was conducted to determine if there was association between nonadherence and province variables. This test is a non-parametric hypothesis testing for association between two categorical variables. The chi square test was chosen since two categorical variables are analysed. The test is as follows:

Assumptions/Requirements:

1. Two categorical variables.
2. Two or more categories for each variable.
3. Independent observations.
4. The sample must be relatively large, i.e. all expected frequencies must be greater or equal to 1 and 80% of the expected frequencies must be greater or equal to 5.

Hypotheses.
Null Hypothesis (H_0): There is no association between the two variables. Knowing a value for one variable must not enable one to be likely to predict the value of the second variable [21].
Alternative Hypothesis (H_1): There is an association between the two variables Knowing a value for one variable enables one to be likely to predict the value of the second variable [21].

Test Statistics

$$\chi^2 = \sum_{i=1}^{R} \sum_{j=1}^{C} \frac{(o_{ij} - e_{ij})^2}{e_{ij}} \qquad (1)$$

Decision
Reject H_0 if $\chi^2 > \chi^2_{\alpha,\,df}$, otherwise, fail to reject H_0.
where.

- $\chi^2_{\alpha,df}$ is the chi square critical value at a chosen level of significance (α) and degrees of freedom (df = (R 1)(C 1)) which is the number of values in the calculation of a statistics that can vary.
- R is the number of rows (i.e., number of categories of the variable represented by the rows).
- C is the number of columns (i.e., number of categories of the variable represented by the columns).

Conclusion
If H_0 is reject, there is enough statistical evidence to conclude that there is association between the two variables, otherwise, there is not enough statistical evidence to conclude that there is association between the two variables.

3 Analysis

The incidents were observed and recorded from 27 March 2020 up to 29 May 2020. The data collection process stopped because SA was moving to Alert level three in June and the restrictions were eased making it difficult to observe the nonadherence incidents at this level of the lockdown. The following subsections provide an overview of the incidents that were recorded, highlighting the frequency of the occurrences based on different factors, pointing out the top three incidents and showing them in graphical form.

3.1 Trends

The following graphs highlight some of the nonadherence incidents that occurred during the observation period. The most frequent nonadherence categories that the stories fell into were 'breaking social distancing' and 'Moving around unauthorised' respectively. 'Crime incidents' (consists of 'Looting' and 'Fraud') was also prevalent and was identified as third highest. The listed incidents were both merged into one category 'Crime Incidents' to reflect on the overall crime incidents that occurred over the lockdown period. Figure 4 shows that some of the observed residents in SA were moving around unauthorised in the first few weeks of the lockdown. This was partly because it was just unnatural for human beings to be forced to stay at home and so some moved around for no real reason other than being rebellious. On the morning of the first day of lockdown (27 March 2020), people were already breaking the regulations. Jogging was prohibited during the first phase of lockdown, however people were still going for their jogs (mostly witnessed in the suburbs) and some would loiter at nearby malls.

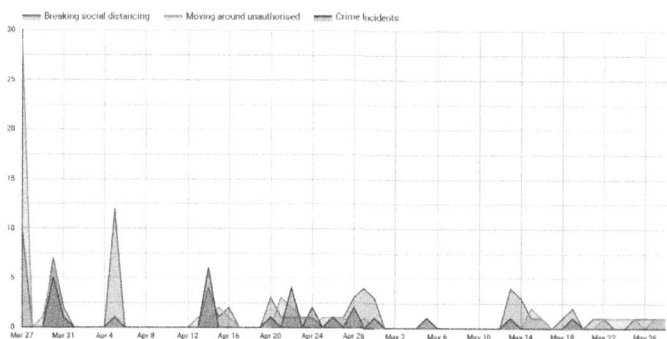

Fig. 4. Prevalent Nonadherence incident categories.

Lockdown was perceived differently in various parts of the country i.e. suburbs, rural and townships. People acted differently, for example, in townships people were going about their businesses as usual. Nothing had changed, to them it seemed like there was no lockdown in place and more importantly, no COVID-19 that they had to protect themselves from (which was reported in various news platforms). The sale and distribution of alcohol was prohibited during Alert level five of the lockdown and so it did not take long for people to start breaking in at liquor outlets, hence the 'Crime Incidents' category depicted in Fig. 4 recorded in the beginning of the lockdown.

The Government started giving out food parcels to curb the poverty that had been exacerbated by the regulations. However, it was observed that this initiative was being tainted with fraudulent activities where parcels did not reach the intended recipients due to corrupt Government officials. At the beginning of May, the Country moved to Alert level four, which meant freedom of movement. Thus, the 'moving around unauthorised' incident, dropped significantly during this period as the regulations were eased, however, people still contravened them.

As time progressed, the recorded incidents declined, due to eased regulations. The following section provides analysis on how the lockdown impacted the Country, in terms of the identified nonadherence incidents and how it generally affected the running of the Country.

3.2 Test of Association Between Nonadherence and Province Variables

Before we conducted the chi square test for independence, we plotted a bar chart to display the number of nonadherence incidents per province. If there is no association between the two variables then the counts for the nonadherence variable categories within each province should be similar or equal, otherwise, there is association [20].

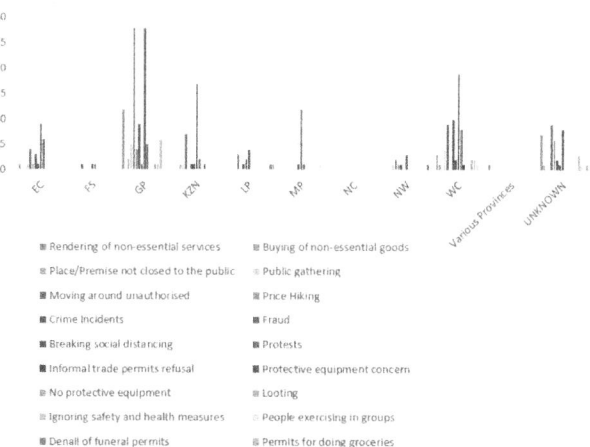

Fig. 5. Number of nonadherence incidents per province.

From Fig. 5, it is evident that the counts of nonadherence categories within each province are not equal, this suggests that there is an association between the two variables. The next step was to check if the test's assumptions were met. The first two assumptions were met since both variables are categorical and have more than two categories. To meet the third assumption of independence of observations, we had to make sure that each story fell in only one category. Therefore, the stories that were classified in more than one nonadherence category, were classified under the first category it appeared in. Some of the categories for both variables were combined to meet the test assumptions:

1. All expected frequencies must be greater or equal to 1.
2. At least 80% of the expected frequencies must be greater or equal to 5.

This resulted to:

1. The Province variable having four categories, namely, Gauteng (GP), Western Cape (WC), Eastern Cape and KwaZulu - Natal (EC & KZN) and other, which is made up of Free State (FS), North West (NW), Various Provinces (VP) and UNKNOWN.
2. The nonadherence variable having six categories, namely, Rendering of nonessential services, Public gathering and Protests, Moving around unauthorised, Price hiking and Crime incidents, Breaking social distancing and Other (included the rest of the categories).

The resulting observation and expected frequencies between the categories of the two variables are tabulated in Tables 2 and 3 respectively.

Table 2. Observed frequencies

Provinces	Rendering of none-essential services	Public gathering and protests	Moving around unauthorised	Price hiking and crime incidents	Breaking social distancing	Other	Total
GP	12	10	28	13	28	11	102
WC	3	12	9	10	19	9	62
EC&KZN	1	10	11	5	26	4	57
Other	8	3	15	11	28	14	79
Total	24	35	63	39	101	38	300

Table 3. Expected frequencies

Provinces	Rendering of nonessential services	Public gathering and protests	Moving around unauthorised	Price hiking and crime incidents	Breaking social distancing	Other	Total
GP	8.16	11.90	21.42	13.26	34.34	12.92	102
WC	4.96	7.23	13.02	8.06	20.87	7.85	62
EC&KZN	4.56	6.65	11.97	7.41	19.19	7.22	57
Other	6.32	9.22	16.59	10.27	26.60	10.01	79
Total	24	35	63	39	101	38	300

The chi squared test statistic, $\chi^2 = 27.25$ and chi squared critical value at $\alpha = 0.05$ and df = 15, $\chi^2_{0.05,15} = 24.99579$. Therefore, since the test statistic is greater than the critical value at at $\alpha = 0.05$ the null hypothesis is rejected and conclude that there is enough statistical evidence to infer that there is association between nonadherence and province. From the results, we can conclude that nonadherence varies with province.

3.3 Impact of the Identified Nonadherence Stories

The lockdown was enforced as a mechanism to slow down the spread of the virus in SA. As 'breaking social distancing' ranked highest when tallying all the incidents from beginning to the end of the observation period as seen in Fig. 6, it was the first one to be analysed. It started off with high numbers in the beginning of the lockdown and dropped as there were a lot of law enforcement agents who were enforcing the rules in public spaces. Certain events led to peaks observed in this category i.e. social grants collection which usually occurs at the beginning of each month. This is where most of the social distancing was broken attributable to very long queues.

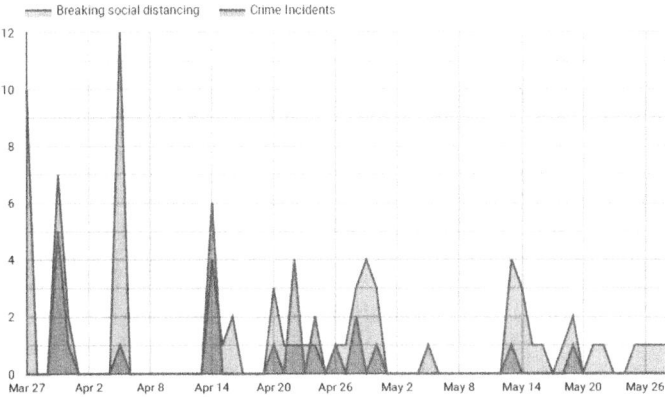

Fig. 6. Overview of the top 2 nonadherence categories.

Different types of crime incidents were recorded throughout the observation period which included looting and fraud. These ranged from those who posed as healthcare workers to deceive South African residents and rob them, to some robbing ambulances. A unique one was that of a lady that wrote an email saying she had intentionally gone to a shop knowing she had tested positive for COVID-19. As much as in her email she was apologising and practicing honesty, what she did was considered illegal [22]. Looting became very prominent, and this ranged from looting shops (to steal food in cases where they could not afford to buy it), to even stoning and looting trucks delivering food stock to supermarkets.

The last category under crime incidents is fraud, which involved certain Government officials distributing food parcels meant for South African citizens to their loved ones only. Other officials required citizens to make payments prior to receiving these parcels, some took the food for themselves and some of the food items ended up on shelves of some shops. From the three most frequent categories, we can see the impact posed by them. However, these are not the only categories that were observed. Twenty categories were identified as depicted in Fig. 7. An analysis was performed to highlight how the areas with higher recorded incidents were affected by the virus. Looking at these incidents, most, if not all, encouraged the spread of the virus as there were always large numbers of people with no social distancing.

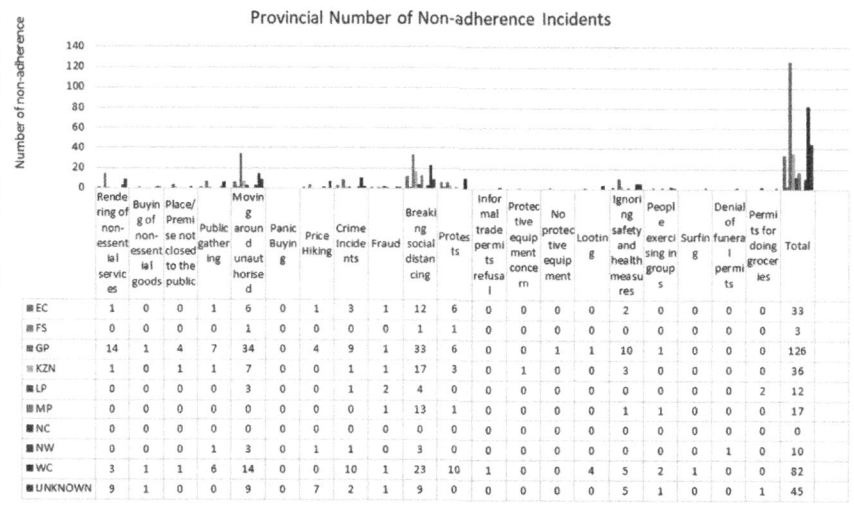

Fig. 7. Provincial number of nonadherence incidents.

Around 29 May 2020, the Coronavirus statistics portrayed that the Western Cape (WC) had the highest number of confirmed cases at 17754, followed by Gauteng Province (GP) with 3329 and the Eastern Cape (EC) which had 3306. This supported the conclusion that, the virus spreads more in places where there are more incidents occurring [23]. Figure 7 shows which of the nine provinces in SA had recorded incidents. With the 20 categories recorded, some incidents could not be allocated to a province because some of these incidents did not have location details. According to Fig. 7, these three provinces also appeared in the top four provinces that had the highest number of recorded nonadherence incidents. GP was leading by 126 overall incidents, followed by WC with 82, KZN with 36, followed closely by the EC with 33 overall recorded incidents. Where 'Breaking social distancing' was the top nonadherence incident in all four provinces. The following subsection describes the impact that was caused by the lockdown on different sectors in the Country.

3.4 Impact of the National Lockdown on Various Sectors

The lockdown had a general impact on the country as a whole and not just in reference to the regulations that were passed. Several sectors were affected by some of the regulations and below are some of the identified sectors in SA that were negatively affected during this period.

Economic Sector

The national lockdown has had a damaging effect on the South African economy. According to the Southern Africa-Towards Inclusive Economic Development (SA-TIED) [24], the lockdown caused many nonessential markets to be closed, leaving only a few essential markets open, such as food, electricity, water, healthcare services, etc. The Gross Domestic Product (GDP) dropped by 34% overall, which had a ripple effect on the overall wages, which dropped to 30% [24]. This caused the economy to be in shock and even the essential sectors had a decline of between 10–30% indirectly because of the reduction in economic activities [24]. The international exports were not affected much, but a decline of 60% or more was recorded in sectors such as tobacco, alcohol, tourism, steel manufacturing, etc. [24]. A R200 billion loan was introduced by the President shortly after the lockdown was announced [25]. This loan was used to mitigate the impact the lockdown would have on the small and medium business owners that were financially distressed [25]. This was also to assist with preparing the healthcare system for the pandemic.

Education Sector

To assist in reducing the spread of the virus, many educational facilities remained closed and announced the extension of vacation time. Schools were scheduled to reopen in phases with the grade 12 s going back on the 1st of June. The other grades would then follow [24]. With the revised schedule of reopening schools, the learners would have lost between 25%-57% of normal school depending on the grade of the learner, especially with school resuming from 7 August 2020 [24]. This was going to affect the learning and cognitive growth of most learners, especially those in lower grades as they were the most affected [24]. For schools to be reopened, basic measures had to be followed and several schools were exposed to inadequate supply of running water. More than 100 schools in KZN could not open due to this [26]. The Government tried to mitigate the problem by providing water, which did not completely solve this problem as some schools opened but they still did not have water [27].

Most higher learning facilities were also closed, but they turned to online learning as the students are deemed to be responsible enough to keep up with this new learning system. Lecturers were conducted virtually, and students could write tests and submit assignments online, which had a positive effect as most courses continued [28]. Despite this, challenges had emerged and required addressing. This includes ensuring that all students had the required resources such as laptops and internet to access classes and putting security measures in place to curb cheating during online tests [28]. The universities contributed by offering students data bundles according to the students' needs. The National Student Financial Aid Scheme (NSFAS) was able to provide laptops to students that needed them [29].

Health Sector

One of the main reasons why the lockdown was implemented was to give the healthcare sector time to best prepare for an upsurge in cases. The healthcare system was struggling to offer primary healthcare for serious illnesses such as Tuberculosis (TB) and the Human Immunodeficiency Virus (HIV) infected patients, as the COVID-19 spread worsened, creating an imbalance in this sector [30]. There were shortages in staff and facilities for isolation purposes, there was also a need for PPE [30]. According to the Investec Focus report [30], the lockdown was the best way to curb the rise in infections by 2 million.

4 Recommendations

Tracking and monitoring nonadherence incidents during the lockdown in SA assisted in identifying the regulations that were not adhered to, as far as the recorded incidents gave insight. This yielded recommendations that may assist government entities to better enforce the regulations for better management of the spread of the virus. This may be applied in different situations where a lockdown is enforced. This paper recommends that:

- More effort should be placed in monitoring the movement of everyone during a hard lockdown. The deployment of law enforcement should not focus on certain areas, as it was observed that people move around unauthorised regardless of the area they live in [31].
- There should be visible law enforcement in areas where people will be forming long queues, e.g. social grant collection points, so that people do not break social distancing.
- Entities providing products and services should be monitored by law enforcement to ensure that lockdown regulations are enforced.
- The distribution of food parcels should be governed by a strategic plan so that government officials do not misuse their power and leave the poor to fend for themselves. This will help ensure that the food parcels reach the intended recipients.
- Areas which have been identified as hotspots for crime during a lockdown should be closely monitored by law enforcement so that it is difficult for people to resort to crime during such a time.
- There should be more effort done to educate the public. The little knowledge about the virus and enforced regulations in communities such as rural areas and townships was, very concerning. There is a definite need for innovative and effective communication strategies, to be developed and used to enable the continuous dissemination of information to these communities.
- The economy participants, such as industry, should be included in decision making and given an opportunity to contribute to the strategy handling the pandemic crisis not just the Government.
- A strategy favouring SA's healthcare sector, should be developed, now that the shortcomings that exist in it have been identified. An action plan for the healthcare service preparedness, in all provinces, needs to be implemented.
- A strategy that favors SA's educational sector, should be devised. Many vulnerabilities have been uncovered in this sector such as the unpreparedness of schools to handle this crisis. However, should there be a similar crisis in future, the government needs to have standards in place to ensure that; learners and teachers are sufficiently prepared to deal with the changes and adapt to technology. Infrastructure that meets the current

learning requirements is a necessity. These standards should be streamlined to enable the adjustment in the advancement of the digital age.

5 Limitations

In conducting this study, a few limitations were encountered. One of the limitations was the incomplete representation of the populace, i.e. in terms of rural areas there were not a lot of reports as most people from these areas are not active on social media. The focus was directed mostly towards social media platforms particularly Twitter, due to its richness of information through various discourses. Research shows that SA has a 60% internet penetration and 36% of the population on any type of social media [32]. If the focus is on Twitter, SA has just over 2.3 million users on Twitter [32], out of an estimated total population of 59.62 million [33]. Therefore, only a portion of that data could be gathered. This number also includes people that posted the same story differently and could also be found in other platforms such as Facebook, WhatsApp, and the data collectors had to sift through those to ensure uniqueness in the stories or data. Despite this, adequate results for this study could still be drawn. Also, although social media is known to be very useful when gathering information about popular and concerning topics [34], the users of this network are also likely to delete their posts which leads to loss of evidence even if the post was available when data was collected. Once the user deletes the post, certain ethical standards should be adhered to. Fiesler and Proferes [35] recommended that deleted content should not be used in a research study as their findings indicated a high level of discomfort when the respondents expressed their views on this topic. This is also explicitly stated in the Twitter Developer's Agreement [36]. Depending on the relevance of this information, this was mitigated by searching for similar information that exist on other online platforms.

Finally, readily available tools and methods were used to collect, analyse and verify data discussed in Sects. 2.1 and 2.2, due to the urgency of the study. Nonetheless, for further research additional data collection and analysis tools will be employed since considerable insights have been gained.

6 Conclusion

Within the timeframe of this work, the researchers investigated the people's communication via social media platforms during the period of the global pandemic COVID-19 in SA. The Government took measures and introduced lockdown regulations to curb the spread of the virus as well as ensure that the health sector is well prepared. Thus, for this study the aim was to monitor, via online media platforms, how SA residents responded to these regulations. Platforms like Facebook, WhatsApp, Twitter, and news websites were used to collect data for this study. Twitter later proved to be the best platform to use for collecting data as events were added as soon as they occurred. As a first contribution, a dataset of nonadherence events or stories was collected and pre-processed (verified) to analyse and highlight useful insights or trends. As a second contribution, the dataset was analysed to yield descriptive and inferential statistics. From the analysis, it can be observed that trends in topics changed throughout the timeframe of collecting data and other topics remained for the duration of the work. These trends were caused by the change in lockdown alert levels which introduced new regulations or eased some of the regulations.

A detailed analysis of the study was presented along with recommendations that could be employed in the future if the need arises. With that, the researchers are aware of limitations experienced during the timeframe of this study and these have been discussed in detail. The study shows that social media, especially Twitter, can be leveraged for information by studying the evolving public discussions and sentiments during times like the COVID-19 pandemic. Realtime monitoring and analysis of these discussions and concerns can be used for addressing challenges in different governmental departments and coming up with solutions for the future. Reacting to real concerns from the public can enhance trust between the governmental departments and the public, as well as prepare for future emergencies. For future work, the researchers plan to explore data mining techniques for the purposes of improving data collection and analysis.

References

1. Li, Q., et al.: Early transmission dynamics in Wuhan, China, of novel coronavirus–infected pneumonia. N. Engl. J. Med. **382**(13), 1199–1207 (2020)
2. Chauhan, S.: Comprehensive review of coronavirus disease 2019 (COVID-19). Biomed. J. **43**(4), 334–340 (2020)
3. WHO Director-General's remarks at the media briefing on 2019-nCoV on 11 February 2020. https://www.who.int/dg/speeches/detail/who-director-general-s-remarks-at-the-media-briefing-on-2019-ncov-on-11-february-2020. Accessed 14 Sept 2020
4. WHO Director-General's opening remarks at the media briefing on COVID-19. https://www.who.int/dg/speeches/detail/who-director-general-s-opening-remarks-at-the-media-briefing-on-covid-19. Accessed 10 Sept 2020
5. Liu, Y.C., Kuo, R.L., Shih, S.R.: COVID-19: the first documented coronavirus pandemic in history. Biomed. J. **43**(4), 328–333 (2020)
6. FIRST CASE OF COVID-19 CORONAVIRUS REPORTED IN SA. https://www.nicd.ac.za/first-case-of-covid-19-coronavirus-reported-in-sa. Accessed 30 July 2020
7. A ticking time bomb': Scientists worry about coronavirus spread in Africa. https://www.sciencemag.org/news/2020/03/ticking-time-bomb-scientists-worry-about-coronavirus-spread-africa
8. Update on Covid-19, 28th May 2020. https://sacoronavirus.co.za/2020/05/29/update-on-covid-19-28th-may-2020/
9. Statement by President Cyril Ramaphosa on measures to combat COVID-19 epidemic, http://www.thepresidency.gov.za/press-statements/statement-president-cyril-ramaphosa-measures-combat-covid-19-epidemic
10. Global novel coronavirus death toll reaches 1,383 as China purges officials in Hubei. https://edition.cnn.com/2020/02/14/asia/coronavirus-covid-19-update-intl-hnk/index.html. Accessed 08 Sept 2020
11. President Cyril Ramaphosa: Measures to combat Coronavirus COVID-19 epidemic. https://www.gov.za/speeches/statement-president-cyril-ramaphosa-measures-combat-covid-19-epidemic-15-mar-2020-0000
12. President Cyril Ramaphosa meets with political parties to combat Coronavirus COVID-19. https://www.gov.za/speeches/president-cyril-ramaphosa-meets-political-parties-combat-coronavirus-covid-19-18-mar-18-mar

13. Department of Basic Education, Government Gazette Staatskoerant, Gov. Gaz., **583**(37230), 1–4 (2014)
14. About alert system. https://www.gov.za/covid-19/about/about-alert-system. Accessed 16 Sept 2020
15. Social Media Analysis: Utilization of Social Media Data for research on COVID-19. https://www.researchgate.net/publication/340511574
16. Sentiment Viz: Tweet Sentiment Visualization. https://www.csc2.ncsu.edu/faculty/healey/tweet_viz/tweet_app/. Accessed 02 Sept 2020
17. Republic of South Africa: Disaster Management Act (57/2002): regulations made in terms of section 27(2) by the minister of cooperative governance and traditional affairs. Ment. Health Care **480**(43258), 3–36 (2020)
18. Schifferes, S., Newman, N., Thurman, N., Corney, D., Göker, A., Martin, C.: Identifying and verifying news through social media: developing a user-centred tool for professional journalists. In: The Future of Journalism: In an Age of Digital Media and Economic Uncertainty, pp. 325–336
19. GUIDE: How to verify a Twitter account. https://africacheck.org/factsheets/guide-verify-twitter-account/. Accessed 30 July 2020
20. SPSS TUTORIALS:CHI-SQUARETEST OF INDEPENDENCE. https://libguides.library.kent.edu/spss/chisquare. Accessed 01 July 2021
21. Chi-Square Test of Independence and an Example. https://statisticsbyjim.com/hypothesis-testing/chi-square-test-independence-example/. Accessed 28 June 2021
22. Joburg pet shop closed after customer claims to have visited store after testing positive for Covid-19. https://www.iol.co.za/news/south-africa/gauteng/joburg-pet-shop-closed-after-customer-claims-to-have-visited-store-after-testing-positive-for-covid-19-45859492. Accessed 09 Aug 2020
23. Minister Zweli Mkhize confirms second case of Coronavirus Covid-19 in South Africa. https://www.gov.za/speeches/minister-zweli-mkhize-confirms-second-case-covid-19-south-africa-7-mar-2020-0000
24. Impact of Covid-19 on the South African economy: An initial analysis | IFPRI: International Food Policy Research Institute. https://www.ifpri.org/publication/impact-covid-19-south-african-economy-initial-analysis
25. South Africa extends COVID-19 loans for struggling businesses. https://www.reuters.com/article/us-health-coronavirus-safrica-loans/south-africa-extends-covid-19-loans-for-struggling-businesses-idUSKCN24R09T. Accessed 28 Aug 2020
26. More than 100 KZN schools still closed due to water shortages. https://www.news24.com/news24/southafrica/news/more-than-100-kzn-schools-still-closed-due-to-water-shortages-20200608. Accessed 28 Aug 2020
27. Schools have tanks – but no water. https://mg.co.za/education/2020-06-26-schools-have-tanks-but-no-water/. Accessed 28 Aug 2020
28. Covid-19 and South African universities: A raft of problems to ponder. https://www.dailymaverick.co.za/opinionista/2020-04-09-covid-19-and-south-african-universities-a-raft-of-problems-to-ponder/. Accessed 28 Aug 2020
29. Covid-19 financial impact on SA universities stands at over R3.8bn. https://www.iol.co.za/news/politics/covid-19-financial-impact-on-sa-universities-stands-at-over-r38bn--f41d76f5-27d0-4071-9c6e-f725cfe0e861. Accessed 28 Aug 2020
30. Is SA's healthcare system prepared for Covid-19? https://www.investec.com/en_za/focus/beyond-wealth/is-south-africas-healthcare-system-prepared-for-covid-19.html. Accessed 03 Sept 2020
31. No army back-up for city. https://www.news24.com/witness/news/no-army-back-up-for-city-20200331. Accessed 05 April 2021

32. DIGITAL 2020: 3.8 BILLION PEOPLE USE SOCIAL MEDIA, Digital 2020 Global Overview Report (2020)
33. Statistics, S.A.: Mid-year population estimates 2020, no. 8–9 (2020)
34. Ghosh, S., et al.: Temporal topic modeling to assess associations between news trends and infectious disease outbreaks, Sci. Rep. **7**(1), 40841 (2017)
35. Fiesler, C., and Proferes, N.: "Participant" perceptions of Twitter research ethics. Social Media + Society **4**(1), 2056305118763366 (2018)
36. Developer Agreement and Policy. https://developer.twitter.com/en/developer-terms/agreement-and-policy

Regression Model-Based Energy Prediction Approach for IoT Oriented System

Khanyisile Mkhonza[1(✉)], Sizakele Mathaba[2], and Adigun Mathew[3]

[1] University of Zululand, Durban 4001, Republic of South Africa (RSA)
khaxmkho@gmail.com
[2] University of Zululand, Empangeni, Republic of South Africa (RSA)
[3] University of Zululand, 4 Anthony Crescent, Empangeni, Republic of South Africa (RSA)

Abstract. The increasing use of renewable energy sources has presented challenges for energy management in IoT-based systems. Efficient energy management is essential for enhancing overall system performance. Machine learning techniques, such as Load Forecasting (LF), are increasingly applied to predict and regulate energy consumption. However, many existing methods fail to adequately address prediction errors and accuracy in short-term intervals. To bridge this gap, a study aims to develop a Regression model and compare its performance with Gated Recurrent Unit (GRU) and Long Short-Term Memory (LSTM) algorithms.

The proposed model is designed to forecast energy consumption for the upcoming day and week, utilizing historical data from the Moroccan buildings' electricity consumption dataset (MORED) dataset. Experimental evaluations on Hourly Energy Prediction (HEP) and Weekly Energy Prediction (WEP) tasks show the superior performance of the proposed Regression model compared to recent deep learning models. The results include HEP evaluations with a rootmean-square error (RMSE) of 0.603, MSE of 0.364, MAE of 0.5091, MAPE of 13.60%, and an accuracy of 86.40%. For WEP evaluations, the RMSE was 0.071, MSE was 0.0052, MAE was 0.0657, MAPE was 1.60%, and the accuracy was 98.40%. The study recommends this model for real-time datasets in Africa.

Keywords: load forecasting · energy inefficiency · and Machine Learning

1 Introduction

This study focuses on leveraging regression models to forecast energy consumption within systems integrated with the Internet of Things (IoT). As IoT devices become increasingly prevalent in smart homes, industrial facilities, and other connected environments, there is a growing need for accurate and efficient energy management solutions. By utilizing regression models, this approach aims to predict energy usage patterns based on data collected from IoT sensors, ensuring optimized energy consumption, cost reduction, and enhanced system performance.

In such systems, large volumes of data are continuously generated by IoT devices, encompassing various parameters such as temperature, humidity, occupancy, and appliance usage. Regression models, being highly effective for numerical prediction, can be applied to this data to create reliable energy forecasts. This predictive capability not only supports real-time energy monitoring but also enables proactive decisions for energy conservation, reducing operational costs and enhancing the sustainability of IoT-based infrastructures.

Due to the tremendous increase in urbanization in the past years, it is necessary to employ smart, energy-efficient, and sustainable solutions for customers. IoT-Based systems must be able to utilize energy efficiently and handle all challenges [2]. To perform any manufacturing, inhabiting a building requires energy consumption. A comprehensive intelligent energy management system triggers minimizing costs, improved stability, reduced CO_2 emission, and improved energy consumption [4].

Forecasting accuracy is of great significance for a utility company's operational and managerial loading. Inefficient load forecasting happens if energy prices fluctuate, inadequate energy generation, and climate change. Conducting research that can design a machine learning model for efficient forecasting of short-term energy consumption can bridge a gap of inefficient energy consumption in IoT-based systems.

Smart cities are facing the challenge of developing an accurate and reliable load forecasting approach for a variety of load data including industrial, commercial, and residential data sectors [2]. The existing LF methods are inadequately investigated and provided in IoT-edge computing scenarios. Investigating more LF methods can significantly enable the effective interaction between communicating devices through IoT Networks for energy consumption.

This research recommends an intelligent LF model that will predict the future energy consumption of smart cities in South Africa using a regression model. The study will use MORED historical data to predict future energy consumption. The model will address the issue of loss of power and accuracy to ensure reliable future energy consumption prediction for short-term intervals.

2 Related Work

The study [8] intends to provide an optimal machine learning regression model that will perform the context of energy load forecasting for the short-term horizon. The proposed work will implement important features such as pre-processing techniques and decision-making methods to deal with any nature of energy consumption data [2]. A historical dataset will be used to train a robust regression model to predict future short-term energy predictions. This model is also intended to be compared with the benchmark models to validate the performance of the model.

As stated in [11], the accuracy of prediction in load forecasting is highly dependent on smart grid capacity and characteristics. The literature also revealed that data-driven models for energy pricing prediction assist decision-making in energy-providing companies. Nowadays, the large amount of data available from smart grids has also led to an increase in artificial intelligence methods as compared to traditional methods.

The micro-grids, smart grids, and buildings have gained much attention in shortterm load forecasting. Short-term energy load forecasting plays a significant role in energy management, energy storage operation, shortage risk reduction, and loss of power [14]. Exponential smoothing and Autoregressive models have proven to be the baseline of time series prediction for several years. Moreover, the models have driven deliberate election slacken input variables to identify validly.

An Adaption Autoregressive Moving Average (ARMA) model developed by Chen et al. [12] to predict day-to-day ahead of the work reported a superior performance when compared with the Boost model. It was observed that these time series approaches suffer from accuracy dropping and require frequent model training. Noticeably Artificial neural networks ANN has been widely used in various energy forecasting because of its quality of non-linearity [4]. Machine learning performs better than traditional time series and regression approaches. It is very imperative to improve the energy forecasting model while ensuring high accuracy and prediction stability. Our claim concludes that an optimal machine model produces more accurate predictions as compared to those with shallow structures [13].

The intelligent techniques involving load forecasting play a significant role in reducing energy crises and loss of power. These methods include a deep learning based sequential mechanism such as Long-short term memory (LSTM). LSTM is a type of recurrent neural network (RNN) that is commonly used for many computational domains such as video analytics, etc. [7]. Deep learning also has a hybrid approach incorporating fuzzy neural inference systems in genetic algorithms using spatial and temporal features assimilated for housing energy prediction [8].

The prominent challenge there is to find an exactness in forecasting accurately and the algorithm is also not implemented over the edge nodes [9, 10]. Intelligent forecasting can handle the energy demand fluctuating from energy producers and customers by providing a common platform for effective communication. The literature has also revealed that the higher the rate of errors in energy prediction the higher the loss of power in smart grids. In response to that it will be wise enough to propose a model that will minimize the error rate in load forecasting.

The Literature has revealed that energy load forecasting is one of the most complicated studies for both engineers and academicians and is still an ongoing area of research. The literature has also revealed that there are not enough studies on energy forecasting in African countries, and it is still an ongoing area of interest for researchers. The research will use historical energy consumption data to predict future energy consumption.

3 Case Study

The data accomplishment campaign was conducted from 2019 to 2020 during the summer and winter seasons. The data collection was based on the Moroccan country in different cities and the data samples were reflecting energy consumption. The participating residents gathered preliminary to attain data. Moreover, invisibility/obscurity was maintained in all collected samples to protect the resident's rights to privacy. It was observed that all Moroccan households are served 220 V̇ 50 Hz two-wire single-phase power circuits except affluent neighbourhoods since they are served with a three-phase voltage supply.

Morocco is still a growing country with a great portion of individuals purchasing low power. However, high-energy-consuming loads such as air conditioners, geysers, etc., especially the ones used by affluent households. Electricity load patterns and load types highly depend on socio-economic status. The MORED dataset has been categorized by considering the size, type, and location of the premises. MORED.

Dataset has also taken into consideration the apartments from affluent and disadvantaged households. We call these chosen samples Whole Premise (WP) and it was collected from 13 households. The Data samples consist of the following input variables: power (P), Voltage (V), and duration (t).

3.1 Motivation of the Study

Accuracy and reliability in the load forecasting approach face a challenge in Smart cities for a variety of load data including industrial, commercial, and residential data sectors. Accuracy and reliability will go a long way to increase efficiency by maximizing the planning process of power-generating industries. A deep learning model was proposed for intelligent energy management to predict future energy consumption for short-term intervals [1–3]. Energy prediction is aimed at enabling electricity distributors, suppliers, and generators to prepare effectively ahead.

It also promotes energy conservation among customers. However, the existing works have not considered error rates, prediction confidence, and accuracy for shortterm intervals. These factors can cause unreliable and inaccurate future energy consumption predictions. Having unreliable energy prediction can lead to high excessive energy distribution from the smart grid.

Error rates and term intervals are factors that can affect the accuracy of energy prediction. Therefore, this research will introduce a machine learning load forecasting model that will address the error rates and accuracy for short-term intervals. This study will introduce a machine learning model that will predict short-term future energy consumption using historical household energy consumption data stored from smart grids. Smart meters are used in IoT networks to allow the execution of efficient responses to energy requests.

Regression Model-Based Energy Prediction Approach

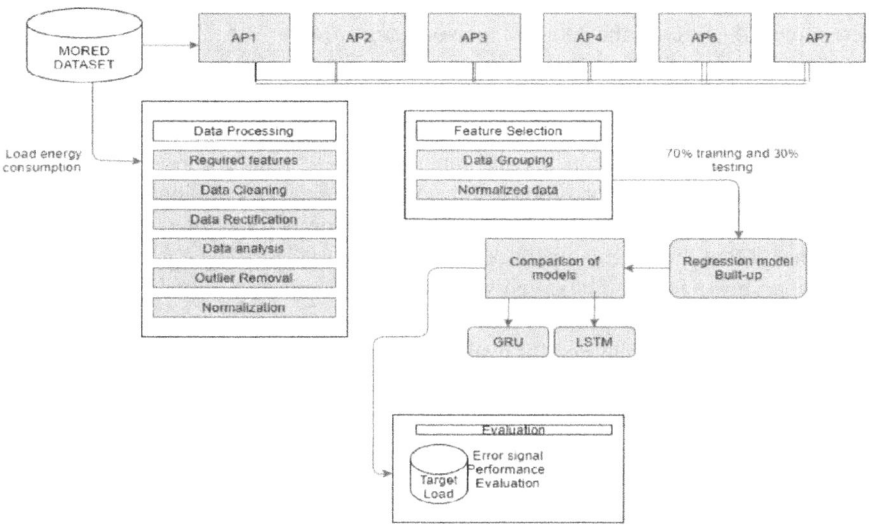

Fig. 1. An Intelligent Prediction Framework

3.2 Designed Model

In our methodology design, we have 3 sections (see Fig. 1) Data Processing, feature selection, and Evaluation. In this study, we have collected a MORED Dataset that has the recordings of 6 apartments with the energy consumption readings collected from smart meters. After collecting the dataset, we had to undergo data processing in preparation of our data for evaluation. After processing we have to undergo feature selection to ensure we meet the research goal. Lastly, we will evaluate the results by comparing our model and the other two models named GRU and LSTM.

The Framework shown in Fig. 1 has different components named as Dataset called MORED dataset. MORED dataset consists of 6 Apartments named as AP1, AP2, AP3, AP4, AP6 and AP7 (See Fig. 1). AP1, AP2, AP3, and AP4 were taken from disadvantaged households, and AP6 and AP7 were taken from affluent households. The MORED dataset has energy consumption readings taken from each apartment. The following architecture is also extended into three sections as Data Processing, Feature Selection, and Evaluation.

Data Processing

This section consists of the following sub-components named as required features, data cleaning, data rectification, data analysis, outlier removal, and normalization. Data processing is responsible for preparing MORED raw data and making it usable for the linear regression model. The significance of using this stage is to clean data, read data, and present data in a formatted way. To apply data preparation, we use Pandas.

This section serves as a preparation stage (see Sect. 6). All features and variables were populated using Jupyter Notebook. This section is responsible for data reading to observe all the variables to be used to satisfy the aim of the study. Statistical analysis was done to check the relationship of the variables between the variables. The outliers were removed to rectify the data and to avoid data noise.

Feature Selection

Feature selection consists of two sub-components: data grouping and normalized data. This stage is crucial for reducing the input variables to those most suitable for the regression model used in load forecasting. At this point, relevant features, such as the duration (the time taken to record energy consumption per apartment), were selected. It was noted that the timestamps were measured in seconds. Data grouping was then applied (as shown in Fig. 1) to align with the study's objective, organizing the data by weekly, hourly, daily, and monthly load demands.

After selecting the features for evaluation, the data samples were split, with 70% allocated for training and 30% for testing the regression model. The model is ultimately designed to predict future load demands. The evaluation section will assess and validate the model's effectiveness. The model's performance will be measured in terms of accuracy and error rates. Finally, the computed results will be compared with those obtained from two existing machine learning models, specifically the GRU and LSTM models.

4 Correlation Analysis and Data Preparation

The procedures used for data preparation in predictive models are common, especially in the preparation stage. To initiate the preparation, it must be indicated in the variables selection by separating both independent and dependent variables. The chosen data for this study are numeric. All outliers were identified from the dataset using a machine-learning method called Dixion's Q test. Dixion's Q test has two assumptions.

The first one assumes that all variables are taken from the same population, and the alternative assumption says that the biggest and smallest variables are considered to be outliers at a 0.1% significant level. For single linear regression, this stage was applied to contemplate mainly the predictors that are strictly at 95% confidence. A descriptive analysis must be obtained especially the coefficient of skewness (CS). When the CS ranges from −0.5 to 0.5, this clarifies that the data values are relatively symmetric. Table 1 below outlines the full descriptions of the data samples taken from the WP of the MORED.

Table 1. Data Acronyms

Variables	Description
Estimated Hourly Load Consumed (EHLC)	The estimated hourly energy for different Apartments (Kw)
Estimated Weekly Load Consumed (EWLC)	The estimated weekly energy for different Apartments (Kw)

(*continued*)

Table 1. (*continued*)

Variables	Description
PML	Previous month's load for Apartments (Kw)
PWL	Previous week's load for Apartments (Kw)
PDL	Previous day's load for Apartments (Kw)
P24Hr	Power Consumed for 24 h (Kw)
Duration	Time taken to record energy consumption (s)

5 Applied Model

Linear Regression algorithm is one of the best algorithms to be used to design the regression model. This algorithm is used to check the relationship between the variables it is also used for univariable linear regression analysis to fit linear equations in a given data. If data consists of more than one variable, then it applies multiple linear regression (MLR). MLR keeps one constant value from one of the predictor values. There is an association between two variables meaning that the relationship between the response variable and predictor variable does not significantly imply that the predictor produces a response variable. Two linear regression algorithms are depending on the complexity of the data.

The chosen SLR model permits an automatic assessment of a household's energy loads. The benefit of using this model is to minimize the amount of input data compared with the physical model, it avoids tedious work, and no powerful informatics equipment is required. The equation of the simple linear regression is presented as follows.

$$Z = P0 + XP1 + e \tag{1}$$

Where Z is a response value, X is a predictor value, P is a regression coefficient or parameter, and e is an error to measure the divergence between predicted data from Eq. 1 and actual data. The equation for the predicted value is derived from Eq. 1 as presented below.

$$Z = P0 + XP1 \tag{2}$$

Where $Z^\wedge$ is the predicted value or computed value $P^\wedge$ is an estimated regression coefficient. The difference between fitted and predicted values is that the fitted value occurs in predictor variables corresponding to N observation from observed data but the predictor value is taken from any predictor value different from observed data.

$$in \sum_{i=1}^{N1} (yi - \sum_{j=1}^{N2} xijPj - P0)^2 \tag{3}$$

This Model uses the least square method aimed to minimize the sum of the least square errors (see Eq. 3.) between actual and predicted energy loads.

This study will examine the following statistical errors:

$$MAE = \sum_{i=1}^{N} |xi - yi|^2 \tag{4}$$

Mean Absolute Error denotes the mean significance of the forecasting errors deprived of the respective directions and is computed as the average of the absolute divergence between predicted and real values. Helps in assessing how close the predicted energy consumption is to actual usage. A lower MAE indicates better model performance.

$$MSE = \sum_{i=1}^{N} (xi - yi)^2 \tag{5}$$

Mean Square Error represents the average squared variation between the expected and the real values.

$$RMSE = \sqrt{\frac{1}{N} \sum_{i=1}^{N} (xi - yi)^2} \tag{6}$$

The root MSE (RMSE) represented in Eq. 6 measures the standard deviation corresponding to forecasting errors and is frequently applied in prediction/regression analysis. Particularly useful when large deviations in energy consumption (such as spikes or extreme values) are critical to the prediction. It is more sensitive to outliers, highlighting any large deviations from actual consumption.

$$MAPE = \sum_{i=1}^{N} \frac{1}{N} \frac{|xi - yi|}{xi} \tag{7}$$

The Mean absolute percentage error (MAPE) represented in Eq. 7 calculates the prediction accuracy of the model as expressed in percentages.

The mathematics equations mentioned above named MAPE, MAE, RMSE, and MSE permit us to compare the discrepancies between the actual and predicted energy load of the households. The last three are based on absolute errors so it's impossible to find the best fit of the model but the smaller the values of the errors the more it resembles the effectiveness of the model. MAPE is more significant compared to the one mentioned above [15]. Statistical metrics play a crucial role in the prediction of energy consumption by enhancing the accuracy, efficiency, and reliability of forecasts. Accurate predictions are essential for optimizing energy use, minimizing waste, and planning for future demand, allowing analysts to fine-tune models and select the best-performing algorithms.

Reliable energy forecasts also empower businesses, governments, and utility providers to make informed, data-driven decisions regarding infrastructure investments, energy purchasing, and sustainability efforts [15]. Furthermore, precise predictions contribute to cost efficiency by ensuring that energy supply aligns with demand, avoiding both over-provisioning and under-provisioning of resources. They also support demand-response management by forecasting peak usage times, which aids in better grid management and reduces strain during periods of high demand. Ultimately, these accurate predictions help design energy-efficient systems, reduce consumption, and lower carbon emissions, promoting environmental sustainability.

6 The Experiments

The growing adoption of renewable energy sources has introduced significant challenges for managing energy in IoT-based systems. Effective energy management is crucial for optimizing overall system performance. Machine learning techniques, such as Load Forecasting (LF), are increasingly employed to predict and manage energy consumption. However, many existing approaches do not sufficiently address prediction errors or accuracy in short-term intervals. In response to this issue, a study has been conducted to develop a Regression model and assess its performance in comparison with Gated Recurrent Unit (GRU) and Long Short-Term Memory (LSTM) algorithms.

The proposed model is intended to predict energy consumption for the following day and week, based on historical data from the MORED dataset. Experimental assessments conducted for both Hourly Energy Prediction (HEP) and Weekly Energy Prediction (WEP) tasks have demonstrated the superiority of the Regression model over recent deep-learning models. The results for HEP include a root-mean-square error (RMSE) of 0.603, MSE of 0.364, MAE of 0.5091, MAPE of 13.60%, and an accuracy of 86.40%. For WEP, the RMSE was 0.071, MSE was 0.0052, MAE was 0.0657, MAPE was 1.60%, and the accuracy was 98.40%. The study advocates for the application of this model to real-time datasets in Africa.

The findings in Table 2 GRU model demonstrate the best performance based on both MSE and RMSE, while also performing reasonably well in MAE and MAPE, which indicates it is a reliable model overall. In contrast, the LSTM model exhibits higher error metrics across all categories compared to GRU and the proposed methods, making it the least effective model in this comparison. The Proposed Regression (HEP) model shows moderate performance; although it does not surpass GRU in terms of MSE and RMSE, it achieves the best MAPE value (46.99%), indicating superior performance in percentage-based error.

Table 2. Results Findings.

Models	MSE	RMSE	MAE	MAPE (%)
GRU [1]	0.21	0.518	0.389	65.2
LSTM [4]	0.413	0.643	0.409	67.8
Proposed Regression (HEP)	0.3635	0.6029	0.5091	46.99
Proposed Regression (WEP)	0,0052	0.0721	0.0657	82.84

On the other hand, the Proposed Regression (WEP) model boasts exceptionally low MSE, RMSE, and MAE, but its higher MAPE of 82.84% suggests that while it performs well in terms of raw error, its percentage-based error may indicate inconsistencies in specific cases. Overall, GRU emerges as a strong performer, striking the best balance across most metrics. Meanwhile, Proposed Regression (WEP) excels in raw error, though its higher MAPE raises concerns in certain scenarios. Lastly, Proposed Regression (HEP) stands out in percentage-based error (MAPE), making it a suitable choice when proportional accuracy is a priority.

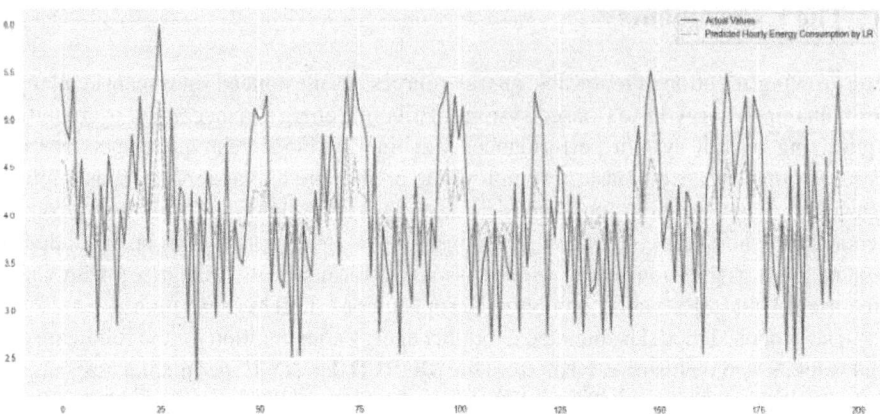

Fig. 2. Visual depiction of real data and load Hourly predictions generated by Regression Model.

The graph (see Fig. 2) presents a comparison between the actual values and the predicted hourly energy consumption using a Linear Regression (LR) model. The actual values, represented by a blue solid line, show significant fluctuations over time with notable peaks and troughs, reflecting the true variability in energy consumption. In contrast, the predicted values, shown as a dashed yellow line, are relatively smoother. While the predictions generally follow the overall trend of the actual values, they miss capturing the more extreme fluctuations. The Linear Regression model performs reasonably well in capturing the broader trend but struggles to handle rapid changes, such as sudden spikes or drops in energy consumption.

Notably, at points where the actual values exhibit high peaks (around the 20th and 120th intervals) or deep drops (around the 70th interval), the predicted values fail to align closely, indicating that the model smooths over the volatile parts of the data. Although the predictions follow the general pattern, the mismatch at extreme points suggests that the model may not be wellsuited for highly variable or noisy data, consistent with the limitations of linear models in handling non-linear or fluctuating patterns.

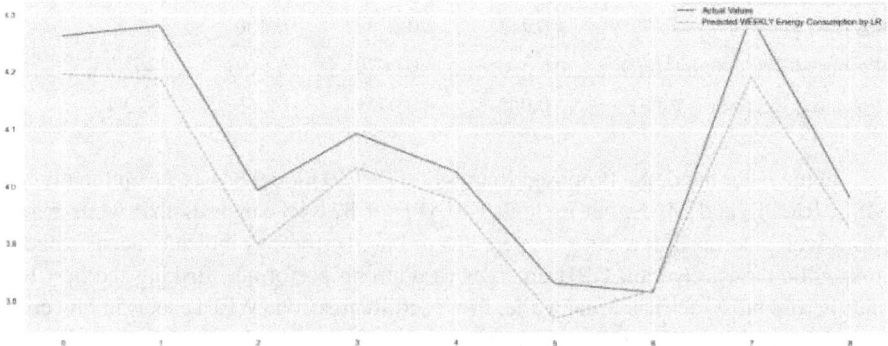

Fig. 3. Visual depiction of real data and Weekly Energy predictions generated by the Regression Model.

The graph (See Fig. 3) compares actual weekly energy consumption with the predicted values using a Linear Regression (LR) model. The actual energy consumption fluctuates over the week, starting with a rise in week 0, then a decline from week 1 to week 5, and a sharp increase around week 7 before a slight drop at the end. The predicted values generally follow the overall trend of the actual data but are smoother, particularly around peaks and troughs.

The Linear Regression model captures the general pattern but fails to accurately reflect the sharp fluctuations seen at extremes, such as the steep rise around week 7 and the dip at week 5. While the model performs well in estimating the overall trend, it does not fully capture rapid changes in consumption, indicating its limitation in handling short-term variations. Nonetheless, the model provides an adequate prediction for general trend analysis.

7 Conclusion

The study designs an accurate load forecasting linear regression model that predicts hourly and weekly energy consumption. This model ensured accurate and error-free energy predictions. The Regression Model proposed achieved strong performance across all metrics, surpassing all competing models, thereby demonstrating its superior effectiveness in predicting energy consumption during the learning phase. To validate the effectiveness of this model it will be compared with the GRU and LSTM models.

Acknowledgment. This work was supported by the Center of Excellence sponsorship. We acknowledge the contribution of the supervision that was led by the staff members from the University of Zululand in the Department of Computer Science.

References

1. Han, T., Muhammad, K., Hussain, T., Lloret, J., Baik, S.W.: An efficient deep learning framework for intelligent energy management in IoT networks. IEEE Internet Things J. **8**(5), 3170–3179 (2020)
2. Abdel-Basset, M., Hawash, H., Chakrabortty, R.K., Ryan, M.: Energy-net: a deep learning approach for smart energy management in IoTbased smart cities. IEEE Internet Things J. **8**(15), 12422–12435 (2021)
3. Liu, Y., Yang, C., Jiang, L., Xie, S., Zhang, Y.: Intelligent edge computing for IoT-based energy management in smart cities. IEEE Network **33**(2), 111–117 (2019)
4. Tan, M., Yuan, S., Li, S., Su, Y., Li, H., He, F.: Ultra-short-term industrial power demand forecasting using LSTM based hybrid ensemble learning. IEEE Trans. Power Syst. **35**(4), 2937–2848, July 2020
5. Forecasting of renewable energy sources. In: 2020 IEEE International Conference on Big Data and Smart Computing (BigComp), pp. 240–246. IEEE (2020)
6. Kosunalp, S.: An energy prediction algorithm for windpowered wireless sensor networks with energy harvesting. Energy **139**, 1275–1280 (2017)
7. Jeschke, S., Brecher, C., Meisen, T., Özdemir, D., Eschert, T.: Industrial internet of things and cyber manufacturing systems. In: Jeschke, S., Brecher, C., Song, H., Rawat, D. (eds.) Industrial Internet of Things. Springer Series in Wireless Technology. Springer, Cham (2017). https://doi.org/10.1007/978-3-319-42559-7_1

8. Bouktif, S., Fiaz, A., Ouni, A., Serhani, M.A.: Optimal deep learning LSTM model for electric load forecasting using feature selection and genetic algorithm: comparison with machine learning approaches †. Energies (MDPI) **11**, 1–20 (2018). https://doi.org/10.3390/en11071636K.Elissa. Titleofpaperifknown, unpublished
9. Kuhba, H., Al-tamemi, H.A.H.: Power system short-term load forecasting using artifcial neural networks. Int. J. Eng. Dev. Res. **4**, 78–87 (2016)
10. Zahid, M., et al.: Electricity price and load forecasting using enhanced convolutional neural network and enhanced support vector regression in smart grids. Electronics **8**, 122 (2019). https://doi.org/10.3390/electronics8020122
11. Ahmad, W., et al.: Towards short term electricity load forecasting using improved support vector machine and extreme learning machine. Energies **13**, 1–17 (2020). https://doi.org/10.3390/en13112907
12. Zakarya, S., Abbas, H., Belal, M.: Long-term deep learning load forecasting based on social and economic factors in the Kuwait region. J. Theor. Appl. Inf. Technol. **95**, 1524–1535 (2017)
13. Ciulla, G.; D'Amico, A.: Building energy performance forecasting: a multiple linear regression approach. Appl. Energy **253**, 113500 (2019)
14. Ahajjam, M.A., Bonilla Licea, D., Essayeh, C., Ghogho, M., Kobbane, A.: MORED: a moroccan buildings' electricity consumption dataset. Energies **13**(24), 6737 (2020)
15. Lü, X., Lu, T., Kibert, C.J., Viljanen, M.: Modeling and forecasting energy consumption for heterogeneous buildings using a physical–statistical approach. Appl. Energy **144**, 261–275 (2015)

Author Index

A
Adama, Samassi II-295
Adehan, Anziz I-315
Adinsi, Alfred II-143
Agbahoungba, Symphorien I-37
Agoyi, Eric I-37
Ahouandjinou, Arnaud I-293
Ahouandjinou, Sèmèvo Arnaud R. M. I-232
Ahouansou, Maurice I-37
Ametepe, Adoté François-Xavier I-232
Angaman, Jean Cyrille Koffi I-52
Appoh, Kouamé II-295
Assogbadjo, Achille Ephrem I-37
Augustin, Touré Kidjégbo II-295

B
Ba, Aboubacry Hamat II-162
Ba, Mamadou I-159
Badiane, Ndeye Mery Dia II-162
Baelongandi, Ange Taboria I-87
Bagula, Antoine I-263, II-240
Bah, Issagha I-52
Bampende, Marivaux Nzaji I-87
Barry, Mamadou Alpha II-81
Baruni, Kedimotse I-249
Beni, Robert Makila II-58
Bernard, Saha Kouassi II-3
Bikienga, Moustapha I-3
Bissyande, Tegawendé F. II-182
Bissyandé, Tégawendé F. II-256
Bissyande, Tegawendé F. II-281
Bissyandé, Tégawendé F. II-319, II-334
Boateng, Thato II-344
Boris, Zouneme II-267

C
Charlemagne, Kopoin N. D. II-267
Chicapa, Eusébio I-199
Ciss, Mamadou II-162
Coly, Adama I-278

Corenthin, Alex II-113
Coulibaly, Fatimatou I-52

D
Dabo, Abdoul-Rachid I-172
Dagba, Théophile I-315
Dagou, Koffi II-267
Dama, Theodore II-182
Damoue, Zacharia II-81
Degila, Jules I-37, I-293, I-315, II-71
Désiré Dao, Goya Alama II-334
Diagne, Oumar II-13
Diallo, Mohamed Bobo I-52
Diatta, Abel II-13
Dieng, Ousmane II-162
Dione, Déthié I-52
Diongue, Dame II-162
Diop, Ibrahima I-191
Diouf, Nicolas Djighnoum II-162
Djoko, Kely Maxime Motue II-34, II-197
Dlamini, Nelisiwe II-344

E
Edwige, Johnson Grâce Yénin II-304

F
Fall, Assane G. II-162
Fam, Pape Abdoulaye II-128
Faty, Lamine II-13
Faye, Ibrahima II-128
Fofana, Vazoumana I-52

G
Gandonou, Jean-Baptiste I-315
Guel, Désiré I-15, I-142
Guinko, Ferdinand Tonguim I-172

H
Houngue, Pélagie II-143

J
Jérome, Diako Doffou II-304
João, Adalberto I-199

K
Kabore, Abdoul Kader II-182, II-281, II-319, II-334
Kafando, Rodrique II-256, II-281, II-319, II-334
Kamagaté, Aladji I-66
Kamenan, Koffi A. I-66
Kassé, Bassirou II-113
Kiki, Probus M. A. F. I-232
Kondengar, Thierry I-159
Koné, Douatia I-66
Kone, Ismael II-95
Kone, Tiémoman I-118
Kouraogo, P. Justin I-142
Kpoze, Aurélie I-293
Kyamakya, Kyandoghere I-87

L
Lungenyi, Nicodème Kabongo I-87

M
Maaradji, Abderrahmane I-52
Macedo, Joaquim I-199
Mahlasela, Oyena I-249
Makila Beni, Robert II-240
Manari, Unarine I-105
Mantsi, Motlatsi II-344
Marcelin, Sandjé II-304
Marcellin, Brou Konan II-295
Mathaba, Sizakele II-363
Mathew, Adigun II-363
Mbale, Landry I-263, II-240
Mbaye, Maïssa I-278
Mbaye, Maissa II-162
Méné, Niangoran Médard I-66
Mensah, Patrice E. II-304
Mkhonza, Khanyisile II-363
Mkuzangwe, Nenekazi II-344
Mondjo, Ghislain Dorian Tchuente II-34, II-197
Mthethwa, Sthembile I-217, II-344
Mudilu Kafunda, Jean-Claude I-87
Mukala, Patrick II-58
Myaka, Siphelele I-249

N
N'guessan, Behou Gerard I-118
Nabi, Rasidatou I-191
Nana, Emile I-172
Ndiaye, Abdourahmane II-81
Ndiaye, Mamadou Lamine II-128
Ndiaye, Mamadou Moustapha II-81
Ndong, Joseph I-52
Nelufule, Norman I-105
Ngejane, Cynthia Hombakazi I-217
Ngom, Aminata II-220
Ngom, Ndeye Fatou II-220
Niang, Oumar II-220
Ntshangase, Sthembile I-249
Ntumbwa, Jonathan Kabemba II-58

O
Olowo, Venceslas M. I-232
Ouédraogo, Tounwendyam Frédéric I-52, II-3
Ouédraogo, Zonabo II-281
Ouya, Samuel I-159

P
Patricia, Anassin Chiatsè Mireille II-3
Petey, Kragbi Olivier I-118

S
Sabane, Aminata II-182
Sabané, Aminata II-256
Sabane, Aminata II-281, II-319, II-334
Salako, Valere I-37
Sankara, Karzoum Arsène I-3
Sarr, Edouard Ngor II-13
Sarr, Idrissa II-113
Sbihi, Nada I-52
Senamela, Pertunia I-105
Sene-Wade, Mariama II-162
Senou, Rosaire II-71
Shadung, Daniel I-105
Shibambu, Avuya II-344
Sidibé, Samba II-220
Silue, Donilèmin Jules II-95
Sodedji, Frejus Ariel I-37

Somda, Flavien Herve   I-142
Somda, Flavien Hervé   I-15
Somda, Metouole Mwinbe Yves Ghislain   I-159
Sounouvou, Marius   I-37

T
Tapsoba, Lydie Simone   II-281
Tchouangang, Evrard Cabrel Nguemeyou   II-113
Thiam, Fatoumata   I-278
Tognisse, Ida Sèmévo   I-37, I-315
Tougma, Manegaouindé Roland   I-3
Traore, Papa Silly   II-128
Traoré, Yaya   I-191

W
Wandji, Thierry   I-315

Z
Zampaligre, Rabiatou   II-319
Zerbo, Boureima   I-3, I-142

Made in the USA
Monee, IL
03 May 2026

49438645R00221